late Pleistocene – gl[...]
humans fir[...]

Holocene 10,000 – 5,[...]

oaks filled in [...] ev[...]
conifers again moved [...]

Mt. Mazama 6,000 yrs. ago

general stability
p. 30 → early 18th c. – horses — bison exterminated 1830s
early 19th c. – fur trade   beaver nearly exterminated "

Cook 1778 – disease to Indians
1830-33 malaria

Weyerhaeuser Environmental Books

William Cronon, Editor

Weyerhaeuser Environmental Books

Weyerhaeuser Environmental Books explore human relationships with natural environments in all their variety and complexity. They seek to cast new light on the ways that natural systems affect human communities, the ways that people affect the environments of which they are a part, and the ways that different cultural conceptions of nature profoundly shape our sense of the world around us.

The Natural History of Puget Sound Country
Arthur R. Kruckeberg

Forest Dreams, Forest Nightmares:
The Paradox of Old Growth in the Inland West
Nancy Langston

Landscapes of Promise: The Oregon Story, 1800–1940
William G. Robbins

Weyerhaeuser Environmental Classics

The Great Columbia Plain: A Historical Geography, 1805–1910
D. W. Meinig

Mountain Gloom and Mountain Glory:
The Development of the Aesthetics of the Infinite
Marjorie Hope Nicolson

Cycle of Fire by Stephen J. Pyne

World Fire: The Culture of Fire on Earth

Vestal Fire: An Environmental History, Told through Fire,
of Europe and Europe's Encounter with the World

Fire in America: A Cultural History of Wildland and Rural Fire

Burning Bush: A Fire History of Australia

The Ice: A Journey to Antarctica

LANDSCAPES

OF PROMISE

THE
OREGON
STORY
1800–1940

WILLIAM G. ROBBINS

Foreword by William Cronon

UNIVERSITY OF WASHINGTON PRESS   SEATTLE & LONDON

Landscapes of Promise has been published with the assistance of a grant from the Weyerhaeuser Environmental Books Endowment, established by the Weyerhaeuser Company Foundation, members of the Weyerhaeuser family, and Janet and Jack Creighton.

Library of Congress Cataloging-in-Publication Data

Robbins, William G., 1935–
Landscapes of promise : the Oregon story, 1800–1940 / William G.
Robbins ; foreword by William Cronon.
p.   cm.
Includes bibliographical references (p.   ) and index.
ISBN 0-295-97632-2 (alk. paper)
1. Oregon—Environmental conditions—History.   I. Title.
GE155.07R63   1997
333.7′09795—dc21   97-16531
CIP

For Aubrey *and* Kelly,
Larry,
Jody *and* Dina,
and Billy G. *and* Jason

Contents

Foreword: Dreams of Plenty
William Cronon

O regon has long been one of the most resonant national icons of the United States. Known as a land of journey's ending since at least 1805, when Lewis and Clark first set eyes on the Pacific Ocean after their long march across the continent, the Oregon country seemed a kind of lush oasis on the far side of the Rocky Mountains for nineteenth-century Americans thinking of pulling up stakes and heading west. Lewis and Clark and subsequent explorers brought back the news that the lands west of the Missouri River were anything but well-watered, and might prove dangerous indeed for anyone trying to set up a farm and make a living there. The report of Stephen Long's 1820 expedition went so far as to describe the Plains as "The Great American Desert"—hardly an inviting prospect. But beyond this arid country was Oregon, a moist green Eden perfectly suited to the Jeffersonian vision of yeoman farm families tilling the soil and fulfilling the democratic promise of the young American nation. And so the first great overland migrations were not to California and the Gold Rush but farther north, to the country at the mouth of the Columbia River and along the fertile banks of the Willamette.

The story of those journeys is that of the Oregon Trail, a name that still looms as large in the mythic and historical consciousness of the American people as any in our history. As such, Oregon is central to some of the deepest and most fiercely held narratives of American frontier history: families leaving their homes and loading their most precious belongings into covered wagons, struggling with gritty determination in the face of terrible hardships, finally to arrive at the promised land at the end of the trail. In its most familiar forms, this is a story of ordinary folk rising to meet great challenges, of fertile lands rewarding their inhabitants with bounteous plenty, of communities improving themselves and thereby fulfilling the dream of American progress. The stories Americans have wanted to tell about Oregon are the stories they have most wanted to believe about themselves, and about America itself.

That is why William Robbins' compelling new book, *Landscapes of Promise: The Oregon Country, 1800–1940*, is such an important contribution not just to the history of the Pacific Northwest but to American history generally. This volume offers one of the most ambitious and creative syntheses of Oregon history we have seen in a generation, and manages to find much that is unexpected in material that might otherwise seem all too familiar. Robbins recognizes right from the outset that mythic stories about Oregon's past are in fact a crucial part of its history, for what people believe most deeply about a place can powerfully affect the way they relate to and use its environment. He acknowledges how central the dream of progress and agrarian community has been to Oregonians and to Americans generally but then proceeds to demonstrate the complex tensions between that dream and the historical realities of the region. By combining a sensitive understanding of regional ecology with a critical analysis of economic change, he offers a much fuller understanding of how the Oregon country developed between the arrival of Lewis and Clark and the advent of World War II.

As such, *Landscapes of Promise* is a benchmark achievement in William Robbins' already impressive scholarly career. One of the nation's leading western historians and a pioneer in developing the new field of environmental history, Robbins has authored a series of books on different aspects of the ways Americans have used and manipulated the ecosystems around them. His *Lumberjacks and Legislators: Political Economy of the U.S. Lumber Industry, 1890–1941* (1982) is a significant and highly critical study of interactions between lumber corporations and American politicians. *American Forestry* (1985) examines the interactions between national forest policy and the United States Forest Service on the one hand and state and local forest managers on the other. *Hard Times in Paradise* (1988) is a richly textured and evocative local history of Coos Bay, Oregon, as members of its community sought to weather the booms and busts of lumbering in the local economy. And his *Colony and Empire: The Capitalist Transformation of the American West* (1994) offered a bold synthesis of the entire West as a case study in economic colonialism, social struggle, and environmental degradation. Along the way, Robbins also served as editor of *Environmental Review* (now renamed *Environmental History*) and helped consolidate its role as the journal of record for the field of environmental history.

Throughout these many works, William Robbins has steadfastly held to certain intellectual commitments and perspectives that shape the way he retells the story of Oregon in this book. Even when he writes of a small local area like Coos Bay, he is always acutely aware of the external forces that shape its life and economy. Never one to romanticize the autonomy or heroic self-sufficiency of rural places, he invariably tries to embed the people and communities whose lives he studies in the context of the much larger system of which they are part. During the period about which he writes in this book, that system became modern corporate capitalism, and Robbins is a firm critic of the social inequalities and environmental harms that capitalist markets, institutions, and social relations have produced in places like Oregon and the American West. Believing that even the most abstract of human ideas and the loftiest of human dreams cannot help but be grounded in material relationships and in the soils of the earth that sustains them, he seeks always to show the political economic connections that bind people to each other and to the ecosystems they inhabit.

All of these ideas lie near the heart of *Landscapes of Promise*, marking it as a book that few other authors could have written — a quintessential expression of William Robbins' ideas and scholarship. In place of the mythic dream of Jeffersonian farmers making their way into the fertile bounty of a virgin wilderness, he shows us an Oregon already long-modified by native peoples with complex trading relationships with European traders and markets for fur. The transformations that ensued when the overlanders finally arrived on the Oregon Trail were intricate indeed, and can hardly be attributed merely to the individual labors of yeoman farm families. Government explorations and surveys soon laid the groundwork for an ever-expanding development process, and railroad corporations led the way toward new technologies and new corporate forms of organization that quickly came to dominate many sectors of the regional economy.

Robbins demonstrates better than any scholar before him the ways in which the agrarian myth of the Oregon country was increasingly at odds with the capitalist and urban-industrial realities that actually characterized the region. More importantly, though, he shows how agrarian dream and capitalist reality both expressed an even deeper and nearly unshakable American faith in progress and the ability of science and technology to control nature. Over and over again, this book shows how farmers, workers, railroads, lumber companies, government bureaucrats, engineers, politicians, and other Oregonians intervened to "improve" their condition by exploiting the landscape. Faced with ecosystems that seemed to place limits on the possibilities of economic growth and social progress, most Oregonians sought ways to overcome those limits with new technologies, whether on the farm, in the forest, or in the city. The technologies they adopted and the changes they made did in fact bring prosperity and remarkable change to the region, but at an ecological cost whose full scale remains unknown and whose future sustainability this book is inclined to question.

By the time *Landscapes of Promise* ends, in 1940, the distinctive features of modern Oregon were already largely in place. Dramatic change would follow after World War II, and we have reason to hope that Robbins will tell that story in a successor volume . . . but one finishes this book more impressed by the continuities than the discontinuities. The phenomena that Robbins describes—the commodity markets, the industrial technologies, the city-hinterland connections, the ideologies of growth, the powerful economic forces external to the region that have pervasively shaped its environment and the life of its people and other creatures—none of these had their origins in the years since 1945. The capitalist transformation of the Oregon country (and beyond Oregon, of North America itself) has been going on for a very long time, and the environmental challenges that Oregonians face in the twenty-first century have roots that are deep indeed. Even those who are well informed about the problems may not fully appreciate the complex historical processes that have produced them. To understand those problems, to try to figure out where they came from and how we might most responsibly confront them, one could do a lot worse than to ponder the lessons of this book.

Acknowledgments

This book had its beginnings during my four-year hitch with the U.S. Navy. Through the mist and fog of an early October morning in 1955, I hitchhiked north on U.S. Highway 101 and crossed the border into Oregon, courtesy of a friendly, shirt-sleeved log-truck operator who preferred driving with both windows open. I was filled with fuzzy notions about tall timber and rivers teeming with fish, and southern Oregon's coastal mountains appealed to my romantic notions about the great Pacific Northwest. The countryside seemed large, different. In truth, the rugged, mountainous countryside adjacent to the Smith, Illinois, and Chetco river valleys is a spectacular setting, especially to one whose childhood memories were nurtured in southern New England's Berkshire foothills. Although I recall writing home that much of the original coastal forests of northern California and Oregon appeared to have been cut over, there was something about the place that prompted me to return eight years later. By that time I was armed with a teaching degree and had developed a growing interest in the serious study of history. After spending much of my life in Oregon, I can now say with conviction that it is a move I have never regretted.

This study originated in a conversation with David Brooks, a social scientist with the Pacific Northwest Research Station of the United States Forest Service. In the fall of 1992 David invited me to provide historical context for the federal government's big Eastside Forest Ecosystem Health study. With time away from the classroom during the winter of 1992–93 and with the assistance of Don Wolf, I completed the research and wrote a lengthy essay about the changing landscape of the region between the Cascade Mountains and the Idaho border.* It immediately became evident that I was already well launched into an exciting book project. For those and other reasons, I am grateful to David Brooks and the U.S. Forest Service for suggesting the potential for such a study.

Oregon State University provided critical assistance during various stages of this project: the Research Office funded support for a graduate research assistant to photocopy documents, reports, and census data in the university library; a Center for the Humanities fellowship relieved me of classroom responsibilities in the spring of 1994; and the university's Research Office again provided support toward the close of the project in the search for maps and illustrations. Finally, an Oregon Council for the Humanities fellowship in the summer of 1994, a sabbatical leave from the university during the academic year 1994–95, and a fellowship from the National Endowment for the Humanities freed me from regular academic work to pursue research and writing full time.

This study reflects the growing volume of innovative scholarship on the western American landscape. I am especially indebted to the insights and ideas of William Cronon, Patricia Limerick, Stephen Pyne, James Ronda, Carlos Schwantes, Elliott West, Richard White, and Donald Worster. As usual, I am grateful for the advice and careful reading of a small group of historians: Richard Maxwell Brown for an important and critical review of the entire manuscript; Bob Bunting for valuable insights and for generously sharing copies of his own rich trove of research materials; Don Wolf for being a diligent research assistant in the early stages of the project and for his clinician's insights into important sections of the manuscript; Amy Sievers Fackler for her research skills in tracking down hard-to-find documents; Bill Cronon for his excellent stewardship of this series and for suggesting that I provide proper "signposts" for the study; and Bill Lang for sharing professional forums on several occasions and for our always "friendly" disagreements.

Over the last several years I have enjoyed the friendship and support

---

* See *Landscape and the Intermontane Northwest: An Environmental History,* U.S. Department of Agriculture, Forest Service, Pacific Northwest Research Station, General Technical Report PNW-GTR-319 (February 1994).

of two exceptional administrators. Paul Farber, chair of the Department of History, encouraged this project from its inception and willingly offered his wit and wisdom on matters natural and cultural. Paul, the glass of Oregon Trail Ale is on me this time. And Kay Schaffer, dean of the College of Liberal Arts and the best of all possible bosses, has been understanding and supportive about my obsession with doing history.

Perhaps my greatest debt is to Jerry Williams, a sociologist and social historian with the United States Forest Service in Portland, Oregon. In addition to his extensive bibliographies of Forest Service, conservation, and environmental history, Jerry is an avid collector of historical photographs of the Oregon country. The illustrations in this book are testimony to both the scope and breadth of his collection and to his generosity. Jerry is a model of the selfless public servant whose professional work bridges the public and private sector.

I also want to express my gratitude to Henry Sayre and his wife Sandy Brooke. Henry suggested that I use the Bierstadt painting as the jacket illustration, and Sandy risked life and limb to take the picture that appears at the end of the photo section.

Staff personnel in Oregon State University's Valley Library, its branch unit at the Hatfield Marine Science Center in Newport, Oregon, and the University of Oregon's Knight Library were helpful in locating census information, government documents, and a myriad of other pieces of historical literature. In ways large and small, I am also grateful to the always friendly and helpful staff in the History Department, Marilyn Bethman and Sharon Johnson, and to Mecila Cross in the Dean's Office.

My appreciation to the many present and former graduate students—especially Katrina Barber, Ron Gregory, Linda Hahn, Lindon Hylton, Jackie Martain, Christine Morita, and Don Wolf—who continue to challenge me to think in new and different ways about conventional historical questions.

Finally, my thanks to Lita Tarver, a treasured friend and managing editor of the University of Washington Press, and to Lane Morgan for curbing most of my stylistic excesses.

Landscapes of Promise
The Oregon Story
1800–1940

Prologue: The Essence of Place

Space is transformed into place as it acquires definition and meaning.
— *Yi-Fu Tuan*[1]

M ore than we ever believe," the writer Raymond Williams observed, "we understand life from where we are."[2] We draw upon the actual, the real, and the symbolic from our immediate social experience and weave them into a pattern of larger stories. I begin by citing Williams in order to argue that our perceptions of human cultures, of time and place are intertwined, enmeshed in an intricate choreography involving memory, experience, and understanding. History is a study of the complexities of human thought and action and an attempt to understand how our own cultural perceptions inform the way we view the past. That is certainly true of the narrative constructions that have centered on the Oregon country and the state of Oregon over the last 150 years or more. The intruders who came to dominate the region by the mid-nineteenth century carried with them powerful cultural prescriptions about the proper ordering of their new surroundings. Those mostly white newcomers imposed on their adopted homelands a new language, a discourse steeped in the politics of power: that defined the intruders favorably against the native residents, that vested landscapes with special meaning and purpose, that carried with it heavy suggestions about transforming the land itself. The collective force of that new cultural vision led to new definitions, new bounds of reckoning, and new perceptions about place. These were manifested in changes to the landscape and in the development of a literary tradition that emphasized optimism and the prospects for human betterment.

Nineteenth-century newcomers to the green western valleys of the Pacific Northwest were ecstatic about the region's mild climate, long growing season, and fertile soil. But they also saw themselves as part of a larger epic, one that is centered in the great myths of the American narrative. Indeed, the effusive stories that grew out of those early recollections fit the mythical representations that appear in the writings of Frederick Jackson Turner, arguably America's most celebrated theorist of material, cultural, and political progress. Turner's most productive years embraced the period from 1890 to 1920, and his stories outline a progression from primitive beginnings to great achievements in the westering movement of white Americans. Representations of progress were ubiquitous in his writings. Hunting for subsistence, trapping fur-bearing animals, and building rough-hewn log cabins quickly gave way to frame buildings, fenced prairie land, and acres of wheat. The plowed field, the church, the schoolhouse, the stagecoach, and the railroad all were signs of progress.[3]

Those Turnerian nineteenth-century narratives emphasized the natural abundance of Oregon and the Northwest and the notion that white settlers were in the process of building a civilization and laying the groundwork for progress. A midcentury Vancouver, Washington, newspaper saw those changes in terms of providential design: "the western coast is to be peopled; the treasures of her forests, her rivers, her rich soil, . . . are to be developed for the expansion of civilization." The first newspaper published in the region, the *Oregon Spectator*, put progress and civilization in a racial cast in an 1850 article: "The Indian retreats before the march of civilization and American enterprise; the howling wilderness is fast becoming fruitful fields." One year later the Reverend Gustavus Hines viewed the dramatically declining Indian population through a similar ethnocentric lens: "the hand of Providence is removing them to give place to a people more worthy of this beautiful and fertile country." And A. W. Campbell, speaking at the opening of Oregon State Normal School at Monmouth in 1883, contrasted the Indian and the Anglo-Saxon and remarked that the wigwam always retreated in front of the American schoolhouse.[4]

A careful reading of early journals and diaries makes clear that white settlers in the Oregon country firmly believed they represented the rising trajectory of those stories. At the onset of the twentieth century, the survivors among those early comers could recall the environment of the 1840s: the Indians' autumn burning of the prairies; the meandering, debris-filled rivers; and the seasonal floods that turned the landscape into a vast wetlands. And when they recounted those experiences, they expressed great pride in what they had accomplished. No matter how exaggerated their achievements, historian Richard White points out, "their story became the American story."[5] To the writer Dayton Duncan, the substance of those "national" narratives has always embraced elements of determination, of prospects, of getting there, "the quest for the unreachable." In the name of progress—to obtain free land, to gain access to grazing and mining areas, to extend the bounds of an expanding nation—the intruding whites displaced the First Americans and confined them to colonial reserves in their once vast homelands.[6]

While the outlines to that story are familiar, the details become less clear the closer we move to home. For the Pacific Northwest, we now recognize that the human experience has been more complex than an unmitigated tale of success, that there were (and are) multiple stories to be told about the groups who have inhabited the region. For the larger trans-Mississippi West, according to historian Elliott West, we should look past the "pioneer experience" that has dominated narrative discourse to a more complex view of the western story, to "its severe limitations and continuing conflicts, its ambivalence, and its often bewildering diversity." Indeed, if we move beyond the heroic and romantic blush of conventional accounts about the Oregon country, we recognize that tragedy preceded the later, triumphal accounts: I refer to the epidemic diseases that caused the deaths of thousands of Indian people in the Pacific Northwest. Elliott West refers to the percentages of fatalities in that catastrophic population decline across North America as "the greatest die-off in the human record."[7]

In conventional histories of the Oregon country, heroic men and women built a civilization from a primitive but abundantly endowed landscape. Those narrative accounts begin with sawmills, grist mills, increased acreages of "improved lands," and then the story moves to the region's first sizable American settlement at Oregon City. To recently arrived white settlers, the new valley towns and the changes taking place on the prairies and hillsides were signs of advance and forward movement. In that sense, progress was the antithesis of the status quo, the enemy of native environments that whites defined as primitive, pristine, and natural. Statistics reflect some of that newly emerging demographic, cultural, *and* ecological world: the number of immigrants, the acreages of improved land, the productions of the soil, and the number of livestock being grazed on the prairies and foothills. To protect their domestic animals and crops, settlers waged campaigns against wolves, cougar, bear, and elk. Killing wolves in particular was a sign of progress, part of an effort to extend the bounds of civilized space. An optimistic and confident lot, settlers saw everything to gain and nothing to fear from those activities.

As time passed, land increasingly became a commodity, a tool of production of central importance to the settler-farmers' expanding market output. Farmers organized agricultural societies to disseminate up-to-date information about wheat culture, animal husbandry, horticultural advances, and marketing news. To speed the movement of grain, especially to Portland, shippers on the Willamette River funded the removal of obstructions in the river, the building of canals, and the construction of dikes. Although those nineteenth-century alterations set in motion the progressive industrialization of the river, they were modest in comparison to the changes that eventually took place on the Columbia River and its tributaries beginning in the 1930s.

The completion of the nation's first transcontinental railroad, the famous Union Pacific–Central Pacific line in the spring of 1869, was greeted everywhere as a stunning achievement. That effort, the building of a railroad up the Willamette Valley in 1870, and the extension of a transcontinental line to Portland in 1883, brought the awesome forces of the industrial world to the Northwest and further integrated the region with the world beyond. The narratives of that period are particularly interesting for the words defining human relationships with the natural world—the increasingly popular idea that human destiny was intertwined with the ability to reorder natural systems.

By the early years of the twentieth century—in the midst of explosive industrial growth—influential Americans had developed an almost transcendental belief in the efficacy of the unlimited manipulation of the natural world. That practical and commercial view of nature embraced Progressive-era conservationism: a belief that orderly, scientific, and engineering approaches would bring an endless bounty of riches; a conviction that human technical genius would combine with an abundant landscape to improve the quality of life for future generations. That scenario, played out in the Pacific Northwest until well after the Second World War, elicited few questions about unseen and unintended consequences.

Long after it had been subject to global market forces, Oregon's material environment was still tied to the myth of an unspoiled Eden. A British planner who visited Oregon in 1978 concluded that "if an Ecotopian society were to develop anywhere, then Oregon would be one of the most likely spots on the globe." Peter James of the University of Nottingham obviously liked what he saw: snow-capped mountain peaks towering over one of the most productive agricultural valleys in the world; seemingly endless stretches of evergreen forests; and "salmon-teeming rivers" that sliced through the rugged coastal mountains. In an essay that appeared in the *New Scientist,* James emphasized that the people of this widely varying landscape were an outdoor folk who loved nature and displayed a clear sense of superiority over their more material-oriented neighbors. Using the region as a real-life metaphor for Ernest Callenbach's utopian best seller, *Ecotopia,* James informed his readers that this "almost frontier country" had good reason to call itself "the most ecologically conscious area in the world." [8]

At the moment Peter James made his brief visit, the Oregon landscape was something less than a harmonious and pristine earthly paradise. Indeed, the British scholar's romantic description of the state would appear to fit Yi-Fu Tuan's precept that myths tend to prosper where precise knowledge is lacking, that stories take on a life of their own when they lose touch with material reality. [9] But the British visitor's account, however embellished

and devoid of realistic descriptive evidence, did offer a tangible identity to
a politically bounded, late-twentieth-century place. And despite the superficial and fanciful word play, James did capture elements of Oregon's material life: "Even the industries . . . logging, fishing, food processing, tour-
ism," he remarked, were "close to nature."¹⁰ That James would accentuate
the state's natural abundance and its "still almost frontier" qualities suggests that those mythical phrases continued to enjoy wide currency among
observers, especially those with a distant and at best limited knowledge of
the Oregon countryside.

More recently another planning expert, Kevin Kasowski, offered a more
sober and informed assessment in the pages of the state's leading newspaper, the Portland *Oregonian*. By the late twentieth century, Kasowski
observed, the celebrated wagon ruts left by the 350,000 migrants who traveled west on the Oregon Trail had become symbols of ambivalence toward
the natural world. Although many citizens cherished the famous ruts as a
valuable cultural treasure, to other people the wheel marks left by the wagons represented little more than the defacing of the landscape. Kasowski's
principal worry was that "our own much larger footprints on the land . . .
are scarring the land's beauty and productivity." Once scenic wonders—
such as American Falls on the Snake River and Celilo and Kettle Falls on
the Columbia—had been flooded behind dams, all in the name of human
progress and material comfort. And while hydroelectric power production
had made possible technological advances that had eliminated much of the
drudgery of daily life, Kasowski argued that those innovations and similar
modifications to the landscape had exacted a heavy price in sharply dwin-
dling salmon runs and a generally worsening biodiversity crisis.¹¹

Where Kevin Kasowski writes about a bioregional "Oregon Country,"
linked by river systems, climate patterns, and a shared recent history of
settlement, James was referring to a well-defined, clearly delineated physical
space, one that is easily recognizable on standard highway road maps. Oregon's physical boundaries, like most others of their kind, are the product of
history, imperial rivalries, politics, and geography. And precisely because
the state's boundaries involve a mix of geopolitical reality and historical
circumstance, not all of those markers follow definable natural attributes,

especially those of a bioregional or topographical character. But for most kinds of environmental history, carefully bounded places—geographical, ecological, cultural, or political—are the beginning point for understanding human/cultural relationships with the natural world. Indeed, some of the best environmental monographs to date are studies of particular places during specific periods of time.[12]

In his study of the English colonial settlements in the South, Timothy Silver used both cultural and political boundaries to define his work. Because most environmental change was local, he reasoned that its extent and reach varied with topography, climate, and patterns of settlement. Using cultural and political bounds to define the parameters of his inquiry proved a satisfactory compromise for Silver and a workable framework for doing environmental history.[13] Because stories about particular environments have physical dimensions, the critical question is how to bound that geography in designing a study. Considerations of human/environmental relationships in well-defined areas, however, must always reckon with the fact that humans and their ideas have never been place-bound. Quite the contrary, they have been notoriously mobile.[14]

In the strict definition of the phrase, the identification and meaning we attach to politically bounded places are primarily culturally constructed. In that sense, I generally agree with historian Dan Flores who argues that "with rare exceptions, the politically-derived boundaries of county, state, and national borders are mostly useless in understanding nature."[15] Although Oregon and the Oregon country gained wide recognition as a vaguely understood geographic region during the early nineteenth century, imperial negotiations between the United States and England and the subsequent political maneuverings of Congress in creating territories and states shaped its present boundaries. With the exception of the Pacific Ocean to the west and the Columbia River on the north, only in a crude way do those clearly delineated political boundaries conform to broader, "natural" geographic features. Indeed, the early nineteenth-century missionary Gustavus Hines argued that the Forty-ninth Parallel separating the United States and Canada was most "unnatural," because it failed to include the entire drainage of the Columbia River. "In crossing the great valley of the

Columbia," the boundary put "asunder that which the God of nature has joined together."[16]

For the last several millennia the Great River of the West has sliced through both time and terrain along its winding passageway to the ocean. The Columbia has provided a physical arterial linking the interior reaches of the Pacific slope and the oceanic highways beyond, and it provided a definitive geographic description for the region that came to be called the Oregon country. But it never served as a cultural or political borderland until 1853, when the United States Congress decided to use the Columbia River as part of the boundary dividing the territories of Oregon and Washington. With the stroke of a pen, the river was made an arbitrary point of human reckoning, and the cultural/historical meanings attached to "Oregon" as opposed to "the Oregon country" became a well-defined geographical place. The *Columbian,* published in Vancouver, Washington Territory, observed that nature had "pointedly divided the territory by the Columbia river."[17] In the same piece of legislation the federal overseers, who were attempting to partition the western landscape into neatly arranged geometric lines, decided upon the twisting contours of a section of the Snake River to fashion Oregon's northeastern boundary.[18] By their use of the two great river systems to establish the bounds for Oregon and its adjacent territories, the imperial policy makers in the nation's capital *did* reckon with certain obvious geographic realities. But neither the Columbia nor the Snake systems provide coherent and defining features for a bioregion or greater regional ecosystem. Great waterways of their kind have the annoying habit of flowing through multiple and diverse zones of geology, climate, and ecology.

The southern markers to politically bounded Oregon acknowledged treaties between expanding and declining empires — the United States, Spain, and Mexico — and the subsequent division of the victor's spoils into convenient political and organizational districts. With its political boundaries fixed by 1853, Oregon became a political and administrative fact in the life of an expanding and aggressive national state. In terms of a distinct geography, however, it lacked common definition. The territory and state embraced a myriad of climatic zones from the rain-forest bioregion

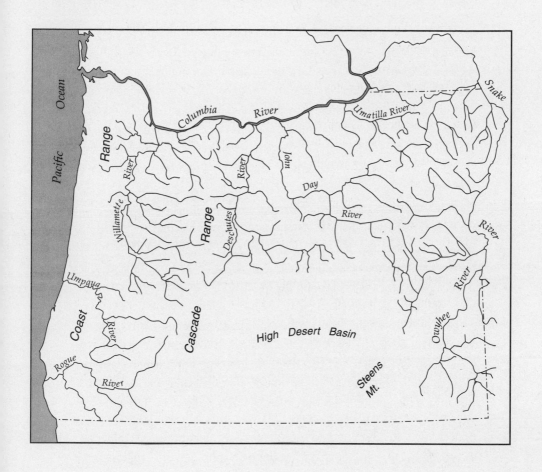

Oregon's major river systems. *University of Wisconsin Cartographic Lab*

along the Pacific Coast to the arid and semiarid desert country of the great Harney Basin. Its geography and landscape embraced the humid zones of the coastal and Willamette valleys, the Cascade Mountains dividing western from eastern Oregon, and a series of rugged, forested mountain ranges and plateaus in the northern and eastern section, areas that contrasted sharply with the relatively flat and arid lowlands nearby. To the degree that place-bound, "natural geographic systems"[19] provide the only proper context for doing environmental history, politically bounded Oregon makes little sense.

But I would argue that there are viable and useful strategies beyond those associated with natural geography for exploring the environmental history of politically contrived places. That would be especially true for inquiries that involve regional landscapes during the last two hundred years or so, a period that coincides with the expansion of market and then industrial capitalism to the far corners of the earth. Under the influence of that progressively expanding global system, political units, no matter how diverse their internal geographical and ecological features, increasingly became culturally scripted places, reflecting the common purposes and designs of capitalism,[20] an economic culture that views the natural world in terms of its commodity potential. Those prescriptions include an entire complex of ideas that define and model human behavior toward a broad panoply of relationships. Under capitalism the conceptual ideas shaping human conduct tend to reduce the natural world to simplified abstractions that center on the personal ownership of material things. Moreover, as industrial metaphors become more firmly embedded in our thinking about the physical world, human societies become increasingly indifferent to the uniqueness of place.[21]

Culture, therefore, in the sense that it is infused with economic influences that prescribe human activity, provides intriguing insights about the way we define geography. To Fernand Braudel, the use of geographical space to explain phenomena affected all historical realities, including "states, societies, cultures, and economies." Using the rise of capitalism as an integral part his work on the Mediterranean world, Braudel argued that of all the ways to understand space, the economic was the easiest to define. All social realities, he contended, were "concerned with the working of the economy." Once Europe set out upon the great oceans of the world, it began the process of opening up and extending its influence across the waters of the Atlantic to "the wastes of America." With its rapidly evolving capital institutions and because of its dominant position, Braudel contended, Europe enjoyed privileges of choice. The influence of its capital resources and borrowing capacity and its communications complex combined to make the European presence a formidable one.[22] Like Braudel, I am interested in using geographical space and the introduction of capitalist exchange relations to explain environmental change. Unlike him I also wish to focus on the ecological and human costs involved in that expanding geography of market values, which were beyond the scope of his study.

Capitalism, it must be remembered, has always been more than an economic system; it is a mode of production, a particular take on the world that attaches ultimate significance to material effects and the manipulation and transformation of those domains for the purposes of profit taking.[23] Scholars should pay more attention, I am convinced, to the culture of capitalism, especially its propensity to reduce the complexities of the natural world to simplified abstractions about exclusive property rights.[24] In an age in which capitalism and its cluster of values have been the preeminent influences in global affairs, it seems appropriate to study a region that includes multiple ecological zones and different forms of cultural adaptation to reach some larger truths about relations between culture and the natural world. Examining social, geographical, and biological phenomena that are politically bounded, therefore, has the potential to provide unique insights about the influence that capitalism has exercised in structuring both human and ecological systems. I believe that the study of different ecological zones rather than those with common natural features provides a plausible way to reach some larger conclusions about human relationships with the natural world under the capitalist mode of production.[25]

The time frame for this book, roughly 1800 to the onset of the Second World War, encompasses the period from the first inroads of market influences in the Pacific Northwest to the increasing integration of the region with the global capitalist system as the twentieth century advanced. During those years, the Oregon country witnessed the progressive destabilization of the aboriginal social system and of its widely varying and diverse ecosystems.[26] The strategy adopted in this study is to view that century and a half as an organic whole, to focus on the incipient market influences of the early nineteenth century and their subsequent growth and maturation as the Pacific Northwest was integrated first into continental economic networks and then the larger arena of global affairs.

As the preeminent industrial power in the world at the close of the Second World War, the United States had developed an aura of supreme self-confidence, an overweening hubris, a widespread belief and conviction in the capacity of humans to order the world to their advantage. For the Oregon country, the advent of the big dam era serves as a symbol of that new techno-cultural paradigm, the stage setting for an age in which human culture itself became the dominating influence in directing systemic ecological and even climatic change. Although this book includes references to the years following the Second World War, its thematic and organic framework embraces the period from the maritime fur trade to the construction of Bonneville and Grand Coulee dams.

To see the natural world in terms of its commodity value, Richard White insists, "is to see lumber in trees, minerals in mountains, winter forage for animals in grasslands." [27] Therefore, even though a region's boundaries might be politically fashioned and absent of what Dan Flores calls "deep time," [28] the intrusion in particular locales of the cluster of values associated with capitalism provides a useful strategy for examining changes to common landscapes and ecosystems, for explaining the dramatic cultural and biological modifications that accompanied the subordination of nature—the colonization of the natural world—to the requirements of the metropolitan-based centers of global capitalism.[29]

Focusing on the kind of bioregional particularism that Dan Flores calls for does little to contribute to larger understandings about the intersection between culture (especially the culture of capitalism) and the natural world. As we close on the end of the twentieth century, it is obvious that capitalist cultural influences have prevailed around much of the globe. For North America, whose eastern seaboard was integrated into the Atlantic trading system in the seventeenth century, it is far more instructive to examine the larger framework of values, the shifting modes of production, and environmental change in fixed and bounded places commencing with the first appearance of market influences. Beginning in the late eighteenth century, the forces unleashed by capitalism have progressively destabilized both human cultures and environments on America's North Pacific slope. How better to study its influence as an agency of transformation than through the examination of a variety of environmental stresses (i.e., the disruption of riparian ecosystems, the disappearance of species, and other phenomena). This inquiry, therefore, is an exploration of the spectacular modifications to Oregon's human and natural world between the late eighteenth century and through the decade of the Great Depression.

The workings of global economic forces in Oregon were not the first cultural modifications of the environment. Although earlier cultural systems—the subsistence groups of fishers, hunters, and gatherers—were less intrusive in terms of their environmental influence, nevertheless a mounting volume of evidence indicates that native people left a considerable imprint on their natural surroundings. But the capitalist mode was more inclusive: it dictated patterns of settlement; it prescribed certain changes to the land; it reflected a move toward more exclusive notions of property; and it subsequently contributed to the commodification of all natural phenomena. In telling the story of the great changes that have occurred during the last two centuries, my *modus operandi* is centered in the belief that a material understanding of the world, the physicality of modern life, is central to comprehending the human relationship with the natural world.[30]

Ideologies, and especially the choices that are rooted in ideology, have exercised a profound influence in shaping the Oregon that we inhabit in the late twentieth century. "All human groups," historian William Cronon argues, "consciously change their environments to some extent." During the last two centuries, the successive cultural cohorts occupying the Oregon country have lived in landscapes shaped to some degree by previous dwellers.[31] Each of those groups, operating from deeply rooted beliefs and values, has in turn molded in varying degrees the places it occupied. The centerpiece of this study is the influence of those ideological prescriptions and the human activities they fostered in particular locales. The interface between humans and the natural world *is* the story, but a critical subset to its telling is the history that humans themselves have inscribed on the landscape over the last two centuries. Although the prospectus for this investigation outlines a chronological approach that covers the period from about 1800 through the 1930s, the major theme addressed in the broader inquiry is the imposition of a culturally preconceived ordering on a common geographic and political unit.

As a physical area, Oregon exists in relation to other places, to other biological, cultural, economic, and political entities. As such, it is impossible to understand the vast biological changes and other modifications that have taken place in Oregon without looking far beyond its political bounds. This inquiry, therefore, will reflect the wider network of market, capital, technological, industrial, and political influences, and the manner in which those investment and exchange relationships, new technologies, and political and economic decisions combined to transform local environments. A vast demographic shift, the dynamic forces of the market, and new and more productive forms of technology combined to transform local ecosystems into human-centered, utilitarian landscapes.

The persistent theme argued in this book, then, is the nearly century-and-a-half relationship between culture and landscape, between human activity and environmental/ecological change in a politically bounded place. The study begins with a general reconstruction of the landscape at a particular moment in historical time. From there the argument shifts to a discussion of native people and their special behavior and adaptation to the region's widely varying ecological zones. The story of the Euro-American penetration and subsequent domination of the region comprises the remainder of the narrative. This is an inquiry into relationships between the cultural and the natural. It is an account of change and much more; it is a story about culture and nature, the study of the intersection between a particular set of values and a disparate natural world. It posits the argument that culture has been a powerful force in shaping the place we call Oregon; it also suggests that the ever-expanding cultural influences of the last two centuries have vastly accelerated the pace and scope of change with the passage of time.

Readers should be cautioned, however, that this is not an exercise in the reductive study of mere change in which humans are simply one species among many competing species in the great natural order of things. As the biologist Edward O. Wilson contends, I believe humans have arrived at the point where the machine, a decidedly *human* creation, is in the Garden and is in the process of vastly accelerating an already rapid pace of change. If culture is now a factor in climate change; if instrumentalism is now the ultimate mark of value; and if human ingenuity oftentimes leads so easily to environmental tragedy, then I agree with the cultural historian Simon Schama: we may indeed be "trapped in the engine of our self-destruction."[32] To leave humans beyond the pale of responsibility for the dramatic alterations that have taken place in the Oregon country during the last two centuries would have the effect of excusing people from the history they have created. Simply put, it evades questions of politics and raises suspicions that environmental history is depoliticized history.[33]

At the close of a long and distinguished career as a professor of agriculture at Oregon State University, E. R. Jackman addressed the Corvallis Friends of the Library in 1961 on the subject, "Oregon: A State of Mind." During the course of an evening's lecture spiced with anecdotes, homilies, and tributes to a mythical past, Jackman outlined the unique features of his adopted homeland:

Oregon is a remarkable state, climatically, geologically, and botanically. Rainfall here runs from six inches up to thirty times as much, or 180 inches, and some spots can be found where the average is at any point in between. Curry County grows palm and eucalyptus trees, but some spots in the state have frost every month in the year. Farming is carried on from sea level up to 9,000 feet, and every elevation in between.

The resources of the state, including trees, he said, were largely related to land and what it produces. Despite the existence of an expanding volume of records about those human-land relationships, Jackman told his audience that something more was needed: "a systematized story showing Oregon's use of its land, including the stories of agriculture, forestry, [the] marketing of products," and related investigations in irrigation, mining, and geology.[34]

Jackman concluded his talk with a plea for the publication of articles about "the history and use of our land." He told the Friends of the Library gathering that he could envision advanced-degree students engaged in research on "all sorts of things": the Indian use of plants; innovations in farm machinery; the recorded efforts to find oil in the state; the history of the canning of salmon and fruit; the vegetation of Steens Mountain; the story of irrigation works; and the evolution of the beef industry.[35] In brief, Jackman was interested in the broad historical effects of human relationships with the natural world and with Oregon's myriad local ecologies.

Life in nineteenth-century Oregon—for native people and Euro-American newcomer alike—was intimately connected to the land. Its resources were essential to human existence. Fishing, hunting, farming, mining, and cutting trees were elemental, physical activities that placed individuals in the midst of a daunting and imposing natural world of great valley bottoms, turbulent waterways, magnificent mountains, and an amazing profusion of flora and fauna.[36] The Oregon writer Robin Cody put it this way: "Nature was fearsome. Nature was to be conquered, to be triumphed over. Heroes were the woodsmen and homesteaders and railroaders who cleared the last American wilderness."[37] The stories associated with that mix of people and natural settings are, to a degree, stories about nature, environmental narratives, accounts of people struggling to find their way in their newly adopted places of habitation. That link to what I have called "nature's industries" was to remain a constant in the life of the region, at least until the late twentieth century when machines of a very new order, those linked to the telecommuter "Information Age," became a critical factor in a vastly different set of economic/environmental relations.

In the process of defining and then reshaping the Oregon landscape over the course of two centuries, the incoming culture—slowly at first and then with gathering momentum—began the transformation of the very material conditions under which life itself was maintained: vast river systems were pooled and re-created into technical artifices; forest lands were harvested, replanted, and redesigned into monocultural, market-driven models under the rubric of forest science; swamps and marshlands were diked, drained, surrounded with diversion canals, and turned into plots of industrial efficiency. The transformation of Oregon's landscape over the past two hundred years was the effort of individuals and groups of people who were in the process of disrupting, creating, and changing the world about them.[38] The cultural underpinnings for that work included a firm belief in progress and the efficacy of human advancement through the endless appropriation and manipulation of nature.

The writer William Kittredge, who grew to maturity in southcentral Oregon's Warner Valley, described the set of mind, the mentality that it took to transform that landscape into a modern, systematized setting for agribusiness:

> An ancient world was changing, and my people were on the leading edge of the conversion. They not only knew it, but also gloried in it. The idea that they were connected to important doings and improvements in the world inhabited them and drove them forward.[39]

The Kittredge family and their neighbors shaped the world around them according to their mythology, a story line that carried with it implicit instructions about bringing civilization to a seemingly savage country. But instead of a benign parable of pastoralism, of having created a good place, according to Kittredge, that reordering of humans and landscapes turned out to be little more than "a rationale for violence — against other people and against nature."[40]

There is a somber even brooding tone to the stories of people like William Kittredge, writers who are in many instances only a generation or so removed from the great engineering transformations wrought on Oregon's landscape. In a sense, those recent lamentations about environmental change represent a wistful case of the lost cause, the paradise squandered, the good life frittered away in a spate of material gluttony. Barry Lopez, an author of nature-oriented books who has made Oregon his adopted home, is another literary figure who is disheartened by what he calls a "crisis of culture, of character," a spirit that seems endemic in Oregon and elsewhere. Because Americans have made such an enormous investment in "mining the continent" — with its endless profusion of jobs in gathering, processing, and selling the products of nature — Lopez fears that citizens "cannot imagine stopping."[41]

That new temperament is remarkably different from the pride and self-confidence, the aura of purpose and conviction that prevailed in Oregon for more than a century and a half. As recently as forty years ago there were few who questioned the essential rightness of remaking and remodeling a seemingly discordant world into a managed, regulated, and more orderly setting to serve the purposes of human welfare. The reflections of Kittredge, Lopez, and others provide a kind of literary mapping that marks a significant departure from the formerly dominant narratives that focused on human progress and the broadly shared goal of mastering difficult natural worlds, of gaining power over nature.

The first Euro-American stories about America's North Pacific slope begin with a strikingly different spirit, a set of assumptions centered in what historian James Ronda has called "Ouragon—the fabled land of promise." To the ambitious and to those who dreamed of earthly Elysian fields, Oregon was a mythical place with the potential "to fulfill the dreams and calculations of every prophet, promoter, and visionary," a setting that "promised . . . nature beyond measure." [42] As the eventful twentieth century draws to a close, the old stories about western America as the land of promise, a place where earthly dreams would come true, seem distant and removed from our contemporary world of vanishing species and diminishing resources. For the first time since the nation's inception in the late eighteenth century, a sizable public in the United States is beginning to question and rethink the deeper meaning of the idea of progress. Today those who have been the more thoughtful about the scope and scale of environmental change tend toward the darker view of matters. The story that follows will explore the background and wider meaning of that former landscape of hope. [43]

The Early Historic Period

I

The Native Ecological Context

We crossed . . . a steep and high mountain, called the Blue. . . . The whole mountain is densely covered with tall pine trees, with an undergrowth of service bushes and other shrubs. . . . the grass has been lately consumed, and many of the trees blasted by the ravaging fires of the Indians. These fires are yet smoldering, and the smoke from them effectually prevents our viewing the surrounding country. — *John Kirk Townsend*[1]

The early fall weather was warm and even more so during the midafternoon as the stonemason's son proceeded southward through a gently rolling landscape interspersed with "beautiful solitary oaks and pines." It would all "have a fine effect," the traveler wrote in his journal, except for "being . . . burned and not a single blade of grass except on the margins of the rivulets." The wandering sojourner was David Douglas, a Scot in the employ of the Horticultural Society of London and one of the most famous of all exploring botanists. The year was 1826 and the peripatetic Douglas was passing through the Willamette Valley with Alexander McLeod and the Hudson's Bay Company's southern trapping expedition. Along his route of travel the inquisitive Douglas busied himself collecting plant specimens and confiding daily observations to his journal. For nine long days from late September into early October Douglas and the small party passed through burned and charred terrain, an experience that prompted the only discordant entries among his Willamette Valley notes. When the group neared the southernmost reaches of the valley, Douglas complained in his journal that his "feet were very sore from the burned stumps of the low brush-wood and strong grasses."[2]

The charred and blackened landscape that Douglas described was the result of deliberate burning. Because lightning storms are rare events in the Willamette Valley proper, and especially so during the late summer and early fall months, the extensive areas of burned grasslands and rolling hills that Douglas witnessed were most certainly the work of human activity. The Scot was quick to acknowledge that truth in an oft-quoted passage:

> Some of the natives tell me it is done for the purpose of urging deer to frequent certain parts, to feed, which they leave unburned, and of course they are easily killed. Others say that it is done in order that they might the better find wild honey and grasshoppers, which both serve as articles of winter food.

When the McLeod party headed southward into the Umpqua Valley on its way to California in November, Douglas reversed his course and back-tracked to Fort Vancouver through a dramatically transformed and re-newed landscape of lush, green prairie whose appearance was broken by occasional marshes and lakes abundant with waterfowl.[3]

That burned valley landscape and its seeming rebirth following the fall rains fit the "cultural grasslands" thesis advanced by the geographer Carl Sauer more than fifty years ago—that native people made strategic use of fire to enhance their hunting prospects for animals and for a variety of other purposes. A careful reading of seventeenth-century North American literature convinced Sauer that fire was a widespread and general feature of Indian practice, except where conditions were too humid for burning or too arid to produce fuels. At the time of the European intrusion in North America, historian Stephen Pyne concludes, the role of fire in sus-taining grassland and open savanna landscapes is incontestable.[4] Although the historical record clearly shows that anthropogenic activity such as fire profoundly influenced Indian landscapes, scholars have long overlooked its cultural role.[5] The evidential literature is less clear in underscoring the long shadow cast by those practices.

Because floral and plant successions were critically important to hunting-and-gathering economies, native people regularly used fire to successfully manipulate the proper environmental conditions to enhance their subsistence prospects. According to anthropologist Henry Dobyns, "fire constituted the principal technology that Indoamericans possessed for modifying natural environments in order to augment their food supplies."[6] There is also abundant evidence to suggest that native fires were strategically set when seasonal and fuel conditions were conducive to low-intensity burns. It is also reasonable to assume that the rationale for burning varied with climate, topography, and vegetative conditions, and that native people used fire for a variety of purposes: (1) to stimulate new growth for browsing wildlife and waterfowl; (2) to enhance the development of a variety of plant foods; (3) to assist in hunting animals; (4) to maintain clearings for easy travel; and (5) once they acquired horses, to improve grazing prospects for their herds.[7]

Those cultural modifications to the landscape existed everywhere across the terrain that was to become Oregon. Archaeological evidence indicates that purposeful human manipulation of the environment was geographically widespread long before the observations of travelers like Douglas.[8] As William Cronon points out, "Historical 'accidents' — many of them anthropogenic — cast long shadows." It would appear to be an incontestable fact, therefore, that Indian cultural practices had profoundly influenced the character of the landscapes that Europeans reported. An abundance of data, one scholar argues, indicates that "humankind has influenced the composition and structure of nearly all North American ecosystems for nearly ten thousand years."[9] The great weight of scientific evidence argues against the notion of the Americas as a pristine, Eden-like world where the human imprint was barely perceptible.[10]

Indian subsistence activities, through conscious practices that encouraged some plant and animal species while discouraging others, influenced the extent and composition of forests, established and extended grassland areas, and altered arid environments. All the evidence indicates that indigenous peoples manipulated and shaped their environments to suit their subsistence needs.[11] According to geographer William Denevan, the important question is "the form and magnitude of environmental modification rather than . . . whether . . . Indians lived in harmony with nature and with sustainable systems of resource management." The historical and archaeological record shows indisputably that the paradise Columbus reported in the Western Hemisphere "was clearly a humanized landscape."[12]

Both natural and cultural processes have been involved in shaping the world about us. But culture did not become a factor in environmental change until the emergence of modern humans during the middle of the last glacial period, say 40,000 years ago, when the members of genus *Homo sapiens* were in the process of colonizing most of the earth. For thousands of years, however, population numbers and technological practices limited the human imprint on environmental change, with the possible exception that humans may have contributed to Pleistocene extinctions. The latter issue has been a problematic one for scholars, because the disappearance of several species of large mammals occurred between 11,500 and 9,000 years ago, a period when the North American climate was warming rapidly and humans were spreading across the continent. Whether the extinctions were cultural, environmental, or a combination of both, megafauna such as the mastodon and the mammoth have been extinct for several thousand years.[13]

The rather abrupt warming conditions that occurred during the early Holocene epoch (10,000 to 5,000 years ago) also marked the general northward advance of forest ecosystems and plant life, "one of the great stories of the Earth's recent natural history," according to geographer Neil Roberts. Coinciding with the warming climate, cultural influences in the natural world also become much more noticeable in the archaeological record. The more favorable climatic conditions for plant and animal species extended the range of ecological niches suitable to human habitation and enabled people to manipulate their surroundings to their advantage. But more than any other factor, the advent of Neolithic agriculture accelerated the human role in environmental change in many parts of the world. Beginning about 10,000 years ago in the Middle East and much later elsewhere, the Neolithic revolution accelerated population growth and set in motion more intensified use of the land, cultural intrusions that wrought major disruptions to native flora and fauna.[14] Those changes, however, were a long time in coming to the Pacific slope of North America.

As elsewhere in the Northern Hemisphere, the end of the Pleistocene epoch brought cataclysmic changes to the landforms and topography of the greater Pacific Northwest.[15] When the huge ice mass receded from the upper reaches of the Columbia River drainage, it left in its wake an enormous inland lake that periodically burst through its dam of glacial ice and unleashed a series of catastrophic downstream floods. The scouring effects of that huge volume of water created the channeled scablands of eastern Washington, including the famous Grand Coulee, and contributed to the physical configuration and buildup of silt deposits in the Willamette Valley. The most recent of those floods probably took place toward the end of the glacial period. In the now-arid basin and range country further to the south, massive glaciers still covered higher elevations such as Steens Mountain during the late Pleistocene; in the basins proper, vast lakes were slowly diminishing in size.[16]

With the recession of the glaciers and the gradual draining of the interior lakes, spruce, fir, and other conifers appeared over broad areas of the country. Pollen samples from the immediate postglacial period indicate that sagebrush was a dominant plant growing across Oregon's high desert; the same records also show that fir, spruce, and other conifers formed scattered stands of subalpine woodlands. The northern basin and range country, however, changed dramatically with the transition to warmer temperatures. The Pleistocene lakes disappeared, leaving only remnants such as Summer Lake, Lake Abert, Malheur Lake, and smaller ones in Warner Valley. As the climate continued to warm between 7,000 and 4,000 years ago, grassland and sagebrush cohorts replaced the retreating alpine and subalpine plant communities.[17]

Similar changes took place west of the Cascade Mountains, especially in the Willamette Valley, where Douglas fir, grand fir, ponderosa pine, and western hemlock emerged following the gradual recession of the late Pleistocene floodwaters. Under those warming and drying conditions, the marshlands and lakes of the valley proper diminished in size and grasslands and oaks began to appear across the landscape. In the rugged southwestern mountains and valleys of Oregon—a sort of ecological borderland between moist rain country and the dryer conditions of the Californian province— the same postglacial warming conditions prevailed with the appearance of oak savannas in the bottomlands and along mid-elevation areas. There also are indications that the moderating, slightly cooler conditions of the last

5,000 years have witnessed the expansion of the coniferous forests to lower elevations.[18]

Several archaeological finds, including one in Oregon's Fort Rock area on the periphery of the Great Basin,[19] indicate that humans first entered the greater Pacific Northwest during the late Pleistocene when glaciers still covered much of the mountainous country of the interior. Before the dramatic warming of the climate between 11,000 and 9,000 years ago, now-extinct animals—the giant ground sloth, the giant bison, the camel, and a prehistoric horse—were still present in North America. Those species intermingled with present-day animals—antelope, deer, mountain sheep, and a wide variety of bird life.[20] Over the course of the next several millennia, the postglacial climate varied in temperature and in precipitation—with cooler and moister conditions alternating with warmer and dryer patterns. But for most of the last 9,000 years, it is fairly accurate to say that the prevailing climatic regime has resembled that of our present age.[21]

Although it is generally acknowledged that human environmental influences in prehistoric North America were considerable, it is also widely understood that the Columbian encounter triggered vast biological and technological changes with worldwide repercussions. Following the epic event of 1492, an expanding global network of economic and biological exchanges emerged whose "international energy flows," according to Carl Butzer, favored the emerging centers of the industrial revolution. As those industrializing sectors gradually extended their technological reach, forces were set in motion that introduced immense social and environmental changes worldwide.[22] During the last several centuries, therefore, succeeding modes of production—hunting/fishing/gathering, peasant agriculture, and the industrial/postindustrial mode—have increased the extent and scope of the human influence in the natural world.[23]

By the sixteenth century, the onset of the modern era, human-manipulated agricultural regimes had replaced natural systems in many parts of the globe. But economic, environmental, and ecological changes taking place elsewhere were delayed in the Pacific Northwest. Until the very recent past, the region was simply beyond the reach—or at best on the periphery—of the immense market-induced global ecological exchanges of the post-

Columbian world. History and geography, especially the region's isolation from major routes of transoceanic commerce, conspired to place the Northwest beyond the reach of Europe and even the neo-European settlements along North America's Atlantic seaboard. Indeed, what is striking about the region is the *very* recent and *very* rapid pace of human-induced environmental disturbance over *very* extensive areas in a *very* brief span of time.[24]

For America's North Pacific slope, the hunting-gathering way of life remained dominant until Europeans began to impose a new set of cultural arrangements on the landscape. The region was an anomaly in one other respect as well: Neolithic agricultural practices were absent during the Indian period of domination. Richard White has argued, however, that the rapidity with which the Salish peoples of Whidbey Island adapted to the cultivation of potatoes "reflects the extent to which their gathering practices had already approached true agriculture." But the degree to which native people in some areas of the Northwest were approaching agricultural behavior is not the issue. Fisheries and wildlife scientist Dean Shinn emphasized that unique conjuncture of historical circumstances in the region: "we are still relatively close to the early history of the region, and to the events which caused environmental change there."[25]

The particular historical configuration of events and circumstances in the Northwest provides exceptional opportunities for studying precontact landscapes, for examining ecological conditions at the onset of large-scale Euro-American migration, and for placing in a broader perspective the human-induced changes that have occurred during the industrial age. Because the postcontact history of the region is telescoped into such a brief span of time, it is possible to learn—through conventional historical records, such as journals, diaries, government surveys, and travel accounts—a great deal about ecological conditions at the time of Euro-American entry. That scholars are increasingly turning to pollen and soil records and traditional archaeological evidence further enriches the potential for building a realistic and viable profile of landscapes and environments.

Once the postglacial regime established itself, environmental conditions in the Northwest remained *relatively* stable for at least 10,000 years—with the exception of the cataclysmic explosion of Mount Mazama (circa 4,000 B.C.), which formed Crater Lake. That is not to deny what the anthropologist Eugene Hunn calls "the biogeographical consequences of climatic change." But he points out that differences in climatic patterns, because they were not extreme, merely required adjustments in hunting and gathering strategies rather than dramatic social and economic change. Richard White makes a similar argument for the native people of Puget Sound, who inhabited a "relatively stable and productive environment" for centuries before the arrival of white settlers. For most of the Pacific Northwest, therefore, the archaeological record permits a consensus of sorts: cultural and social changes were modest until the historical period, with subsistence patterns largely centered on terrestrial and riverine environments. Only the northward spread of Spanish horses in the early eighteenth century, the entry of the market-oriented fur trade in the early nineteenth century, and the introduction of the exogenous diseases that ravaged indigenous peoples disrupted that stability.[26]

But relative social and cultural stability does not imply the absence of native influence in the natural world. Indeed, extensive archaeological and other historical evidence suggests quite the opposite. Native people in the greater Oregon country[27] inhabited humanized landscapes, ecosystems that were purposefully modified. Richard White points out that natives in Puget Sound's Whidbey Island used fire as a tool to enhance the growing of bracken and camas, staple vegetables in their diet. "Rather than being major Indian food sources because they dominated the prairies," he concludes, "camas and bracken more likely dominated the prairies because they were major Indian food sources." There is abundant evidence to indicate equally human-influenced landscapes elsewhere in the region.[28]

The archaeological record indicates that early Pleistocene hunters in the Northwest used burning thousands of years ago, and the early narratives of the region also include frequent references to fires and burned landscapes. Fires alter ecosystems in several ways, affecting the composition and distribution of species and selectively favoring some over others, especially early successional types. Still extant stands of old-growth forests show evidence of previous disturbances, with fire being one of the most prevalent of all recurring disturbing agents. It is fair to say, then, that the fire regimes and forest types of historical Oregon were the consequence of repeated fires, some natural and others of human origin, of variable rates and intensity.

Although historical sources do not reveal with any precision the ratio between human and naturally caused fires before large-scale white settlement in the Pacific Northwest, the evidence suggests that Indian incendiarism was a significant factor in the burning of both grassland and forest.[29]

Fire ecologist James Agee has found that the role of anthropogenic fire in the Pacific Northwest varied with climatic regimes. Native influences varied according to subregion, with their role in the forests west of the Cascades less clear because of the moist marine environment. Nevertheless, Indian burning practices definitely were significant in shaping the ecology of the prairies and the rolling oak and savanna grassland country in the Willamette Valley and even into the foothills of the Cascade and Coast ranges. Although the historical record is less revealing, anthropologist Henry Lewis is convinced that native fire routines in the Umpqua and Rogue River drainages created similar environments. Despite the relative dearth of information, he reasons that "habitat fires were no less important for the Shasta, Umpqua, and other tribes of the south and southwestern part of the state." Like the Kalapuya in the Willamette Valley, Indian groups in the Umpqua and Rogue valleys fired the landscape to enhance their subsistence gathering prospects, or as Henry Lewis points out, to better their chances of obtaining food through the periodic firing of grassland and forest environments.[30]

Except for the extremely arid regions of North America, the historian Stephen Pyne contends that the continent's grassland environments were also the result of the Indian's calculated and routine use of fire. From the coastal plain of Massachusetts southward to Florida and westward to Texas, from California's great Central Valley to Oregon's Willamette Valley, grasslands flourished as a consequence of Indian incendiary activity.[31] The first narrative portraits of the Willamette, Umpqua, and Rogue valley landscapes, therefore, describe culturally influenced physical settings. When Hudson's Bay Company operative John Work traveled southward through the Willamette Valley in 1834, he made frequent references to vast open areas and fine interior valleys with neither "a stone & scarcely a shrub to interrupt the progress of the plow which might be employed in many places with little more difficulty than in a stubble field." South of the present town of Amity, Work reported an uninterrupted plain where "wood here & there juts in points out to the Plain, and there are patches of oak here & there." In the vicinity of Corvallis, the Bay Company trapper confided to his journal: "Here is an extensive plain on both sides of the river, and the mountains to the w. are nearly without wood."[32]

Over several millennia, seasonal burning routines in the Willamette Valley created vast open prairies like those reported by Work, interspersed with scattered groves of fire-resistant oak. Corridors of mixed deciduous and conifer forests lay adjacent to the major waterways, and scattered throughout the valley, but especially prominent toward the north, were low-lying marshes and lakes most likely the result of seasonal flooding. The great stands of Douglas fir forests, so characteristic of the modern era, were confined to the higher, mountainous elevations on each side of the valley.[33]

George Emmons, an official with the United States Exploring Expedition of 1841, left a strikingly graphic word picture of that valley landscape prior to white settlement, probably from the vantage of the Eola Hills to the northwest of Salem:

[These] are a little singular being the only hills of any magnitude that rise from the great Walamat Valley—in an extent of Prairie from 60 to [1]00 miles either way. . . from the top of these at an alt. of about 1000 feet—had a panoramic view . . . prairie to the south as far as the view extends—the streams being easily traced by a border of trees that grew up on either bank. . . white oak scattered about in all directions.[34]

Lt. Charles Wilkes, the commander of the government-sponsored expedition, traveled up the valley to the Willamette Mission in June of that year and wondered about the open stretches of prairie land. He quickly concluded: "Fire is no doubt the cause." His subordinate, Emmons, verified his commander's judgment two months later when he offered a vivid description of native influences in shaping the ecology of the Willamette Valley in the vicinity of present-day Newberg:

. . . the country becoming smoky from the annual fires of the Indians—who burn the Prairies to dry & partially cook a sunflower seed—which abounds throughout this portion of the country & is afterwards collected by them in considerable quantities & kept for their winter's stock of food. The forests are also frequently burnt to aid them in entrapping their game—these two burnings combined formed the greatest obstacle the travellers encountered in this country—one blocking the way—& the other destroying the food of the animals [i.e., the expedition's horses].[35]

Lt. William Peel, the son of the famous British politician, was among the many who confirmed the prairie, oak savanna, tree-lined waterway configuration of the valley landscape when he traveled through the Willamette country at the onset of white occupation. Peel described a rich and well-watered land, generally bare of timber with "fine luxurious grass" covering the prairies, "divided by belts of timber running along the Banks of the Rivers and Streams." In the "oak openings" scattered throughout the valley, Garry or white oak was the dominant species with an understory that included a mixture of grasses, forbs, and small shrubs occasionally intermixed with ferns and hazel and oak saplings. Away from the timbered waterways and the scattered oak groves, all was grassland, presenting, in the words of Charles Wilkes, "one of the most striking appearances . . . its Prairies in some instances a dead level for miles in extent."[36]

In the late spring and beyond the densely wooded riparian areas, luxurious grasses and clover covered the valley's prairie landscape: blue wildrye, Idaho bentgrass, California oatgrass, California danthonia, and needlegrass. Where the soil was well drained, red fescue was the most common bunchgrass, while the tall, tufted hairgrass grew across the valley's extensive areas of poorly drained soil. The camas plant, whose starchy bulb was a staple food in the Indian diet, grew in marshy valley areas that were subject to seasonal flooding. During the late spring the widespread flowering of the blue camas was a beautiful sight to behold. The grasses and plants that grew in both floodplain and upland prairie alike provided an abundance of food for browsing animals such as deer and elk and the numerous flocks of waterfowl that passed through the valley.[37]

The anthropologist Robert Boyd has found a consensus among scholars that frequent firing was the principal ecological factor in maintaining the oak and savanna environment that dominated the Willamette Valley landscape. Pollen studies indicate that the oak savanna regime dominated the valley for more than 6,000 years, an estimate that is generally consistent with the widely accepted scientific view about the long-term ecological stability of the greater Pacific Northwest. The native Kalapuyas, whose ancestors may have lived in the valley from 6,000 to 10,000 years ago, were the principal actors in maintaining that oak savanna environment into the historic period.[38]

The more heavily timbered zones in the valley proper were largely riparian, floodplain woodlands that varied in widths up to one mile on each side of the main stem of the Willamette and to a lesser extent for smaller streams. Those streamside, bottomland forests were dense, gallery-like communities of white ash, black cottonwood, willow, bigleaf maple, Douglas fir, and western red cedar with an understory vegetation comprised of a variety of shrub species: salmonberry, elderberry, and Oregon grape. The land survey notes compiled by the General Land Office during the early 1850s detail the character of that bottomland vegetation. In the low-lying area along the Willamette River in present-day West Salem, a surveyor reported:

river bottoms overflowed in high water of the Willamette, 10 to 15 feet deep. Timber in bottoms w ash, maple, balm of gilead, fir, etc. Undergrowth hazel, vine maple, crabapple, etc. North of bottoms scttering w. oak.

In an adjacent section along the same riparian tract the surveyors reported a similar growth of fir, ash, willow, and maple, with an undergrowth of hazel, vine maple, briars, and nettles. Those same bottomlands, the report continued, "are overflowed in high water of the Willamette from about 10 to 20 feet in depth."[39]

At the time the General Land Office conducted its surveys of the Willamette Valley, white settlements in the area were well advanced. And while the survey notes for the Willamette countryside appear to have a good degree of scientific reliability, they also reflect floral and faunal conditions at a point when new cultural forces were beginning to alter the valley's landscape. Except for the areas immediately adjacent to a few of the fledgling communities along the Willamette River, however, it is likely that the composition of the riparian zones had changed little since the turn of the century. The trees in the bottomlands were very large and difficult to fall; the river flooded to various stages during the rainy season; and little had been accomplished in the way of stream "improvements." At the time of the surveys, the river still reflected its old character of multiple, meandering channels filled with snags and fallen trees and a riparian forest of varying widths.[40]

With some differences due to areal variations in precipitation and climate, the Indians of the Rogue, Umpqua, and Willamette valleys were a gathering, hunting, and to a lesser degree a fishing people. Those native groups lived in the midst of a strikingly diversified subsistence base that provided a variety of root foods. Principal among them was camas. Harvested in great quantities in the spring, the onion-shaped camas bulbs were pounded into a mash, baked in subterranean rock ovens, and stored for winter consumption. Other staples of the native diet — roots, nuts, seeds, and berries — were all fire-nurtured foods. Several species of animals supplemented the plant foods, including black-tailed and white-tailed deer, elk, and a variety of waterfowl and other bird life.[41]

Although the historical record is less revealing, there are striking resemblances between the Willamette Valley and the cultural/landscape paradigm of the Rogue and Umpqua valleys, despite moderately different climatic patterns and some dissimilarities in the floral composition of forests and grasslands. Passing from the Willamette into the Umpqua drainage in mid-September 1841, Henry Eld, a surveyor with the Wilkes Exploring Expedition, reported that the weather continued "thick and smoky the sun seen only occasionally." After several hours of hunting for their horses through bottomlands obscured with smoke, the party traveled "through valleys . . . principally oak trees with grass growing under them. . . . The prairies mostly today are on fire, winding its course slowly with the wind across the plains and up the hills." [42]

As the group continued southward through the homeland of the Athapascan speakers of the middle Umpqua and into the Takelma-controlled area of the middle Rogue River country, the chronicling of Indian burning continued. Eld reported that the company camped on the banks of the South Umpqua River "on a piece of very narrow prairie ground with very little vegetation or grass and that very dry & burnt, affording an exceedingly scant allowance for the animals." The hills surrounding the valley proper, according to Eld, were "12 to 1500 ft in height with grass extending to their summits and their tops scattered with pines and oaks." For the next two days as the party worked its way southward, expedition member George Emmons described a countryside so smoky and burned that "I feel that I am groping my way along half blindfolded."[43]

When the exploring party descended into the Rogue Valley, a drier ecological regime and cultural transition zone of sorts, the naturalist Titian Ramsay Peale added to the group's voluminous reportage of a "country . . . mostly burned by Indians." Finally, as the small band of interlopers moved into the Siskiyou Mountains on September 28, Peale witnessed an Indian woman "so busy setting fire to the prairie & mountain ravines that she seemed to disregard us." He also reported that the woman "had a large funnel-shaped basket which they *all* carry to collect roots and seeds." Although Peale failed to make the connection in this instance between fire and food gathering, his is a revealing description. The seeds from tarweed, a sunflower-like plant that grew widely throughout the interior valleys of western Oregon, were staples of the Indian diet. When the seeds were ready to harvest in late summer, the tarweed was set on fire and the seeds beaten from the stalks into baskets.[44]

What Peale and his companions regarded as a difficult, food-deprived, and scarred landscape was in fact a culturally nurtured and productive environment for its native inhabitants. George Riddle, who settled on a tributary of the South Umpqua River in 1851, remembered Indian women gathering seeds during the summer months, "of which the tar weed seed was the most prized." When the seeds were ripe in the autumn, the Indians burned the prairie bench lands of the valley, leaving "the plant standing with the tar burned off and the seeds left in the pods." Indian women then collected the seeds, beating them from the pods into a basket. The tarweed seeds were subsequently mashed with a stone pestle and stored for later consumption.[45]

As it was for the Kalapuya in the Willamette Valley, tarweed was a major food source for the Athapascan and Takelman speakers of the Umpqua and Rogue valleys and for many California Indians as well. All of those groups practiced prescribed burning of the tarweed gathering grounds to enhance their harvesting prospects. The annual burns, which nurtured rather than destroyed the highly valued plants, suggest that native people in the interior valleys exercised a remarkable degree of ecological manipulation. Successful harvests *required* burning; therefore, because of its limited availability in some areas and because it was a desirable foodstuff, Robert Boyd argues that "plots of wild tarweed, unlike other food plants, might be considered family or personal property." [46] Although native people burned the western valleys for a variety of reasons, tarweed culture was certainly a major motivation for their incendiary activity.

As an agent of disturbance, fire is both natural and cultural, destructive and restorative. In its cultural form, historian Robert Bunting contends, "the way fire is employed reveals a great deal about the cultural precepts of the people who live upon the land." For Indian people in the Oregon country, fire was central to the processes of gathering and hunting. Native burning activities followed an annual pattern, with most of the incendiarism taking place in August and September. The point to be emphasized is the *intentional* torching of prairie and woodland alike to shape regional vegetation patterns to suit native subsistence needs. Fire enhanced browsing prospects for foraging animals like deer and elk; provided tender grass shoots in the fall for migrating waterfowl; and increased the acorn production of oak trees. Less consciously, Bunting points out, those practices also reduced the risk of the high-intensity fires that have characterized the region in the aftermath of white settlement.[47] Regular burning diminished the buildup of debris and undergrowth that feeds dangerous wildfires.

The general character of the Umpqua Valley, according to Overton Johnson who traveled through the region in the early 1840s, "is very similar to the Willamette Valley, excepting that its surface is more undulating." Johnson described a woodland and prairie landscape, "but prairies occupy the greater portion, the timber being principally along the water courses and on the bordering Mountains." The Rogue Valley, too, was "much like that of the Umpqua; but is more level . . . and is covered with good grass. . . . Here, as in the Umpqua Valley, the timber is on the streams, and the prairies are between them." [48]

Native land-use practices in the Little Applegate River watershed, part of the extensive Rogue River system, offer a vignette of the reciprocal relationship between human occupation and the natural world. Indian subsistence routines that measurably influenced the Little Applegate setting included fishing, horticultural activities (the growing of tobacco), communal hunting of deer and elk, the intensive use of certain plants, and the conscious and regular use of fire in all of those processes. Human fires shaped the Little Applegate bottomlands into a savanna and oak woodland landscape, kept the upper-slope pine zone clear of underbrush, and maintained certain high-elevation openings where native people regularly harvested beargrass, the latter valued for its edible rhizomes and its leaf fibers used in basket making. A newspaper account in the *Ashland Tidings* in 1892 indicated the effects of that human-fashioned landscape—with its absence of underbrush, open grasslands, and plentiful deer—on historical memory: "old settlers in Southern Oregon claim that the Indians kept the country looking neater than the whites do."[49]

The native people of the western interior valleys do not fit the cultural profile associated with the Northwest coastal groups who were dependent on salmon and shellfish. Nor did their lifestyles mirror the Plateau people to the east, many of whom were horse mounted by the early eighteenth century. The Athapascan speakers who lived in the extensive Umpqua River drainage, especially in the upstream areas, exhibited a blending of several cultural traits. Unlike the Indians of the lower Umpqua, who depended largely on marine sources for their sustenance, the interior valley people relied on fishing, hunting, and gathering in approximately equal measure, their principal foods being camas, salmon, and deer and elk meat. The dietary conventions of the Takelman-speakers who lived adjacent to the long arm of the South Umpqua River and its several tributaries included small amounts of salmon, deer and elk, and abundant use of acorns and camas, supplemented with a variety of seeds, nuts, and berries.[50]

Native influences in modifying forest and grassland environments across the mountainous and high-desert country of eastern Oregon and in eastern Washington's "Great Columbia Plain"[51] are also too obvious to ignore. Indeed, the effects of native fires east of the Cascade Range may have been even more pronounced than they were in the marine-influenced environment to the west. For desert ecosystems, fire ecologist Lee Eddleman contends, "human caused fires were of greater consequence" than natural ones. Other scholars agree about the significance of cultural influences in shaping arid and semiarid environments: fire "was a natural component of the native ecosystem."[52] Indeed, early nineteenth-century travel accounts mention fire with such regularity as to create a mental picture of a ravaged, charred, and ruined land.

The vast intermontane region extending north and south between the Rocky Mountains and the Cascade and Sierra Nevada ranges—from the southern reaches of the Great Basin to the northern extent of the Columbia Basin—is the land of the "cold desert." Except for the coniferous forests at higher elevations in the north, this was a variegated, sagebrush-dominated landscape with an understory of perennial grasses. Early whites who traveled through the interior country referred to all shrublike species as sage or wormwood. The classic sage/bluebunch wheatgrass section embraced an extensive region that included the Malheur and Harney basins in the south to the Columbia Basin in the north. This was also a fire-maintained region, where native cultural practices shaped the ecological association between plants and grasses.[53]

Fire played an essential role in the character and distribution of big sagebrush throughout the intermontane region. Identified as *Artemisia tridentata* by the British naturalist Thomas Nuttall, big sagebrush is a three- to six-foot-tall, woody-based shrub that will not sprout after it is burned. As two fire ecologists point out, "the effect of wildfires in sagebrush/grasslands is to eliminate the landscape's dominant shrub." The function of fire in the big sagebrush/bluebunch wheatgrass country of eastern Oregon, therefore, was to remove competition and to enhance and nurture the growth of perennial grasses, especially that of the bunchgrass variety. Both the historical record and scientific evidence show conclusively that fire was the dominating influence in shaping and sustaining both plant and animal communities in those arid and semiarid ecosystems.[54]

Except for the introduction of Spanish horses in the early eighteenth century, bison were the only large herbivore to inhabit the eastern country just prior to the coming of whites. Bison evidently grazed from northern Nevada through the Malheur and Harney basins to the Columbia Basin, roughly the extent of the bluebunch wheatgrass range. Promiscuous killing by Hudson's Bay Company and American trapping parties and an increased take by native hunters with rifles most likely exterminated the bison population west of the Rocky Mountains sometime during the 1830s. When the Hudson's Bay Company trapper Peter Skene Ogden ventured

[handwritten margin note: except that this picture is probably skewed to include only areas frequented by humans. On a more vast, regional scale, a different picture might emerge.]

into the vicinity of Harney Lake in November 1826, he recorded in his journal that "Buffal have been here and heads are to be seen," a reference that might indicate that the animals already had been eliminated from the area. But even when the bison herds were at their peak, ecologist Lee Eddleman argues, large grazing wildlife had little effect on vegetation.[55] As the eighteenth century advanced and the size of Indian horse herds multiplied, some evidence suggests that the influence of grazers on specific locales may have been much more intrusive.

One of the most important documents in the early literature on the Oregon country, the journals of Lewis and Clark were the first to reveal the complexities of Indian environmental influences, especially the important role of fire to the horse-mounted hunter-gatherers of the interior country. On their return trip upriver in the spring of 1806, Meriwether Lewis reported that the plains of the Columbia were covered with a "rich verdure of grass and herbs from four to nine inches high." As the party drew closer to the Walla Walla River, the journal entries note the absence of firewood, the Indian use of shrubs for fuel, an abundance of roots for human consumption, and favorable references to the availability of grass for horses. Writing some distance up the Walla Walla River, William Clark remarked that "great portions of these bottoms has been latterly burnt which has entirely distroyed the timbered growth."[56] To attribute all of that early season greenery to Indian burning practices is unreasonable, yet the historical literature shows a fascinating juxtaposition of human incendiary activity in the fall and rich vegetative growth the following spring.

Native people east of the Cascade Mountains readily fired arid landscapes just as their counterparts did in the western valleys to enhance hunting and the gathering of roots and berries. Peter Skene Ogden, who led a trapping party through the upper Crooked River and into the Harney Basin in 1826 and 1827, repeatedly declared the country "overrun by fire" and pointed what he deemed to be a finger of guilt at native culprits. In the vicinity of the Crooked River in late September 1826, Ogden reported that the party's hunters were experiencing difficulty finding game, because "all the Country appears lately to be overrun by fire." As the group passed through the Harney Basin a month later, Ogden observed "the Country being burnt for a long distance in advance." But Ogden's greatest disappointment about those summer conflagrations centered on a different cultural perception of the role of fire, the widespread destruction of beaver habitat (and beaver):

Many small Streams have been discovered in the Mountains and were not long since well supplied with Beaver but unfortunately the Natives have destroyed them all and probably by the aid of fire which is certainly a most distructive mode of exterpating them for scarcely ever one escapes particularly when the Streams are not wide enough, and from what I have seen in this my last years travels I will venture to assert without exaggeration the Natives have distroyed and principally by fire upwards of sixty thousand Beavers and of this number not a Hundred have reached any Establishment but all have been lost.[57]

Ogden saw the regional landscape through a sharply different cultural lens from that of eastern Oregon's Paiute people. The Paiute practice of burning *for Indian purposes,* in his view, was irrational because it contributed to the destruction of beaver, an animal with a commodity value in distant markets.[58] Ogden's eyewitness reportage suggests, however, the significant influence of native-caused fires in shaping the eastern country's high-desert, shrub-steppe ecosystems. Prior to white settlement, plant and animal communities survived in the midst of culturally generated annual fire regimes that recycled nutrients in the soil and contributed to a diverse landscape with a particular vegetational pattern. Bluebunch wheatgrass and scatterings of big sagebrush covered those fire-maintained shrub-steppe lands across Oregon's high desert, a setting, according to one scientist, that "assumed an environmental balance maintained by the continuation of customary broadcast burning."[59]

It is important to recognize that native people's strategic use of fire sustained a complex hunting-gathering system that persisted until white settlers progressively imposed a new set of cultural arrangements on the landscape in the last half of the nineteenth century. Evidence suggests that Paiutes in the northern basin used fire as an aid in hunting deer and to improve forage for the following season; they also employed fire to enhance the production of plant foods, especially to increase the yield of certain types of edible seeds. The burning of riparian vegetation that Ogden reported may have reflected an effort to improve streamside stands of willow, a deciduous shrub that produces vigorous and straight canes in the aftermath of fire. Indian people used willow for making vessels of various types, infant cradles, headgear, and domestic utensils.[60]

Anecdotal evidence also indicates that native people farther north in the Columbia Basin country made widespread use of fire. John Kirk Townsend, a Philadelphia-based naturalist and traveler on the Oregon Trail, provides one of the most vivid word pictures of Indian burning practices in the Columbia River region. When his westward-bound party camped about fifteen miles downstream from the mouth of the Umatilla River on the evening of September 3, 1835, Townsend reported that the Indians had "fired the prairie" on the opposite side of the river, thereby brilliantly lighting the night sky:

Here I am sitting cross-legged on the ground, scribbling by the light of the vast conflagration with as much ease as if I had a ton of oil burning by my side; but my eyes are every moment involuntarily wandering from the paper before me, to contemplate and admire the grandeur of the distant scene. The very heavens themselves appear ignited, and the fragments of ashes and burning grass-blades, ascending and careering about through the glowing firmament, look like brilliant and glowing birds let loose to roam and revel amid this splendid scene.[61]

Standing on a hilltop at the mouth of the Walla Walla River the following spring, the Reverend Samuel Parker described a landscape "covered with the fresh green of spring vegetation." A few miles to the north at the juncture of the Snake River, he remarked again about "the fresh verdure, which is springing up, luxuriantly, at this early season." A few years later, looking toward the Columbia River from the western slopes of the Blue Mountains in mid-October 1840, United States Army reconnaissance officer John C. Fremont reported that "smoky and unfavorable" weather conditions obstructed "far views with the glass." And before descending to the Walla Walla River, he observed what he deemed to be the salutary aftereffects of burning: "the grass very green and good; the old grass having been burnt off in the autumn."[62]

Although the preceding discussion has focused on native burning practices in arid basin landscapes, there is abundant evidence that culture played an important role in shaping the ecology of intermontane forests as well. That native-modified forest landscapes extended well beyond the Puget and Willamette lowlands to the eastern slope of the Cascades is simply too obvious to ignore. Indians used fire as an effective tool to enhance the production of a variety of foodstuffs, including nutritious herbs and shrubs such as black mountain huckleberry and its near relatives, grouseberry and blueberry. Those natural and human fire-created niches stretched north and south along the Cascades and attracted browsing animals such as deer and elk, abundant sources of protein in the Indian diet.[63] Widespread native burning practices, along with lightning-caused fires, created a forest environment of open glades and park-like settings on the eastern slope of the Cascades, a descriptive refrain that runs through virtually all of the nineteenth-century travel and survey literature.

For the greater Blue Mountain area, early travel accounts—many of them Oregon Trail narratives—provide copious testimony to the ecologically intrusive presence of Indians throughout the region. Stories of fire and ash are literally strewn along the section of the trail from the juncture of the Boise and Snake rivers to the Columbia.[64] After leaving the Grande Ronde Valley in a northwesterly direction through the Blue Mountains in late August of 1834, John Kirk Townsend remarked about the stately pine trees with a scattering of underbrush of "service bushes and other shrubs." What most offended Townsend, however, was the burned grass and trees "blasted by the ravaging fires of the Indians. These fires are yet smoldering, and the smoke from them effectually prevents our viewing the surrounding country."[65]

The ubiquitous and controversial Capt. Benjamin Bonneville crisscrossed the Snake River–Blue Mountain country that same year and later made his notes available to Washington Irving, who wrote an account of Bonneville's travels. According to Irving's rendition of the captain's field observations, during the summer months the party witnessed "the season of setting fires to the prairie," with fire and smoke apparent on every hand. The frustrated captain's troop subsequently spent two weeks camped in the Grande Ronde Valley because fires in the surrounding hills blocked egress from the area.[66]

Passing through the high country dividing the Powder River and Grande

Ronde valleys in August 1835, the westward-bound missionary Jason Lee described a forest landscape "covered with a heavy growth of pitch pine, very large, tall, and beautiful." The only feature that distressed the Methodist pastor was evidence that fire "had recently been making its destructive ravages over the whole mountain." After ascending the Blue Mountains and traveling across the summit, Lee reported that the party's vision was obscured "by smoke, which was [so] dense that we could discern objects only a few yards." Four years later Thomas Jefferson Farnham followed the west bank of the Snake River and then moved into the hills along a small stream where he noted that Indians had recently burned the countryside. Farnham likened the smoke-filled atmosphere to "Indian summer-time in the highlands of New England." [67]

By the time the large emigrant train of 1843 was en route to the Willamette Valley, late-summer Indian fires were familiar sights to newcomers traveling through the interior region. The trapper James Clyman, who accompanied an 1844 emigrant party to Fort Boise and then pressed on ahead to Oregon, observed "verry Smoky" weather in the Powder River Valley and even worse conditions in the Grande Ronde Valley, where "Indians as is their habit . . . set fire to the grass." Moving northward from the Powder River, Clyman and his group "nearly suffocated with smoke & dust," and upon descending into the Grande Ronde Valley, they witnessed "the whole mountains which surround this vally completely enveloped in fire and Smoke." Despite the smoky and acrid conditions, however, Clyman reported that the "vally was nearly covered with horses . . . of which the Kyuse tribe of Indians . . . have great numbers." [68] But the juxtaposition of the "ravaging fires" of the natives and large Indian horse herds held little meaning to travelers who judged fire only for what they deemed to be its destructive qualities. To whites who were passing through the Blue Mountains, according to environmental scientist Nancy Langston, "burning seemed like careless destruction, not the labor of serious adults." [69]

There is an ironic twist to much of the scientific and technical literature on the influence of fire in shaping ecosystems in the Pacific Northwest. Virtually all writers recognize that Indians used fire as a tool to fashion grassland and forest environments for a variety of purposes. Despite that acknowledgment, those same writers discuss "fire and its role in the pristine environment" as if the manipulations of native people were part of nature itself. One authority on fire history, while conceding "significant Indian influence," refers to nineteenth-century forests as "unmanaged" and "natural" environments. In this view, before the advent of modern forest management, Northwest woodlands were not humanized places. As Richard White has observed: "Perhaps the most important decision Europeans made about American nature . . . was that they were not part of it, but Indians were." Moreover, he argues, even when the newcomers encountered human-influenced ecosystems, they "tended to deny that Indians could have created them."[70]

After the United States established sovereignty over the country south of the Forty-ninth Parallel in 1846, the government undertook a series of boundary, military road, and railroad surveys, many of which centered on the Cascade Mountains. Those inquiries provide further evidence of ecosystems heavily influenced by human activity. The reports of the Northwest Boundary Survey Commission, although describing the mountainous area north of the Columbia River, offer an excellent portrait of the transition in forest types on the western and eastern slopes of the Cascades. On the western side, where the human use of fire was less apparent, the timber was dense, "being a heavy growth of pine and fir that in many places stands over a fallen forest not yet decayed." But east of the summit, the commission observed that in fire-nurtured ponderosa pine, "The timber becomes more open, and survey operations less difficult."[71]

Lt. Henry L. Abbot's 1854 survey of a prospective railroad route from the Sacramento Valley to the Columbia River offered detailed descriptions of fire-nurtured landscapes, firsthand observations of Indian burning practices, and frequent reference to sizable Indian horse herds. Through the entire route of its travel on the eastern flank of the Cascades from Klamath Lake northward, the Abbot survey found "excellent bunch grass. . . . Whortleberries, elder berries and service berries," specimens that survive in the aftermath of fire. A decade later, officials of the Oregon Central Military Wagon Road surveyed a route from Eugene southeast through the Cascade Mountains to the headwaters of the Deschutes River. Although the party struggled through the dense forests on the western slope, once east of the summit the terrain leveled off, the higher elevations "covered with black pine, clover grass in abundance, and great quantities of meadow grounds." The surveyors observed places where the forest had been "killed by fire" and elsewhere found little evidence of undergrowth, either in the black pine or in the yellow pine timber to the southeast. On The Dalles–Fort Klamath trail, they saw signs where a large band of horses had camped the previous night, "and from the character of the horse tracks and mockasin tracks accompanying think it is Indians."[72]

The federal railroad surveys for the Washington Cascades provide a strikingly similar description of landscape: dense underbrush and thickly spaced trees in the higher elevations, gradually giving way on the eastern slope to open spaces and a clean understory in the fire-nurtured, ponderosa-dominated stands at lower elevations. During the month of August, 1853, Isaac Stevens's survey party also encountered "a profusion of berries of several kinds, which the Indians were engaged in collecting." The Stevens report mentioned what may have been a cultural factor influencing the particular character of that landscape: large forest fires at lower elevations. As forest scientist Thomas Quigley has indicated, the huge open stands of ponderosa pine in eastern Washington and eastern Oregon reflect ecological conditions that differed sharply from the coniferous forests west of the Cascades. The ponderosa forests, he notes, evolved in an ecological environment "of low-intensity, high-frequency fire."[73]

By the early nineteenth century, native people in the interior Northwest had acquired sizable numbers of horses, with some tribes—the Yakima, Cayuse, and Nez Perce—possessing especially large herds. The diffusion of horses across western North America originated in the Spanish colonies in what is now New Mexico. When the Pueblo Indians revolted in 1680 and drove the Spanish out of the Rio Grande country, they liberated the Spaniards' horses, which quickly found their way northward. Along the western slope of the Rocky Mountains, the animals passed from the Utes to the Shoshones on the upper Snake River, to the Flatheads by 1720, and most likely to the Nez Perce and Cayuse the following decade.[74]

That the acquisition of horses dramatically increased Indian mobility (and thereby affected Indian economic and social life) is well known; what is more difficult to discern is the extent and magnitude of ecological change that should be attributed to the horse. Some scholars argue that much of the grassland niche in western North America lay vacant and "underutilized" in the wake of the Pleistocene extinctions. The dispersal of horses, according to that view, took place over areas absent of large grazing animals and consequently had little appreciable influence on those settings. Yet the evidence presented here strongly suggests that the introduction of horses, especially as the herds assumed sizable proportions, intensified Indian burning practices. Until the large-scale western emigration of the 1840s, therefore, it seems reasonable to assume that both horses and fire represented an Indian-mediated presence in the landscape.

The early and numerous references to the abundance of Indian horses strongly suggest that humans used fire as well as other means to shape intermontane ecosystems. Through the acquisition of horses, they had in fact introduced a new species to the region. Struggling through the snow-clad Blue Mountains north of the Grande Ronde Valley in the winter of 1811–12, the Astorian Wilson Price Hunt observed "horse-trails used by Indians" on every side of their route. When party members reached the Umatilla River, they visited an Indian camp of thirty-four lodges with an estimated two thousand horses in the surrounding area. The presence of copper kettles and pots about the dwellings and the wearing of bison robes and buckskin leggings also indicated extensive travel by horseback and trade with distant peoples. Passing down the arid stretch of the Columbia River between the Umatilla and Great Falls (Celilo Falls) in September 1834, John Kirk Townsend reported seeing "large bands of Indian horses. . . . beautiful animals . . . almost as wild as deer" and marked with "strange hieroglyphic looking characters" to indicate ownership.[75] Nearly every Oregon Trail travel account mentions sizable numbers of Indian horses throughout the Blue Mountain region. Writing from a camp on the Walla Walla River in 1843, emigrant James Nesmith mentioned hunting down cattle and horses that strayed during the night, "the Indian horses being so numerous made it difficult for us to find our own."[76]

When Thomas Jefferson Farnham's group passed through the Blue Mountains in 1839, the members encountered a Cayuse family returning from a buffalo hunt to the east. The man and woman and their two children had seventeen horses in tow, "splendid animals," Farnham wrote, "as large as the best horses of the States, well-knit, deep and wide in the shoulders."

When he reached the south bank of the Columbia River, he noticed that "groups of Indian horses occasionally appeared." And at the onset of the settler movement to the Willamette Valley in the early 1840s, the inveterate preacher-traveler Samuel Parker recorded in his journal that he saw several "bands of Indian horses as well as deer and antelope."[77]

John C. Fremont, who reached the Walla Walla River in October 1834 with his reconnaissance troop, reported "several hundred horses grazing on the hills, . . . and as we advanced on the road we met other bands, which Indians were driving out to pasture also on the hills." A month later, journeying along the eastern slope of the Cascade Mountains, Fremont observed a village of Nez Perce "who appeared to be coming from the mountains, and had with them fine bands of horses." Fellow army officer Major Osborne Cross, on the Umatilla River in September 1849, witnessed everywhere "large droves of horses, . . . stout, well built, and very muscular." And a decade later in the Grande Ronde Valley, George Belshaw wrote in his diary about the "quantities of Indians and Poneys" in "this butiful valey."[78]

That Samuel Parker and other observers lumped horses, deer, and antelope as part of the natural world points to a fundamental problem in distinguishing between the natural and the unnatural. Horses, unlike deer and antelope, were, of course, *unnatural* to the region; they were Indian cultural adaptations of the relatively recent past; they were exotic, large grazing ungulates. Moreover, as an alien introduction, they unquestionably represented a new and intrusive agent in their adopted places of habitation. Although the research and literature on Indian horse herds as agents of ecological change is not large, a growing body of evidence suggests that the rapid diffusion of horses in western North America, contrary to some opinion, introduced considerable ecological change. When substantial numbers of the animals frequented particular areas, and especially in the arid and semiarid intermontane region, they unquestionably would have taxed the carrying capacity of their surroundings. In that context, it seems obvious that Indian burning served to renew the grazing capacity of particular localities.[79] Because human agency was responsible for the introduction of horses, Indian use of the animals should properly be considered another culturally engendered force shaping the landscape of the Indian Northwest.

With the arrival of ever-increasing numbers of Euro-Americans after

1800, the relative cultural and ecological stability of several millennia in the Oregon country began to erode. The writer Philip Shabecoff has remarked that Lewis and Clark represented the opening wedge of a relentless push "that would tame, transform, and with innocent ferocity, transmute the landscape that both men found so enchanting." Possessing unique social and economic attributes, the newcomers initiated dramatic cultural and biological modifications that continue to the present day. The aging former president John Quincy Adams, speaking on the floor of the House of Representatives in favor of settling the Oregon boundary question, may have expressed that newly emerging set of convictions best: "We claim that country—for what? To make the wilderness blossom as the rose, to establish laws, to increase, multiply, and subdue the earth, which we are commanded to do by the behest of God Almighty." [80]

The intruders, slowly at first and then with gathering momentum, imposed on the indigenous people and the regional landscape a markedly different cultural vision, one that led to the gradual and sometimes spectacular modification of ecosystems both east and west of the Cascade Range. In the words of one scientist, the last 150 years have witnessed "an unprecedented acceleration" in the ever-changing ecosystems of the region. And because it was the factor most responsible for precipitating those changes, Richard White asserts, "white settlement destroyed the Indian Northwest." [81]

The Great Divide

These Southern Valleys of Oregon, . . . notwithstanding their wildness and dangers, offer inducements, (deadly to the native,) for which, ere long, the stronger hand of the white man will beat back the present wild and implacable inhabitants, and make them homes of civilization. — *Overton Johnson (1843)*[1]

When the members of the Lewis and Clark expedition floated into the Columbia River near the end of their epic journey in the fall of 1805, they entered the great waterway at a critical season in the subsistence cycle of the people who lived along its banks. As they coursed downstream from the mouth of the Snake River during the next three weeks, the observant captains sketched in their journals a remarkable story of abundance, especially of the fall salmon runs and the prodigious number of fish taken by native people whose lives centered on the river. When the expedition passed Celilo Falls, Clark reported large quantities of pounded fish neatly preserved in blankets lined with dried salmon skin:

those 12 baskets of from 90 to 100 w. each (basket) for a Stack. thus preserved those fish may be kept Sound and Sweet Several years, as those people inform me, Great quantities as they inform us are Sold to the whites peoples who visit the mouth of this river as well as the nativs below.

In their travels on the Columbia below the Wenatchee River, Lewis and Clark encountered more than a hundred native fishing stations, and as they descended the river on one remarkable fall day, they passed twenty-nine mat lodges where Indians were preparing and drying fish.[2]

But Lewis and Clark brought more than disinterested scientific reportage to their accounts about the Columbia River country. Like the British sea captains James Cook and George Vancouver and the American sea-otter merchant Robert Gray, Lewis and Clark viewed the Great River of the West and its adjacent countryside through a cultural lens that differed sharply from that of the region's native residents. The Corps of Discovery and the merchant adventurers who followed—the Astorians, the Northwest Company, and Hudson's Bay Company operatives—represented an expanding world of capitalist enterprises, trading and commercial ventures that were literally probing the farthest corners of the globe. For the Oregon country, that odd miscellany of explorers, governors, field governors, factors, fur-brigade leaders, and occasional freebooters produced a corpus of writing that hinted at the larger market prospects for the region, the "inevitability" of the decline of the native population, and glowing descriptions of the area's potential for "progressive" people who would bring civilization to the shores of the Columbia. Prior to the departure of Lewis and Clark up the Missouri River and far removed from the field of action, the imperial-minded Thomas Jefferson[3] provided context and potential meaning for an expanding American republic in a letter to John C. Breckinridge: "The future inhabitants of the Atlantic and Pacific States will be our sons."[4] With planning for the Lewis and Clark expedition already well under way, Jefferson's declaration was an omen of sorts for the great demographic, cultural, and ecological changes that would follow.

When the expedition returned to St. Louis in September of 1806, Lewis reported to President Jefferson that the Corps of Discovery had accomplished its goal of locating "the most practicable rout which dose exist across the continent" by means of the Missouri and Columbia rivers. And although their findings did not sustain the president's original notion of an easy passageway across the great divide between the two waterways, Lewis did recommend that the United States establish a trading post on the Columbia to gain an advantage over the "British N.West Company of Canada." Doing so, Lewis reasoned, would give the Americans an advantage in obtaining and shipping "the furs not only of the Missouri but those also of the Columbia." If the United States policy makers deemed the fur trade of the Missouri River country important, Lewis advised, the moves of the Northwest Company "must be vigelently watched." For the native people of the region and for the future course of the American empire, geographer John Logan Allen contends, Lewis's words were prophetic: the "American response led to the Astorians, the Rocky Mountain fur trade, and ultimate American victory in the imperial conflict over the Oregon country."[5]

The American overlanders, of course, were not the first to suggest the rich potential that would be gained in joining the region's natural wealth to distant markets. Sailing with Captain James Cook on his epic (and last) voyage in Pacific waters nearly thirty years earlier, New England-born Corporal John Ledyard of the Royal Marines was the first to praise the material wealth of the Northwest. In his questionable journals of Cook's passage along the North Pacific Coast, including nearly a month's stay in Nootka Sound in April 1787, Ledyard reported "no plantations or any appearance that exhibited any knowledge of the cultivation of the earth, all seemed to remain in a state of nature." It was a country, he wrote, "intirely covered with woods, . . . mostly with well grown pine," and would "appear most to advantage respects the variety of its animals, and the richness of their furs," especially for the price they would bring in Canton, China.[6]

When the British sea captain George Vancouver sailed northward from the mouth of the Columbia River in 1792, he described the view from his ship as a "luxuriant landscape," a country of "continued forest extending as far north as the eye could reach." After his lieutenant, Peter Puget, made an extensive survey of the inland sea subsequently named in his honor, Vancouver recorded what was to become common in the narrative descriptions of the region:

The serenity of the climate, the innumerable pleasing landscapes, and the abundant fertility that unassisted nature puts forth, require only to be enriched by the industry of man with villages, mansions, cottages, and other buildings, to render it the most lovely country that can be imagined; whilst the labour of the inhabitants would be amply rewarded, in the bounties which nature seems ready to bestow on cultivation.[7]

Although Vancouver portrayed the Puget Sound country as uncommonly attractive, the significance of his observation is his emphasis on the region's *potential* for improvement, the degree to which nature could be assisted and improved through human labor. In that respect, Vancouver's description of the Oregon country paralleled the narratives of the British and the Americans who followed, whether they came overland or by sea. In that set of cultural assumptions, natural abundance represented opportunity, promise, a belief in the potential for both human and environmental improvement, and most of all that great material reward would come to those who capitalized on that wealth.

But it was the land-based fur traders who left the most lasting narrative descriptions, stories that provided the building blocks to what became familiar and popular images of the Oregon country by the 1840s. Ross Cox, who arrived on the Columbia River in 1811 to clerk for John Jacob Astor's Pacific Fur Company, expressed "pleasure" about the "productions of the country, amongst the most wonderful of which are the fur trees." The climate of the Willamette Valley was "remarkably mild . . . [and the valley] possesses a rich and luxuriant soil, which yields an abundance of fruits and roots." Like most of his contemporaries, Cox thought the native people in the valley were inferior, recommending that missionary societies extend "their exertions to the northwest coast" to rescue those who were "still buried in deepest ignorance."[8] The efforts of civilized humans, he hinted, would benefit both the native population and the valley landscape alike.

After he had made his way beyond "the impervious and magnificent forest [that] darkened the landscape" of the lower Columbia River, fellow Pacific Fur Company clerk Alexander Ross remarked that the "Wallamitte" valley was the most favorable spot for agriculture, "salubrious and dry" and with sufficient heat "to ripen every kind of grain in a short time." The abundant Columbia River salmon, a fish he described "as fine as any in the world," also attracted his attention. Because the fish were "caught in the utmost abundance during the summer season," Ross reasoned that salmon offered great potential: "were a foreign market to present itself, the natives alone might furnish 1,000 tons annually." To another Astorian, Robert Stuart, the country above Willamette Falls was "delightful beyond expression," with bottomlands "composed of an excellent soil" thinly sprinkled

with cottonwood, alder, white oak, and scatterings of pine along the ad-
joining hills "to give variety to the most beautiful Landscapes in nature."
Like his colleague Alexander Ross, Stuart was impressed with the productive "first rate salmon fishery" on the Columbia. But the unwillingness of
the local Indians to hunt for fur-bearing animals frustrated Stuart and his
associates on the lower Columbia: "the natives both from inexperience &
indolence seem as yet little inclined to reduce [the animals] in number."[9]

Stuart and other traders failed to recognize the obvious: sea otter and
beaver had no commodity value to native people. They hunted and traded,
as historian Robin Fisher and others have indicated, to a set of cultural
norms that differed sharply from the values of their European counterparts.
When Indians did participate in the fur trade, Fisher argues, it was for purposes that were central to their lives, "because they perceived there were
benefits to be gained," and not because they yearned to participate in market exchanges for personal accumulation.[10] But that was not true for the
likes of Robert Stuart and the fur traders, the early salmon merchants, and
subsequently the settler-farmers who flocked to the Oregon country. The
acquisitive and aggressive newcomers brought with them a very different
set of values, precepts that attached special significance to the manipulation and transformation of the physical world for personal gain.

Although there were important national differences between England
and the United States, the principal imperial powers contending for influence in the Oregon country, historian Robert Bunting points out that
both nations "shared broadly construed cultural understandings."[11] For the
most part, the intruders treated the region as a vast commons, a spacious
arena they were free to enter and occupy, irrespective of the resident native
people and their subsistence and cultural needs. John Jacob Astor's New
York–based Pacific Fur Company, with its main post at the mouth of the
Columbia River, was a short-lived enterprise that reverted to the Montreal-
controlled Northwest Company in the midst of the War of 1812. And when
the Northwesters and the Hudson's Bay Company engaged in open conflict for control of the rich fur-producing region in British North America,
the British government ended what it deemed destructive competition and
forced the smaller firm to merge with the more powerful Hudson's Bay
Company. Under field governor George Simpson's shrewd management,

the Bay Company began constructing its regional trading headquarters at Fort Vancouver in 1824.[12]

Whether those early interlopers were British or American, Hudson's Bay Company employees or Pacific Fur Company clerks, their collective descriptions of landscape followed cultural conventions that looked with favor on humid environments and reserved special praise for physical settings that reinforced images already deeply ingrained in their cultural repertoire. The common features outlined in those early narrative representations — virtually all of them describing the area west of the Cascade Mountains — sketched a landscape of incredible bounty. All that was required to transform and improve the new land to suit more productive human purposes was an energetic immigrant population. Aside from commercial interest in the great fishery on the Columbia River and in the immense forests adjacent to the region's waterways, most of those initial observations emphasized a mixed landscape of the sylvan and pastoral.

Few of the early travelers captured that mood better than John Work, one of the Hudson's Bay Company's most enterprising and capable traders. When he made his renowned trapping expedition from Fort Vancouver to the Umpqua River in 1834, Work was already a veteran of several company expeditions.[13] His descriptions of the Willamette Valley sparkle with bright prospects for agriculture. Near present-day Hillsboro in late May, he wrote that the slightly rolling and open countryside presented excellent prospects "for abundant crops of every kind of grain [and] would amply reward the labor of the husbandman." Work also thought the land "well adapted for [the] pasture of cattle and sheep." Camped near Amity on the western side of the Willamette Valley a few days later, he described an extended plain, uninterrupted except for trees along the streams, "capable of yielding pasture for immense herds of cattle." Finally, in the vicinity of the Marys River and present-day Corvallis, he observed "large tracts of open ground" and an extensive plain on both sides of the river covered with grass.[14]

Despite the Hudson's Bay Company's exclusive interest in fur-bearing animals during its early years in the Columbia region, its factors and brigade leaders were quick to notice the potential for agriculture and other enterprises beyond the peltry trade. Indian-maintained open landscapes became plausible farm sites for future settlers; stands of Douglas fir offered promise and opportunity should regional markets be developed; and the abundant salmon in the Great River itself suggested great rewards to those with the ingenuity to develop the commerce. No person was more alive to those possibilities than John McLoughlin, the shrewd and efficient person who headed the Bay Company's Columbia District operations for two decades. In concert with his immediate superior, George Simpson, McLoughlin developed strategies to make the Fort Vancouver establishment self sufficient in foodstuffs and other goods, and he aggressively expanded land and sea trading contacts with native villages.[15] The long-range consequences of those cultural practices for specific locales was the dramatic decline in the native population, the rapid elimination of fur-bearing animals, especially beaver, and the subsequent alteration of riparian environments.

Perhaps the best known of the Simpson-McLoughlin geopolitical strategies was their decision to create a "fur desert" to discourage Americans from trapping and then colonizing regions that bordered the company's territory. That effort focused on the Columbia's two great tributaries, the extensive drainages of the Snake and Willamette rivers. Decisions that were made thousands of miles from the Oregon country brought profound environmental and political change to the region and considerable profits to the coffers of the Hudson's Bay firm. The remarkable thing about the company's scheme was the dispatch, efficiency, and effectiveness with which its trappers carried out the decree. Both British and American travelers reported that beaver stocks declined rapidly virtually everywhere south of the Columbia River by the 1830s and early 1840s. The person with the best information, Chief Factor McLoughlin, informed Simpson in the spring of 1831 that beaver in the Snake River country "were getting nearly exhausted."[16]

Well before the establishment of a permanent American settlement in the Oregon country, the aggressive designs of the Americans concerned both Simpson and McLoughlin. Simpson worried in his famous "Dispatch" of 1829 that news about "the Wilhamot Country, as a field for Agricultural speculation, had induced many people in the States to direct their attention to that quarter." For the forseeable future, however, he concluded that nature's geography—difficult travel through "a rugged and barren country of great extent"—would discourage travel across the continent. But it was McLoughlin, even more than Simpson, who fretted about Americans competing in the Saskatchewan trade and who encouraged the Bay Company to "salt" salmon for the commercial market. "It is certain if the Americans come," he warned, "they will attempt something in this way."[17]

The worldwide expansion of market capitalism was the great driving force in the transformation of the human and natural world of the Pacific Northwest. First came the fur men in their quest for sea otter and beaver pelts, deliberately creating the infamous "fur deserts" in some instances to drive competitors away from the region. The decimation of the beaver population occurred early in the Euro-American presence in the Northwest, with consequences for riparian ecosystems that scientists are only beginning to understand today. The fur traders also unknowingly trafficked in other items that effected enormous ecological and demographic change, especially the introduction of human contagions and exotic plants. According to anthropologist Eugene Hunn, the story of Indian-white relations in the mid–Columbia River country "has been first and foremost a history of the ravages of disease . . . which drastically reduced aboriginal populations."[18] And, he might have added, opened the way for the repeopling of the region with immigrants whose cultural views and practices set in motion vast ecological changes.

Robert Boyd, an anthropologist who has written extensively on the lethal pathogens that devastated the native populations of the Northwest, points out that the celebrated Columbian voyage of 1492 opened up a Pandora's box of biological disease pools that proved deadly to the natives of the Americas. Native Americans had previously been relatively free of the lethal epidemic diseases. Columbus's trek across the Atlantic ended the Western Hemisphere's physical isolation and introduced clusters of exogenous diseases—smallpox, measles, whooping cough, typhoid, malaria, cholera—to a people who lacked genetic immunity. Until the close of the eighteenth century, however, the Oregon country remained relatively isolated from the pandemics that ravaged Indian populations elsewhere in the Americas. It is reasonable to assume, Boyd argues, that for some time the Rocky Mountains and oceanic barriers limited access to the region.[19]

When Spanish ships first touched base along the Northwest Coast in 1774, that isolation began to erode. Although there is some evidence that

disease

exogenous diseases reached the Northwest in the sixteenth century, Boyd believes that the introduction of the horse among the Nez Perce in the 1730s provided the opening wedge for Old World disease pools. Acquiring horses enabled the Nez Perce and other groups of the Inland Plateau to travel through the Rocky Mountains to the Plains. That greatly enhanced mobility brought the Plateau Indians into contact with people who were already infected with introduced diseases. Infected tribes to the east spread smallpox to the Nez Perce and other Plateau groups in 1781–82. For most native people in the Oregon country, however, the Spanish coastal explorations of 1774 and the later voyage of James Cook, who spent a month at Nootka Sound in 1778, were more disruptive. Beginning in the late 1770s a succession of diseases ravaged Northwest Coast populations; the most notable among them were smallpox in the 1780s and malaria in the early 1830s. Because those epidemics took place at a relatively recent moment in the region's history, there is a considerable body of documented evidence to indicate the extent and influence of the diseases.[20]

Smallpox was the most deadly of all the invisible killers. Rapidly spread through the respiratory system, smallpox can be 100 percent fatal among people lacking genetic immunity. Smallpox is especially dangerous because of its incubation period; seemingly healthy people can be efficient carriers of the disease. The first smallpox epidemic along the Northwest Coast occurred during the late 1780s and infected people from the Tillamooks on the Oregon coast to the Tlingits far to the north. For some time scholars believed that ocean-going sea-otter traders were responsible for introducing the disease, but more recent evidence suggests that it may have spread from the Plains tribes via the horse. During their winter stay at the mouth of the Columbia River, Lewis and Clark reported that a recent smallpox epidemic had greatly reduced the local Clatsop people. Whether by sea or land, it is fair to say that new forms of transportation aided and abetted the spread of smallpox and the disease pools that followed, such as chicken pox, measles, and whooping cough.[21]

The best documented of the major pandemics in the Oregon country—and a major cause of native population decline in the region—was the series of malaria outbreaks that took place between 1830 and 1833. Spread by mosquitos, the malarial parasite was carried first from West Africa to the mid-latitudes in the Americas. The initial outbreak of what was called "fever and ague" in the Oregon country first appeared in the area around Fort Vancouver in August of 1830, and from that point it returned annually to ravage Indian and white populations alike. But while the Euro-Americans normally developed only fever and sickness and then recovered, the disease proved lethal to native people. Before ditching, diking, and flood-control dams came to the Willamette Valley, the vast wetlands stretching across the valley proved an ideal breeding ground for mosquitos, making the summer months perilous for residents.[22]

One source estimates that in the Willamette Valley and the lower Columbia Valley as many as 6,000 Indians died during the malarial outbreaks between 1830 and 1833. Fewer than 1,000 survivors remained in the Willamette corridor by 1835.[23] John Kirk Townsend, who visited Fort Vancouver in September 1835, provided a firsthand account of the human tragedy: "The depopulation here has been truly fearful. . . . Probably there does not now exist one, where, five years ago, there were a hundred Indians." In the Rogue Valley, 200 miles to the south, Townsend reported that "the Indians are said to be in a . . . flourishing condition" and hostile toward whites, believing that "we brought with us the fatal fever which has ravaged this portion of the country."[24]

In a letter to Hudson's Bay Company officials during the early stages of the epidemic, John McLoughlin estimated the native death rate in the vicinity of Fort Vancouver at 75 percent. The peripatetic David Douglas left a similar description in October 1830: "A dreadfully fatal intermittent fever broke out in the lower parts of this river about eleven weeks ago, which has depopulated the country. Villages which had afforded from one to two hundred effective warriors, are totally gone; not a soul remains!" Two years later the American merchant Nathaniel Wyeth reported on Sauvies Island at the juncture of the Willamette and Columbia rivers: "a mortality has carried off to a man its inhabitants and there is nothing to attest that they ever existed except their decaying houses, their graves and their unburied bones, of which they are in heaps." Wyeth made similar observations at the Cascades of the Columbia River in October 1832: "the Indians are all dead only two women are left—a sad remnant of a large number—their houses stripped to their frames are in view and their half buried dead."[25]

The journals of Samuel Parker, a clergyman who traveled along the Columbia in 1835, provide a kind of summary report of the scope of the epidemic:

> I have found the Indian population in the lower country, that is, below the falls of the Columbia, far less than I had expected, or what it was when Lewis and Clarke made their tour. Since the year 1829, probably seven-eights, if not as Dr. McLoughlin believes, nine-tenths, have been swept away by disease, principally by fever and ague. . . . So many and so sudden were the deaths which occurred, that the shores were strewed with the unburied dead. Whole and large villages were depopulated; and some entire tribes have disappeared, but where there were any remaining persons, they united with other tribes.

Parker estimated that the "great mortality" extended "from the vicinity of the Cascades to the shores of the Pacific" and north and south in both directions, even into California. The incredible death rate eventually abated, he wrote, only "from want of subjects." [26]

By the time the seasonally recurring epidemic had run its course, Robert Boyd calculates that the Indian mortality rate had reached the neighborhood of 90 percent of an estimated preepidemic native population of approximately 14,000 people for the lower Columbia River and the Willamette Valley. Boyd estimates that the Indian population of the Pacific Northwest in 1770 was approximately 300,000; by the close of the American Civil War the tribes numbered about 60,000 people, an 80 percent decline. [27]

When he visited the region in 1841, Lt. Charles Wilkes counted 575 Chinook survivors on the Columbia and 600 Kalapuyans in the Willamette Valley. Later epidemics continued the carnage, with the attrition rate especially high among children. The ever-increasing number of white immigrants traveling west on the Oregon Trail in the early 1840s included large numbers of children, carriers of childhood diseases new to the region: chicken pox, whooping cough, and measles. Hence, the introduction of those later pathogens struck disproportionately against children and skewed the average age of the native population.

In retrospect, we can say with some certainty that the epidemic diseases had thinned the native population at a critical moment in the history of the Oregon country. Sometime during the mid-1830s, the region passed a demographic, cultural, and ecological divide of sorts, a transition that appears to have been discernible to many contemporary observers. The stage was set for the first great wave of Euro-American immigration. In a lengthy memorandum to the governors of the Hudson's Bay Company on November 18, 1834, John McLoughlin reported the recent arrival at Fort Vancouver of the Boston merchant Nathaniel Wyeth, who was making a second effort to capitalize on the region's natural wealth. On the day following Wyeth's arrival, two Methodist missionaries, Jason Lee and his nephew Daniel Lee, and two naturalists, the Britisher, Thomas Nuttall, and the Philadelphian, John Kirk Townsend, also called at the fort. Still others were en route to the Columbia River region. In a remark that would prove prophetic, McLoughlin observed that the missionaries "present in the Willamette country expect to be joined by some more of their country men next year." [28]

McLoughlin had good reason for concern because the fecundity of the soil already impressed the Reverend Jason Lee, who was interested in the bright prospects that appeared to be in the offing for those with enterprise and initiative. When the missionary party arrived at Fort Vancouver in mid-September, Lee expressed delight "in viewing the improvements of the farm. . . . and was astonished to find it in such a high state of cultivation." He praised the dinner, including the "fine muskmelons and water melons and apples [that] were set before us." Later that evening, he took a "turn in the garden" with his host and noted that fruit so burdened the branches of the trees that they "would break if they were not prevented by props." A few days later when he made his first venture up the Willamette Valley to the Tualatin Plains, Lee reported ample grass everywhere and the Bay Company's horses and cattle doing "exceedingly well." [29]

In truth, the valley landscape was already beginning to take on a different hue. Former employees of Astor's Pacific Fur Company and the Northwest Company and retired Bay Company engages had been hard at work since the early 1820s establishing subsistence farmsteads along the Willamette system. Mostly French Canadians, the ex-trappers first exploited the valley's abundant wildlife for food; only later did they begin to take advantage of the soil's ability to produce grains. For the Hudson's Bay Company, dominant in the region by the mid-1820s, the valley provided excellent grassland for cattle and horses, and it served as a source for deer and elk hides. When McLoughlin himself visited the lower valley in 1832, he remarked that it deserved "all the praises Bestowed on it as it is the finest country I have seen." In the midst of that increased Euro-American activity in the valley, Bay Company official Francis Ermatinger declared, "the Willamette is getting much in vogue."[30] But those modest and seemingly insignificant modifications to the Willamette ecosystem began to accelerate as the seasonal reoccurrence of malaria continued to decimate the native population and as people steeped in the acquisitive values of a different cultural world began to resettle the valley landscape.

During his first trek to the "Wallamet" country in 1832, Nathaniel Wyeth proved himself an astute observer of the transformation that was under way. In addition to the appalling attrition rate among the Kalapuya Indians, Wyeth witnessed other harbingers of change in the valley. Twenty-two miles above Willamette Falls he found three or four Canadians, "old engages of the Co.," who had recently established farms, built houses and barns and were raising cows, horses, and hogs. Ten miles farther upriver he reported another group of settlers and observed, "if this country is ever colonized this is the point to begin." The Boston merchant then went on to paint a glowing description of the valley's agricultural potential:

this country seems a valley between two mountains to the East and West of about 50 miles wide including both sides of the river and is very level of nearly uniform soil extremely rich equal to the best of the Missouri lands. . . . I have never seen country of equal beauty except the Kansas country and I doubt not will one day sustain a large population.[31]

The growing number of American citizens who were on the move to the Oregon country during the 1830s were little more than the advance guard in what eventually would become a floodtide of overland immigrants pouring into the Willamette Valley. The groundwork for that increased interest in the region rested in the convergence of a well-known series of historical events and circumstances that originated in the sea-otter trade of the late eighteenth century and gathered momentum with the Lewis and Clark expedition. In the decades that followed, American politicians and publicists used the Corps of Discovery's journey for both commercial and strategic geopolitical purposes.

Eight years after the short-lived Astor venture of 1811–12, a subcommittee of the U.S. House of Representatives issued a flattering, albeit greatly exaggerated, report about the agricultural efforts of the Astorians: "The soil was found to be rich, and well adapted to the culture of all the useful vegetables found in any part of the United States." The committee characterized the larger Columbia region from "a commercial point of view . . . of the utmost importance," singling out for special praise its fisheries, the fur trade, and the area's proximity to potential markets in China. The committee described the great waterway and its surrounding countryside in terms of superlatives: "a smooth and deep river running through a boundless extent of the most fertile soil on this continent." The "safe and easy navigation" of the Columbia provided access to a region of valuable fur-bearing animals that had already enriched others. In addition to the rich soils and the abundant mammal life, there were luxuriant grasses for raising horses and magnificent forests "well calculated for ship building." Finally, the committee urged the government to establish a settlement to "give this country the advantage of all its own treasures, which otherwise must be lost forever, or rather never enjoyed."[32]

The most single-minded and obsessive American to promote the imperial occupation of the Oregon country was the Harvard-educated New England schoolmaster, Hall Jackson Kelley. During the 1820s he wrote numerous letters to eastern newspapers and published a pamphlet extolling (and exaggerating) the virtues of the region. He applied those messianic promotional efforts to an equally visionary scheme when he organized a group to encourage the establishment of Christian settlements on the Columbia River.[33] Besides Kelley, the most prominent American to advertise the Eden on the Columbia was the Missouri senator, Thomas Hart Benton. Through newspaper articles, but especially on the floor of the Senate, Benton persistently directed public attention to the Oregon country. Following the publication of the House report in 1820, Benton proclaimed that "the first blow was struck . . . in the public mind which promised eventual favorable consideration."[34] For the next two decades and beyond, Benton worked tirelessly in the cause of westward expansion, but especially to the Columbia River country; in that effort he portrayed the region as an earthly paradise.[35] His fellow Missourian, Sen. Lewis F. Linn, echoed his pronouncements.

The firsthand reports of visitors and the boosters set in motion a great demographic movement that ultimately brought dramatic changes to the human *and* ecological communities in the Oregon country. To explain those connections, historian Alfred Crosby uses the metaphor of folklore, the old song about Sweet Betsy from Pike County, Missouri, who crossed the western mountains "with her lover, Ike, with two yoke of oxen, a large yellow dog, a tall shanghai rooster, and one spotted hog." The symbolism in Betsy's party, Crosby points out, is the host of colonizing species in her entourage. "Betsy came not as an individual immigrant," he argues, "but as part of a grunting, lowing, neighing, crowing, chirping, snarling, buzzing, self-replicating and world-altering avalanche."[36]

The immigrants who arrived in the Willamette Valley in increasing numbers during the 1830s began the slow and arduous work of imposing a different ordering on the landscape. The newcomers, sometimes purposefully and oftentimes by accident, disturbed and destroyed plant and animal communities and thereby severely disrupted Indian subsistence assemblages. White farmers modified both the biological (plants) and the physical (soil). As incipient agriculturalists, their mental world embraced social and economic values that had broad ramifications.[37] Although they were not the first humans to purposefully interfere with natural processes in the region, the white settlers' influence differed both in quality and in kind from the practices of native people. As Richard White points out, incoming Euro-Americans "altered the direction of that change and increased its pace." Under the influence of the new cultural presence in the region, indigenous plant and animal species that had no utility to whites were dubbed "weeds" and "pests."[38]

Most European species easily adapted to the mild and humid climate of the Douglas-fir region. Indeed, the Willamette Valley, today a major exporter of grains, grass seeds, and meat, is an ideal fit for Alfred Crosby's description of a Neo-European landscape: thousands of miles from Europe proper and an area (in 1800) without "wheat, barley, rye, cattle, pigs, sheep, or goats."[39] Scientists today are only beginning to understand the complexities of the elimination of some species and the introduction of others. We do know, however, that Euro-American practices created disturbances that in the short run favored the newcomers' preferred flora and fauna. Whites who came to the Willamette Valley in the 1830s and in succeeding decades plowed the prairie lands, grazed cattle, horses, and sheep on the grasslands, and cut timber from the surrounding hillsides. In doing so, they disturbed some native plant communities, destroyed others, and created ideal situations for invading species.[40]

Despite repeated gold discoveries across the region, there is little question that the humid agricultural lands of the western valleys attracted most of the white immigrants who traveled the Oregon Trail between 1840 and 1860. In fact, to the would-be migrants of eastern North America, the lush Willamette Valley became a synonym for the larger region when the term "Oregon Country" became popular during the 1840s. Played out in exaggerated and embellished language in earlier journal and travel reports, its attractions were especially appealing to people in the Mississippi River Valley who were suffering in the midst of a prolonged agricultural depression. That immigrant, agricultural-minded population, already well versed in the cultivation of wheat and other grains, found the Willamette Valley an ideal setting for the production of familiar crops. Moreover, the mild maritime climate west of the Cascade Mountains—as boosters never failed to point out—made it possible in most years to winter livestock without shelter or the need to put up reserve supplies of hay. To a certain extent, the Willamette Valley was a microcosm of other temperate zones around the world, settings where European success, as Alfred Crosby asserts, had "a biological, an ecological, component."[41]

The newcomers who flocked to the Northwest during this period "husbanded the familiar," in Richard White's words. That is, they brought with them a panoply of well-known and easily adaptive species. For the immigrants, the positive side of that story is obvious: the particular form of husbandry they practiced worked exceedingly well in the western valleys. Despite some areal differences in the seasonal distribution of rainfall, adaptation took place within the context of generally familiar climatic conditions. Unlike the very high percentage of failures among the farmers who occupied the arid reaches of the Great Plains following the Civil War, those who emigrated to the Oregon country's western valleys in the 1840s and 1850s were mostly successful in establishing subsistence farmsteads.

The Willamette Valley was more attractive to settler-farmers than the arid interior for obvious reasons. For one, emigrants left the Midwest in the month of May, with the full and radiant bloom of spring apparent on every hand. By the time they reached the great stretch of the Snake River country, daytime temperatures were hot and the surrounding countryside appeared parched and lifeless to those accustomed to the humid summers of Illinois, Iowa, or Missouri. Indeed, once they reached the high plains, travelers saw little greenery until they entered the Powder River and Grande Ronde valleys of eastern Oregon sometime in September. And despite the arduous physical work of passing through the Blue Mountains, the latter provided a welcome respite from the desert country the migrants had recently experienced. On ascending the Blue Mountains in the late summer of 1853, Phoebe Goodell Judson remarked about the welcome transition to the forested countryside:

This great change from the desert sage plains, where there was no verdure to refresh the soul, or to screen us from the hot rays of the sun, made us feel we had come into a new world and among kind friends, for a tree comes as near being human as any inanimate thing that grows.[42]

Once the parties reached the arid Columbia plain, however, the descriptions of the surrounding terrain once again assume a discordant note. The Oregon Trail writings of Illinois resident Thomas Jefferson Farnham provide a good example, reflecting dramatic changes in mood as the travelers made their way through the Blue Mountains toward the Columbia Basin in the fall of 1839. Before descending to the low country, Farnham and his party stopped for a midday meal adjacent to a "sweet clear" stream where he enjoyed a "dish of rich cocoa, mush and sugar, and dried buffalo tongue, on the fresh grass by a cool rivulet on the wild mountains of Oregon!" In a spate of noonday ecstasy, he exclaimed: "Nature stretched her bare and mighty arms around us!" But once in the Walla Walla Valley, Farnham's literary mood darkened and he expressed dismay at the clouds of dust, the "dry and brown" countryside, and the dead vegetation. At the point where the Walla Walla enters the Columbia River, he wrote bitterly in a well-known passage about the "ugly desert; designed to be such; made such, and is such." Although there was "some beauty and sublimity in sight," the disgruntled Farnham remarked that the land lacked fertility.[43]

Those who traveled with the large emigrant party of 1843 formed judgments that parallel Farnham's assessment. Talmadge Wood observed that travel became exceedingly more difficult beyond Fort Hall where the road was *"very rough* & grass in many places *very scarce."* Although the area from the Platte River to the Blue Mountains was "entirely unfit for the residence of civilized man," Wood believed that the mid–Columbia River country was "peculiarly adapted to grazing purposes." To James Nesmith, a member of the same immigrant train, "the barrenness of the surrounding country" between the Walla Walla and Deschutes rivers was most striking. While the Columbia River itself was beautiful, the adjacent landscape had "an arid, barren appearance, without timber or grass." Toward the close of September two years later, Joel Palmer formed a similar impression of the arid Columbia plain: "the whole distance we have traveled since we first struck the river cannot be regarded as more than a barren sandy plain." Palmer concluded that the "country [was] very barren" and provided no forage for animals, "the grass being completely dried." Like others, Palmer's party "suffered great inconvenience from want of fuel" and resorted to the use of scatterings of driftwood and weeds to cook their food.[44]

Those late-summer Oregon Trail narratives reflected both natural and historical events. During the autumn months, the long, hot days withered and diminished the volume of grasses and browse available for animals. But as time passed and the number of people and animals on the trail continued to mount, cultural forces increasingly came to play a part in reducing the volume of forage. Over a relatively brief period of time, as Elliott West has indicated, the annual passage of large numbers of immigrants created a veritable environmental wasteland along the route of travel, with grasses, shrubs, and firewood all in short supply. For the Platte basin, according to West, "streams of horses, mules, oxen, sheep, and milch and beef cattle" chewed their way toward the Rocky Mountains "eating away forage by the thousands of acres." Through their activities in falling and cutting firewood, the emigrants themselves added to the new cultural forces brought to bear on the Platte Valley.[45]

Once westbound travelers passed beyond the Cascade Mountains, most of the narratives assume a more positive tone. Those more favorable assessments very likely reflected anticipation that the end of the long and arduous journey was near, the expectation of renewed contact with friend and kin, and the prospect of seeking out a land claim. But those more receptive narratives suggest something more, and it rests in the comfort of being in the midst of a more familiar setting and climate, one that more closely fit their expectations. Within three weeks of his arrival in the Tualatin Valley in 1843, Iowa native M. M. McCarver concluded, "no country in the world of its size . . . offers more inducements to enterprise and industry than Oregon." While its soil was equal to that of Iowa, in fertility and production the valley was "far superior, particularly in regard to wheat, potatoes, beets, and turnips." Even in its native condition, McCarver observed, the Tualatin prairie was covered with a rich grass, "perhaps the most nutritious in the world." [46]

To a people accustomed to the mixed woodland and prairie environments of Indiana, Illinois, and Missouri, settings where both water and wood were easily accessible, the arid West was an alien, forbidding, and psychologically disturbing place. Once the emigrants breached the Cascades, however, journal and diary narratives assume a different temper. Joel Palmer's account of his party's struggles through rain and snow in the Cascades south of Mount Hood in late October 1845 provides a graphic story of the difficulties of negotiating incredibly rough terrain prior to the building of the Barlow Road. His journal also provides one person's insights and reflections upon entering the Willamette via the western slope of the Cascades.

Palmer's group was one of several attempting the land route around Mount Hood in the fall of 1845. Because of the difficult passage, people from the fledgling community at Oregon City had begun to hack out a rough road to meet the struggling immigrants. Indeed, the travelers ahead of him were so numerous that Palmer reported difficulty finding sufficient forage for his animals, because "the numerous herds of cattle which had passed along had . . . ate up the grass and bushes." But once below the snow line, the migrants began to find patches of good grass and then, the best news of all, on October 28 they connected with the new road that led to Oregon

City. As they descended along an upper portion of the Sandy River, and before they had reached the open prairies below, Palmer's spirits rose:

The soil is good, and is covered with a very heavy growth of pine and white cedar timber. I saw some trees of white cedar that were seven feet in diameter, and at least one hundred and fifty feet high. I measured several old trees that had fallen, which were one hundred and eighty feet in length, and about six feet in diameter at the root. We passed some small prairies and several beautiful streams, which meandered through the timber.[47]

For the next two days Palmer and his small entourage passed "alternately [through] prairie and fern openings," the soil "of a reddish cast, and very mellow," the sort, he thought, that "would produce well." After more "rolling and prairie country" and an occasional sighting of settlers' homes, the group entered the Clackamas Valley proper where "the soil looks good." Finally, on November 1, 1845, Palmer's band reached their objective, "the place destined at no distant period to be an important point in the commercial history of the Union — Oregon City." [48]

The increasing number of people moving along the Oregon Trail in the early 1840s were potent carriers of biological and ecological change. All along their winding route of travel, the westbound groups were instruments of transformation: they encroached on Indian lands; they killed or drove away game animals and other wildlife; their livestock overgrazed and destroyed grasslands that had been the province of Indian horse herds; and they brought waves of new diseases. The whites who followed the westward trails toward the sunset were efficient carriers of cholera, smallpox, and measles, diseases that spread outward from the primary migration route along the Oregon Trail from the Platte Valley to the lower Columbia.[49] George B. Roberts, who settled just north of the Columbia River in the Cowlitz Valley, remembered the anxiety of local Indians in the fall season when new immigrant groups arrived:

Every year they [the immigrants] brought something new. . . . Whooping cough, measles, Typhoid fever etc. . . . the country was free from all these maladies till then — when first introduced they seemed much more violent than now. . . . All these things we think so lightly of now scourged the poor Indians dreadfully.[50]

The infamous measles epidemic that led to the death of Marcus and Narcissa Whitman, supposedly spread by Oregon Trail migrants, is more problematic. According to Robert Boyd, the Hudson's Bay Company post at the mouth of the Walla Walla River first reported the disease in late July 1847, well before the arrival of the overland migrations of that year. Boyd reasons that Cayuse and Walla Walla Indians may have carried the infection with them when they returned from trading ventures in California. But whoever transmitted the disease, the contagion devastated Indian people. The measles spread outward from the mid-Columbia to the vicinity of Fort Vancouver and then to the Cowlitz Valley by the winter season. The following spring, measles outbreaks occurred in Puget Sound and as far north as Fort Victoria. Boyd contends that the Hudson's Bay Company supply ship *Beaver* may have spread the disease to the company's northernmost posts. The measles epidemic reduced the Cayuse population by one third and other groups to a lesser degree.[51]

Apart from the pathogens that were persistently reshaping the region's demography, the most extensive changes were taking place in the Willamette Valley. The Hudson's Bay Company trader James Douglas warned his superiors in the late 1830s about the growing influence of the American settlements, especially those clustered around the mission at Champoeg:

No sort of manufacturing is yet introduced, but the restless Americans are brooding over a thousand projects, for improving the navigation, building steam Boats, erecting machinery and other schemes that would excite a smile, if entertained by a less enterprising people.

Although the "vagrant Americans respect[ed] power and integrity," Douglas worried that Jason Lee and the Methodists nourished "secret views, at variance with our interests." The real intentions of the Americans, he wrote, were difficult to anticipate, but the company should be aware that they "have the power of seriously injuring our business."[52]

When Charles Wilkes and his United States Exploring Expedition conducted a reconnaissance of the Oregon country in 1841, he estimated the population of "whites, Canadians, and half-breeds" in the region to be between 700 and 800 people. Of those, approximately 150 were United States citizens, most of them associated with mission settlements at the falls of the Willamette and further up the valley, at Clatsop on the lower Columbia, and at The Dalles. The missionaries in the Willamette Valley, Wilkes reported, had made little progress in Christianizing natives but were "principally engaged in the cultivation of the . . . farms and the care of their own stock." Most of the newcomers, he remarked, had selected lands and "seem more occupied with the settlement of the country and in agricultural pursuits than missionary labor." Wilkes concluded his report with what was fast becoming a standard reference to the Willamette Valley: few sections of the globe offered more opportunity for "the happy abode of an industrious and civilized people."[53]

Because agriculture involves modification of the biological and physical world, those initial farming activities were beginning to effect visual changes in the Willamette Valley landscape. In addition to the expanding agricultural activities at the mission establishments, the oldest Euro-American population—the "Canadian Settlement" at French Prairie and the small number of ex-trappers on the Tualatin plains (numbering about 100 people in the late 1830s)—had begun to remake the ecology of the valley. Geographer James Gibson estimated that those farms produced more than 7,000 bushels of wheat on approximately 566 acres of tilled land in 1836. Because those mostly subsistence farmers wanted to barter their small surpluses of wheat, the Hudson's Bay Company built a small warehouse at Willamette Falls to receive grain. Gibson's calculations also showed that those same operations owned 156 horses and 384 hogs. In the short run, however, the increasing number of Bay Company cattle being grazed south of the Columbia River represented the most intrusive agent of ecological change. Ever since the company established its post at Fort Vancouver in the mid-1820s, it had carefully nurtured its cattle herds. When their numbers grew too large, the HBC pastured animals on Wapato (Sauvie) Island and subsequently on the Tualatin plains. In his government-sponsored reconnaissance of 1841, Charles Wilkes reported approximately 3,000 cattle grazing in the vicinity of Fort Vancouver.[54]

The Americans who were arriving in ever greater numbers accelerated the still relatively slow pace of environmental change in the Willamette Valley. Hudson's Bay Company personnel, some of whom had been in the region for nearly two decades, were amazed at the number of overlanders suddenly in their midst. From Fort Nez Perces on the Walla Walla River, Archibald McKinlay noted that the Americans were getting "as thick as Mosquettoes in this part of the world." And after the large emigrant group of 1843 arrived in the Willamette Valley, the usually taciturn McLoughlin expressed alarm that the country was "settling fast" with Americans. James Gibson estimates that the valley's Euro-American population numbered approximately 500 people in late 1841 and then increased to 809 early in 1843. Willamette settlers farmed 6,284 acres of "improved land" in 1842 and produced 31,698 bushels of wheat. According to Gibson's calculations, the newcomers' animals vastly expanded the number of domestic livestock in the valley: 3,519 cattle, 2,683 horses, 1,733 hogs, and 135 sheep.[55]

Oregon City was both a symbol and representation of the transformation taking place in the lower Willamette Valley. The growing settlement at Willamette Falls served as a market and processing point for commodities from the surrounding farmlands and forests and as a point of transshipment and exchange with oceanic markets beyond the Columbia River. John McLoughlin established a land claim "at the Falls of the Willamatte" in 1829. Two years later the HBC opened a water-powered sawmill at the falls, with McLoughlin promising that cargos would be ready for "exportation" on a regular basis. But the Americans who passed through the area in ever-increasing numbers in the early 1840s brought the greatest change. The Methodists established a mission at Willamette Falls and the fledgling settlement grew from a single building in 1840 to several more wooden structures early in 1843. And then, following the large influx that comprised the "Great Migration" of 1843, the newly named Oregon City had seventy-five buildings by the end of the year.[56]

Peter J. Burnett, one of the leaders of that emigrant group, wrote James G. Bennett of the New York *Weekly Herald* in 1844 that Oregon City had four stores, two sawmills, one gristmill and another, owned by John McLoughlin, under construction. "There is quite a little village here," he reported. The commercial-minded Overton Johnson and William Winter, with a greater flair for poetic fancy, informed readers of their travel guide (published in 1843) that Oregon City was busy with the "hum of industry; the noise of the workman's hammer; the sound of the woodsman's axe; the crash of falling pines." The vast amount of water power available at Willamette Falls, the authors' estimated, "is alone sufficient to propel an immense machinery." [57]

By the time Joel Palmer made his way down the western slopes of the Cascades to Willamette Falls in 1845, Oregon City was a village of about 100 houses, "most of them not only commodious, but neat." Located on the east side of the river below the falls, the town of approximately 300 residents possessed two conspicuous public buildings — a Methodist church and a Catholic chapel — and the usual array of services:

four stores, two taverns, one hatter, one tannery, three tailor shops, two cabinet-makers, two silversmiths, one cooper, two blacksmiths, one physician, three lawyers, [and] one printing office.

Of the two grist mills, the one owned by John McLoughlin had three sets of buhr runners and compared "well with most of the mills in the States." Palmer also reported that the two sawmills were cutting "a great deal of plank for the use of emigrants." [58]

Sawmills and grist mills, of course, are mechanisms for turning the productions of nature into commodities to be sold at market; as such they imply varying degrees of ecological disturbance to places far beyond the sites where logs are sawed into boards and wheat is ground into flour. When Joel Palmer first visited Oregon City, settlements extended along both sides of the waterway above Willamette Falls all the way to the relocated Methodist mission at Chemeketa, the present site of Salem. Still other concentrations were located in the vicinity of Champoeg and in the Tualatin Valley. The newcomers located most of those subsistence farmsteads at the edge of woodland and prairie, along the margins of the grasslands where fuel, building materials, and spring water from the foothills were present. One early resident remarked that such land claims were convenient and made common sense:

All of the first settlers to this valley chose their homes on the foot-hills of the Cascades or about the various buttes. The reason was that good springs and plentiful wood was found there and they could live conveniently and still pasture their stock all over the open valley.[59]

Indeed, the first non-native settlers in the Willamette Valley, the small Canadian colony at French Prairie, established land claims at the margins between the heavily wooded lower valley and the first upriver prairie, a selection process that prevailed through most of the 1830s and 1840s. Less prone to flooding and easy to plow, those sites were ideally suited to mid-nineteenth-century agriculture. Unlike North America's eastern woodlands, where settlers had to do the hard work of clearing brush and timber, Willamette Valley homesteaders found that the burning practices of the Kalapuya had created vast areas of open prairie, a ready-made environment for cultivating the soil. The General Land Office surveys of the mid-1850s confirm that settlers located the great majority of their land claims at the topographic and vegetative edge between forest and prairie.[60]

As they did in other newly occupied places, white settlers distinguished between improved land, usually within the confines of the crude but effective Virginia worm fences, and the unimproved lands beyond. Both spaces, however, were subject to cultural disruption: plowing under native grasses and introducing "domestic" plants dramatically altered the ecology of the land inside the fence; the area beyond the fence, left to grazing animals and root-digging hogs, underwent a slower transformation. "The fence," Richard White has argued in his study of Island County, Washington, "became both an actual and symbolic boundary line." Farmers consciously controlled activity within its confines and made persistent efforts to expand the extent of fenced or "improved" acreage. Meanwhile, cattle and horses grazed outside the fence and pigs rooted through fields of camas.[61]

Changes to the ecology of the Willamette Valley grasslands can be traced to the earliest Hudson's Bay Company's cattle on the Tualatin plains in the late 1820s. While those small herds produced limited environmental effects, the influence of grazers on the native grasses began to accelerate when Ewing Young and a small company of men journeyed to California in 1838 and returned overland with more than 630 head of Spanish longhorns. Following Young's venture, other drovers trailed Spanish herds northward to the valley, all before the arrival of the "Great Migration" of 1843 and its sizable number of cattle. Those mostly black longhorns adapted well to the grasslands of the Willamette Valley and many of them eventually became feral. In addition to the increasing herds of domestic cattle, James Clyman reported in 1845 that there were more than 2,000 head of wild cattle "runing in the hills" near the Yamhill River. When an American officer, Lt. Neil Howison, conducted a reconnaissance through the Willamette Valley in 1846, he remarked that only a small portion of the country was in cultivated fields, but that "outside the fences is a common range for cattle." Although emigrant parties had introduced large herds of cows and oxen, Howison estimated that "the far greater number in the Wilhammette valley have sprung from a supply driven in from California." [62]

Geographer William Bowen points out parallels between the herding economy of the Spanish Southwest and that of the Willamette Valley: "Without care or need of winter feeding they ran half wild, a terror to anyone afoot. Once or twice a year riders brought all the animals of a neighborhood together for branding." The Methodist settlement at Chemeketa, with a herd of more than 1,000 head in the early 1840s, grazed its cattle in the vicinity of Mill Creek and along the hills to the south. The largest cattle herds, conservatively estimated at more than 1,200 head, belonged to Hamilton Campbell, who assumed control of the longhorns at the Methodist mission when the latter liquidated its stock holdings in 1844. Campbell's animals roamed throughout the country from Salem south into Linn County. [63]

The transformation of the million-acre grassland prairies of the Willamette Valley was part of more general systemic changes occurring elsewhere in the Far West. California's great Central Valley, where exotic grasses and weeds such as wild oat and yellow mustard had invaded the grasslands as early as the 1830s, provides a laboratory of sorts. Described by the earliest Spanish travelers as waving tall in the wind as far as the eye could see, the valley's original grasses and forbs were largely destroyed by the time of the gold rush. Whereas native perennials could not withstand the combined forces of drought and heavy grazing, the seeds of the invading annuals could lie dormant in the dust and litter until the rains returned. In the Central Valley, according to biologist Raymond Dasmann, "heavy grazing and dry cycles paved the way for widespread invasions by exotic plants." The destruction of the perennial grasses, therefore, was directly related to the expansion of commercial cattle raising in California. That process began with the ever-increasing size of the Spanish cattle herds during the mission period and then ecological change gathered further momentum and became systemic when wheat production boomed in the late 1860s.[64]

Unlike native browsers such as deer and elk, which prefer leaves and brush, the cattle and horses brought into the Willamette Valley were grazing animals, and along with sheep, their close cropping of native grasses, especially during the dry summer months, created opportunities for the introduction of exotic species. Although the historical record is spare by comparison with California, there is evidence to suggest that the transition from native species—blue wildrye, Idaho bentgrass, California oatgrass, California danthonia, needlegrass, red fescue, and tufted hairgrass—to exotic grasses in the valley's open prairie lands occurred during a relatively brief span of time. The *Oregon Statesman* reflected in 1862 that the lush grasses of the Willamette Valley provided ample subsistence feed for the earliest immigrants to winter their stock. The newspaper lamented, however, that "the grass is eaten up and mostly rooted out," because livestock "have been altogether too abundant in every locality to subsist on the product of the wild grass." A scientific study carried out in 1919 indicated that most of the grass vegetation in the Salem area was "composed largely of introduced species."[65]

Statistics reflect to a considerable degree the essence of the Oregon country's newly emerging demographic, cultural, and ecological makeup at midcentury: the size of the incoming population, the total acreages of improved land, and the number of livestock being grazed on the prairies and foothills. But most of those changes were limited to the great north-south valley along the Willamette where the great bulk of the immigrants who arrived during the late 1830s and 1840s had settled. Except for the occasional fur trading post and mission establishment, the introduction of a limited array of Euro-American trade items, and the exotic diseases that wrought such devastation among native people, the cultural and ecological landscape of the Oregon country beyond the Willamette Valley remained relatively unchanged.

The United States census for 1850 lists the population of Oregon Territory at 12,093, with an adjusted figure of 11,873 people living in settlements south of the Columbia River. The Indian population of the Oregon country is nearly impossible to calculate for 1850, because the census marshals operated under vague and limited instructions and because Indian numbers were in sharp decline. In the Willamette Valley, the area of principal white settlement, William Bowen estimates the Indian population at fewer than 500 at the time of the first federal census. The Commissioner of Indian Affairs added more confusion to the numbers game when he declared that the total native population for the United States "does not profess to be accurate," and that the numbers for Oregon and a few other states and territories "are confessedly 'estimates.' "[66]

In the vicinity of the newly dominant clusters of settlements in the Willamette Valley, the process of change was moving at a brisk pace. The census of 1850 lists 132,857 acres of improved land and another 299,951 acres of unimproved land for all of Oregon Territory. The new settlements, most of them located south of the Columbia River, included more than 41,729 head of oxen, beef, and milk cattle; 8,654 head of horses; 15,382 sheep; and 30,235 hogs.[67] Clearly, great change was in the offing; where there were only a few hundred head of livestock in the valley twenty years earlier, now there were thousands of animals grazing in the areas beyond the settlers' fences. The rapid and continuing increase in those numbers further escalated the remaking of the local ecology.

The natural world of the Willamette Valley was being altered in still other ways. To protect their domestic animals and crops, the new settler population waged wholesale campaigns to liquidate wolves, cougar, bear, and elk. To accelerate the extermination of wolves (and later coyotes), settlers laced deer carcasses with strychnine and left them in locations easily accessible to the predators. When Daniel Waldo first settled near Salem, wolves killed several horses one spring. "Cattle would fight them," he recalled, "but horses would run; the wolves would run them. I got some nux vomica that killed them off in about two months. We just rubbed it on a file and put it on a piece of meat."[68] The loosely structured Provisional Government of 1843 placed the first bounty on wolves. Subsequently county, territorial, and state governments adopted similar practices. But removing wolves and bears posed another dilemma: in the absence of natural predators, pigs multiplied to the point that they too had to be legislated against.[69]

Killing wolves, of course, was a sign of progress, of improvement. To those who were in the process of establishing farms, villages, and towns along the Willamette, such work implied extending the bounds of civilized space. An acquisitive, optimistic lot, settlers saw everything to gain and little to fear from the improvisations they were effecting in the valley. And why should they raise questions when, in the words of Lieutenant Howison in 1846, "continuous ranges of prairie lands, free from the encumbrance of trees or other heavy obstacles to the plough, stretch along, ready for the hand of the cultivator." Building an agricultural paradise in the Willamette Valley required only a two-horse plow to ready the soil for a crop of wheat. Although the population was widely dispersed, Howison reported that "over these clear lands, . . . there is, notwithstanding, a mere fraction cultivated."[70]

Settler Occupation and
the Advent of Industrialism

Prescripting the Landscape

The sweet Arcadian valley of the Willamette, charming with meadow, park, and grove. In no older world where men have . . . recreated themselves for generations in taming the earth to orderly beauty, have they achieved a fairer garden than Nature's simple labor of love has made there, giving to rough pioneers the blessings and the possible education of refined and finished landscape, in the presence of landscape strong, savage, and majestic. — *Theodore Winthrop (1862)*[1]

For the last millennium and more, agricultural practices have wrought revolutionary changes to global ecosystems. For North America, in both the intentional and accidental introduction of exotic plant and animal species, agriculturalists both subsistence and commercial unquestionably were in the vanguard of ecological change.[2] In addition to their disease pools, westering Euro-Americans carried with them cultural habits and practices as well as familiar plants and animals. The combined effects of that mix of ideas and organisms initiated the transformation of their newly adopted places of habitation. The historical evidence also shows that where climate and soil permitted, native people readily adopted the agricultural practices of the newcomers. Beyond the gardens and fields of the Hudson's Bay Company post and the mission establishments on Puget Sound, Indians were growing potatoes in several locations by the 1830s, and Samuel Parker reported in 1836 that the Spokane Indians were cultivating a small field of potatoes, beans, peas, and other vegetables.[3]

Although those early agricultural enterprises did little to disturb existing ecosystems, they represented the opening wedge to the more invasive practices of the settler-farmers who arrived in the Willamette Valley in increasing numbers during the 1840s. In the end, however, it was the link between agriculture and the market, the shift from subsistence and barter to commercial operations, that set in motion the wholesale transformation of the Willamette Valley, the repeopling of the Umpqua and Rogue river valleys, and the first incursions of white graziers east of the Cascade Mountains. Events and decisions in faraway places—the 1846 boundary treaty with England, the Oregon Territorial Act of 1848, congressional enactment of the Oregon Donation Land Act in 1850, the California gold rush, and judgments made in San Francisco, eastern United States, and transatlantic boardrooms—increasingly integrated Oregon's natural world with distant markets.[4]

The growing volume of white emigrant traffic along the Oregon Trail during the 1840s merely suggested the cultural and physical changes that would take place in the Pacific Northwest in the next few decades. When sufficient numbers of the newcomers had congregated in the lower Willamette Valley, their concerns turned to acquiring title to their land claims and establishing legal mechanisms to protect them. Hitherto, a sharply declining native population had enabled French Canadians, retired Hudson's Bay Company trappers, and members of the Methodist Mission to hold land through simple preemption and use. But in the face of the increasing movement of newcomers along the Oregon Trail, the older settler population drafted formal standards to legalize their land claims.[5] Article 3 of the Provisional Government's Organic Code established the basis for land ownership:

No individual shall be allowed to hold a claim of more than one square mile, of 640 acres in a square or oblong farm, according to the natural situation of the premises; nor shall any individual be allowed to hold more than one claim at the same time.[6]

The Organic Code of 1843, amended slightly the following year, became the legal basis for all land transactions until well after the United States and England settled the boundary issue in 1846.

Because the Oregon Territorial Act had nothing to say about the preemptory and charter land-claim situation, white settlers in the Willamette Valley continued to press for a resolution. The region's first newspaper, the Oregon City *Spectator*, warned that residents were sensitive about the land issue because they had come to the valley "under every assurance . . . that they would receive liberal grants of land." Moreover, the paper argued, settlers had "a right to expect an unconditional grant of their full claims of 640 acres of land each." When the territorial legislature elected Samuel R. Thurston as its first delegate to Congress in 1849, the legislators commissioned him to secure passage of the desired land law.[7] Thurston achieved his constituents' objective with surprising speed and good fortune when Congress passed the Oregon Donation Land Law in September 1850; the measure was a virtual facsimile of the bill Thurston had recommended. The legislation validated legal title to land already claimed by white settlers (most of it in the Willamette Valley) and served as an inducement to encourage additional immigration to Oregon Territory. Before the act expired in 1855, it is estimated that 25,000 to 30,000 immigrants, mostly of Euro-American descent, entered the territory, an increase in that population of nearly 300 percent.[8]

Valid legal title to land was the centerpiece to settler ambitions, occasionally as a matter of conscience but more often to legitimize those claims in the eyes of larger constituencies—to enhance its market value and to keep other grasping interlopers from interfering with established legal rights. The newly constructed legal arrangements redefined landscapes that native people had formerly treated as a commons, valley bottom and upland places that had served as gathering grounds for foodstuffs such as camas, tarweed, bracken fern, and an assortment of berries. Land increasingly became a commodity, a thing of value in the marketplace. To justify that new set of conditions, the newcomers refurbished the old argument that they practiced superior methods of cultivation and represented a more advanced civilization. The rights of native people, who enjoyed the legal status of "prior occupancy" under constitutional law, entered the debate only when incoming white settlers pressured the federal government to extinguish Indian title to the land.[9]

Because the appropriation of native land was well advanced in the Willamette Valley, the federal government's problem was to establish constitutional procedures for "extinguishing" Indian title before it could legally become part of the public domain. The boundary treaty with England in 1846 recognized native title to land and specified that "settlers are not to settle on or occupy land in use by the different Indians until such land is ceded to the United States by treaty." The Oregon Territorial Act of 1848 further guaranteed the Indian right to property "so long as such rights shall remain unextinguished by treaty between the United States and such Indians." The territorial legislation, in fact, declared null and void "all laws heretofore passed in said territory making grants of land."[10]

America's imperial policy makers were well aware of the constitutional requirements for the transfer of Indian title to land. When Congress passed the Donation Land Act, the matter of Indian legal claims to land had already been resolved by a previous enactment that authorized the negotiation of treaties with native people in Oregon "for the Extinguishment of their claims to lands lying west of the Cascade Mountains." Sometimes referred to as the Indian Treaty Act, the measure allowed the president to appoint commissioners to negotiate treaties, "and if they find it practicable . . . they shall remove all these small tribes . . . and leave the whole of the most desirable portion . . . open to white settlers." Territorial delegate Samuel Thurston told Congress that Indian removal was the "first prerequisite step" to settling the Oregon land issue.[11]

The California gold rush increased pressure on the Indian land base when prospectors in northern California moved across the border in the winter of 1851–52 and found gold along several southwestern Oregon streams. In addition to the large numbers of miners working numerous Rogue River tributaries, the Oregon Donation Land Law also began attracting settlers to the fertile soils of the Rogue and Umpqua valleys. The intruders quickly set about destroying Indian dwellings, fencing in native camas fields, and contributing to the increasing scarcity of wildlife. What took place in the Rogue Valley between 1853 and 1856 was akin to race war; miners and ruffians organized themselves into volunteer troops and waged hunt-and-destroy forays against the native Takelmas. Finally, after being harassed through the winter and spring of 1856, the Takelmas surrendered to a contingent of United States Army troops in the canyon country of the lower river. The end result was the forced removal of *all* native people from the Willamette, Umpqua, and Rogue valleys and their relocation to the newly established Grand Ronde and Siletz reservations. As executive-order rather than treaty reservations, both of those native enclaves could be reduced in size at the whim of presidential decree.[12]

The Indian bands in the Umpqua Valley who lived on the periphery of the violence to the south were forced to sign a treaty with Oregon's super-intendent of Indian affairs, Joel Palmer, early in 1855. Like the native people of the Rogue Valley, the Umpquas reluctantly ceded their land to the United States government and then were forcibly moved to a reservation. Palmer dictated another treaty with the Confederated Tribes of the Willamette Valley that conveyed title to 7.5 million acres to the United States for $200,000; Palmer reported, however, that the Willamette Indians would not agree to leave their homes for a smaller expenditure: "Promises of the government they say are not good, as they have before been deceived."[13]

Despite a considerable volume of criticism from white settlers, Palmer defended the Grande Ronde and Siletz reservations because they were physically separate from the Willamette Valley, inaccessible from the sea, and because they lacked agricultural potential. A visiting army officer said much the same in a letter to the Secretary of War: "[The] area abounds in game of various kinds, is well watered . . . contains sufficient arable land . . . is heavily timbered and rich in nuts, roots, and other articles of food as these Indians have always been accustomed to, — and has not yet been considered as worth occupying by the whites."[14] In truth, the effort to control and then confine western Oregon Indian people to isolated land reserves sharply cir-cumscribed and limited their hunting/gathering, communitarian mode of existence and opened thousands of acres to the transforming agency of the market. Confinement to reservations and the continued ravages of disease reduced Indian numbers from about 4,000 people in western Oregon in 1856 to just over 700 survivors in 1900. And while the growing white settle-ments were reordering the landscapes beyond the reservations, reformers were busy extending the blessings of "civilization" to diminishing numbers

of native people on the reserves. "All that native people had to do," Robert
Bunting concludes, "was to shed their own culture."[15]

The human tragedy wreaked upon Indian people in the Umpqua and
Rogue valleys during the 1850s also marked the onset of dramatic ecological changes in those valley settings. Among the external forces reshaping
the landscape of the Oregon country, the greatest catalyst and immediate
stimulus was the California gold rush. Hundreds of thousands of people
flocked to California, triggering an immediate demand for foodstuffs, lumber, and other materials. That instant market stimulated commercial agriculture and lumbering activity in the Willamette Valley and Puget Sound,
contributed to the white settler movement into the Rogue Valley in the
early 1850s, and led to subsequent gold rushes to the Oregon interior in the
early 1860s.

United States officials repeated the policy carried out in Oregon's western valleys and negotiated a series of forced treaties ceding huge areas
of Indian land in the interior Northwest to the federal government. And
perhaps anticipating the subsequent inrush of miners to eastern Oregon
and the Snake River country, federal troops conducted extensive military
campaigns to confine the scattered surviving Indian population to reservations.[16] The census for 1860 shows only two white "colonization clusters"
east of the Cascade Range, one centering on the Columbia River around
The Dalles with a population of 1,340 and another on the Walla Walla River
of 1,393; the mining boom that ensued quickly made those figures obsolete.[17] By that time, however, the ecological transformation taking place in
the humid western valleys was already far advanced.

The displacement of peoples and cultures in the Umpqua and Rogue
valleys took place in an extraordinarily brief span of time. The new cultural imprint on the southwestern Oregon landscape witnessed an inrush
of white settler-farmers and equally hectic activity at the federal land offices
as donation claimants filed for legal title to property. Jesse Applegate, who
settled in the Umpqua Valley in the late 1840s, reported in 1851 that "three-
fourths of the inhabitants of Umpqua are immigrants of the present year."
From the vantage of his new claim on the eastern fringes of the mid-
Willamette Valley, Wilson Blain wrote that the immigration of 1853 had

"taken up all the land that is of any value for agricultural purposes in the Willamette Valley." The same, he said, appeared to be true of the Umpqua and Rogue valleys as well. A newly arrived settler in the Rogue Valley confirmed Blain's suspicions, observing that all the good land had been "fenced-up" by 1853."[18]

To the incoming groups who were settling the Umpqua and Rogue valleys during the 1850s, the increasing white population and the filing of land claims signaled progress, the sure signs of home, farm, and community building.[19] As the settlers went about establishing mixed-farming homesteads in Oregon's southwestern valleys, they dramatically altered the landscape and ecology of their newly occupied lands. Within a decade, the scattered oak openings and prairie grasslands in the valley bottomlands, formerly subject to Indian burning in the autumn, were turned into farms with small cultivated fields and larger fenced areas of pastureland. But the alterations to the ecosystems in the Rogue and Umpqua valleys, while significant in contrast to the Indian period of occupation, were still limited when compared to the changes that would take place in the twentieth century.

The Applegate clan, three married brothers with their wives and an extended family that eventually numbered forty children, were among the first white immigrants to homestead in the Umpqua Valley. The Applegates staked out claims in 1849 and 1850 in the small Yoncalla Valley just south of the Calapooya divide, the low hills separating the Willamette from the Umpqua watershed. Although it is likely that the malaria epidemic of the early 1830s had sharply reduced their numbers, several surviving members of the Yoncalla band of Indians, the southernmost linguistic group related to the Kalapuya, still lived in the area. To Jesse Applegate, the greater Umpqua Valley in 1850 was "a land just emerging from a state of barbarism . . . where the recently and rudely constructed log cabin of the emigrant stands beside the ruder wigwam of the aborigines."[20]

The Applegates and their neighbors in the Yoncalla used a technology that can best be described as rudimentary. Animal power and human labor accomplished most of the plowing, hauling, and digging tasks. Jesse Applegate's oldest daughter, newly married Roselle Putnam, who still lived in the family household, wrote to friends in the fall of 1849 describing her husband's efforts to build a rough-hewn cabin:

he has succeeded in getting five thousand rails made a few acres of land plowed and the body of a log cabin built. this cabin consists of one room the roof is of boards just as the fro* left them the floor is of puncheons hewed with the axe, the crevaces between the logs are still open there is neither window door shutter nor chimney. . . . there is neither chair table nor bed a few blankes complete the furniture.

Before he bought a team of his own, husband Charles borrowed his father-in-law's oxen to haul rails sufficient to fence twenty acres of land beyond the house. Finally, after a trip to the Willamette Valley, he returned with several fruit trees, a plow, and a team of oxen. Before those purchases, Roselle wrote, Charles owned "but one tool that is *axe*, with this he is working out his apprenticeship in labor."[21]

When the Applegates first moved to the Yoncalla area, Roselle Putnam reported that there were "but three families [to] . . . share our unlimited sovereignty over these beautiful hills . . . the land all around us is our own." For those early white residents in the Umpqua Valley, the key markets for surplus agricultural goods and labor were the numerous mining camps in northern California and around the periphery of the Rogue Valley. "All the products of the farm bring immense prices in the mines," Putnam declared, "tis this that settles Umpqua any man can live well that will cultivate a small farm & he that has not the means to improve his claim can go to the mines and make them." Jesse Applegate agreed with his daughter's assessment: "the principal market for the products of the farm is found in the gold mines of the Klamath and Rogue rivers." To her eastern relatives, Roselle Putnam boasted that area residents "have all the necessities of life with less labor than they can be produced in any other country."[22]

Because they were largely subsistence farmers, the Yoncalla residents took advantage of the abundant deer population to augment their meat supply, with Jesse Applegate reportedly killing more than forty deer during his first three years in the valley. The Applegate clan were also active killers of wolves; Roselle Putnam reported that a great number of wolves were killed in the winter of 1851–52 "with strycknine, Charles put out upwards of thirty doses of it, and I suppose every one killed a wolf." Although the

---

* The fro, or froe, is a knife used to split cedar shakes for roofing.

wolves "do frequently kill cattle & horses," she noted that "they have never killed any of our cattle."[23] The Applegates and their neighbors, like white settlers everywhere across the American West, were attempting to eliminate species that threatened their mixed agrarian, pastoral economy. Wolves, coyotes, and cougars were predators—"vermin"—that had no utility, no commodity value in the calculus of a people whose objective was to raise cattle, sheep, and pigs for market. Indeed, predators ultimately became the foil for *all* stock losses, even those killed by the settlers' dogs.[24]

George Riddle and his family entered the Umpqua Valley from a southerly direction in 1851 and immediately established a claim along Cow Creek, a large tributary that joins the South Umpqua River from the southwest. The Riddles selected land with black soil and two mountain streams crossing a small valley, "the nearness of the mountains furnishing a splendid out range for cattle." Within a year of their arrival, an epidemic spread through the Cow Creek band of Indians and more than half of them died. "The Indians who were not affected with the fever," Riddle remembers, "scattered into the mountains, leaving some of the sick who were not able to follow to shift for themselves." Riddle, who was on good terms with the local Indians, observed other changes that were detrimental to native subsistence practices. The settlers' hogs rooted up the camas bulbs, an item central to the Indians' diet.[25]

But Riddle's memories of those years were mostly optimistic. And he had no reason to think otherwise when the ribby cattle the immigrants brought with them that first year "were fat by Christmas time." Riddle reflected many years later that his family "had . . . reached the promised land":

[The land] was ready for the plow. There was no grubbing to do. In all the low valleys of the Umpqua there was very little undergrowth, the annual fires set by the Indians preventing young growth of timber, and fortunately there was plenty of material at hand for house and fencing.

Like the extended Applegate family to the north, the Riddles and their growing number of neighbors struggled to cobble together agricultural equipment, especially workable wood and steel moldboard plows to till the soil. Despite those difficulties, by the summer of 1852 most of the arable land in the valley was taken up in claims, and the Cow Creek country soon began to take on the look of permanence with homes and fenced fields, "all with split rails laid up in worm fashion." [26]

Because of the influx of white settlers to the upper Umpqua region, the territorial legislature created a new county in 1851 that embraced the drainage of the Umpqua River. A correspondent to the *Oregon Statesman* predicted in midsummer of that year that land claims in the upper valley would "smile on lord and master" within a few months, whereas "twelve months since but two or three were taken." The records of the donation land titles filed for the area indicate that most of the claims in the Umpqua Valley north and south of Roseburg were taken by 1852 and 1853. In brief, settlers had claimed the best land within three years of the passage of the land law of 1850.[27]

When George Riddle and his emigrant party passed through the Rogue Valley in the summer of 1851, he recalled that "its primitive beauty had not been marred by the hand of the white man." Indeed, there were no white settlers or prospectors in the valley until gold was discovered in the fall of 1851. That event, according to Riddle, "caused that country to settle up rapidly in 1852." Historian Wallace Farnham has concluded that "the great wagon trains of 1853 . . . devoured the good lands" in the Rogue Valley. By the end of the following year, one settler observed, the valley was all "fenced up." Because of the large white settler inrush to southern Oregon's two great westward-trending river valleys, the territorial legislature abolished existing Umpqua County and created two new political units, Douglas and Jackson counties, early in 1852.[28]

In an essay published in the *Oregon Historical Quarterly* shortly after the turn of the century, James R. Robertson argued that nineteenth-century Oregon had passed through two different forms of industrial life and social development—a fur trader society based on the "utilization of a superficial resource," and a more deeply rooted agricultural society—"from an industry adapted to the support of a small population to one capable of supporting large numbers." In Robertson's view, Oregon's development had evolved toward "forms of social life that were better and higher," a remarkable accomplishment, a "work of heroism . . . as great as anything ever done." The migration of 1843 initiated the agricultural stage of Oregon's industrial life, Robertson contended, and then with the California gold rush and the opening up of commercial markets, it shifted to a more mature stage.[29]

Robertson's use of an evolutionary metaphor to describe agricultural expansion parallels Jesse Applegate's remark of 1851 that Oregon was "a land but just emerging from a state of barbarism." [30] Whether the new cultural practices were in fact "better and higher" is irrelevant to this discussion, but we can conclude, nevertheless, that agricultural "progress" meant an increase in the ecological changes taking place; it also implied other alterations associated with tertiary activities linked to those practices. For Oregon's new residents, cultivated fields, cleared and fenced pastureland, rapidly expanding trading and commercial centers, and improved overland and waterway transportation arterials represented progress.

By the mid-1850s the more accessible bottomlands in the Willamette, Umpqua, and Rogue valleys reflected the work of that new cultural presence. Immigrants who came later and who were looking for unclaimed land to settle were forced into coastal lowland valleys or into higher-elevation interior valleys, and finally by the 1860s, to eastern Oregon.[31] But there was little that was unique or different about the farms and towns that appeared with regularity during the middle years of the nineteenth century. The farmsteads themselves reflected the form and function of the built environments left behind in the Midwest, and community-building efforts followed similar conventions. As the 1850s drew to a close, the introduction and increasing use of mowing machines, threshers, and wheat separators suggests that farmland being worked beyond the settlements was also beginning to display the marks of the new and improved technology.[32]

The California gold rush provided an instant commercial boost to Oregon agriculture, creating instant markets where none had existed before. A vigorous lumber and flour trade opened up on the lower Willamette River, replacing what had been local and limited market exchanges, primarily with the Hudson's Bay Company. Where only seven ships sailed into the Willamette tidewater area between 1840 and 1846, fifty ships entered in 1849 alone, offering to purchase timber and grain products at virtually any price demanded by merchants and farmers. A writer for the *Oregonian* later re-

flected that the discovery of gold in California brought "a marked improvement in the manner of living among the farmers in Oregon." Although
small river steamers could make their way above Willamette Falls all the
way to present-day Corvallis by 1851, the middle and upper valley produced
little wheat for export until the late 1850s when steamers extended their
service to Eugene. In the interim, immigrants who settled the grasslands
in the southern Willamette Valley went heavily into livestock production,
especially cattle and hogs, animals that could be walked to shipping points
on the lower river.[33]

Those who were already established cautioned newcomers to the Willamette Valley not to expect a "second Eden." The Portland *Oregonian*
warned in 1852 that immigrants who made the trip west usually arrived
in the valley at the beginning of the rainy season, "when all things wear a
gloomy appearance — when a deep melancholy appears to pervade the face
of nature." Because most of the travelers were exhausted after the "long
and perilous journey," they should be advised not to expect a land of gaiety
and sunshine, but to learn patience, be watchful, and make a closer examination of their surroundings. In the end, the newcomer would realize,
the newspaper concluded, that "this territory is without a rival in point of
natural advantages." The "neat cottages of the hardy yeoman" settled along
the route between Portland and Salem and "the spontaneous succession of
crops year after year" were testimony to agricultural success. What Oregon
residents expected from immigrants were the industry and energy to take
advantage of the valley's rich soils which are "always sure to reward the
hand of toil."[34]

The "rapid improvements" made by settlers in western Oregon, according to contemporaries, signaled an astonishing and "radical change for the
better."[35] Moreover, the ever-increasing number of new arrivals during the
1850s continued to extend the physical boundaries of that new set of cultural assumptions, and the valley landscape began to take on a very different physical hue. Because settlers had largely eliminated the annual autumn
fires from the Willamette Valley, brush and small trees began to creep down
the slopes and onto the grasslands proper. There they expanded and colonized everywhere beyond the fences of tilled land. Heavy grazing in some
areas disturbed the soil and created ideal conditions for germinating the

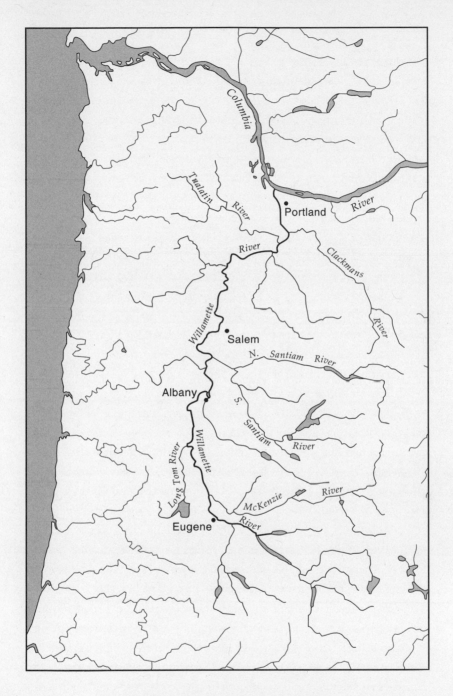

The Willamette River and principal tributaries.
University of Wisconsin Cartographic Lab

wind-blown seeds from trees and shrubs. Late in life George Goodell remembered that the Willamette Valley and its rolling hills provided excellent grazing for cattle because Indians burned the hills every autumn. But "the white man," he noted, "neglected to do this, and now in many places the grass has given way to moss and timber." [36]

Despite the more intensive and consumptive human and animal presence in the valley, woodlands actually expanded in the years following extensive white settlements. "Where the prairie was unplowed," geographer Jerry Towle points out, "oak woodland replaced grasses." Joseph Brown, who emigrated from Illinois in 1847, reflected that there was more prairie when he first arrived in the Willamette Valley: "This growth of oak and fir has grown up since pretty much. . . . When I came to Salem 30 years ago you could ride these hills anywhere." The aging John Minto, whose residence in Oregon spanned the entire settler era, recalled a conversation in 1847 about the prospective timber supply in the valley. As nearly as he could remember, one of the discussants pointed to the huge original stands and argued that pasturing cattle on the grasslands would cause "grass fires [to] . . . cease and timber would come up in plenty." Minto added with a note of hindsight: "and that was precisely what was taking place at that very time." [37] In brief, the ambitions and cultural aspirations of its new residents were increasingly beginning to shape the physical contours of the valley landscape.

Beyond the grasslands of the western valleys, the wooded coastal regions also began to mirror the new set of cultural realities. The city of San Francisco, important both for its insatiable appetite for goods and materials and as a source of investment capital, quickly extended its influence northward along the Pacific Coast. Because of the difficulty of hauling lumber over the bar of the Columbia River, San Francisco capitalists sought more accessible sources for wood materials. As a consequence, Bay Area entrepreneurs began looking to the coastal forests. Among the more notable and venturesome were newly arrived New Englanders Frederick Pope and William Talbot, who built a steam-powered sawmill at Port Gamble on Washington's Puget Sound. That new settlement of workers was one of the region's first satellite lumbering communities to depend on the powerful California market. Similar rich stands of Douglas fir, Port Orford white cedar, and Sitka spruce attracted San Francisco capital to the Coos Bay region on the southern Oregon coast.[38]

The Coos estuary is a maze of sloughs and tidewater streams where lush forests once reached to water's edge. For centuries the Penutian-speaking Coos Indians lived around the extensive waterway, subsisting on a rich variety of shellfish, other marine life, and foodstuffs from the forests. Already sharply reduced in number from exogenous diseases, the Coos saw their relatively stable world come to an end when the area was integrated into the investment and marketing network that extended outward from San Francisco. The region's huge timber stands and its convenient physical location impressed those who were anxious to take advantage of its forested wealth. A visitor observed in 1853 that the Coos waterway was "certain and safe," and that the area abounded in excellent coal and timber. "As a commercial point and depot, it is second only to San Francisco on the Pacific Coast." Another passerby reported "an abundance of the white cedar timber, well calculated for lumber," and "extensive coal banks" that would make the area a "place of great importance."[39]

By the close of the 1850s, ties of investment capital and trade firmly linked the Coos Bay region to the great California metropolis on San Francisco Bay, a marketing outlet for the rich timber stands of southwestern Oregon. Investors turned the extensive waterways that fed into the bay into industrial arterials, transportation routes for floating logs to one or more of the mostly California-owned mills. And although the small farms scattered about the lowland areas represented a transition to "improved" landscapes, logging activity brought the greatest change to the Coos region. At first, hand loggers working without the aid of oxen or steam donkeys felled trees directly into the waterways. Eventually, local mills increased their output, timber fallers moved away from the water's edge and extended the area of "daylight" in the vast Coos timberlands. At the same time, loggers periodically filled the estuaries and streams with logs, and occasionally timbers set loose in the bay became hazardous to shipping. Further disruption to the local waterways occurred when loggers began constructing chutes and splash dams to transport timber to tidewater, techniques that were used into the 1950s. As a consequence of those practices, the Coos estuary ultimately developed one of the greatest wood-sediment problems on the North Pacific Coast.[40]

The changing landscape and ecology of western Oregon during the 1850s and 1860s reflected technical improvements in water transportation, a continued influx of new immigrants, and a sometimes volatile but perpetually growing demand for the products of its soil, rivers, and forests. Through those turbulent years settlers engaged in a persistent effort to refashion the natural world to reflect the habits, conventions, and agricultural practices of the eastern United States. Beyond the expanding acreages of wheat culture, one of the most determined efforts to husband the conventional were the early and numerous attempts at horticulture. When newcomers encountered indigenous fruit or root bulbs, rather than food for personal consumption they saw the potential that their own cultivated varieties promised in the new land. According to an authority on early horticulture in Oregon, the work was carried out "with most gratifying results."[41]

That process of recreation, of imposing a different but familiar vision on the land, began with the Hudson's Bay Company's introduction of the first cultivated fruits and vegetables at Fort Vancouver in 1825. When she visited the post a decade later, Narcissa Whitman and husband Marcus were taken for the customary walk in the company's garden:

What a delightful place it is, what a contrast to the rough barren plains through which we had so recently passed: here we find fruits of every description, apples, grapes, pears, plums, and fig trees in abundance; also cucumbers, melons, beans, pease, beets, cabbage, tomatoes, and every kind of vegetable. Every part is very neat and tastefully arranged with fine walks lined on either side with strawberries.

An Oregon horticultural writer, J. R. Cardwell, observed that the apple and pear trees and grapevines at Vancouver barracks—"hoary chroniclers of time, yet showing a vigorous growth"—were still bearing fruit eighty years later.[42]

Cardwell, who was a practicing physician in Portland at the turn of the century, believed that nothing more thoroughly accented the isolation of early white settlers "than the absence of fruit trees on their newly made farms." The sight of the orchard in bloom, "the waiting and watching for the first ripe fruit," he remembered, had always brightened his childhood years. But the family orchard held even more promise, Cardwell argued: a plentiful supply of fruit was evidence of culture and civilization, of health, morals, and manners, "of love of home and . . . the foundation of all patriotism." Cardwell urged that the foresight and patient work of Oregon's early horticulturists "should be kept green in the memory of those to come after." [43]

The most prominent of those "green" memories and one of the most persistent attempts at conscripting the landscape was the tireless work of Henderson Luelling, an Iowa immigrant, who brought two large boxes of year-old grafted fruit-tree sprouts to Oregon in 1847. Carefully watered and tended in the bed of a wagon during the six-month journey, the yearling trees were planted along the Willamette River upstream from Portland near the town of Milwaukie. Another member of the party, William Meek, brought apple seeds and a few grafted trees. Forming a partnership, Luelling and Meek opened a commercial nursery in 1848. The two men successfully propagated their fruit stock, developed the first extensive nurseries in Oregon, and eventually established an orchard in the Waldo Hills near Salem. Part of their early work involved grafting cultivated root stock to indigenous fruit trees such as Oregon crab apple, wild cherry, and wild plum. That effort proved abortive, however, and the firm did not begin selling trees until 1850. [44]

Luelling and Meek and their allies on the lower Willamette River were not alone; others soon joined in what quickly became a booming horticulture business. Among the many who benefited from the new fruit stock available in Oregon were Charles and Roselle Putnam, the newlyweds staking out their Umpqua Valley farmstead in the early 1850s. After the construction of a crude cabin and using his father-in-law's horses to haul rails to fence twenty acres of ground, Charles, "who was anxious to get a few fruit trees," left for the Willamette Valley early in 1852 to buy trees, a plow, and other necessities. When he returned home, Roselle reported that Charles had purchased "a common two horse plow which required some alteration" and then spent part of a day "setting out his trees of which he only succeeded in getting a few." While the historical record is spare, Putnam's effort unquestionably was one of the initial attempts at domestic fruit cultivation in the Umpqua Valley. [45]

The world of wheat provides yet another metaphor for the ever-expanding and complex interrelationships that developed between Pacific Northwest landscapes and national and international places. That story begins on the small tracts of Willamette Valley land where subsistence farmers prepared the ground in the fall by plowing with wooden, moldboard plows, harrowing with crude wooden-toothed implements, and then seeding the rough ground by hand. Farmers cut those early crops of "Oregon white winter wheat" by hand with a grain cradle or reap hook and then placed the wheat in "shocks" in the field. From that point, farmers gathered the crop and threshed the grains by tramping it loose with oxen or horses. Workers then removed the straw with forks, thereby winnowing the remaining chaff in the wind.[46] That mode of production involved only small acreages of land sufficient to turn out enough wheat for subsistence and barter. But the California gold rush set in motion increasingly more intimate and reciprocal commercial links between San Francisco Bay and the Willamette Valley. More productive technologies — improved plows and harrows, threshers, headers, and binders — meant a dramatic expansion in the acreage of "improved" land.

In the wake of the California gold rush, white settlers sharply increased the amount of land planted to wheat, a process that required farmers to ditch and drain the prairie grasslands to ready those acreages for plowing, harrowing, and seeding. Farmers worked with plows and teams of horses to carry out their ditching work, opening thousands of acres to the plow in the thirty years following the gold rush. One valley resident recalled that much of the land was too wet for farming until "drains had been opened up and the sloughs drained." At that point, "wheat farming became all important."[47] Ditching was hard work and required long hours of seasonal labor, but it was inexpensive and remarkably successful in quickening the run-off of winter precipitation. Although agrarian newspapers like the *Willamette Farmer*[48] drew attention to the merits of underground drainage systems, ditching remained the cheapest and preferred technique for quickly converting land for commercial purposes. Those alterations to the land also imply that larger continental and global forces were significant factors in forcing changes to local ecologies.

We know today, of course, that draining wetlands is detrimental to a great variety of native flora and fauna. John Minto, who was an eyewitness to the changes that had taken place in the Willamette Valley during the last half of the nineteenth century, remarked late in life that ditching and drain-ing for roads, crops, fruits and hops, and ornamental trees "have all tended to absorb the life-giving moisture" so valuable to agriculture in western Oregon. "The general effect," he observed, was that "these damp-land and water fowls and animals, which once found here their breeding places, have gone forever." Minto also warned about the destruction of beaver dams that impeded run-off and kept silt from going to sea.[49] But the loss of nest-ing grounds for migrating waterfowl and soil erosion were not matters of great concern to a society filled with confidence and engaged in building an agrarian paradise.

The route to agricultural success, regional newspapers and magazines pointed out, required a multifaceted approach: improvements in land and water transportation; an aggressive effort to increase production and estab-lish stable markets; the promotion of "mixed farming"; and the devel-opment of regional manufactures to supply local needs.[50] But that effort to energize the local economy was not intended to create a self-sufficient "society devoid of market relations."[51] The Portland *Oregonian* repeatedly made clear that the function of mixed husbandry was not to provide for subsistence needs, but to "enable the farmer to have something on hand that will find a prompt and paying market." And while it persistently urged farmers to "press the production of wheat," the newspaper also advised agriculturalists to keep a keen eye on potential markets for all surplus goods: "The success of their business depends in good measure, in watch-ing the market."[52]

In the quiet October morning mists of 1869, the bark *Adeline Elwood* an-chored in the lower Willamette River and began taking on a cargo of wheat to be delivered directly to Liverpool. According to the *Oregonian*, the event signaled the beginning of an auspicious trading venture between Portland and the great industrial centers of the world. Opening direct trade with Europe, the publication promised, would be of great importance to "our agricultural and commercial progress." The trading venture indicated that Portland and the Northwest were "breaking away from the domination of

San Francisco" and extending trade to new markets. The Portland newspaper added that shippers already were conducting a sporadic but direct
trade with China, Australia, and New York. If farmers were wise and kept
their prices reasonable, the *Oregonian* concluded, local producers could expect to "secure constant and remunerative markets for our products."[53]

For several months Portland merchants had attempted to establish marketing outlets for the increasing wheat surpluses produced in the Willamette Valley. A consignment of several hundred barrels of flour destined for
New York early in 1867 represented the first effort of Portland traders—
mirroring their San Francisco counterparts—to link the productions of the
valley with distant markets. A few months later a New York sales agency
reported that Portland flour was "as good as anything in this market and
superior to the California flour." Despite a surplus of unsold valley wheat
in late October 1867, the *Oregonian* cited the attractions of a potential eastern market to encourage farmers to expand production:

If the amount of wheat which the State now has to dispose of were twenty-fold
greater, we should have a better market, because buyers would know where to come
to purchase. We ought to produce more of everything than we have ever yet done.[54]

Although Adam Smith might quarrel with the economic logic of that statement, there is little question that such sentiments accelerated changes to
Oregon's landscape.

Wheat output in the Willamette Valley increased from fewer than
200,000 bushels in 1850 to 660,081 bushels in 1860 and then burgeoned to
2,086,826 bushels in 1870.[55] That dramatic increase in production reflected
substantially larger acreages of ditched and drained, "improved" cropland
as well as major alterations to the transportation arterials that enabled
farmers to market grain and other products. Because the Willamette waterway was the critical factor in the movement of wheat from upriver points
to Portland, the federal government funded the construction of a steam-
powered "snag puller" to remove obstructions to river navigation, especially in the area above Willamette Falls. Built at Oregon City in 1871, the
snag puller worked ceaselessly when water conditions permitted to remove
snags from Oregon City upstream to Corvallis. In those places where large
trees were embedded in the bottom of the river, operators used dynamite to

loosen the trunk, according to the *Oregonian,* "thus rendering its removal quite an easy task."[56]

Snag-pulling operations on the Willamette River marked the beginning of human efforts to reconfigure and channelize the waterway to meet the requirements of commercial traffic. Along with the diking and revetment work that soon followed, the Willamette and its major tributaries were in the process of being converted into rationalized components of a transportation infrastructure that linked the material abundance of the Willamette Valley with distant markets. Removing obstructions from the stream freed the river to steamboat traffic and set in motion the industrialization of the extensive valley waterway. But the engineering work targeted for the Willamette was only one element in ever-more ambitious water management schemes that eventually would be carried out at the mouth of the Columbia River and in the Portland Harbor area.

The increasing volume of wheat reaching Portland was the immediate and primary explanation for the transformation of western Oregon's valley landscape, but the expanding wheat output along the Willamette also marked the wholesale turn toward commercial agriculture. Continued gold discoveries in the interior country and the hint of lucrative foreign markets generated an interest in market reports, new agricultural implements such as plows, seed drills, movers, and reapers, and the latest practical and scientific advice in modern farming techniques. The publication of the *Willamette Farmer,*[57] a weekly newspaper devoted primarily to the interests of agriculture, signaled to a growing audience that land was little more than a commodity, a vehicle to obtain financial security and profits, a central objective of the valley's ever-expanding market farming.

The appearance of fledgling agricultural societies to disseminate up-to-date information to farmers about wheat culture, animal husbandry, horticultural advances, and a broad variety of marketing news was another indication of the shift to commercial agriculture. During the 1850s farmers organized a few small groups that eventually coalesced to form the State Agricultural Society in 1860. The latter, according to John Minto, "united all interests of the soil" and provided the organizational framework for the annual state fairs that served as a forum for displaying the rural arts.[58] But in a larger sense, the agricultural associations suggested more fundamental transformations that were taking place along the rivers and valleys of western Oregon. The advertisement, display, and promotion of headers and binders meant changes to both land and riverine environments as an increasing volume of wheat moved toward the warehouses and shipping facilities at Portland.

The sudden emergence of Portland as the leading trading center on the Willamette River was tied firmly to the California gold rush and the ensuing increase in commerce. Situated near the confluence of the Willamette and Columbia rivers, Portland enjoyed strategic advantages as a distributing center by virtue of its natural water routes to upstream markets on the Columbia and Willamette and across the Columbia bar to the oceanic highways beyond. With only five or six commercial houses in 1850, Portland expanded to more than forty mercantile establishments by 1853. In addition, the booming town had four steam sawmills, a planing mill, and several small manufacturers, while sailing vessels from San Francisco arrived daily. And where a single steamboat plied the Columbia and Willamette between Astoria and Portland in 1850, three years later that number had increased to fourteen.[59]

Confined mostly to the west side of the Willamette River about twelve miles from its junction with the Columbia, Portland attained a population of 2,874 in 1860, more than three times the size of any other settlement in the Pacific Northwest. Portland became "The Oregon Emporium," according to the prominent regional publication, *West Shore,* because it captured the trade of its interior at the time of the California gold rush. The magazine was referring to wooden macadam roads constructed during the 1850s to the rich prairie lands west and south of the town. It was the Portland business community's genius, *West Shore* reported, to unite "the external commerce of the country, . . . to bring the prairie schooner and the ocean-going vessel together." In point of fact, Portland possessed a deep water harbor, a natural advantage that its upriver rivals lacked. The city's population surged to 8,292 in 1870 as local merchants capitalized on a series of gold discoveries on upriver tributaries to the Columbia. Its major newspaper, the *Oregonian,* boasted in 1867 that Portland was "more distinctively a commercial city" than any other in the state, the signs of maturity and domination over an expanding tributary region.[60]

TABLE ONE

Population of Oregon Towns, 1850–1870

	1850 Census	1860 Census	1870 Census
Albany			1,722
Corvallis	—	700	
Eugene City			861
Jacksonville	—	892	
Oregon City	933	889	1,832
Portland	805	2,874	8,292
Roseburg	—	835	
Salem	291	625	1,139

As it grew in size and importance, Portland developed a strategic infrastructure that fronted on two worlds, one that faced outward to the Pacific and oceanic markets and sources of capital, and a second that looked inward to a vast hinterland linked to Portland by the magnificent Columbia River and its tributary, the Willamette. Portland was an intermediary settlement, a point of exchange between distant centers of global capitalism and its own hinterland, the latter with a natural abundance that could be turned to advantage in oceanic markets. Lesser population centers in the interior Northwest paid tribute to Portland, just as Portland paid tribute to San Francisco. Although the Willamette community was a mere village compared to the California metropolis, historian Dorothy Johansen eloquently underscored its early significance and influence:

Portland has been appropriately described as the "city that gravity built." Down the Willamette flowed the produce of the Valley; down the Columbia came the immigrants and the riches of Idaho mines and the interior's wheat fields. California ships brought goods to Portland for distribution to the Valley and for transshipment on sternwheelers up the Columbia.[61]

Until transportation magnates built railroads up the Columbia River and directed new supplies of wheat to Portland in the 1880s, much of the city's prosperity was tied to grain produced in the Willamette Valley. Although the booming gold camps on the tributaries of the upper Columbia increased the volume of traffic through Portland, the city's primary "interior" region and source of prosperity and wealth lay to its south. Both the *Oregonian* and the *Willamette Farmer* worried about receipts of flour and wheat, improvements in water transportation on the Willamette River and its tributaries, the declining per-acre yields of valley wheat fields, and what the newspapers perceived as an excessive reliance on single-crop production. Despite those concerns, valley farmers continued to increase the number of acres planted to wheat until output reached more than two million bushels in 1870. The biggest advance in production during the nineteenth century took place during the ten years following 1870 when valley harvests reached 5,365,117 bushels.[62] The completion of the Oregon and California Railroad through the Willamette Valley and a greater volume of wheat sales in the British market explain the huge increase during the 1870s.

Before the construction of the rail line, the greatest movement of wheat to Portland took place during the rainy season when shallow-draft steamers were able to navigate the Willamette River upstream as far as Eugene. However, even during the low-water season the river steamers regularly plied the slow-moving waterway to the most productive centers of wheat growing at Albany, Corvallis, and Harrisburg. The removal of trees and the deepening of some of the worst bars in the stream gradually improved commercial travel on the river. To facilitate moving their annual harvests to the Willamette River, farmers also built canals across flat sections of the valley and attempted to make small streams like the Long Tom River navigable. Near Salem, farming interests diverted water from the Santiam River to increase the flow of Mill Creek for purposes of floating sacked wheat to the city. And farmers and merchants in the mid-valley area lobbied for nearly two decades before finally building a small canal from the Santiam River near Lebanon across the valley to the Willamette River at Albany.[63]

Even though farmers and their allies operated with a relatively limited technology, the combined work of deepening bars, clearing snags from the main river, and building modest canals represented an effort to rationalize the natural world, to remodel the valley landscape to aid and abet capital and commodity exchanges between very different and distant places. At the same time, the land beyond the navigable rivers was increasingly equated with money and profits, with farmers occasionally selling surplus land to finance the purchase of new machinery. If there was any mystique associated with holding land in pursuit of some independent yeoman ideal, as one writer claims,[64] the actual course of events in the valley suggests that in most instances such notions were quickly pushed aside in the midst of the growing volume of wheat being shipped downriver to Portland.

As workers were laying the first rails south of Portland, the *Oregonian* pointed to the commercial power of wheat: "This product may be said to be the staple of Oregon and to a great extent the prosperity of our farming community depends upon the profit arising from its production." The newspaper urged farmers to take more aggressive measures to establish firm markets or turn their attention "to the cultivation of something more certainly profitable."[65] George W. Hunt, who farmed near Sublimity east of Salem, was one who enjoyed the benefits of expanding wheat production. In a letter to the *Willamette Farmer,* Hunt suggested that landowners could benefit in several ways:

Times are prosperous with the farmer; plenty of money; wheat on the upland is looking well; stock is poor, but will go through [the winter] with little loss; land is looking up, and rapidly changing hands. I notice that those taking the place of the old settlers, are wide awake; so we will rather gain than lose by the change.[66]

There also are some indications that the introduction of the new steam technology in the valley led to an increase in land speculation.

The industrial aspirations of the region's newspapers and booster groups extended beyond the call for building railroads to the development of manufacturing facilities. Instead of importing agricultural implements, harness and leather, clothing, stoves, and other items, the *Willamette Farmer* urged Oregonians to produce those goods for their own market. Home production and home consumption would reduce the stress on continual croppings, enable farmers to allow land to lie fallow, and thereby permit the soil to recover its fertility. The *Oregonian* observed that residents "produce food in abundance, but produce too few of the other necessities of life." Because there was a close connection between agriculture and manufacturing, it thought the state would be wise to promote the latter. The

Portland newspaper also worried that in the face of an incredibly bountiful land, citizens were less ambitious than they should be: "Wherever nature does most for a country, there the denizens do the least." [67] The *Oregonian* attributed some of the problem to "the restless and roving habits of the people." Since its settlement, residents had been constantly on the move looking to acquire "large and sudden gains," especially in "the mining regions lying on our border." [68]

At the onset of the railroad era the *Oregonian* continued to express alarm about the excessive reliance on wheat as a single cash crop. It was poor policy to rely on "wheat for export as an exclusive industry," the newspaper argued, because a single crop would eventually impoverish the soil. Moreover, a community that depended exclusively on agriculture could never prosper. The great danger in continuing the present course, the *Oregonian* warned, was "the uncertainty of the foreign market for wheat." The solution was to "diversify our employments so as to bring machinery to our aid in the production of manufactures." In a rather equivocal bit of reasoning, it pointed out that developing a manufacturing capability would lead to a profitable home market and a more reliable venue "for our grain than we now enjoy." For its part, the *Willamette Farmer* worried that the Pacific states exported too much precious metal and received little in return, measures "well calculated to . . . impoverish these States." The true source of wealth, it argued, rested in agriculture and manufactures and "the development of the multifarious resources of the State." [69]

The imposition of that new commercial ordering on the valley landscape was revolutionary in terms of the more simplified ecology that it implied. When farmers bounded and fenced land devoted to wheat production, they increasingly restricted the free movement of cattle (and hogs). Peter Boag observes that open-range herds in the southern Willamette Valley declined during the 1860s, and as farmers extended their fence lines, the cattle industry shifted east of the Cascade Mountains. Valley agriculturalists also sought answers "to the best method of destroying ground squirrels and rabbits" and chastised neighbors who were negligent "of co-operation against the common enemy." But the most intrusive and revolutionary changes to the landscape and ecology of western Oregon followed the building of the Oregon and California Railroad. The new technology that Karl Marx referred to as the crowning achievement of industrial capitalism reached Salem in September 1870, Eugene the following year, and Roseburg in the fall of 1872.[70]

The federal census for Oregon lists a population of 12,093 in 1850, 52,465 in 1860, and then in 1870, as the state legislature was disposing of the federal land grant to support railroad construction through the Willamette Valley, Oregon's numbers increased to 90,923. The population figures for the counties west of the Cascade Mountains indicate an areal concentration of white settlement and also imply those settings where the greatest extent of environmental change was taking place. Although the statistics do not reveal the precise arguments that legislators used to carve new counties from existing ones, they do show that western Oregon's population was concentrated largely in those areas with the greatest agricultural potential. With the exception of Multnomah County on the lower Willamette River, there is a direct correlation between population and agricultural production. (See Table Two.)

There is nothing particularly striking about the close link between population and agricultural activity, especially in an age where production was largely dependent on human and animal power. Lane and Linn, two of the most heavily populated counties in Oregon in 1870, also ranked first and second in listings of improved land, and Linn County led in wheat production. Linn County also surpassed all others in "total (estimated) value of all farm productions, including betterments and additions to stock."[71] Human activity was unquestionably most intense where sizable acreages were devoted to the cultivation of wheat and oats, the latter used chiefly for grazing livestock. As a linear progression through time, those cold statistics represent both human enterprise and the influence of human agency in altering the ecosystems and landscape of the Willamette Valley. (See Table Three.)

Exclusive of the Indian population, the census figures for eastern Oregon reveal a slow and scattered increase in numbers until the completion of the Northern Pacific Railroad through the Columbia River corridor in 1883 and the Oregon Short Line across northeastern Oregon in 1884. The 1870 census lists five organized counties east of the Cascades, with Jackson County spilling over on both sides. The figures for Union (2,552), Grant

TABLE TWO

Oregon Population by County, 1850–1870

County	1850	1860	1870
Benton	814	3,074	4,584
Clackamas	1,859	3,466	5,993
Clatsop	462	498	1,255
Columbia	—	532	863
Coos	—	445	1,644
Curry	—	393	504
Douglas	—	3,203	6,066
Jackson	—	3,736	4,778
Josephine	—	1,623	1,204
Lane	—	4,780	6,426
Lincoln	—	—	—
Linn	994	6,772	8,717
Marion	2,749	7,088	9,965
Multnomah	—	4,150	11,510
Polk	1,051	3,625	4,701
Tillamook	—	95	408
Washington	2,652	2,801	4,261
Yamhill	1,512	3,245	5,012

(2,251), and Baker (2,804) counties reflect the rising and declining fortunes of mining camps; those for Wasco (2,509) and Umatilla (2,916) counties represent expanding agricultural settlements. The immigrants flocking to the inland areas, the *Willamette Farmer* concluded, were also pouring their mineral wealth into the city of Portland, furnishing a market for goods going upriver, and "affording us a medium of exchange and capital to carry on trade." In the hinterland region, freight depots like Umatilla emerged as warehousing and exchange points, taking in consignments of goods from the steamers that plied the upper Columbia, and then sending out heavily laden teams to the mining districts.[72]

TABLE THREE

Miscellaneous Agricultural Statistics for Oregon, 1850–1870

	1850	1860	1870
Improved land*	132,857	896,414	1,116,290
Unimproved land	299,951	1,164,125	1,272,962
Percent of unimproved land in farms to total land in farms	69.3	56.5	53.3
Average size of farms	372	355	315
Horses	8,046		51,702
Cattle	41,729		50,766†
Swine	30,235		119,455
Sheep	15,382	86,052	318,123

* All land figures are in acres.
† Includes only milk cows and oxen.

Although the cattle, sheep, and mining interests were in the process of placing a new and different cultural imprint on the streams, grasslands, and hillsides of eastern Oregon by the 1870s, far more dramatic changes were taking place in Oregon's humid western valleys where human cultural practices, the productions of an abundant natural world, and external markets were contributing to the dramatic remodeling of the landscape. Those changes, however, were but a hint of the transformation that would take place when the full presence of the industrial world arrived in the form of the railroad.

Technology and Abundance

We can offer the emigrant a civilization fresh in its newness. . . . we can offer the virgin soil under almost every variety of price and circumstance. The New England man may here find opportunity for trade, or manufactures or farming. We have forests for the lumberman of Maine, and fisheries for the fishermen of Cape Cod. . . . We have the soil whereon to settle hundreds of thousands. Here all these classes of immigrants will find climatic conditions similar to those they leave behind. — *Willamette Farmer, June 28, 1869*

Railroads provided a technical means for mastering nature, for overcoming the seeming inefficiencies of a natural world whose physical obstacles blocked the ambitions of those who wanted to link nature's wealth with urban processing and manufacturing centers. The ribbons of steel that increasingly transected western North America following the Civil War provided the critical infrastructure that liberated investment capital from the restrictions of geography. For the real world of the Oregon country, railroads accelerated the commodification of nature's abundance by making raw materials accessible to the manipulations of distant investors. The rail lines built during the 1870s and 1880s — from Portland south to the California border, eastward through the Columbia River corridor, and across northeastern Oregon into Idaho — were an entrepreneur's dream. Carlos Schwantes has properly concluded that railroads "functioned as engines of empire." In brief, railroads were vehicles for incorporating nature, for extending the awesome forces of the industrial world to distant and relatively unpopulated areas.[1]

As the proudest symbol of industrial capitalism, first in England and western Europe and then in the United States, the railroad marked the onset of increasingly intrusive patterns of human activity in the natural world. In terms of heavily capitalized and broadly based transportation and extractive enterprises, the railroad represented a vastly accelerated move to take advantage of the region's natural bounty. At the same moment, distant places like Chicago, New York, Minneapolis–Saint Paul, and even London, Berlin, and Paris assumed increasing importance to activities that took place in the interior Northwest. If "history happened fast" in the region, then steel rails were the transcendent medium for that quickening pace of activity.

The initial railroad construction in the Northwest was accomplished in halting and piecemeal fashion. The Oregon Steam Navigation Company (OSN) solidified its shipping monopoly on the Columbia River in 1862 when it completed a six-mile portage railroad at the Cascades and another fourteen-mile road to bypass the rapids that extended from The Dalles upriver beyond Celilo Falls. The OSN's key to success was its ability to control the two strategic natural obstacles to river travel at the Cascades and The Dalles. To the Portland *Oregonian,* the portage railroads represented "a great improvement, of vast value to the upper and lower country," developments that would eventually prove to be of great public importance. From the vantage point of Oregon's Umpqua Valley, Jesse Applegate argued that the portage railroads were the first step in the important work of building a northern branch of a transcontinental link through which "Oregon will become a great, prosperous and independent State." But when it came to the proposed route from Portland to Sacramento, Applegate was suspicious, because the road might "bind us in vassalage to our strong neighbor forever."[2]

Railroads, then, held multiple promises: they were physically and economically liberating, firmly linked to issues of improvement and progress; and the more enthusiastic promoters argued that they contributed to advancing the cause of civilization itself. Without acknowledging any hyperbole, the *Oregonian* portrayed railroads as "an indispensable adjunct of civilization." At the same time, the metaphorically more earthbound *Willamette Farmer* argued that "the progress of new countries depends . . .

upon their railroads, and their connection with extensive railroad systems." Still other railroad proponents believed that a line through the Willamette and Umpqua valleys was needed to "attract attention from the commercial world" and "make Oregon a great State."[3]

Amidst all the excesses of that promotional rhetoric, however, there were more realistic expectations: railroads would redound to the benefit of the larger centers of commerce, increase land values, speed the transition to commercial agriculture, bring an end to open-range cattle grazing, and introduce agriculture to places where none existed before. During the 1870s and 1880s some farmers brought more acreage into production, while others sold their surplus land to prospective agriculturalists and used the capital to invest in new machinery. There was also a growing conviction among property holders in the western valleys that land should be equated with the money and profits that it would yield. In effect, the acquisition of wealth for its own sake became one end to agricultural enterprise. "As that shift proceeded," historian Dean May argues, "land lost its magic and became . . . simply one of many possible ways to make a living."[4]

"Developing our vast, dormant resources," the Oregon booster David Newsom explained, was the railroad's one great virtue. Building roads across Oregon would provide the needed transportation arterials for shipping the state's vast reservoir of natural riches "to the great outside world."[5] Its supporters argued that the proposed rail lines would intensify and expand agricultural production, open "new" territory to commercial ventures, increase the population along the rail corridors themselves, and bring permanent "improvements" everywhere across the state. But even with the arrival of the transcontinentals, the *Oregonian* complained of Oregon's "remoteness and isolation," circumstances that placed the region "far behind the progress of industry and commerce in other states." What Oregon needed, it concluded, was "the introduction here of a knowledge of the methods of industry and business."[6] In conventional economic thinking, Oregon and much of the American West were the nineteenth-century equivalent of "developing" countries, areas poor in capital but with an abundance of "dormant" natural wealth.[7] It is important to remember, then, that European and eastern United States capital investments greatly influenced and accelerated the pace of change in backcountry areas.

The transformation of the hinterland West from preindustrial economies to functional components in global exchange relationships involved
technological advances other than the extension of rails through the region. Technical improvements in steamship transportation, the successful
laying of the transatlantic cable in 1867, and the simultaneous building of
telegraph lines across the vast expanses of the West accelerated the speed
of travel and communication. E. J. Hobsbawm has suggested the extraordinary achievements of that quickened pace of activity: "From the journalistic point of view the middle ages ended in the 1860s when international
news could be cabled freely from a sufficiently large number of places on
the globe to reach the next morning's breakfast-table."[8] It can be said with
some accuracy that the symbols marking that transition in the American
West were the pony express and the telegraph. The former, "the most famous and the most ephemeral" of all western communication systems,
quickly became obsolete when the first transcontinental telegraph line was
completed in 1861.[9]

That infinitely more rapid and increasingly sophisticated communications infrastructure quickened exchanges in information and vastly advanced the capitalist transformation of the outback. Oregon joined that
new world of the rapid dispersal of the latest intelligence when William
Ladd and Henry Corbett's Portland firm completed a telegraph line to
Sacramento in 1864. The Portland *Oregonian* celebrated the event shortly
thereafter when it published news from the east that was twenty hours old.[10]
But a more auspicious moment for the Far West took place in the spring of
1869 when the last miles of the nation's first transcontinental railroad, the
Union Pacific and Central Pacific line, were joined in Utah's Great Basin.
Although the new route lay well beyond the more heavily populated centers
of the Pacific Northwest, the completion of the road stirred a great deal of
excitement in the region because it was viewed as "the sure forerunner of an
early extension to us of a branch line." Sixty years ago, the Portland *Oregonian* observed, it took one month to travel from Philadelphia to Pittsburgh:

But now one week will suffice for the whole journey across the middle of the continent from the Atlantic to the Pacific. *Time and space have been actually annihilated
by the industry of man* [emphasis mine].[11]

The prospects of railroad building in the Pacific Northwest stirred the imagination of Frances Fuller Victor, an astute observer of Oregon's historical development and one of the principal writers for Hubert Howe Bancroft's publishing house in San Francisco. In a travelogue and promotional tour of the Oregon country in 1871, Victor observed what she called the stirrings of industrial activity: the incipient salmon canning business on the lower Columbia, Washington's "unrivalled facilities" for lumber production, and the latent potential of Oregon's commercial forests. But the promise of improvement, of the betterment that rail construction would bring to the Columbia River country, inspired her the most. "The silent grandeur of the Columbia," she predicted, "is to be made busy with the stir of human labor, and the shriek of 'resonant steam eagles.'" Linked to distant places by rail and oceangoing vessels, the Northwest would offer its goodwill to the "nations of the world in bales of merchandise." The joining of the Far West to oceanic markets, Victor concluded, was "the dream of Jefferson and Benton realized."[12]

The completion of the Union Pacific and Central Pacific railroads preceded by only one year the building of the Oregon and California Railroad (O & C). The colorful stagecoach entrepreneur, Benjamin Holladay, built the state's first major rail line from Portland southward through the Willamette Valley, eventually terminating in Roseburg in the fall of 1872. Although the O & C was not completed through to Sacramento until 1887, it attracted a rush of immigrants to Oregon's western valleys, contributed to a huge boost in agricultural production, and accentuated Portland's significance as a commercial center. One scholar suggests that the railroad introduced the golden era of agriculture to the Willamette Valley, with the area's population rising from about 61,000 in 1870 to more than 233,000 in 1900. The number of farms nearly tripled during the same period. Statewide, Oregon's population more than quadrupled from 90,704 in 1870 to 413,536 at the turn of the century. Those statistics also suggest significant changes to the physical landscape of western Oregon. Although the euphemism was "progress," one writer hinted at a larger spirit of transformation at work: "More than one farmer who took donation land in the Willamette Valley . . . lived to eat his supper by electric light and ride to town in his automobile."[13]

Even as the prospect of the railroad loomed on the horizon, the *Willamette Farmer* suggested that the Pacific slope offered "the emigrant a civilization fresh in its newness," with land available for everyone and a climate similar to that in the eastern United States. As work crews busied themselves building the O & C connection to Roseburg, newspapers, magazines, and promotional publications praised the bright prospects for the region: the fertility of Oregon's western valleys, the availability of additional good land, and the water power available for the development of manufacturing industries. But "railroads, and their connection with extensive railroad systems," the *Willamette Farmer* bragged in 1872, were true measures of progress, the symbols of improvement and betterment in a new country.[14]

Wheat production in the Willamette Valley had risen to more than 5 million bushels in 1880, a year when a rust-like fungus infected the crop. With passenger and freight cars running twice daily between Portland and Roseburg, the O & C Railroad vastly speeded the movement of agricultural goods to the big export warehouses on the Portland waterfront. In that first decade of rail travel, the population of the Willamette Valley increased 62 percent to nearly 100,000 in 1880, a larger rate of growth than the 57 percent of the previous decade. During that same ten-year period (when wheat production in the valley more than doubled), the census indicates a 53 percent increase in the acreage of "improved" land.[15] Even before the first transcontinental rail line reached Portland, cultivated grain fields, orchards, farm houses and outbuildings, and patterned and fenced boundaries characterized the valley landscape.

The census figures that differentiated between improved and unimproved places reflected well-known cultural practices that segmented, classified, and provided definitions for identifying landscapes. The language and categories in the census reports reflect larger cultural relationships with the natural world, with the land itself and its rivers, forests, and other flora and fauna. Newspapers, magazines, political sermons, and public forums across the Oregon country all reveal comparable rhetorical tendencies. Cultivating the soil, altering the course of rivers, enlarging the built environment, and similar cultural influences were improvements to the natural order and indicated to the settler population advances in the state of civilization itself.

In a celebration at Aurora of the annual gathering of "pioneer" settlers in June 1874, the *Willamette Farmer* mused that Oregon's Elysian fields were "made by the joint hands of Nature and of man." While nature had taken centuries to provide a luxurious growth of forests and grasslands, it required human labor and ingenuity to "thin the exuberance of Nature's growth," to clear the way and give "breathing space for the native grasses." What the pioneers and their friends were celebrating, the newspaper exclaimed, was "the triumph of man over Nature in Oregon."[16] The hard work of redeeming the wilderness, the magazine *West Shore* asserted in one of its early issues, placed Oregon in the enviable situation where it "now gives its unequalled wealth of breadstuffs to the nations of Europe." Its productivity had garnered it a "foremost place as a producing State." The journal praised the state's growing lumber trade, its "unequalled Salmon fisheries," growing manufactures, and improvements in transportation that were "far in advance" of what the most prophetic pioneers would have anticipated.[17]

The ebullient and prolific David Newsom, while agreeing that Oregon's resources were "almost boundless," cautioned prospective immigrants that "each one is expected to 'paddle his own canoe.'" And although residents had already claimed much of the good agricultural acreage, newcomers could still locate rich land in the "interior districts." Because of its boundless resources, there was "a great diversity of ways and means by which persons can acquire comfortable livings here and enjoy it well." Newsom then proceeded to praise the state's abundance:

Upon the western slope of the Coast Mountains, and along the ocean for over 200 miles, are large boundaries of timber and brush lands, very rich, well watered and productive; healthy and capable of being utilized in many ways. The timber is excellent; vast coal mines abound; there are oyster, salmon and cod fisheries; and upon the marsh or tide lands fine wild grasses for hay and grazing.[18]

In the view of most boosters, Oregon's most significant attribute was its vast potential for future development. A. J. Dufur, an unabashed promoter and featured speaker at the State Agricultural Society meeting in 1877, told the gathering that the state had "just entered on the era of . . . industrial development." Although farmers had successfully introduced "tame grasses" in their meadows and had established orchards and vineyards on the hillsides, Dufur pointed out that Oregon's mineral wealth, its timber and ship-building resources, and its fisheries remained virtually undeveloped. The state also had an unlimited capacity to produce flax and wool, and it had the water power to turn the raw material into finished products. "Who," Dufur exclaimed, "is able to foreshadow, or even comprehend the greatness of our future destiny!"[19]

As one might expect, works and projects associated with the practical side of "improvements" occupied a great deal of space in the regional press. David Newsom, a farmer and self-appointed public adviser on all matters having to do with agriculture, was particularly active in this regard. Born in West Virginia in 1805, Newsom emigrated to Oregon in 1851 and settled on rolling Howell Prairie, northeast of Salem, where he became a successful farmer, operated a sawmill, and established a large and thriving orchard. But over the years Newsom gained most of his public notoriety through his letter writing to newspapers and magazines in Oregon and elsewhere. Shortly after Newsom died in 1882, his friend John Denison offered the following obituary in the *Pacific Christian Advocate:*

> More than fifty years ago he began writing for the press, and has devoted much time to that occupation, never receiving any cash remuneration from any source. He has corresponded with over fifty papers in Oregon and has been, at one time, correspondent for a dozen papers east of the Rocky Mountains. . . .
> Of late his contributions have been much sought for by the press. The great corporations and syndicates have given him free passes over every line of travel in Oregon and Washington Territory, and have urged him to travel and write up the country. This he has done, visiting in the last year every part of our country, and writing hundreds of articles for the press.[20]

In agricultural circles Newsom would have been cast as a progressive. He advised farmers, primarily those in the Willamette Valley, on a multitude of issues: (1) the use of manure on fields and pastures to maintain the quantity and quality of crops; (2) the appropriate care of fruit trees; (3) the building of shelters for livestock, especially for milk cows; (4) the proper methods for plowing the valley soils; and (5) workable techniques for ditching and draining fields. "Of all countries," he said of his adopted homeland, "this most needs natural or artificial drains." Because of the valley's heavy winter precipitation, permanent ditches were necessary to drain the land and make it ready for the plow: "A great benefit can be derived here from a small amount of labor and care." And finally, Newsom warned that farmers who failed to vary and rotate their crops regularly were exhausting the soil.[21] Through articles and letters, Newsom offered this information to readers of the *Oregonian, Willamette Farmer,* the Salem *Statesman,* and *West Shore.*

Although Newsom was an unabashed boomer and promoter of his adopted land, he also provided his audiences with a variety of homilies on proper stewardship and techniques of adaptation. Because "wild grasses in Western Oregon are mostly eaten out," he wrote in the *Willamette Farmer* in 1872, he advised farmers to plant "tame grasses" such as timothy to produce summer feed and winter forage for livestock. To provide sufficient hay to keep animals through the sometimes difficult winter conditions in western Oregon, Newsom argued that the cultivation of "tame grass is of paramount importance." Farmers should persist in their work of replacing "wild grasses" with "tame grasses," especially in areas of "superior grass lands"—properly ditched wetlands and swales, well-drained swamplands, and brushy hillsides. If they were well cared for, he thought those ideal grasslands would produce two to three tons of timothy hay per acre.[22] Newsom firmly believed that newly introduced grasses were far superior to indigenous varieties; that farmers should practice crop rotation and other progressive agricultural methods; and that those who continued to make improvements and followed his advice would be richly rewarded.

Although there were serviceable railroads through the Willamette Valley and at the portages on the mid-Columbia River by the 1870s, agricultural interests worried about monopoly influence—the Oregon Steam Navigation Company on the Columbia River and the Oregon and California Railroad from Portland south to Roseburg. The solution to those forms of economic oppression, critics argued, was free and open competition, especially that afforded by improving Oregon's waterways as an alternative means of shipping goods to market. The canal and locks at Willamette Falls, according to the *Willamette Farmer,* were "permanent and expensive improvements" that assisted in overcoming a natural and seemingly insurmountable barrier to river navigation. But equally important and a matter of great significance to the valley, the canal and locks "made competition possible." [23]

A consortium of local chapters of the Grange led the initial effort to improve navigation on the Willamette River. The Grangers requested congressional appropriations "to secure a survey of river obstructions" and "to push a demand for their removal in the most speedy manner." The Grange also urged farmers to use the ballot to enlist support from Oregon's congressional delegation in their behalf, especially in the struggle against the new corporate presence in the valley.[24] In the view of agricultural interests and area chambers of commerce, nature's waterways would continue to serve as a potential foil against the monopolistic machinations of the railroads. One correspondent to the *Willamette Farmer* even suggested that valley producers should operate their own boats on the Willamette system:

> The Willamette River was surely placed where it is for the benefit of the country which it drains, and belongs to the farmer by right of purchase, inheritance, and birthright, and will not be sold for a mess of pottage.[25]

Those who opposed monopolies in transportation eventually centered their requests on the Columbia River, where their arguments gained a larger audience.

The success of the canal and locks at Willamette Falls, according to the *Willamette Farmer,* proved that some transportation projects merited public support. Speaking for its agricultural constituency, the newspaper urged the state legislature to appropriate money to build portage railroads at the Cascades and above The Dalles on the Oregon side of the Columbia. Such public works would "open up the Columbia River to free competition and so lessen the cost of transportation to the people of the upper country." Because the federal government's proposals to build canals and locks at the two locations were still in the distant future, the *Willamette Farmer* reminded the state that it had an obligation "to aid the opening of transportation . . . on the Columbia." Such a move would "rapidly build up and improve all Eastern Oregon." But the newspaper's ultimate objective was establishing dual transportation routes along the river. If shippers had access to both a railroad and canals and locks around the rapids, it would be impossible for private interests "to monopolize a majestic river on which so great a region depends for freight and travel."[26] Providing a water bypass around the two major portages on the mid-Columbia would "improve" and rationalize the shipment of passengers and freight; it would also have the advantage of "opening" transportation systems along the river corridor to competition.

"The great primary need" in bringing future prosperity to the region, the *Willamette Farmer* reported in 1877, was "aid for railroad communication and for the improvement of river navigation on the Columbia." In that respect, the *Farmer* took a more advanced and aggressive position than the *Oregonian* in pressing for a transportation infrastructure to promote agriculture. Deepening the bar of the Columbia River and completing the Northern Pacific Railroad, the *Willamette Farmer* contended, would stimulate commerce throughout the interior country. As the reality of the Northern Pacific transcontinental link to the Columbia River neared, the newspaper predicted that the development of the interior country tributary to the Northern Pacific line would bring "numerous branch roads and the progress of this whole region must open up considerable trade with the Pacific Coast States."[27]

Although the expanded railroad networks pleased those who wrote for the *Willamette Farmer* during the 1880s, the newspaper devoted even greater space to improvements in water transportation, especially for the Columbia. Producers, in its view, needed the river "as their free, natural highway, and look with intense desire for the removal of its natural obstructions." The *Farmer* again pointed to the canal and locks on the Willamette as an example of the advantages that would be derived from "making the Columbia navigable for its whole course." But favoring improvements in river navigation did not imply opposition to railroad construction: waterways simply afforded a "much cheaper means of transportation than railroads."[28] For the next century and despite considerable evidence to the contrary, proponents continued to argue that the river provided the most cost-effective means for shipping wheat and grain products to market. What promoters dubbed nature's highway would continue to be the object of development plans and the subject of lofty, windy rhetoric for more than a century.

In the general expansion of capitalism in late-nineteenth-century America, nature in its commodity form was critical to the successes of the Atlantic-centered industrial world and to the sustained economic growth of distant, hinterland places. Collectively, the activities of several disparate groups —agriculturalists, distant investors, and local promoters—revolutionized productive relations and altered the legal status of land, rivers and streams, and subsurface mineral rights. Aided and abetted by the great railroad systems, those combined activities introduced significant ecological modifications and in some instances the systemic remodeling of the most distant reaches of the Oregon country. In extractive and processing works involving large outside investments, such as the timber industry, a crude argument can be made that those activities represented capital at work converting nature into more capital.

A German-born American journalist, Henry Villard, was more important to railroad building in the Columbia River country than any other representative of foreign capital. According to Carlos Schwantes, "no decade would rival the 1880s for miles of track laid, . . . and the person doing most to create a coherent railway system amidst all the building was Henry Villard." [29] Representing German security-holders, Villard first gained control of the financially troubled O & C, and then in a series of shrewd maneuvers, he purchased the extensive holdings of the Oregon Steam Navigation Company (OSN), including its strategic railway portages on the mid-Columbia River. Villard reorganized the OSN in 1879 as the Oregon Railway and Navigation Company with, of course, himself as the chief executive officer. He focused his next effort on linking those newly acquired properties with one of the transcontinental lines, either the Northern Pacific, which was building slowly across the northern West, or the Union Pacific extending westward across southern Idaho toward the Snake River. [30]

Completing a transcontinental line to the region, the *Oregonian* exclaimed, would provide "the key to the great natural channel of communication" that would "develop the commerce of the entire northwest, with

Portland its principal depot." The pending conclusion to hundreds of miles of rail construction also implied other changes. While his crews were laying track at a rapid pace up the Columbia River, Villard purchased the Philadelphia-based ship *Columbia* and directed the steamer to deliver more than 1,000 tons of equipment for the Oregon Railway and Navigation Company. The material included ten locomotive engines, twelve passenger cars, 280 freight cars, turntables, and other railroad fixtures.[31] The arrival of the heavily laden steamship in Northwest waters marked the onset of an expanded industrial presence in the valley of the Columbia.

As construction of the Oregon Railway and Navigation Company railroad line pushed east from The Dalles, in a daring maneuver Villard formed a "blind pool" with eastern financial backers and purchased controlling stock in the marginally solvent Northern Pacific Railroad. Proceeding with great haste, he then directed construction of the Oregon Railway and Navigation tracks to Wallula and across eastern Washington's channeled scablands toward the village of "Spokan Falls." From there the line passed eastward through northern Idaho to join with the Northern Pacific in Montana. Villard completed his transcontinental links in 1884 with a branch road through the Blue Mountains into the Grand Ronde Valley and then southeast, connecting with the Oregon Short Line at Huntington on the Snake River. With the Northern Pacific Railroad now linked to Portland and Tacoma, Villard had directed the investment and building of more than 500 miles of standard-gauge tracks in the Northwest. During that furious pace of construction, the old O & C line, dormant in Roseburg since 1872, was completed to Ashland in 1883. Once the transcontinental network was in place, however, Villard found himself overextended and within the year he resigned from the presidencies of his various companies.[32] The roads themselves eventually passed into the hands of his competitors: the Columbia River route and the Oregon Short Line to the Union Pacific, the Oregon and California to the Southern Pacific, and the Washington, Idaho, and Montana railroads to the revitalized and independent Northern Pacific.

Like its transcontinental counterpart, the Union Pacific–Central Pacific line, the physical task of building the Northern Pacific Railroad was a daunting construction project. Tunneling through mountain barriers, spanning broad rivers, and building trestles across deep ravines was difficult and dangerous work and required a huge labor force. Construction gangs worked through deep winter snows across northern Idaho and western Montana to push the effort to conclusion. In the narrow gorge of Clark's Fork River, laborers dynamited whole mountainsides into the canyon below. Crews accomplished similar feats in building the Oregon Short Line through the Blue Mountains to the Snake River.[33] In brief, constructing railroads across the rugged and mountainous interior country was not an ecologically benign activity.

A month or so before the first through trains traveled the Northern Pacific line, the *Oregonian* boasted that no place was "likely to be more affected by the introduction of the new and powerful force . . . through which there is a possibility of magical transformation." The newspaper predicted that the completed railroad lines would "work great changes upon the country" and speed "activity through every artery of northwestern life." A vast, formerly isolated section of the continent would soon be sending its goods to Portland. Most important, the *Oregonian* suggested, the city's central location enhanced its ability to capitalize upon "the redemption of the great northwest from its isolation."[34] That kind of rhetorical boasting about River City, as Portland enthusiasts affectionately referred to the place, eventually embraced a variety of metaphors involving its hinterland and the "natural" benefits that would "flow" to the city by virtue of its physical setting.

Portland's position as the "RAILROAD CROSS-ROADS" of the Pacific Northwest, the *Oregonian* observed a few years later, was no accident, nor was it "a forced and artificial arrangement." The great transportation lines of the country came to Portland "by the force of the law of commerce" as well as "the physical law which makes water run down hill." Every productive section of Oregon and Washington, the newspaper pointed out, enjoys a level route to Portland: "The situation of the city at the junction of the Willamette and Columbia valleys is invincible." No artificial devices were capable of altering trade "from the great natural channels which lead to and through her." Moreover, any new railroad and river improvement in the region, the *Oregonian* boasted, merely "widens the area of Portland's tributary country."[35]

If Portland was the geographical center of rail and water transporta-

tion, then the vast countryside radiating away from the city was its tributary territory. From Portland's vantage, the hinterland region to the east
and south held a great abundance of riches awaiting transport to River
City, the natural point of transfer for processing goods and making them
ready for shipment to oceanic highways and the beckoning markets of the
world beyond. Into Portland's "expanding clasp," the *Oregonian* enthused,
"is destined to be poured the varied products of a fertile soil . . . and the
accumulated wealth of both eastern and western Oregon, eastern Washington and Idaho." Although the newspaper's boasting was less grandiose than
that of the Portland-based trade publications that began to appear in the
early twentieth century, its writers continued to emphasize the railroad's
important contributions in bringing "a large share of commercial profit"
and "substantial wealth" to the city.[36] In the process of bringing changes to
the countryside, the newspaper believed that the new transportation arterials would ultimately contribute to the public good.

The perspectives that we bring to the past provide intriguing insights
into the disparate meanings that we attach to the effects of technology.
Although it is widely recognized today that railroads were mighty engines
of environmental change, in the late nineteenth century writers for the *Oregonian* saw the building of the great steel roads as part of "the commercial
history of the country." Railroads represented progress; they "opened" new
lands to growth and development; and the Oregon Railway and Navigation
Company in particular helped convert "the tawny, ever rolling sagebrush
and alkali plains [of eastern Oregon] . . . to bloom and blossom as the rose."
Natural obstacles inhibited ease of travel, the transportation of goods, and
"retarded growth and settlement." Now all that was changed, the Portland
newspaper observed. "Oregon has grown up" and a bright future appeared
assured:

> Westward the tide of empire rolls, has been the cry of our great republic, and
> after all these years the great Northwest, of which Oregon is the central figure, feels
> the flow of the tide.[37]

As the new year opened in 1895, the *Oregonian* returned again to its
celebration of Portland's position as "the natural great railroad center of

the Pacific Coast." The passes through the Rocky Mountains provided natural routes of travel down tributary streams to the great Columbia waterway itself. And just "as nature selected the courses for the streams, . . . so engineering science locates the easy, uniform grades for railroad traffic down the Columbia to Portland." Perhaps with an eye to the rapid emergence of Seattle as a major trading center, the *Oregonian* pointed to the "well-founded law of railroading" that directed commerce to follow natural routes with easy grades following the course of rivers "which nature unerringly surveyed many centuries ago." Indeed, the newspaper strongly hinted that Portland, like Chicago, was a natural metropolitan center:

Railroads did not make Portland the metropolis of the Northwest. They made this city their terminal because it was the metropolis. As Chicago is the great railroad commercial center of a vast territory because of its favorable location and altitude as a receiving and distributing market, so Portland similarly situated relative to the great Pacific Northwest, is its railroad center.[38]

While the rail and water routes that terminated in its harbor area enabled Portland to develop a sizable hinterland trade, other towns also generated their own hinterlands, no matter how small the surrounding population. Roseburg boomed when the O & C made the Umpqua Valley settlement the southernmost reach of its operations between 1872 and 1883. Construction of new business establishments, warehouses, and residential dwellings increased dramatically. Just before the railroad reached Roseburg, a local newspaper reported that living space was in great demand: "There is not a vacant house in town and several parties who have recently came in are anxious for some place to live." The following year the paper observed that "immigrants [were] pouring into all sections of our State," with many families locating in Douglas County. With the idea that they would expand their regional trading prospects, local merchants built warehouses in the vicinity of Roseburg's depot grounds.[39]

In practice, Roseburg's rail terminus served as an important shipping point, especially for the annual wool clip and the products of the soil that were en route to the big warehouses and processing buildings on the Portland waterfront. Shortly after the railroad reached the town, the Roseburg *Plaindealer* took note of the community's strategic position:

Its advantages of location are unsurpassed. It is not only the present terminus of the Oregon and California Railroad, but it is the center of a large county trade. At this place the roads . . . all unite. In addition the whole trade of the Southern part of the county comes here." [40]

At first the expectation and finally the arrival of the railroad triggered a period of unprecedented commercial expansion in the upper Umpqua Valley and beyond. One local newspaper estimated that more than a fourth of Rogue Valley farmers purchased their supplies in Roseburg, and A. G. Walling's 1884 booster publication, *History of Southern Oregon,* reported that the railroad unleashed a spate of construction activity in the area:

Warehouses were built at the depot, and the granaries and wool rooms became more and more crowded each year, until the first warehouses became too small and had to be increased or replaced by new and larger ones, with all the modern improvements for preparing produce for the market.[41]

The improved transportation to Douglas County accelerated the flow of goods passing both ways through the Umpqua Valley, and by speeding the delivery of the latest labor-saving farming equipment, the railroad advanced the cause of commercial agriculture. Even before the railroad arrived, one farmer had already imported a Marsh Harvester—a crude horse-drawn mower—via the tidewater portion of the Umpqua River. But with rail transportation available in the 1870s, farmers began purchasing J. I. Case threshing machines and eventually steam-powered tractors, the sure signs that commercial agriculture had arrived in Douglas County. Despite the dramatic expansion in commercial activity, the county proper remained primarily a place of farming and ranching enterprises with nearly half of its citizens listed under agricultural occupations in the census for 1880.[42]

During the critical decade after the railroad arrived, Douglas County's population grew from 6,066 in 1870 to 9,596 in 1880, an increase of 58 percent. At the close of the decade the principal settlement at Roseburg had three newspapers and its trade with the surrounding countryside supported several mercantile establishments, some of them with large warehouses adjacent to the railroad. But the population boom of the 1870s dropped to 24 percent during the following decade when the railroad, now under the control of the Southern Pacific, extended its line through the mountains into the Rogue Valley.[43] Indeed, agricultural production probably had reached an upper limit of sorts by 1880, especially in terms of the extent of land suitable for cultivation or grazing. The county's population did not make another surge until the 1940s when a rapidly expanding lumber industry drew sizable numbers of people to the area. Those who came to work in the woods or in the county's sawmills boosted the population by 120 percent between 1940 and 1950.[44]

David Newsom, who spoke favorably about *all* sections of the Oregon country, paid a visit to "beautifully situated" Roseburg in 1881. He reported that the town had "a thrifty and business appearance" with several expensive dwellings, a schoolhouse, churches, and abundant supplies "at reasonable rates." But what most impressed Newsom about the settlement at Deer Creek and the South Umpqua River was its strategic position as the terminal point of the Oregon and California Railroad.

The effects are manifest in the wealth and growth of the place. It has been the shipping point north to Portland, and by wagons south to Jacksonville and points between here and there. Wool and farm products were hauled here from many parts, for market or for shipping.[45]

The agricultural statistics for Douglas County also reflect changes taking place in neighboring towns and in the countryside beyond Roseburg as rail lines increasingly transected the valley. Even before the Oregon and California line reached the Umpqua Valley, Douglas County ranked fourth in the state in the valuation of farm productions, "including betterments and additions of stock." The railroad, however, was a major turning point: the acreage of land listed as "improved" grew by 234 percent between 1870 and 1880, with an even larger expansion in wheat production, from 104,246 bushels to 439,198 bushels. Douglas County herders led the state in sheep raising in 1870 with 94,963, a figure that increased to 133,319 in 1880, even though sheep owners were beginning to move their herds east of the Cascade Mountains, and both Wasco and Umatilla counties quickly surpassed the Umpqua region in sheep production.[46]

Thirty years after the extended Applegate family initiated white settlement in the Yoncalla area, the Umpqua Valley had a fenced, cultivated, and regularized appearance. The cultural imprint of that settler population was apparent elsewhere as well, especially along riparian areas and hillsides that were progressively being cleared of timber. Trees were cut for building materials, fencing, home heating and cooking, and for a variety of railroad-related uses: fuel, cross ties, trestles, and the like. During the dry summers in the Umpqua Valley, livestock overgrazed the lush grasses and brush that grew along streams and in the process broke down the banks and created conditions for erosion when the seasonal fall storms commenced. Reduced cover and increased siltation raised water temperatures; and the introduction of animal wastes into streams further disrupted aquatic life.

The white settlements scattered across southern Oregon's Rogue Valley differed from the population clusters in the Willamette and Umpqua valleys in several respects. Although farmers quickly developed a thriving agriculture to serve the local mining districts, mining itself was the principal cultural disturbance responsible for altering the valley's landscape. Small-scale placer activity attracted large numbers of prospectors to the tributaries and small creeks of the Rogue River drainage beginning in the early 1850s; soon thereafter, miners began introducing infinitely more intrusive hydraulic mining techniques. Jackson County, created along with Douglas County in 1852, listed a larger population in the 1860 census than its northern neighbor, undoubtedly a consequence of the large number of gold seekers in the Rogue Valley. But when the mining boom slowed in the 1860s, as Table Four reveals, the valley's population increased by fewer than 2,000 people.

The white settlers along the Rogue River occupied valley bottom and lower elevation areas along streams where there were good agricultural and mining prospects. Even before its population nearly doubled in the 1870s, miners had constructed low-elevation ditches to carry water to their rocker-boxes and sluice-boxes. The combination of those activities increased cultural disturbances all across the Rogue basin. The larger placer operations—"hydraulicking" as contemporaries referred to it—appeared in a few locations in the late 1860s and then were in widespread use by the 1870s. Confined mostly to the winter months, hydraulic mining involved the use of gravity-fed water cannons to blast away entire hillsides of glacial and alluvial deposits to get at the valuable minerals therein. As historian

Population of Douglas, Josephine, and Jackson Counties, 1860–1890 *

	1860	1870	1880	1890
Douglas	3,203	6,066	9,596	11,864
Jackson	3,736	4,778	8,154	11,455
Josephine	1,623	1,204	2,485	4,878

*The figures reflect the total population for Jackson and Josephine counties. A sizable number of people resided in Josephine County's Illinois Valley, a center of considerable placer and hydraulic mining. The Illinois River is a tributary to the Rogue but the valley proper is physically distinct and separate, especially in terms of population clusters.

Richard White put it: "hydraulic mining took mountains and washed them into rivers." [47]

Hydraulic operations introduced far-reaching ecological changes that extended far beyond the location of the mining claims themselves. Washing away hillsides quickly filled narrow canyons with gravel and eroded debris. Then heavy winter rains combined with melting snow to flush the accumulated wastes downstream, clogging rivers and flooding low-lying areas with rocks and gravel deposits that are apparent in many stream beds to the present day. In contrast to sluice-boxes, hydraulic mining required the construction of lengthy, large-capacity ditches to carry water considerable distances to high terrace deposits. In some instances, the operation meant diverting water from mountain streams and transporting it via flumes across ravines to iron pipes that led directly to the water cannon. In the more heavily worked areas, miners cleared away riparian vegetation to expose the banks of streams; they also cut the timber through right of ways for the lengthy contour ditches that carried water to the placer deposits. [48]

One hydraulic operation, the "Sterling Ditch" on the Little Applegate River, was nearly twenty-five miles long with a capacity of seventy-five second-feet (2,000 miner's inches). Another mining set-up on the Little Applegate, the Chinese-owned "Gin Lin" system, sluiced away nearly four miles of the lower river over the course of two decades. During the winter months when the two operations were being worked full time, Jacksonville newspapers reported on several occasions that the Applegate River was "running brick red" with mining debris. Jeff LaLande, the author of an environmental history of the Little Applegate watershed, contends that the combined effects of the Sterling and the Gin Lin operations were considerable:

This activity . . . poured hundreds of thousands of cubic yards of silt and rock into the river during the December-May mining seasons. In 1878, the Sterling Mine reported its two giants moved compacted deposits at the rate of 800 cubic yards a day.

Although miners extracted most of the easily accessible gold from Rogue tributaries during the 1870s, hydraulic activity continued at a less intensive pace for the remainder of the century.[49]

Hydraulic mining obviously played havoc with fish populations, especially the anadromous chinook and coho salmon that spawned throughout the Rogue basin. The silting over of breeding grounds and the great sediment load carried in the streams during the winter months created adverse conditions for juvenile salmon. Cole Rivers, who conducted a study of fish populations in the Rogue basin for the Oregon State Game Commission, concluded that mining "was one of the first inimical factors contributing to the decline of the Rogue River fishery." Although the heavy commercial take on the lower river also may have been detrimental to salmon runs, Rivers argued that fish-packing records show a direct correlation between heavy hydraulic mining and declining numbers of anadromous fish. The virtual absence of fish screens at places where water was diverted into mining ditches (and later irrigation ditches as well) further exacerbated the problems for salmonid populations.[50]

The Rogue basin also was one of the earliest settings for extensive irrigation works in the Oregon country. Because the average precipitation for the lowland areas in the valley is just over twenty inches a year, with most of it coming during the winter, it is necessary to water crops during the hot, dry summers to make agricultural undertakings a commercial success. The extensive mining ditches in the Rogue River drainage, used mostly in the winter, were turned into seasonal irrigation ditches as well. The large volume of immigrants entering the valley in the 1870s included sizable numbers of farmers who began converting many of those old water carriers to permanent agricultural use. One local authority concludes that the early mining history of many of the irrigation ditches has been obscured because they were later converted to agricultural purposes. The Sterling and Gin Lin ditches on the Little Applegate River, whose water rights were established during the 1870s, later served as two of the more important sources of irrigation water in the area.[51]

Except for a few complaints about its unstable economic character, those promoting development in the Rogue Valley do not appear to have been prejudiced against mining. Indeed, one booster wrote the *Willamette Farmer* in 1872 praising the rich mineral resources of the region, the ease with which "water can be carried [to] our mines by means of ditches," and the "rich boon" that awaited those with capital who were willing to invest in such ventures. Although the mines were not as productive as they had been in the past, the writer insisted that great wealth remained beneath the surface, needing only "some thorough, go-ahead and enterprising men who have sufficient capital to open the portal to industry and enterprise."[52]

Other changes to the ecology of the Rogue Valley were more incremental and less dramatic, albeit no less extensive. Following cultural precepts similar to those practiced in the Willamette and Umpqua valleys, early white settlers along the Rogue eliminated fire from the valley proper, thereby allowing brush and trees to colonize areas formerly kept open by low-intensity Indian fires. But the dryer climate in the Rogue basin and the brush that rapidly occupied the areas beyond the settler's fence created conditions that were conducive to the rapid spread of fires. Within two decades, these practices created new fire regimes. Much larger, more destructive conflagrations replaced the more frequent and nurturing fires of the Indians. The Jacksonville *Intelligencer* reported in August 1864 that there was more fire in the valley than at any other time since white settlers had arrived. And John Leiberg, who surveyed forest conditions for the federal government at the turn of the century, concluded that before active suppression, fires were frequent and destructive over large areas.[53]

"A brighter day is dawning for the people of . . . Josephine and Jack-

son counties," David Newsom wrote as construction crews were busy laying railroad tracks into the Rogue Valley: "Life and animation, population
and wealth, follow in the wake of our railroads, and the iron horse will
soon draw the commerce of these large districts to first-class markets." The
Oregonian observed that the extension of the O & C route to the Rogue
Valley would advance "the railroad progress of Oregon" and would be of
"incalculable convenience and benefit to the people." Although the rail line
reached Ashland in April 1884 and then was completed through to Sacramento in 1887, its immediate influence in the valley was limited. The population growth for Jackson County averaged about 23 percent for each of the
last two decades of the nineteenth century. A much larger growth spurt occurred between 1900 and 1910 when the county's population grew by 88
percent to 25,756. Those numbers reflect the expanding acreages planted to
orchards in the vicinity of Medford.[54]

Still, in ways large and small, the railroad brought change to the Rogue
Valley. When Southern Pacific railroad executives decided to pass through
the tiny post-office community of Medford and to bypass Jacksonville four
miles to the west, the former quickly emerged as the largest commercial
center in the upper Rogue Valley. Over the years the old mining town
itself declined in numbers, eventually becoming an historical relic, a visiting place for antiquarians and tourists. Elsewhere in the valley the railroad
brought other new communities into existence, with commercial activity
usually concentrated around the newly built depot. Because mining activity
peaked during the 1870s, agricultural pursuits undoubtedly explain much
of the increase in the number of people who moved to the valley between
1880 and the turn of the century.[55]

The transportation magnates who controlled waterborne and rail
movement along the great Columbia waterway were not the only ones who
placed a commodity value on the River of the West. The seemingly limitless
multitudes of salmon that plied the Columbia and other large rivers of the
Northwest had excited earlier entrepreneurs such as George Simpson of the
Hudson's Bay Company and the Boston trader Nathaniel Wyeth. George
Catlin, who traveled upriver to The Dalles shortly after England and the
United States settled the boundary issue, observed the stirrings of that new
spirit afoot in the land:

The fresh fish for current food and the dried fish for their winter consumption, which had been from time immemorial a good and certain living for the surrounding tribes, like everything else of value belonging to the poor Indian, has attracted the cupidity of the "better class," and is now being "turned into money."[56]

But distance from major population centers, the absence of viable markets, and a limited technology inhibited for a time even the most aggressive and imaginative entrepreneurs from turning that natural abundance to advantage.

Although shipments of packed and salted Columbia River salmon increased during the 1850s, the salmon business remained a commercial sideshow. That is, until the convergence of a series of circumstances and events unleashed open season on the abundant salmon populations of the North Pacific coast. Most of those influences were linked to a distant and industrializing world: (1) the growth of a sizable market in the working-class, industrial centers of Great Britain and the eastern United States; (2) the development of efficient technologies for processing and preserving salmon; (3) advancements in ship design and speed of travel; and (4) the extension of transcontinental railroads to the Columbia River.

In effect, ties of capital, technology, and markets effectively linked global industrial sectors with the natural world of the Columbia River. The different mood that George Catlin observed assumed new dimensions in the year 1866 when William Hume, "a practical fisherman" from the Sacramento River, established a cannery on the lower Columbia and "put up 4,000 cases of four dozen one-pound cans each" on behalf of Hapgood, Hume, and Company. Three years later, the *Oregonian* reported that the Portland firm of Corbett and Macleay had shipped 100 cases of Columbia River salmon to England and Scotland "for the purpose of introducing that article to the markets of the Old World." In what proved to be a remarkable understatement, the newspaper predicted that once Europeans sampled the fish, "our Columbia river salmon will be in such demand as to make a market for all we have to send away."[57] From those meager beginnings, the salmon industry was off and running.

Adapting procedures used for canning lobster along the New England coast, Hapgood, Hume, and Company had perfected a technique at their Sacramento River operations for inexpensively sealing (and preserving) salmon in air-tight cans. As it turned out, canned salmon was especially suited for easy and efficient transportation over long distances, providing a relatively cheap and nourishing food, one especially suited (and priced) to working-class tastes. In little more than a decade after Hapgood and Hume opened their Columbia River operation, the *Oregonian* called the rapidly increasing salmon business "the largest industry, save wheat growing, in the Northwest." More salmon were put up on the Columbia River, it boasted, than "all other localities in the world." [58]

At the front end of the industry—the taking of fish from the Columbia and other Northwest rivers—operators developed highly efficient systems of harvest. Fishers used gillnets, made initially of linen and later of nylon webbing, from the mouth of the Columbia upriver to Celilo Falls. Stationary fish traps attached to posts driven into the river bottom at strategic locations were also popular. Another highly productive method was the use of seines, devices that were most effective at low tide. Five to seven teams of horses, with crews ranging from twenty to forty workers, were used to haul in the huge nets.[59] But the most impressive of all the devices for taking salmon from the Columbia River was the fishwheel. Powered by the current, the elaborate Ferris wheel–like structures literally scooped fish from the water. First used on the Columbia in 1879, the highly efficient wheels (both stationary and mounted on scows) pumped salmon from the river, with the giant Phelps wheel at The Dalles taking 227,000 pounds of salmon during a three-month period in 1894.[60]

From beginning to end the Columbia River salmon industry was a tremendously productive operation. As Anthony Netboy has indicated, virtually every Oregon coastal stream had canneries:

By 1874 there were twelve between Astoria and Portland, and by 1883 fifty-five on or near the Columbia, packing 630,000 cases of 48 one-pound cans valued at $3 million, using only chinook. . . . The chinook catch reached a peak of 43 million pounds on the Columbia in 1883, coincident with the operation of the maximum number of canneries.

Hapgood and Hume dominated cannery production on the lower Columbia; further upriver in the vicinity of The Dalles the Seufert brothers and their big fish wheels controlled the best fishing spots and led all other shippers.[61]

But in the midst of the muscular rhetoric about production figures and the size of the giant chinooks, there were voices of caution, suggestions of foreboding about the future. In a remarkable and well-known letter to the U.S. Senate Committee on Commerce in 1875, Spencer Fullerton Baird of the United States Commission of Fish and Fisheries surveyed the problems of salmon worldwide and addressed the more problematic issues associated directly with the Columbia River. "In all probability," Baird predicted, "the experience of the salmon fisheries of the Columbia will be similar to that of many other noted streams in the eastern United States and in Europe" where formerly abundant stocks had been exterminated. The causes of those extinctions were overfishing, the building of dams, and "some changes in the physical conditions of the stream." Baird reviewed the requirements for successful natural spawning: "gravelly beds, under a more or less rapid current of water, in which the fish can excavate channels for the deposit of their eggs." Dams, he pointed out, blocked migrating fish and contributed to the siltation of spawning grounds.[62]

Other factors responsible for the decline of anadromous fish, Baird contended, were "changes in the physical condition of the country, consequent upon the progress of civilization." The destruction of forests and underbrush and other alterations to the landscapes of river basins, he argued, were harmful to the reproduction of salmon: "With the clearing up of land the whole physical condition seems to be altered," ultimately covering gravel with silt or otherwise destroying spawning beds. "Warned by these facts," Baird asserted, "we can readily appreciate the change which threatens the salmon fisheries of the Columbia river." To avoid "this threatened evil," he advised the Oregon legislature to restrict salmon harvests and to begin the artificial propagation of fish.[63]

Baird believed, however, that it would be difficult to restrict the Columbia River fishery because there were too many political jurisdictions involved. Moreover, restrictive legislation would be expensive to enforce and would create "ill feeling." The wiser procedure, in the fish commissioner's opinion, "would be to employ the now well-understood methods of artificial multiplication of fish" and to build inexpensive hatcheries on the Columbia River. Invoking the idea that human engineering genius could effectively counter the excessive catches and environmental problems, Baird concluded that there was little doubt that building hatcheries would "maintain the present supply of fish indefinitely" and "increase it if desirable." [64]

Spencer Baird, along with a few fish culturists, believed that science had the potential to enhance salmon reproduction and thereby solve the problem of declining runs. With the news that the first salmon hatchery on the Clackamas River was completed, an Astoria resident informed the *Willamette Farmer* that the salmon population would be stabilized, "made permanent and greatly increased over the present run." Livingston Stone, who directed the building of the Clackamas hatchery, wrote Spencer Baird in 1872 that artificial propagation was "the one great work, above all others, in the restoration of salmon to American rivers and lakes." Two decades later, a U.S. Fish Commission employee argued that artificial propagation had "passed beyond the experimental stage," especially on the Columbia River where it had proved beneficial. What emerged during the late nineteenth century was a reification of science, a belief that scientific and technological applications could resolve problems associated with human disruptions to the natural world. [65]

Aside from Spencer Baird's excessive optimism about the role that hatcheries could play in sustaining salmon runs, we know today that he correctly identified the larger ecological issues associated with the survival of anadromous fishes. His words of caution came at a point when the impact of urban pollution and the effects of industrial practices in the Columbia drainage were still in their incipient stages: railroad building in the region was only beginning; agricultural operations, despite the expanding acreages involved, still depended on animal and human power; there were no steam logging machines prowling cutover hillsides; irrigation projects were in their infancy; and the use of heavy capitalized equipment in mining operations awaited the development of rail transport. In brief, the industrial influences that Baird warned about were still in the future for the Pacific Northwest. One can say with some assurance, therefore, that at least until the turn of the century, the huge commercial salmon catch in the Columbia River was the single most important stress on salmon populations.

Although the canning and packing of salmon had developed into a business of great importance, the *Willamette Farmer* warned in 1877 that industry leaders realized the fish runs would begin decreasing "unless some precautions is taken to propagate the fish and so replenish the stock." Despite the persistent decline in the salmon pack, however, new canneries continued to open on the lower Columbia River and on lesser waterways that emptied into the Pacific Ocean. The *Willamette Farmer* urged that "sufficient hatcheries should be placed at an early date" on the Rogue, Umpqua, Coquille, Coos, Siuslaw, and other rivers. Because fish culture was "an easy science," the agricultural newspaper also urged the introduction of shad into the Columbia system. "Now for a trifle," it declared, "we can possess all the best fish of Northern seas here in Oregon." If the experiment worked successfully elsewhere, "why not have it done for Oregon?"[66]

For the most part, the region's newspapers paid little attention to declining fish runs and the ecological disruptions that would eventually play havoc with spawning habitats everywhere. Most writers for the press continued to associate change and industrial progress with the property value of the canneries, the size of the salmon pack, and the health of distant markets. As Table Five indicates, the salmon pack for the Columbia River increased steadily through the mid-1880s when it began to fluctuate wildly.

The *Oregonian* reported in 1881 that the "direct" market for canned salmon was almost exclusively confined to Europe; additional shipments to New York and Australia were made through San Francisco. Of the 550,000 cases of salmon shipped from the Columbia River through August 1881, nearly 300,000 cases were consignments to England. In a fit of regional chauvinism, the newspaper accused retail grocers in the eastern United States of failing to discriminate between "genuine Columbia river salmon and the bogus brands." The latter, it complained, drove prices down and brought hard times to the industry. With proper marketing, however, the demand for Columbia River brands would increase; because the supply was limited, "it would not take the Chinook salmon very long to reach the supremacy of the market and hold it until the end of time."[67] That early faith in the self-regulatory ability of the market to sustain the resource in perpetuity would persist for several decades.

TABLE FIVE

Oregon Salmon Pack, 1866–1887*

(In cases of 48 one-pound cans)

Year	Pack	Year	Pack
1866	4,000	1877	460,000
1867	18,000	1878	460,000
1868	28,000	1879	480,000
1869	100,000	1880	530,000
1870	150,000	1881	550,000
1871	200,000	1882	541,300
1872	230.000	1883	329,400
1873	230,000	1884	620,000
1874	350,000	1885	553,800
1875	375,000	1886	448,500
1876	450,000	1887	356,000

*These figures appear in the *Oregonian,* September 8, 1881, and August 11, 1887.

At other times the *Oregonian* appeared to be more concerned with the industry's failure to produce lasting social benefits than it was with the prodigious number of salmon taken from the river. If "product and profit be the criterion," it argued on one occasion, salmon packing ranked second to agriculture in the Northwest. But even with those impressive numbers, it still was not an industry that "builds up and benefits the state"; the Chinese and nonresident white workers who did most of the labor "come with the salmon run and go at its close, carrying their earnings away"; the industry produced only wage workers; there was no room for individual enterprise; and although it made a few people rich, "it builds but few houses."[68] The *Oregonian's* sometimes arrogant sermonizing aside, the size of the salmon pack continued to be a vital component of the Columbia River economy.

When the diminishing size of the salmon runs first became apparent, the great fishery on the river became a special cause for worry and concern to some. Before the turn of the century both Washington Territory and the state of Oregon made timid efforts to regulate the length of nets and the location of traps, weirs, and seines. Despite the virtual absence of biological information about anadromous fish, Washington and then Oregon began regulating fishing seasons in the late 1870s. "For practical purposes," Anthony Netboy concludes, "the statutes were really dead letters." The Oregon Board of Fish Commissioners (created in 1887) reported in 1889 that it lacked the funds to enforce state laws because of the huge area under its jurisdiction: "In order that the literal law may be enforced it would be necessary to station a river police at the principal centers" of fishing. Because of the heavy fines for fishing during the closed season, the commissioners reported, they "were advised by good authority not to enforce this part of the law." [69]

"INDUSTRY IN GREAT DANGER," the *Oregonian* headlined when the salmon pack plummeted in 1887. The newspaper surveyed the various "theories" for the steady decline in the seasonal salmon runs since the peak year of 1884 and concluded that the river was being fished out; "there can, indeed be no reasonable doubt about it." The Columbia River fishers, in its view, were repeating practices on rivers in England and Scotland, in the state of Maine, and more recently the Sacramento River: "We are face to face not only with a problem," the *Oregonian* pointed out, "but with an emergency." The industry would ultimately fail unless state and federal authorities took stronger measures to protect salmon. Existing laws were ineffective and unenforced, the newspaper concluded, and those who believed that artificial propagation would "supply the place of nature's method" had not proved their case. The only proper response to the crisis was to "keep 'hands off' from the river and give the fish a chance." [70] That sentiment, expressed with even greater voice in the following decades, would prove equally ineffective in preserving the runs.

"There is a subtle sentiment in the calling of the fisherman," a writer for the *Oregonian* remarked in the midst of those first public concerns over declining salmon runs. "Like wine making, it has the tone and flavor of romance," the newspaper intoned. "Historical, classical and religious traditions cluster about it." [71] Despite its romantic and mythical side, however, the salmon business on the Columbia River in the late nineteenth century had all the earmarks of a dinosaur. The thriving commercial fishery produced record catches and packs, and it employed thousands of people, but as a profit-making enterprise, the thirty-year-old industry was already in trouble. An Oregon fish and game official reported in 1894 that it would be "only a matter of a few years under present conditions" until the Columbia River chinook would be as scarce as Oregon beaver:

For a third of a century Oregon has drawn wealth from her streams, but now, by reason of her wastefulness and lack of intelligent provision for the future, the source of that wealth is disappearing and is threatened with annihilation. . . . Salmon that ten years ago the canners would not touch now constitute 30 to 40 percent of the pack.[72]

Despite the noticeably declining fish runs and occasional public expressions of concern, an aura of unlimited abundance prevailed in most quarters. Samuel Clarke's remark during the industry's early commercial years still expressed the prevailing cultural ethos: "The immense supply of the chinook salmon that forms the staple of this great commerce is to be had for the taking." The catch for all species of salmon did not reach its high mark of 46,629,000 pounds until 1911, but the take of the more valuable chinook had already peaked more than a quarter century earlier. Puget Sound fishers produced an even larger output, one that did not peak until 1917, and the Alaska fishery, which got off to a later start, eventually surpassed both. For its part, Columbia River landings for all species indicate a steady and appreciable decline after 1925.[73]

In retrospect, we can say with some certainty that until the Second World War, conditions in the salmon business paralleled similar circumstances in the lumber industry: too many producers, virtually unlimited access to an abundant resource, and periodically glutted markets that encouraged waste and kept prices down. That scenario explains the strictly economic side of the ledger. But beyond the voracious appetite of the canneries, the increasing number of sports fishers, and the expanding fleet of ocean trollers, there were other forces at work in the Northwest that would eventually place even greater stress on the steadily diminishing salmon runs in the Columbia system.

The coming of the industrial age to the Pacific Northwest unleashed new and still more intrusive cultural influences on the landscape and ecology of the Oregon country, including the vast breeding habitat of its anadromous fishes. The completion of the first transcontinental railroad in 1883 and the simultaneous extension of hundreds of miles of branch roads quickened changes that were detrimental to the region's salmon populations. The introduction of mechanized (and more environmentally intrusive) farming and logging machines further accelerated disruptions to riverine and land ecosystems. The adaptation of steam power to logging operations, especially with the steam donkey, dramatically speeded-up the yarding of logs — and disturbance to riparian environments. But it was the *combined* farm, range, mining, and forest activities that ultimately proved so disruptive to the region's waterways.

Into the Hinterland

It was only lately that we confidently said that the Willamette Valley was Oregon. . . . The most sanguine mind had no conception . . . or dreamed it possible that a railroad system would develop the whole Upper Country; that instead of that wide region being only fit for stock raising, it was about to become the favorite home of agriculture, and would be, as it now is, looked to as the most desirable region for settlement in all the far West.
— *Willamette Farmer, June 23, 1882*

A s the 1860s drew to a close, great changes were in the offing for the country east of the Cascade Mountains. A series of gold strikes provided the immediate catalyst, causing an inrush of people to the interior region in search of the seemingly ubiquitous "dust." Beginning in the early 1860s, prospectors found gold on several tributaries of the Snake River, along the streams in Oregon's Blue Mountains, and farther east in emerging mining districts like Montana's Last Chance Gulch. The sudden increase in human traffic up the Columbia River spurred the organization of the Oregon Steam Navigation Company (which soon gained a monopoly on river transportation). The interior gold-rush phenomenon further boomed the city of Portland as a major point of transshipment; expanded the economic prospects for The Dalles and Walla Walla, Washington, as satellite towns to Portland; and led to the establishment of several small trading centers — Lewiston and Boise City, Idaho, and Baker City — as "jumping-off" places for the mines.[1]

That great spurt of human activity was the opening wedge in what can best be described as the systemic, culturally induced transformation of intermontane ecosystems. Mining practices in the nineteenth century were especially disruptive; they sluiced away entire hillsides, silted over salmon breeding grounds, and destroyed riparian habitats. The local demand for construction timbers—trusses for mine tunnels and wooden viaducts to carry water—brought the first large-scale cutting of inland forests. Within a year after the discovery of gold in the John Day Valley (June 1862), an enterprising person opened a sawmill to cut lumber for miners who were building flumes and sluices.[2]

Theodor Kirchoff, who passed through the eastern Oregon mining region in 1868, offered a glimpse of the new ecological reckoning that was taking place: "elevated troughs, long sluices, uprooted ground, raw piles of sand and tailings, heaps of cleanly washed stone, and water for mining rushes in ditches and wooden conduits among bolders and trees." In Rye Valley, Kirchoff reported the existence of shafts and tunnels with piles of tailings on the slopes and "miles of ditches, carrying water to wash gold." What is notable about eastern Oregon's incipient mining industry is the rapidity with which the larger, more heavily capitalized operators replaced the shallow placer miners. The pan and sluice quickly gave way to more intrusive forms of technology—hydraulic pipe, reservoirs, and long canals. It is also important to point out that those changes were well underway before the coming of railroads and steam-powered dredges to the region. The most notable early ditching effort was the construction of a nearly 100-mile waterway from Burnt River to placer deposits near the Malheur River in 1870. During the most productive years of mining activity in the 1860s, the region sprouted a series of short-lived boom towns with colorful names like Sparta, Auburn, Cornucopia, and Susanville.[3]

The gold camps themselves, usually located along tributary streams in narrow canyons, were instant communities of crude, makeshift shelters. The discovery of gold on Canyon Creek, a tributary of the John Day River, attracted more than 300 miners during the initial rush of activity in the summer of 1862. Miners staked claims along the entire lower section of the creek and worked the placer deposits with the rudimentary equipment they had packed in. Canyon City, located two miles up Canyon Creek, was a thriving community within a few months. Canyon City actually extended downstream to the location of the present town of John Day (originally called Lower Town). Miners sluiced away the river banks in the search for precious metal, destroying the riparian vegetation along the occupied stretch of the stream. Later placer and hydraulic mining activity on Canyon Creek, Long Creek, and other tributaries of the upper John Day River proved even more disruptive to riverine ecology, eroding stream banks, silting in breeding habitat for fish, and in other instances speeding run-off that subsequently contributed to the gullying of waterways.[4]

The most important transportation arterial to the interior mining districts was, of course, the Columbia River. At the onset of that rush of human traffic to the interior, boats moving upriver from Portland reported 15,000 passengers in 1861, 24,500 in 1862, and 22,000 the following year. Although the population figures are speculative, Dorothy Johansen estimates that there were more than 75,000 miners in the region during the peak of prospecting. And for the first time since the heyday of the fur trade, freight traffic moved downriver as well, this time in the form of mineral wealth extracted from the stream beds and hillsides of the interior. The Oregon Steam Navigation Company estimated that its monthly shipments of gold to Portland averaged $400,000 during the 1860s. Other market items joined the flow of goods traveling downstream when merchants in Walla Walla experimented in shipping both flour and wheat to Portland. Aided by newly constructed portage railroads at the rapids and the great falls of the Columbia, those first consignments foreshadowed what would soon become a torrent of grain moving downriver.[5]

The external forces driving the ecological transformation of the interior Northwest were twofold: the thousands of newly arrived immigrants who made their homes in the expanding and productive agricultural districts, *and* the external market demand for the commodities that attracted them to the region in the first place. The sharp increase in traffic moving through the river corridor pushed the population of The Dalles from 252 people in 1856 to more than 2,500 in 1864. And like the seasonal tourist towns of our present age, The Dalles had a much larger transient group staying for brief periods. Farther in the interior, the village of Walla Walla emerged as a transfer point for the movement of people and supplies to the Snake

River mining country. That dusty settlement along Mill Creek soon had the largest population in Washington, and for a time the community rivaled Olympia in its aspirations to serve as the territorial capital. Astride the best overland route to the deep interior, Walla Walla enjoyed advantages of early Euro-American occupation and provided, in Donald Meinig's words, "an ever expanding scale and variety of businesses and services."[6]

While miners, incipient wheat farmers, and town builders in the eastern country went about the work of reordering their immediate landscapes, an expanding market demand for beef and wool eventually brought equally systemic change to the arid grasslands away from the rivers and mining districts. In a movement that paralleled the mining push east of the Cascade Mountains, stock farmers began driving large numbers of cattle and sheep onto the sagebrush grasslands of central and eastern Oregon. Because of soaring beef prices in the mining districts, herders began grazing their cattle along the creeks and grassy lowlands in the vicinity of The Dalles. Still others moved their animals into the Deschutes, John Day, Umatilla, Walla Walla, and Yakima valleys. Trailing not far behind were the sheep herders whose flocks eventually numbered in the thousands.[7] Cattle and sheep grazed throughout the intermontane Northwest by the 1870s, with Oregon's southeastern quadrant probably supporting the largest and most spectacular cattle herds.

The gold discoveries in the John Day Valley in 1862 and in several other locations in northeastern Oregon set in motion ecological changes that reached far beyond local mining districts. Some travelers to the mineral lode country from the upper Willamette Valley followed a crude trail along the McKenzie River, across the mountains, and into the Deschutes drainage. Because of the booming market for beef farther east, a few cattle owners began driving their herds through the mountain passes to feed on the lush grasses that grew along the tributary streams in the foothills of central Oregon. Among the earliest were Felix and Marion Scott, who wintered cattle near Hay Creek, part of the larger Trout Creek drainage, in 1863. Other Willamette Valley residents followed, herding their cattle along Trout Creek and in the Ochoco Valley in the late 1860s. The town of Prineville, which grew as the center of a wider stock-raising area, had a population of about 200 in 1876. Elsewhere in central and eastern Oregon's bunchgrass country similar patterns of preemption and settlement took place.[8]

Other white settlers moved their cattle herds to the rich bunchgrass area between the lower Deschutes and the John Day rivers during the 1860s. Among the newcomers, horse and cattle graziers dominated; still others constructed roadhouses and set up ferries at strategic crossings on the Deschutes and John Day, thereby establishing the first crude infrastructures to facilitate travel through the region. The pace of ecological change accelerated in the late 1870s with the arrival of increasing numbers of settlers who were interested in producing crops rather than raising livestock. The Dalles *Weekly Times* reported in the spring of 1880 that the bunchgrass hills between the John Day and Deschutes rivers were "dotted with cabins of settlers." The newcomers represented only a small part of a larger movement into eastern Oregon, which was "fast filling up with an agricultural population." One year later the *Times* remarked that "where one year ago there were but two or three settlers, there are now from 25 to 30 families." The countryside, in its opinion, appeared to be moving in the direction of "an agricultural instead of the grazing region which it has been."[9]

The forces of nature may have hurried the pace of change on the Columbia plateau. A decade or more of overgrazing had seriously depleted the bunchgrass plateau east and south of the Columbia River and in the Klickitat and Yakima valleys to the north. "The tens of thousands of heads that have been roaming at large" through the Umatilla region, an Ohio visitor observed in 1881, had yielded the inevitable. Grasses that once covered its entire surface, the traveler wrote, "are fast disappearing and weeds and thistles are taking their place." Those circumstances and a difficult winter season in 1880–81 inflicted horrendous losses on cattle herds. For the greater Columbia Basin area the mortality ranged from 30 to more than 50 percent, with the actual number of dead cattle probably numbering in the tens of thousands. As geographer Donald Meinig has indicated, this devastating rate of attrition weakened the industry precisely at the moment when the prospects for wheat cultivation appeared most encouraging. With an eye to the best advantage in the market, he points out, farmers "realized that wherever bunchgrass would grow wheat would grow."[10]

The transition from pastoralism to wheat production took place everywhere across the bunchgrass areas of northeastern Oregon and eastern Washington—upland districts of the Great Columbia Plain—during the 1880s. For those who arrived in increasing numbers during the early 1880s, the railroad suggested a new commodity potential for the bunchgrass hills. Farmers now valued land for its ability to grow wheat rather than to produce beef and wool for the market. With a ready transportation outlet via the railroad to Portland and then by ocean steamer to world markets, an infrastructure was in place that eventually would lead to the ecological transformation of the Columbia plateau. In a brief period, several hundred miles of rail construction had been carried out, and in Meinig's words, "historic entryways at three corners of the region were now overlain with steel rails." Products could be shipped out and people brought in "far more quickly, cheaply, and in greater numbers than ever before."[11]

Why acquisitive and enterprising white settler-farmers would find the Columbia plateau attractive should come as no surprise. The upland country of the Great Columbia Plain is a "natural" wheat region. The grain adapted well to the loess soils and continental climate of the interior Northwest, especially to grassland areas where seasonal precipitation was sufficient during average years to produce a mature crop of "winter" wheat. The *Willamette Farmer* alerted its readers as early as 1878 that a considerable amount "of the surplus exports" shipped down the Columbia River came from "the newly opened wheat districts east of the Cascades."[12] Even before rail transportation along the Columbia corridor, a small but thriving wheat-growing industry in the Walla Walla Valley already had tested the capacity of steamboat and portage-railroad shipping facilities.

At the close of the harvest season in 1879, the *Oregonian* reported that boats on the upper river were unable to carry the wheat away as fast as it arrived at the shipping point at Wallula. The newspaper concluded that the failure of the transportation system on the river "to meet the wants of the trade" was the major difficulty. In truth, the increasing volume of traffic on the lower Snake and Columbia rivers was testimony to the expanding acres planted to wheat. Teams of horses and mules hauled the long wagon trains of sacked grain from highland areas to shipping points at the mouths of canyons. In some instances, farmers constructed trams or "grain sprouts" to carry the wheat by gravity flow to river's edge. From that point, merchants shipped the wheat directly to the great grain warehouses on the Portland waterfront.[13]

Downriver commercial groups were vitally interested in the prospects for the upper Columbia region. The *Commercial Reporter,* published in Portland, praised the advances that were taking place beyond the Cascades. The rapid settlement of the eastern quarter of the state, it asserted in 1879, was destined to make the area "one of the great granaries of the West." The *Reporter* pointed to several instances where local interests had recently built narrow-gauge railroads to carry products the short distance to the Columbia River. But even with those advances, the newspaper told its readers, vast acreages of fertile land on the Columbia plateau had yet to be cultivated.[14]

Unwilling to leave their economic fortunes to chance, the great railroad companies aided and abetted settlement in the interior Northwest. The Northern Pacific Railroad employed a skilled public relations writer to attract immigrants to the Columbia plateau. In a promotional book published in the year that Northern Pacific completed its transcontinental line, Eugene V. Smalley praised the potential and the unparalleled fertility and beauty of the great wheat belt in the interior Northwest. Smalley assured farmers that although annual precipitation was "theoretically too scanty for the successful growing of crops," that was a blessing rather than a curse, because "most of it comes in the months when the farmer needs it." And while the average rainfall seldom exceeded twenty inches, most of it fell between October and May. "A summer drought which in most climates is a calamity," the effusive Smalley concluded, "is here a benefit."[15] Along with the lure of a new promised land, Smalley's message did hold an element of truth for practitioners of dryland farming.

As farmers turned grasslands to the plow, they increasingly confined their cattle and sheep to marginal agricultural areas. The lure of distant markets, in fact, played a direct role in remodeling the regional ecology. As one Ohio traveler wrote to the *Willamette Farmer,* the upriver country had one great consolation: "the land can be made to produce fields of grain that no other part of God's earth has ever equaled." From the Umatilla to the Walla Walla valleys, "the whole country [is] a solid field with lines of fences and roads and small pastures breaking . . . the monotony of wheat, barley, and oat fields." The scenery provided a picture, according to the Ohio observer, of "fields of waving grain, giving promise of greater yields than blessed the land of Egypt."[16] Hyperbole aside, themes of renewal and restoration eventually permeated much of the literature about the semiarid interior sections of the Oregon country. Planting fields of wheat in overgrazed, thistle-invaded bunchgrass terrain was hardly an exercise in restoration ecology. But the Ohio writer's larger vision fits the discourse of twentieth-century reclamation devotees who argued that irrigation would restore lifeless acres and bring about a renewal and rebirth of the land.

Agricultural boosters in the greater Pacific Northwest were enthusiastic about increases in the volume of traffic moving in both directions on the Columbia River. For its part, the *Willamette Farmer* applauded the "opening up" of the vast interior and its agricultural potential. At the close of the 1870s, it praised the region's "wonderful fertility" and observed: "Now that the uplands of the Upper Columbia are proved to be capable of producing wheat we may look for the sage plains to be also reclaimed." And when the Oregon Railway and Navigation Company pushed its line beyond Wallula in 1882, the *Farmer* asked, what part of the country east of the mountains "does not invite agriculture?"

Developments show that everywhere in that Eastern country farmers can locate to advantage and stock men may expect to see their ranges converted into farms and homes as rapidly as immigration can find its way there. Eastern Oregon and Washington can furnish farms to hundreds of thousands of people, and the settlement of the country will proceed as fast as railroads can be pushed into these available regions.[17]

Although the *Willamette Farmer* may have been off the mark in its prediction about the number of people the upper Columbia country was capable of supporting, it did recognize an essential element of the new emerging reality: "The Willamette Valley is no longer the granary of the North Pacific." The volume of wheat moving down the Columbia River was proof of that statement. The *Oregonian* reported in the spring of 1886 that shippers had sent *surplus* wheat from the previous season downriver to Portland at the average of thirty-two carloads a day over one five-week period. Moreover, it acknowledged that the volume would have been even greater if more railroad cars had been available. The Portland newspaper also pointed out that the 300,000 tons listed as surplus wheat was a conservative estimate, because it did not include several thousand tons shipped east on the Northern Pacific line.[18]

In a special effort to assess the prospects for irrigation agriculture in the American West, the federal census for 1890 published a general description of eastern Oregon's arid counties and their potential for irrigation. The report was not enthusiastic about the future of agriculture in the region under conventional practices. The federal survey pointed out that the vast plateau area east of the Cascades rarely averaged more than fifteen inches of precipitation annually, most of which fell during the winter months. For the potential grain-producing districts along the Columbia River, the census reported that there was sufficient moisture in only "two or three years out of five to raise fair crops of wheat and other cereals." And even then, success depended "largely upon the care and skill shown by the farmer, and not merely upon the occurrence of fortunate rains." Although irrigation was "not absolutely essential," the census survey concluded that farmers would make at best a precarious living without it. Two of the counties singled out as exceptions to that general assessment were Sherman and Umatilla counties, the leading wheat producers in Oregon. Sherman County, the report said, "apparently has the property of retaining moisture well, and thus, although the rainfall is very small during the summer, nearly all kinds of crops are successfully raised without irrigation."[19]

Sherman County in fact provides a microcosm of the dramatic physical transformation that took place on the Columbia plateau with the shift from cattle and sheep grazing to cultivating the soil. The county is physically unique; bounded by the Columbia River in the north, the Deschutes to the west, and the John Day in the east, the county drops precipitously at each of these edges into deep river canyons. Of its 531,000 acres, 55 percent of Sherman County is presently tillable, the highest percentage of any county east of the Cascade Mountains. Although its loess soils are rich and productive, they are also low in organic materials and therefore especially prone to erosion. Originally deposited by winds, the soils are just as easily

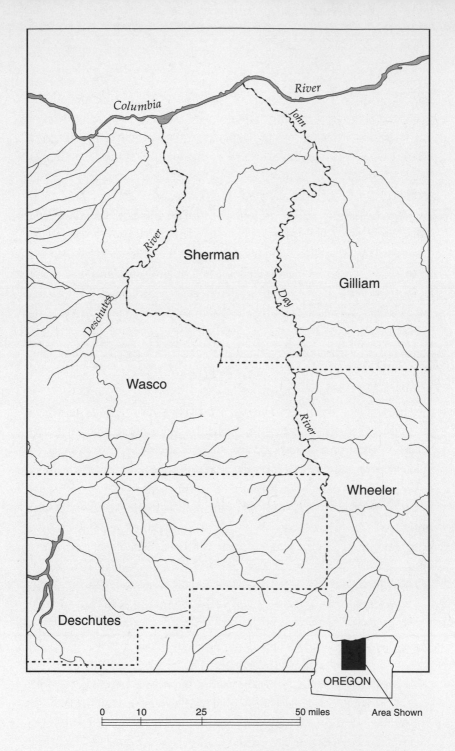

North Central Oregon. *University of Wisconsin Cartographic Lab*

carried away by wind and water. At the onset of the historic period, the plateau grasslands of the future county were lush with the full growth of bunchgrasses during the late spring. Both the graziers who came to the area in the late 1860s and the grain farmers who followed acquired land through the Homestead Act or from the Eastern Oregon Land Company. The latter firm held title to the huge land grant awarded to The Dalles and Boise Military Road Company.[20] Given its profusion of natural grasses and its location adjacent to the Columbia River, it is little wonder that prospective settlers found the area attractive in the years following the American Civil War.

George Doyle, who came to present Sherman County in 1882, was an eyewitness to the alterations that took place after the Oregon Railway and Navigation Company extended its route up the Columbia River. When he arrived, the area from the Deschutes to the John Day rivers was "a stockman's paradise where vast herds of horses, cattle, and sheep grazed to their knees in bunch grass." Doyle estimated the total amount of land under cultivation in the future Sherman County to be no more than 1,000 acres. Three years later the area produced 1,654,210 bushels of wheat. According to a turn-of-the-century history of the region, the railroad brought instant change: "It was not a slow, steady, growth, but the grain enterprise appeared almost spontaneous. Metaphorically speaking," a county history boasted, "Sherman county had been transformed in one night." [21]

Wagons loaded with sacks of wheat hauled the productions of that transformation to the Oregon Railway and Navigation Company depots at Biggs and Rufus on the Columbia River. In the opposite direction, farmers returned with wood, lumber, coal, and a growing volume of farm implements, the material trappings that enabled them to expand their cultivated acreages. Because it required an enormous effort to move the wagon loads of grain north to the river, most of the land in wheat cultivation was not too distant from the railroad shipping points on the Columbia. The combination of the through railroad route on the river and the fecundity of plateau soils eventually attracted sufficient capital to build a winding 26.2-mile, narrow-gauge railroad track. Beginning at Biggs on the Columbia River, the railroad wound southward through the county, eventually terminating at a nondescript place on the plateau that came to be called Shaniko. The completed Columbia and Southern Railroad, according to historian John Due, "was a masterpiece of sophomore-level engineering."[22]

Although its design may have been problematic, the Columbia and Southern revolutionized productive and ecological relations in the southern half of Sherman County. It also marked a shift from a grazing/pastoral economy to commercial agriculture, the latter with an international marketing strategy. Persuaded by the promise of the new rail line, investors in the small town of Moro put up the buildings for the North Pacific Flouring Mills, a firm that began regular shipments to China in 1898. The Columbia and Southern also encouraged the expansion of grazing, especially for the flocks of sheep herded to the south of Sherman County and in the steep canyon country to the southwest. At the end of the line sat Shaniko. Dominated by great warehouses, loading pens, and shops, it quickly emerged as one of the leading wool transfer centers in the United States, sending out more than 500,000 pounds on Columbia and Southern cars in 1902.[23] Shaniko's built environment was pure utility; it held no meaning except as a point of transfer for the cattle, sheep, and wool that came in from the south, and for the wide variety of inbound goods that were hauled away in wagons to facilitate more productions for the market.

The railroad also gave a boost to the three other small towns in Sherman County—Wasco, Moro, and Grass Valley. When the construction crews reached Wasco in October 1897, there were 200,000 sacks of wheat at the railroad siding waiting for shipment. Indeed, from the Columbia River to the terminus of the Columbia and Southern route at Shaniko there were thirty separate warehouses located along the line of tracks. Instead of hauling their wagon-loads of wheat down the tortuous slopes to the river, most Sherman County farmers were within easy striking distance of the railroad. The Columbia and Southern line to Shaniko boomed until the famous Harriman-Hill struggle to build a railroad from the Columbia River up the Deschutes canyon to Bend. When Hill and Harriman compromised their differences and completed their road in 1911, Shaniko and the Columbia and Southern railroad lost the central Oregon wool, sheep, and cattle trade and the inbound traffic to those districts as well. Within a year the volume of goods being shipped over the line dropped sharply.[24]

TABLE SIX

Sherman County Population Figures, 1880–1920*

	Sherman County	Towns			
		Moro	Wasco	Grass Valley	Shaniko
1880	150	—	—	—	—
1890	1,792	—	—	—	—
1900	3,477	335	322	—	—
1910	4,242	378	386	342	495
1920	3,826	418	701	317	124

*These figures are in Due and French, *Rails to the Mid-Columbia Wheatlands,* 46–51.

Raw numbers can only suggest what was taking place on the upland plateau south of the Columbia River. The population figures alone (see Table Six) indicate a sharp increase in activity as farmers turned the bunch-grass countryside into wheat fields. For the kind of extensive agricultural practices that came to dominate much of Sherman County, the increases in cultivated land, the acreages planted to wheat, and the grain production figures all testify to a considerable ecological transformation. Because of the great expansion in acreages planted to wheat along the Deschutes-Umatilla Plateau, by 1900 six of Oregon's leading wheat counties were east of the Cascade Mountains, with Umatilla County ranked first and Sherman County second. As Table Seven indicates, farmers expanded the number of acres planted to wheat by nearly 400 percent between 1890 and 1910. Even more remarkable, the acres of cultivated land in the county has remained relatively constant to the present day.

The rapid building of railroads through the Columbia River corridor during the 1880s introduced economic, social, and ecological changes that were revolutionary in their consequences. Increases in population, the formation of new counties, the spectacular expansion in the acreage of cultivated land, and the advent of large-scale industrial mining enterprises were all part of the story. Rail construction through the Walla Walla Valley and

TABLE SEVEN

Production and Acreage of Wheat, Sherman County, 1890–1920 *

Year	Acreage	Production (bu.)
1890	32,445	148,891
1900	91,000	1,050,400
1910	122,926	1,541,092
1920	116,924	1,838,317

* The figures are in Due and French, *Rails to the Mid-Columbia Wheatlands*, 46–51.

around the fringes of the Columbia plain led to an increase in the acreage planted to wheat to more than 2.5 million acres within a decade. It is important to emphasize that the expansion in tillable land coincided with the emergence of large-scale commercial agriculture, with successful farmers quickly adopting the most advanced machinery of the day. Along the great sweep of semiarid grasslands on the northern margin of the Deschutes-Umatilla Plateau, from the area around The Dalles eastward to Pendleton and northeasterly to the Palouse Hills, wheat—the classic frontier crop—replaced bluebunch wheatgrass and Idaho fescue. A Washington State University scientist concluded that most of the arable land suited to wheat was under cultivation by 1910.[25] As in the Willamette Valley, wheat was a newly introduced exotic to the Columbia plateau; as such, its cultivation eliminated native plants, flora, and grasses. The millions of acres planted to wheat in the interior Northwest reflected the influence of market and industrial forces in reshaping the region's ecology.

By the turn of the century the material and technological effects of that transformation were ubiquitous along the Columbia plateau: the great through railroads and their numerous feeder lines; the depots, the points of transfer for the outbound animals, fiber, grains, and minerals and the inbound goods, much of it from industrial centers; and perhaps the most visible symbol of them all, the increasing number of grain elevators that dotted the countryside. To the Portland *Oregonian,* those developments were extensions of natural processes, because "where bunch grass would

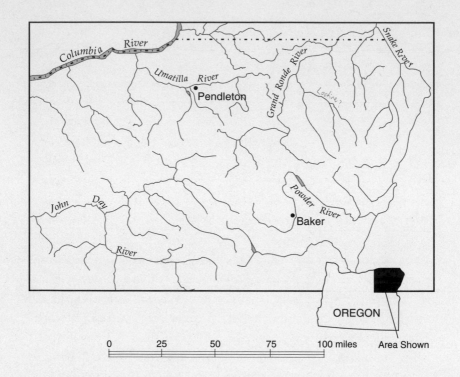

Northeastern Oregon. *University of Wisconsin Cartographic Lab*

ripen wheat would ripen." The light soil along the uplands of the Columbia Basin held the necessary properties to produce the grain in abundance: "Almost as by magic the country was transformed into a checkerboard of cultivated fields, and millions of bushels of wheat are annually contributed to the world's food supply." [26]

Except for several Hudson's Bay Company trapping parties and two large immigrant trains passing through the area, the Harney Basin and much of Oregon's southeastern quadrant remained beyond the reach of permanent white settlement until after the Civil War. The United States Army command at Fort Vancouver sent an expedition under the command of Gen. William S. Harney into eastern Oregon in the summer of 1859 to survey a wagon road route up the Crooked River into the basin subsequently named to honor the officer in charge. As Lt. Joseph Dixon, a topographical engineer with the troop, descended a long and gentle slope, he described a large valley "in many places as level as a house's floor." Dixon estimated the basin to be about eighty miles from east to west and fifty miles in width. The lieutenant singled out the lower Silvies River area for special praise:

. . . a beautiful level valley, covered with a luxuriant growth of bunch grass, wild pea vines, and red clover, interspersed with fields of camus on a rich soil abundantly watered by numerous mountain streams. . . . This wide savannah or grassy meadow makes a picture that would delight the eye of a farmer if he could be content to live in such seclusion as it imposes. Game along this section is abundant: antelope, deer, elk, and several species of grouse, prairie chickens, ducks, geese, etc.[27]

With the onset of the mining rush to eastern Oregon and the Snake River country in the early 1860s, still other intruders passed through the area. Two army expeditions visited the Harney Basin in 1860 exploring the Silver Creek drainage in the north and the Donner und Blitzen River to the south. Other army contingents returned in 1864 and 1867 to remove the Paiute people whose homelands were under siege from all directions. The Army built Fort Harney at the west end of the basin in 1867, the first permanent white establishment in the area. And events were unfolding that would eventually bring a flood of cattle into the valley when the California legislature began enacting a series of "herd laws." [28]

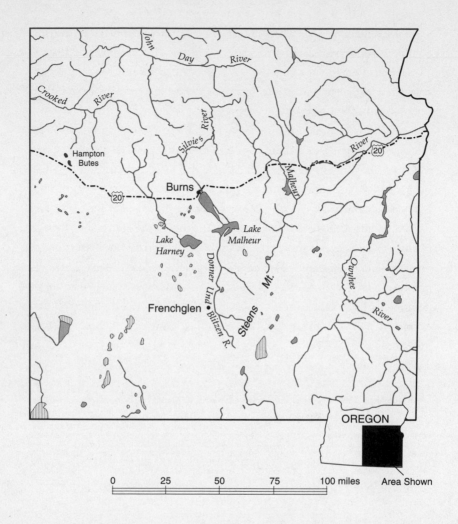

Southeastern Oregon. *University of Wisconsin Cartographic Lab*

The California legislation reflected fluctuating climatic conditions and changing productive relations in the state. With the advent of bonanza wheat farming in the great Central Valley, the newly emergent grain producers used their political influence to convince the legislature to pass several laws that effectively ended open-range grazing in the state. A fence law enacted in 1871 made livestock owners liable for damages caused by their animals. During the same period, several years of extremely low precipitation in the San Joaquin and Sacramento valleys convinced large cattle owners to move their herds into southeastern Oregon and Nevada in search of undepleted, unfenced new grazing land. As one authority makes clear, there was an ecological as well as a legal reason for moving the herds out of the Central Valley: "ranchers preferred to move on if the range became depleted."[29]

Two streams of white intruders entered the Harney Basin in the late 1860s. One group included a trickling of subsistence settlers from the Willamette Valley who occupied small pieces of land along the streams in the northern part of the basin, especially in the vicinity of the Silvies River. At about the same time another cluster of newcomers began camping along the larger streams that drained both the northern and southern slopes of Steens Mountain. Among the latter group were head foremen and their California cattle herds on the lookout for virgin grasslands and good watering places. The cattle drovers were an imperial, flamboyant group representing large corporate interests. John Devine, who came to the bunchgrass country southeast of Steens Mountain in 1869, was the first to move cattle onto the broad alluvial valley along Whitehorse Creek. Another was David Shirk, who drove a herd belonging to John Catlow into the Trout Creek area southeast of the Steens a year earlier.[30]

"Catlow's methods of exploitation," the writer Peter Simpson argues, set the standard for the development of the cattle business in Harney County. Catlow first filed a homestead claim along Trout Creek, a stream that drained the Trout Creek Mountains to the south of Steens Mountain. David Shirk, his foreman, drove 800 head of cattle into the Alvord Basin in the summer of 1868, a herd that increased to 4,000 by the mid-1870s. "By these simple procedures," Simpson points out, "Catlow anticipated the methods of the great 'cattle kings' who came between 1869 and 1873 — French and

Glenn, Todhunter and Devine, Riley and Hardin, and Miller and Lux." [31] As it turned out, each of those enterprises developed into huge, largely self-contained empires, with each of the operators attempting to gain exclusive control of the few streams that drained into the basin.

In a sense the cattle barons treated the greater Harney Basin region as a vast commons free for the taking to those with the courage to enter and occupy. For the large operators, the key to success and longevity was access to and the control of water. The cattle entrepreneurs resolved that problem when they hired dummy entrymen to establish homestead claims along streams in the area. Those water rights were then transferred to the ever-expanding acreages of the principal owner. The cattle tycoons engaged in a power play of the first order, both against the small farmers and as partners with small farmers against the original inhabitants of the land. The United States Army detachment at Fort Harney (under the command of Gen. George Crook) and two lesser posts elsewhere in the region provided a protective screen for the interlopers and their herds. In that respect, the army served an even larger purpose: it acted as a powerful intervening force to oversee the freeing of the land base to market forces.

During the post–Civil War era when the great cattle barons were staking out their huge estates, southeastern Oregon was contested terrain. That was an auspicious moment in the cultural and ecological history of the region. After a military sortie intended to intimidate the Bannock and Paiute people, General Crook forced a treaty on the two groups in 1869 and confined the Paiutes to a vaguely defined area in the basin. Because large ranchers already occupied much of the area when the United States government formally established the Malheur reservation in 1874, the dynamics of power and numbers in the region quickly worked against Indian people. Cattle interests and farmers subsequently forced the Indians to liquidate title to most of the valuable grazing land in the basin proper, thereby opening the former reservation lands to the full force of the market. Several decades later the Indian Claims Commission suggested that during the reservation period, settlers and stock growers had "practically pre-empted the reservation land right from under the Indian." [32]

While the newcomers went about extending their control over the

Harney Basin and the adjacent countryside, their rapidly growing livestock herds were in the process of introducing systemic changes to the region's ecology. When the Central Pacific Railroad built a large shipping facility at Winnemucca, Nevada, in 1875, cattle interests in southeastern Oregon had ready access to a sizable shipping point for marketing their animals. The center for livestock shipments subsequently shifted eastward to Huntington and Ontario on the Snake River when the Union Pacific completed its connecting route into eastern Oregon in 1884. The Oregon Short Line represented a shift in the cattle market to Chicago rather than Winnemucca and its more regional market in San Francisco. In effect, the movement of cattle eastward to Chicago linked southeastern Oregon's grasslands to consumers in America's expanding industrial heartland.[33]

With that transport infrastructure in place, the cattle barons proceeded to load the open ranges with more animals. After only three years, John Devine was reported to have between 15,000 to 30,000 cattle grazing on the Trout Creek ranges. Like each of his peers, Devine assumed that there would be sufficient grass for everyone. For the greater southeastern Oregon area, livestock historian J. Orin Oliphant offered rough estimates for the number of cattle owned by the preeminent corporate groups:

> Todhunter and Devine . . . 40,000
> French-Glenn 30,000
> Thomas Overfelt 30,000
> Riley and Hardin 25,000

All of those outfits were corporate operations, with the owners representing outside capital, especially from California. The famous Miller and Lux outfit from that state eventually gained control of the Thomas Overfelt holdings on the Malheur River in 1875 and then added the Todhunter and Devine operation when the latter went bankrupt in 1889. With the Devine acquisition, Miller and Lux reorganized into the huge Pacific Livestock Company.[34]

During those years, the range cattle industry in southeastern Oregon operated in a Darwinian economic and ecological world, playing footloose and free with federal and state land laws, gaining a stranglehold on water rights, buying out smaller owners to expand their holdings when it was to their advantage, and keeping too many cattle on the ranges when the market was soft. The Portland magazine *West Shore* remarked that the great livestock combines contributed little benefit to the state:

The cattlemen are nearly all non-residents; the cattle are sold out of state and the money used elsewhere; all the benefit the state derives is the presence of the few men need to care for the stock.[35]

In his study of southeastern Oregon's cattle industry, Peter Simpson argues that the open-range method of raising livestock was essentially a speculative enterprise "best suited to bringing the largest return at the least expense." The animals, he observes, "were wagered against weather, disease, and a fluctuating market," and a gamble gone wrong "was paid off at spring roundup when the carcasses were counted against the survivors." [36]

Whether they were cattle barons or settlers, those newcomers to southeastern Oregon confronted both an unpredictable market and an unpredictable climate. The census for agriculture acknowledged in 1880 that "oscillations of climate" in southeastern Oregon had historically contributed to "great changes in the water supply of this area." Settlers who had attempted to raise crops "without an artificial supply of water . . . had generally failed." Moreover, even where farmers had irrigated small acreages, two successive years of drought had "resulted in such a scarcity of water that these lands . . . have been abandoned." The census report indicated two primary problems: (1) the distribution of water; and (2) the complaints of the smaller ranches "that large cattle companies monopolize the present supply and prevent irrigation development." [37]

The federal census for Harney County in 1900 listed 384 farms with an average size of 784 acres per unit, the third largest average statewide. Neighboring Malheur County, with 583 farms, averaged only 379 acres per unit. The census count of the number of cattle and sheep in southeastern Oregon in 1900 suggests an even more intriguing story about those increasingly intrusive cultural influences:

	Cattle	Sheep
Harney	71,260	130,448
Malheur	81,203	294,898

Malheur and Harney counties ranked first and second for both cattle and sheep production in the state. Because few of the sheep operators owned land, most of them were entirely nomadic, making extensive use of easy access to the public ranges throughout the American West. Furthermore, because sheep are more efficient browsers and require less water than cattle, they could be herded to the most remote corners of the two counties to forage for food. With a ready market for wool and lamb in the eastern United States, with low capital requirements, and without the need to control specific areas of land or water, herders began ranging their sheep across the arid West, eventually to the Columbia Basin in the 1870s and to southeastern Oregon a decade or so later.[38]

In a sense, sheep were ecological successors to cattle, especially in areas where the latter had grazed over areas and left invading forbs in their wake. Sheep had certain advantages over cattle: they thrived on forbs of all kinds; they were able to feed farther from streams; and they were easier to herd from valley to mountain slopes as the summer season advanced. The injury that cattle and sheep wreaked upon native grasses, plants, and shrubs was more than a simple function of grazing pressure. As Richard White has indicated, native grasses and browse could withstand considerable grazing stress during years of above average precipitation. However, when semiarid conditions turned to arid, when the periodic cycles of drought returned, the ecological damage from grazing was intense. "The result," according to White, "was a radical change in vegetation and a major increase in erosion."[39]

But the mere numbers of cattle and sheep trailed into southeastern Oregon reveal little about the ecological changes that were in the making during the last quarter of the nineteenth century. Indeed, understanding the dimensions of that ecological transformation is more instructive than the romance associated with cattle kings like Peter French and his buckaroos. Southeastern Oregon is the land of the "cold desert." At the onset of the Euro-American intrusion, the region was a mostly sagebrush-dominated landscape with an understory of perennial grasses. This classic sage–bluebunch wheatgrass section embraced extensive areas of what are now Malheur and

Harney counties and much of the rest of the semiarid country from the Great Basin north to the Columbia Basin.[40]

Although native people exercised a profound cultural influence throughout the basin and range country, it was the incoming whites who introduced dramatic, systemic ecological change to the region. Those modifications to the landscape began with the trapping out of beaver during the 1820s and 1830s. The beaver dams that had normally diminished the velocity of run-off and inhibited stream erosion fell into disrepair and filled with silt.[41] Other changes can be linked to the elimination of deliberate burning after the army confined native people to reservations. But the introduction of cattle and sheep has been the more lasting influence. The animals carried with them the seeds of exotic grasses and plants that for the last century or more have become part of the seemingly "natural" desert. That more intrusive cultural presence ultimately created the conditions for wholesale alterations to riparian environments, changes that we are only beginning to understand today.

Although isolated reports in the late nineteenth century suggested that overgrazing had contributed to erosion and damage in southeastern Oregon, it was not until the early 1900s that a series of federal investigations provided convincing testimony to the systemic alterations that had taken place. In a field reconnaissance for the Bureau of Plant Industry in the summer of 1901, David Griffiths traversed the Harney and Alvord basins and skirted the Steens and southern Blue mountains and their various watersheds. His survey revealed that the control of water throughout the area was "in the hands of the owners of the first ranches settled." Beyond those watering areas, cattle and sheep had closely grazed all of the open-range bottomland, leaving it with "a very unpromising appearance" with "no good feed" to be found. Even the privately owned and more favorably located land was "altogether too closely pastured."[42]

In a three-day tour around Steens Mountain, Griffiths and his party reported an "enormous drain . . . upon these mountains for summer pasture," with sheep causing the heaviest overgrazing. In a rough but remarkable reconnaissance, the Bureau of Plant Industry team counted seventy-three flocks of sheep on the mountain in the summer of 1901, each averaging about 2,500 animals. Accepting Griffiths' calculations of about 400 square miles of mountain, that meant an average of more than 450 sheep per square mile during "a season of pasturage" extending over four months. Nor does that explain the full story of grazing pressure on the mountain. The great cattle ranches located at the base of the Steens, including the French-Glenn estate and the Pacific Livestock Company, ran their animals "into the same region as much as possible during the summer season." The combined effects of too many cattle and sheep grazing on the Steens commons were denuded grasses, extensive areas of defoliated forbs like cinquefoil and Indian currant, and willows "trimmed up as far as the sheep can reach." Griffiths found that the animals even browsed poplar saplings and in some instances completely girdled small trees.[43]

In the summary to his report, Griffiths suggested findings similar to a concurrent study being carried out by the United States Geological Survey. "The destruction of the vegetation," he remarked, was "not the only evil effect" from overstocking the range. Clearing the ground of grasses and shrubbery removed "the protection of the surface soil from the erosive action of water." In a simultaneous inspection of the Snake River Plain for the Geological Survey, Israel Russell reported severe gullying in the streams flowing through the small valleys to the north of Boise. The "numerous lateral depressions and gulches, branching from the larger valleys," according to Russell, were recent and probably originated about 1880. Streams that once were easy to cross and had "smooth, unbroken contours" were now steep-sided gullies ten to fifteen feet deep. "Each rain that comes," Russell observed, "is assisting in their extension and enlargement" and thereby lowering the water table. The consequence is that bottomlands were drying up, causing "the dying out of the formerly luxuriant meadows of wild grasses and their replacement by sage brush."[44]

See next p.

The valleys of southeastern Oregon and southern Idaho share much in common, with grasses and larger vegetational growth inhibiting soil erosion and serving to maintain soil moisture near the surface. But that "delicate balancing of conditions," Russell concluded, "was seriously disturbed" when large numbers of livestock began grazing on the uplands and in the valley bottoms. Russell pointed to one "conspicuous illustration," the broad-bottomed valley of Willow Creek, in the northern part of Malheur County:

This valley, previous to the introduction of stock in excessive numbers, is reported to have been without a dry-season stream channel, and to have been clothed over great areas with a luxuriant growth of rye grass, which was mowed each year for hay. Now, owing to the more rapid escape of rain water falling on the upland, a stream channel 8 or 10 feet deep has been excavated for a distance of a score of miles.

During the summer Russell conducted his survey (1902), the Willow Creek channel was dry and the adjacent land "subdrained" to the point that only sagebrush would grow in meadows that formerly supported rye grass.[45]

The following year Russell resumed his survey, following a route that took him from Burns in the Harney Basin northwesterly through the Crooked River drainage and subsequently to the Cascade Mountains and southerly to the Klamath Basin. During his reconnaissance, Russell recorded detailed observations about Camp Creek and Price Valley, part of the southern watershed to the Crooked River. Russell's findings about the area have been at the center of a considerable body of historical research that raises intriguing questions about environmental change, especially that associated with riparian areas and the gullying of streams. At the heart of that discussion is Russell's description of Price Valley during his 1903 reconnaissance:

Its surface is intersected by arroyos, or small canyons, through which water flows during the wet season. Joining the main trenches are several branches, each of which has the characteristics of a young stream-cut canyon. The main trench, which follows the longer axis of the valley, ranges from 60 to 100 feet in width, is approximately 25 feet deep, and has vertical walls.

According to Russell, the walls of the arroyo revealed silt deposits of recent date, and together with similar evidence of erosion "present facts of much interest." Beyond the stream bank, he noted, the valley floor proper was mostly barren and covered with sagebrush.[46]

Geographer Geoffrey Buckley, who examined the Price Valley area in the early 1990s, remarked that the valley's landscape had changed little since Russell's reconnaissance of 1903. Today Camp Creek holds running water only in the spring; there is virtually no riparian cover; and the vegetation on the valley floor is mostly sagebrush. That assessment contrasts sharply with the observations of Peter Skene Ogden, who traveled through the upper Crooked River drainage and southward into the Harney Basin in the winter of 1825–26. The Hudson's Bay Company trapper reported remarkably rich soil and "in some parts the Grass seven feet high." On two or three occasions he witnessed streams "well lined with willows" with an occasional juniper scattered along the hillsides.[47]

Andrew McClure, a prospector who passed through Price Valley in September 1858, found "several springs of good water," willows growing along the creek, and excellent grass for horses. The following year a military troop also reported wood, water, and grass in plentiful supply in Price Valley. But an army detachment encamped in the valley for two months in 1864 was forced to move: "this place is so thoroughly fed off that any longer stay here was absolutely impossible without starving our stock." When federal officials surveyed the valley between 1871 and 1876, they noted occasional swamp-like conditions, vegetation growing along the stream, and that horses had no difficulty crossing Camp Creek. Oregon's surveyor general recorded a map and compiled survey notes in 1875 that characterized the valley as meadow-like with several marshes. But according to Buckley, the morphology of the stream underwent a dramatic change between 1876 and Israel Russell's visit to Price Valley in 1903. Because the surveys of the 1870s make no reference to Camp Creek flowing through an arroyo, the gullying of the stream very likely took place in the following decade. Moreover, the earlier surveys report that Price Valley was covered with bunchgrass, wild rye, and swamp grass, *not* sagebrush.[48]

During his early twentieth-century reconnaissance through Price Valley, Israel Russell, a trained geologist, reflected that the changes to the valley landscape were of very recent origin, "probably dating back only about fifteen or twenty years." He suspected that the huge volume of water that had turned Camp Creek into a trench was linked to "the introduction of domestic animals in such numbers that the surface covering of bunch grass was largely destroyed, and in consequence the run-off from the hills accelerated." Buckley's reconstruction of the historical descriptions of Price Valley draws a similar conclusion: heavy grazing in the uplands and the valley, especially during a period of severe drought (1885–89), destroyed streamside vegetation along Camp Creek; heavy rains and a rapid snow melt in about 1889 then initiated the gullying process. The fact that the beaver dams that had formerly acted to restrain erosion were gone further exacerbated conditions.[49]

Where travelers through Price Valley once crossed streams with ease, Israel Russell reported sharp, vertical-walled trenches up to twenty-five feet deep in some places. By the early twentieth century, water flowed in Camp Creek only during the winter season. The meadow-like character of the valley with its tall grasses, lush riparian vegetation, and standing pools of water had disappeared; in its place was a sagebrush-dominated plain intersected with numerous arroyos. Although the population of small and isolated Price Valley was limited, herders introduced cattle and horses to the area during the 1870s and sheep the following decade. Ruth Hardenbrook, who homesteaded in Price Valley beginning in 1907, believed that the root cause of the changes to Camp Creek "was too much stock . . . they'd eat the willows and everything and that's what did it. . . . There were too many people with too many cattle. Everybody had cattle."[50]

But the problem of determining cause and effect between human-induced activity and its consequences is not always a simple exercise in observation. As a seasonal employee of the United States Bureau of Forestry in 1902, William T. Cox participated in a study "to ascertain the source and cause of the annual deposits of sand left by the Columbia, which blows out, forming dunes which bury railroads, orchards, vineyards, and fields of alfalfa." The youthful disciple of Gifford Pinchot took his job seriously, traversing the Palouse, Walla Walla, Yakima, Wenatchee, Chelan, Methow, Okanogan, Umatilla, John Day, and Deschutes valleys to account for the drifting and blowing sand. "It is pretty evident," Cox later reported, "that the real cause of the trouble with sand along the Columbia came from crowding of the ranges and breaking up of the sod by sheep and horses." During the early years of settlement, the Columbia River carried "practically no sand," nor could the problem be attributed to cattle. The culprits, according to Cox, were the horses and sheep that caused the Columbia and Snake rivers to develop huge deposits of sand that commenced "to blow inland after the annual subsidence of the streams."[51]

Even a casual perusal of the early observer accounts of the mid-Columbia country would have suggested alternative explanations to that cause-

and-effect relation. Traveling southeasterly from the Walla Walla River on his return trip to the United States in July 1812, Robert Stuart witnessed high winds and blowing sand "sufficiently to produce an almost suffocating effect." David Douglas, after a night of rain in the same vicinity in June 1826, found "great relief, the atmospher being cool and the sand prevented from blowing." The level plain around him, he remarked, was "destitute of timber" and comprised of "gravel and sand." Nathaniel Wyeth, enroute down the Columbia in 1832 with the bright hope of making his fortune in the fur trade, left the Hudson's Bay Company post at Fort Walla Walla and soon encountered "a furious wind" where "the sand flew so as to obscure the air." [52]

The accounts of wind and blowing and drifting sand mount with each successive Euro-American visitor to the mid-Columbia region. John Kirk Townsend, who reached the junction of the Walla Walla and Columbia rivers during the low-water month of September, wrote in his journal that he saw high and rocky banks "interrupted by broad, level sand beaches." Thomas Farnham outdid all others in his rhetorical sketches of a desert-like country of "vast rolling swells of sand and clay," as worthless as the "wastes of Arabia." But the more widely read Fremont described the mid-Columbia/Walla Walla terrain best: "a plain of bare sands, from which the air was literally filled with clouds of dust and sand, . . . this place being one of the several points on the river which are distinguished for prevailing high winds." [53]

Fremont's account also provides an alternative explanation for the deposits of sand visible during the period William Cox called "the annual subsidence of the streams." Moving down the Columbia River from Fort Walla Walla in the fall season of 1843, the lieutenant and his entourage toiled through "loose deep sand. . . . the stream being interspersed with many sand bars (it being the season of low water)." [54] Cox was undoubtedly correct in claiming that some rangelands were being overgrazed; however, his assumption that overgrazing contributed to the problem of sandbars in the river and elsewhere would appear to be wide of the mark. The evidence suggests, rather, that the "drifting and blowing sand" may have been around since the mid-Holocene, or at least since the intermontane climate began to warm.

The exotic animals, introduced in ever-increasing numbers to Oregon's southeastern quadrant beginning in about 1870, initiated changes to the region's ecology beyond the disruption of riparian environments. In their excellent study of the influence of domestic livestock on arid environments, James A. Young and B. Abbott Sparks provide expert witness to the consequences for original plant communities:

The vegetation of the pristine sagebrush/grasslands was rather simple and extraordinarily susceptible to disturbance. The potential of the environment to support plant and animal life was limited by lack of moisture and often by accumulations of salts in the soil. The native vegetation lacked the resilience, depth, and plasticity to cope with concentrations of large herbivores. The plant communities did not bend or adapt; they shattered.

The large herds of cattle and sheep consumed grasses that provided a major fuel source for the annual fires that swept the arid interior. With the elimination of the fires, big sagebrush and juniper proliferated, and exogenous annual grasses virtually eliminated the perennial bunchgrasses.[55] It is accurate to say, then, that before railroads penetrated the interior Northwest in the 1880s, the ecology of the arid grasslands had already undergone extensive change.

Where livestock grazed heavily, they trampled and destroyed native perennial grasses and inhibited plants from flowering, setting seed, and thereby reproducing. Because livestock ruined perennial grasses and refused to feed on big sage, greasewood, or rabbitbrush, shrub vegetation increased. The newly disturbed land then proved excellent ground for nurturing weedy invading species, especially cheatgrass (or downy brome). This aggressive plant, which dies in the fall but leaves its seed behind to reproduce, proved to be an excellent ecological competitor in the high and arid country of eastern Oregon.[56]

Cheatgrass, an annual native to Central Asia, evolved and thrived in the midst of large herds of grazing animals, conditions strikingly similar to those found in the semiarid intermountain region. Although the conditions under which it arrived in the interior Northwest are the subject of debate, it is known that cheatgrass was present in eastern British Columbia, Washington, Oregon, Nevada, and Utah by the 1890s. The plant achieved its present distribution in the Intermountain West by 1930. Wherever the ground in the region of the "cold desert" has been disturbed, cheatgrass easily outcompetes native perennial grasses. There is yet another side to this species: cheatgrass provides ideal fuel for fires, and fires in turn favor the reproduction of cheat over native perennial grasses. The invader sprouts earlier than the native bunchgrass, and in the process exhausts moisture that would be available to the perennials. Two scientists point to the Darwinian irony of those conditions: "the dominance of downy brome after wildfires in sagebrush grasslands resembles the phoenix of an alien life form rising from the ashes to haunt the post-burn environment."[57]

The mining rushes to eastern Oregon initiated the first commercial timber cutting in the region. Enterprising business people established sawmills in the booming mining districts in the John Day, Burnt River, and Powder River valleys in the 1860s to cut lumber for building materials and timbers for bridge, sluice, and mine construction. The modest productive capacity of those early mills was sufficient to meet the local demands of the boom-and-bust mining economy for nearly two decades. Although much of the easily accessible timber adjacent to those small mining communities had been cut, the vast interior of the Blue Mountain forests remained beyond the reach of commercial ventures. The manipulations and maneuvers of distant capitalists, however, soon altered that relatively slow pace of activity.

The completion of the transcontinental railroad in 1884, linking the Columbia River—via the Blue Mountains and Grand Ronde Valley—to the Union Pacific Railroad at Huntington on the Snake River, accelerated industrial activity in the pine forests of eastern Oregon. At the same time, Henry Villard, the financial guru behind the Oregon Railway and Navigation Company railroad across eastern Oregon, initiated a big advertising campaign to encourage settlement in the Powder River Valley and adjacent areas.[58] The Portland *Oregonian* joined that promotional effort with an analogy about apple trees and cities. While the former would be incapable of bringing forth fruit in a desert, cities could not survive in the absence of natural resources. But Baker City would prosper handsomely, the newspaper enthused, because "unlimited resources are capable of giving support to an unlimited population."[59]

David Eccles, already a successful western lumberman, was another who was on the move, in this case to eastern Oregon's timberlands. Using a variety of tactics including dummy entrymen, he began purchasing blocks of timber in the early 1880s to supply railroad ties for the Union Pacific subsidiary, the Oregon Short Line. When the railroad was completed from Granger, Wyoming, to Huntington on the Snake River, Eccles and a group of associates then incorporated the Oregon Lumber Company in 1889, a firm that was soon to emerge as the leading producer of western pine lumber in Oregon. To gain access to the timbered wealth of the southern Blue Mountains, Eccles and his partners formed a subsidiary corporation, the Sumpter Valley Railroad Company; the new company immediately proceeded to build a narrow-gauge line nineteen miles up the narrow Powder River Valley. The first logs rolled down to Baker City and the company's newly constructed state-of-the-art mill on August 1, 1890, establishing a regimen for harvesting, transporting, and milling timber that would last through the Second World War.[60]

In the succeeding years, the railroad pushed deeper into the mountains until the line extended eighty miles to Prairie City and the John Day Valley by 1910. Prosperous mining activity throughout the Sumpter Valley region in the late 1890s created a lively business for the Oregon Lumber Company, especially in the sale of mine timbers. The result was a heavy volume of traffic moving in both directions along the railroad's winding route through the mountains. Because of lucrative marketing prospects, several operators built small sawmills in the town of Sumpter to cut timbers and lumber for the mines. But the area's impressive timber stands were the railroad's long-term, bread-and-butter freight.[61]

Baker County's growing population between 1880 and 1910 reflects the increased human activity along the extensive Sumpter Valley Railroad and its several spur lines. As Table Eight indicates, both mining and lumbering operations attracted people to the area, with the county's numbers growing from 4,616 in 1880 to 18,076 in 1910. The expanding population base and an increasingly sophisticated and productive technology suggest the influence and pace of industrial activity in transforming the landscape of the southern Blue Mountain region. The railroad itself was an intrusive environmental force—linking the physical world of the Blue Mountains, local processing facilities, and markets. But its strategic importance was in fur-

TABLE EIGHT

Population of Baker County, 1870–1930

Year	Population
1870	2,804
1880	4,616
1890	6,764
1900	15,597
1910	18,076
1920	17,929
1930	16,754

ther enhancing the ability of lumbermen to gain access to stands remote from manufacturing sites. H. D. Langille's federal survey of the region in the early twentieth century reported that "the destruction of timber [was] almost complete" along much of the Oregon Lumber Company's railroad.[62]

Although the company did nothing more than the bidding of its directors, a commissioned history of the firm suggests the degree to which the new transportation technology influenced increases in production: "As the rails of the Sumpter Valley Railway were pushed up the Powder River Valley, timber was taken from each gulch and creek along the way." The leading lumber trade journal in the Pacific Northwest, the *Timberman,* noted in 1903 that the Oregon Lumber Company was using "the only steam skidder in the state . . . to *daylight* [author's emphasis] the forest around Whitney." [63]

Less observable in the Oregon Lumber Company's cash-flow statistics were the consequences for the forest lands open to commercial production. For the intermountain pine forests, the pursuit of the bottom line meant production-driven business practices that focused on taking only the best and most marketable timber from the woods and leaving huge amounts of debris on the ground.[64] Waste, as Richard White has indicated, had little economic meaning in an age when the timber supply seemed inexhaustible and operators confronted perpetually glutted markets. To compound those ecological difficulties in the Blue Mountains, miners often set deliberate

fires for mining

fires to clear vegetation and to expose potential outcroppings of minerals. Those practices contributed to some of the worst forest fires in the region's history, fires that were fed in part by the accumulation of heavy fuels lying on the ground. In contrast with earlier conflagrations, the fires that burned through logging debris were hot, consuming duff, seedlings, and standing trees alike. In truth, the new fire regime represented a much more intrusive and threatening element in the forest ecosystem.[65] Those conditions also underscore the powerful and symbiotic bond between economics and ecology in the industrial era.

At the onset of the twentieth century, market influences were apparent over broad areas of central and eastern Oregon. With the transition from livestock grazing to wheat culture, large acreages along the northern margins of the Deschutes-Umatilla Plateau had shifted from pastoral productive relations to commercial agriculture. Land with the potential for growing wheat became increasingly important for its commodity value, both for the volume of grain it might produce and for the price the property itself would exact at market. Farmers bounded, fenced, and thereby "improved" their land, and in the process drastically simplified its diversified ecology. Land put to wheat cultivation transformed the very character of the landscape itself into uniform fields of production to satisfy both the settler-farmer's acquisitive needs and the distant market demand for products from the soil.

For Oregon's southeastern quadrant, the newly imposed pastoral production system introduced equally dramatic and systemic changes. Cattle and sheep were important, in Donald Worster's stark words, only as "impersonal, massed mechanisms for turning grass into money."[66] In pursuit of that complex set of cultural imperatives, livestock entrepreneurs overstocked the arid grasslands, practices that led directly to the introduction of exotic plants and grasses and severe erosion. Just as miners treated the mineral deposits in the Blue Mountains, graziers viewed the bunchgrass area in southeastern Oregon as a mother lode to be mined until it was no longer profitable. As mere livestock production units, the valleys and uplands of southeastern Oregon seemingly had little meaning beyond their commodity value.

Dust Bowl

Far away in Oregon's major metropolitan center, Portland investors and developers had always been enthusiastic about activity taking place east of the mountains. To Portland's boosters and publicists, lands everywhere beyond the Willamette metropolis offered bright prospects for the future; that is, if existing transportation arterials could be improved and railroads extended to the hinterland. Promoters argued that the state could realize its full potential only through initiative, investment, energy, and imagination. Portland's commercial community, in league with the region's leading newspaper, the *Oregonian*, surpassed all others in promoting the "development" of the seemingly limitless wealth that nature had bestowed upon citizens of the state.

Extending the Industrial Infrastructure

Nature's Industries and the
Rhetoric of Industrialism

PEERLESS OREGON

A Marvelously Prolific Soil

Awaits the Farmer

BOUNDLESS MINERAL WEALTH

Commercial Advantages That

Astonish the World

MOUNTAINS CLOTHED IN FORESTS[1]

In conventional literature, material conditions in the late-nineteenth-century West offered up a landscape filled with promise and opportunity, a story line whose direction and focus was imbued with the notion of progress.[2] The Oregon country in particular, according to its boosters, was a land abounding in potential, a place where nature's wealth and human technical genius would combine to forge the good society, to provide decent, stable living for coming generations. The future in that view was full with the expectation of improvement, with the hope that in this special place the next generation would banish want and indigence. That effusive narrative line—pursued in travel and real estate brochures, commercial club and promotional pamphlets, and through regional newspapers—celebrated the seemingly limitless opportunity of the Pacific Northwest.

The transcendent vehicle for that transformation was a lush and abundant landscape in which nature would be put to work to benefit humankind. The entire Northwest, *Pacific Monthly* enthused in 1904, was a field laden with opportunity. Everything that nature could provide or the human imagination conceive was present in the region:

Beautiful and fertile valleys, glorious and majestic mountain and river scenery, wonderful forests, mines of gold, silver, copper, nickel, . . . rivers teeming with fish. . . . We have it; we are in possession of it—this garden spot, this land pregnant with hidden resources, possibilities that almost stagger the imagination, opportunities!![3]

The "material dialectic" of that world was centered in a burgeoning global capitalism, booming industrial development in the eastern United States, explosive economic growth in the greater Oregon country, and a sense of confidence and assuredness that the future would bring rich material rewards.[4]

The narrative accounts prefiguring that remarkable period of change had already served up powerful rhetorical tools that ascribed meaning to conditions and circumstances in Oregon and the Pacific Northwest. It can be said with some accuracy that the rhetoric defining the relationship between culture and landscape, between human activity and environmental/ecological change, assumed a more assertive and confident—even arrogant—tone with the onset of the industrial era. The advent of steam power, expressed especially with the coming of the railroad, marked an increasingly more intrusive cultural presence in the region. Railroads were the primary instrument in the expansion of industrial capitalism across the United States, vehicles, Alan Trachtenberg has argued, that "re-created American nature into 'natural resources' for commodity production." For those areas of North America distant from metropolitan markets, the steam-powered locomotives were even more: they were physical symbols of industrialism, of mechanization, visible representations of change—social, economic, political, and environmental.[5]

For the Oregon country the literal and figurative meaning of industrialism was expressed in terms of nature's industries: that is, enterprises seeking to profit from the region's magnificent forests, its fertile valley bottom soils, the mineral riches that underlay the interior mountains, and the seemingly limitless multitudes of salmon that plied its numerous waterways. A robust and expansive rhetoric that became increasingly more aggressive as the century drew to a close accompanied those narrative prescriptions. That rhetorical discourse linked the region's abundance with the expanding influence of industrial capitalism in the Northwest.

Long before the coming of railroads to the Oregon country, dreamers and other witnesses drew attention to the complementarity between the region's natural abundance and the symbols of industrialism. Peter H. Burnett, an early immigrant to Oregon and future governor of California, gave voice to the industrial potential of the country when he pointed to the "inexhaustible quantities" of timber along the Columbia River "just where the water power is at hand to cut it up." And in the seminal year of the California gold rush, the first newspaper published in the Northwest, the *Oregon Spectator*, underscored the important link between resources (timber) and water power: "With these forests the slopes of our magnificent mountains are densely covered. And down those mountain slopes . . . come tumbling . . . thousands of creeks and rivers affording endless hydraulic privileges." The *Oregon Statesman* made a similar comparison a few years later, praising both the enormous value of the lumber business to Oregon and the "immense" water power nearby.[6] Those images, linking protoindustrial activities to rivers and streams, suggest an affinity between the machinery of production and the natural world of a particular place.

The Pacific Northwest abounded in romantic and ambitious visionaries, promoters whose resourceful and imaginative accounts about "developing" the country knew few restraints. An early emigrants' travel guide published in 1846, Overton Johnson and William Winter's *Route Across the Rocky Mountains*, reported signs of incipient industrial activity on the lower Willamette River. Such bustle and commotion, the guide suggested, was mere prelude to the building of "villages, towns, and cities, with massive walls and glittering spires." The authors looked forward to the time when "the powerful locomotive, with its heavy train, will fly along the rattling railway; when . . . the proud steamer will dash along the majestic river."[7]

A decade later, and in language especially suited to mid-nineteenth-century Fourth of July oratory, Washington Territory's J. W. Goodell envisioned a future where "well cultivated farms adorned with fields of golden wheat" would replace the region's forests, where the "hum of machinery" could be heard near every waterfall, and where the shrill whistle of steamboats echoed dockside as they discharged and received the freight of "flourishing towns":

I behold large cities, with their numerous spires, glistening in the rays of the morning sun, their streets teeming with busy thousands, and their numerous wharves crowded with immense steamers and ships from all parts of the world, receiving and discharging their immense cargoes. I turn my eyes eastward, and behold an immense train of rail road cars thundering down the inclined plain of the Cascades.[8]

For Theodore Winthrop, Boston scion and traveler through the Northwest, civilized humankind had never experienced "a fresh chance of developing itself under grand and stirring influences so large as in the Northwest." His compatriot and pamphleteer, Samuel Bowles, made special mention of the Willamette Valley as "the garden of Oregon," the present bulwark of its prosperity, "its sure security for the future."[9]

The Oregon press aggressively promoted efforts, especially in hinterland areas, to join the industrial realm with earthly abundance. "The progress of new countries depends, to a great degree, upon their railroads, and their connection with extensive railroad systems," the *Willamette Farmer* argued in 1872. In the case of the Rogue Valley, the newspaper praised Jackson County officials for constructing bridges and roads long before the arrival of the railroad. Improvements in transportation, it contended, would promote the development of the area's unparalleled water power and mill sites whose abundance was "sufficient . . . to drive the machinery for the milling and manufacturing purposes of an entire State." This "extensive basin of unsurpassed fertility and loveliness," the *Farmer* exclaimed, had been "supplied by nature" with all the elements necessary to the building of a "dense agricultural, manufacturing and mining population."[10]

The peripatetic David Newsom was one of the most energetic and artful in linking the region's abundance with the development of manufactories. In an essay published in 1876, Newsom praised Oregon's industrial resources, the "vast coal fields" in its southwestern counties and the great fishery on the Columbia River. But the state's "great source of wealth, . . . little appreciated as yet," was its immense stands of timber and abundant

water power. Newsom then outlined an industrial vision that would capitalize on the state's natural wealth:

Capital and brains are needed to utilize them, and [to] erect factories, machine
shops, foundries, fisheries, ship yards, rolling mills, nail factories, woolen mills, etc.,
and to push our commerce to foreign lands.[11]

Still the region's largest circulation newspaper as the nineteenth century drew to a close, the Portland *Oregonian* was equally enthusiastic about
the industrial potential of the Oregon country. "It is the language of truth
and not of exaggeration which describes the great Northwest," the newspaper proclaimed in its inaugural issue for 1890. From timbered sea coast
to wheat fields east of the Cascade Mountains, Oregon offered commercial
advantages that would truly astonish the world. Even in its still sparsely
settled coastal valleys, "the smoke of the settler's hut and . . . the sound
of the woodsman's axe . . . [indicate] that the reign of Civilization is at
hand." But it was along the winding Willamette River—that "exhaustless
storehouse of manufacturing power"—where cities and towns were using
the "power of the river to light their houses, factories and streets, and to
turn the mills that clothe and feed them." With its rich soils, endless mineral wealth, and unmatched scenery, the *Oregonian* concluded, "Oregon is
America in miniature."[12]

Speaking for the small Columbia River town of its name, the *Hood
River Glacier* encouraged the development of manufactures in the community: "We have the water power and natural facilities hundreds of places
have not which carry on manufactures." There were virtues, for instance, in
building a local cannery because it would "keep our money at home which
would benefit all and build up home industries." A cannery in Hood River,
the newspaper observed, would enable fruit and vegetable growers to "put
upon the market a class of canned goods for which we would have no fear
of competition."[13]

As the decades passed, promoters extended those early visions of agrarian
paradise and industrial potential to embrace more inclusive types of enterprise, especially those associated with new and more intrusive forms of

human activity. What the economists refer to as "economic development" first came to the Oregon country with the building of the great transcontinental railroads, transportation arterials that linked the region's natural abundance to riverine and oceanic highways and to the industrial centers of the East.[14] The influence of the new transportation technology reverberated everywhere—from the expanding acreages of wheat in the interior country, to the rich mineral lodes in northern Idaho and the Rossland district in British Columbia, and to the extensive fir, cedar, and pine forests throughout the Northwest.

During the last quarter of the nineteenth century, eastern and foreign capitalists viewed the northern West as a magnificent investment opportunity, a promoter's paradise. More than any other factor, therefore, the heavily capitalized railroads marked the arrival of the industrial world[15] and the subsequent transformation and reordering of the regional landscape. Even in agricultural settings such as Oregon's Willamette Valley—a seemingly nonindustrial environment—railroads vastly advanced the volume of trade, especially in speeding the delivery of modern plows and reapers.[16] As historian Carlos Schwantes put it, the emergence of industry in the American hinterland was "the child of the steel rail."[17]

What is most fascinating about this period is the rhetoric, the language defining human activity and its relationship to particular places—the ongoing dialectic between culture and nature; the idea that the destinies of both people and natural systems were intertwined. In his now-classic work, *Space and Place,* the geographer Li-Fu Tuan observes that culture explains how people "attach meaning to and organize space and place." Furthermore, he argues, myths tend to flourish in the absence of precise knowledge about particular places.[18] A casual reading of the literature promoting the development of an industrial infrastructure in the Oregon country gives substance to Tuan's assertion.

The salutatory issue of *West Shore* listed its publisher and editor as L. Samuel, recently arrived in the city of Portland. From its initial issue in 1875 until the magazine ceased publication in 1891, *West Shore* was the most assertive and widely circulated promotional journal in the Northwest. Within two years of its appearance it was being distributed in thirty-two states and in Great Britain. While *West Shore* paid special attention to the price of agricultural land in Oregon and Washington Territory and regularly carried a section dubbed "Information for Immigrants," Samuel's greatest enthusiasm centered on the region's commercial and industrial growth, especially the building of railroads. Indeed, when Portland celebrated the arrival of the Northern Pacific Railway in 1883, Samuel published a forty-six-page souvenir edition.[19]

In one of its inaugural issues *West Shore* looked back to the 1840s and praised the efforts of that first band of noble adventurers, "brave and enterprising men" who accomplished the magnificent feat of creating a "broad, solid, enduring foundation" from an "unredeemed wilderness." The building of that "superstructure" enabled the Oregon country to provide an "unequalled wealth of breadstuffs to the nations of Europe," an accomplishment that won the region prominence as a producer "in quality as well as quantity." Those early immigrants, the magazine concluded, would never have anticipated the productiveness of the present moment:

Our lumbering trade, our unequaled Salmon fisheries, and our growing and increasing manufacturing enterprises—Iron Mines, Iron Works, Woolen Factories, Machine Shops, Furniture Manufactories, Ship Yards, Flouring, Oil, Paper, and other Mills—and the very lucrative and extensive lines of ocean and river steam navigation.

Two years later *West Shore* again boasted about the region's natural abundance: "Her wheat and wool, lumber, salmon and fruits, make up an aggregate of commercial resources which must be considered extraordinary." An endless wealth of timber "stored up" for future wants and limitless quantities of salmon would provide a perpetual source of revenue.[20]

Other contributors to *West Shore* underscored the importance of water power as the grand attractive feature of the Oregon country, "natural power," as one writer put it, that existed in greater quantity than anywhere else in the United States. The magazine touted the manufacturing productions of a section of the Willamette River in Clackamas County—its six sawmills, woolen mill, tub and bucket factory, paper mill, and iron reduction works—which along with its abundant water power, promised an even greater industrial presence in the future. In promoting the timber resources of Clatsop County, *West Shore* pointed to the juxtaposition of "timber of the finest quality . . . with numerous streams to float it to market." The Portland publication praised agricultural Linn County in the heart of "the great Willamette Valley, the 'garden of the world,'" for its "easy access to markets," made possible because of its proximity to steamboats on the nearby river.[21]

West Shore repeatedly cited the need for investment capital to build industrial enterprises to take advantage of the region's endless sources of wealth. To realize that "undeveloped richness," the magazine insisted that the critical and essential ingredient was capital.[22] *West Shore*'s reasoning suggested, in part, that nature's industries left unadorned would leave the region vulnerable, a potential victim to exploiters from afar. Left unsaid in that equation was the power and influence of distant capital itself.

But it was the steam locomotive that most energized those who wrote for *West Shore*. In an essay praising the natural blessings of the Oregon country—its agricultural productiveness, its unlimited water power, its excellence in fruit growing, and its potential for manufacturing—writer P. B. Simmons observed in 1879 that the region was "only waiting for the magic touch of the iron horse to make it the richest producing section in our country." Writers for *West Shore* were particularly conscious of the revolution that railroads would bring to logging and lumbering operations. Extending a rail line through northwestern Oregon's Columbia County, one author predicted, would bring forth the full promise of its "rich and varied natural resources," especially its abundant timber stands. The absence of rail lines to "sections where the finest of the commercial woods are most abundant," the magazine observed, "has retarded the growth of the lumbering industry." [23]

Waterways, too, were industrial arterials, providing natural routes for transporting the region's earthly bounty to processing centers and then on to national and global markets. The Coquille River on Oregon's southern coast, according to *West Shore*, was "a most beautiful stream having very much the appearance of a natural canal." Once the rocks at the mouth of the river were removed, there would be no obstacles "to the carrying of the immense wealth of this region [timber] out to the markets of the world." Without the river corridor, the area's natural abundance might "lie dormant for generations." Loggers, it should be noted, were among the first to impose an industrial-like regimen on waterways to "flood" timber down smaller creeks to major streams where logs were placed in booms and then rafted to mills.[24]

Of special importance to the region, *West Shore* contended, were the vast resources of coal and iron and "the great quantity of timber on every hand." Moreover, readers were reminded, "notwithstanding her great capacities," manufacturing in the Oregon country had barely made a beginning. But there was a solution to the problem of sending the raw products of nature out to world markets: promote the development of home industries, manufacturing facilities that would turn the region's timber and other primary materials into finished products *before* they were shipped to rail and ocean highways. "Why enrich the laborers of other States at the expense of our fellow-workers?" *West Shore* inquired. "Why stop the wheels of industry, when the skilled operatives are waiting at the doors?"[25] Although the Portland monthly was not alone in promoting the development of the region's bounty, for a time it surpassed all others in its uninhibited boasting.

By the last quarter of the nineteenth century industrial technology in the form of steam power was beginning to reach far beyond railroad locomotives and waterborne stern-wheelers. Nowhere was this more important than in the arduous work of hauling huge timbers from Northwestern forests. The new energy technology also promoted the integration of production and marketing systems: the movement of fleece to woolen mills, shipments of mineral ores to smelters and reduction facilities, and the transport of felled timber to sawmills. Steam-driven engines enabled producers to circumvent the forces of nature, especially in the ability to move natural-objects-turned-commodities through difficult terrain and against riverine and tidal currents. The production and marketing strategy of the Willamette Steam Mills, Lumbering and Manufacturing Company, located on the banks of the Willamette River in North Portland, serves as a prototype for the more expansive enterprises that emerged in the twentieth century.

The Willamette Steam Mills production system originated deep in a Douglas-fir forest somewhere up the Columbia River. Steam donkeys yarded the felled and bucked timber to railroad sidings where the logs were loaded on cars and hauled to water's edge. From that point the logs were floated into booms and rafted down the Columbia and up the Willamette River to the company's large, modern milling facility, a plant capable of turning out 250,000 board feet of lumber every twenty-four hours. The company possessed, according to one source, "exceptional shipping facilities": (1) access to the Northern Pacific Railroad whose tracks passed through its lumber yard, and (2) deep-water wharves that fronted on the Willamette River. The firm sent large quantities of lumber eastward by rail, and it shipped equally sizable cargoes into the Pacific to markets in California, Central and South America, the Hawaiian Islands, and the Orient. From beginning to end, according to *West Shore,* the system wrought a remarkable transformation in the forests adjacent to the Columbia River, converting the products of nature "into cities, towns and farms."[26]

The *Oregonian* promoted agricultural progress (including the expansion of irrigated acreages), railroad building, unrestricted open-river transportation, mineral development, and literally anything that would redound to the "opening up" of Portland's tributary territory. The *Oregonian* boasted that the growing metropolis on the lower Willamette River was a natural community, both in a commercial and in a physical sense. By rail, ocean, and river, Portland was accessible to a vast resource-rich tributary region to the east and oceanic highways to the west; its "advantages of position" signaled that its expectations for the future were invincible.[27]

For several decades the *Oregonian* persistently called for rail and river transportation — the building of an industrial infrastructure — to promote the development of its extensive hinterland. Although the city of Portland provided services and supplies to those vast outlying districts, the great bulk of the wealth of hinterland resources and the attenuated profits would be channeled through the metropolis on the Willamette. "The natural business field of Portland," the *Oregonian* observed on one occasion, also included several ports along the Washington and Oregon coasts. But in order for the city "to hold and control the trade which properly belongs to her," it had to develop and furnish the facilities to attract coastal commerce. The newspaper suggested better communication systems and the construction of small vessels to stimulate the "coasting trade."[28] Beginning in the 1890s and continuing well into the twentieth century, the Portland business community worked tirelessly and through a variety of venues to promote itself and to improve its commercial prospects.[29]

Despite the city's trading prowess, writers for the *Oregonian* were constantly urging the local business community to do more in the way of developing a more broadly based manufacturing infrastructure. On one occasion the newspaper chided the city for being little more "than a depot for exchange of goods produced elsewhere." It accused those with property and wealth in the city of mere "store keeping," of failing to develop the metropolis as a center of production. To become something more than a point of transfer, the local business community had to develop manufactures founded on regional raw-materials industries. If it did so, Portland would attract "the trade of all the surrounding country" and make adjacent communities tributary to its own commerce. "To build up an industrial empire upon the western slope," the *Oregonian* urged Portland entrepreneurs to develop processing facilities, "the raw material for which can be produced upon our own soil." Because the world beyond the city held "every requisite" in the way of raw materials, and because of its ideal natural location at the crossroads of commerce, those with investment capital would be wise to act.[30]

Working up its own wool, tanning its own hides, and canning its home-grown fruit would give the city a manufacturing infrastructure and extend the degree of its influence in the hinterland. Advances in the city's manufacturing and industrial sector eventually convinced the *Oregonian*'s writers that Portland deserved true metropolitan status. As the 1880s drew to a close, the community's financial indexes indicated a 73 percent increase in manufacturing production. "Nothing is so strongly indicative of the progress of a city as its factories," the local press boasted. Railroad passenger lists, the arrival of immigrants and tourists, and increases in trade were all signs of advance, but manufactures demonstrated a city's ability to provide jobs for a large population and to produce goods for the home market and for shipment to hinterland regions. In fact, Portland's growth during the last two decades of the nineteenth century suggests a considerable expansion in local industrial activity. The city's population grew from 17,577 in 1880, to 46,385 in 1890, and then nearly doubled to 90,426 by 1900. By the turn of the century, Portland's increasingly urban and industrial appearance was at one with similar developments in other regional population centers, most notably in Seattle, Tacoma, and Spokane.[31]

The image the *Oregonian* projected for Portland's future embraced both natural and industrial symbols. "Nature could scarcely do more for a state than she has done for Oregon," the newspaper remarked in celebrating the "wonderful diversification" of its resource industries.[32] Because all natural routes of travel and transport led to Portland, the city was the pivotal center, the industrial and commercial depot for the vast area tributary to the Columbia. In a turn-of-the-century editorial urging citizens to "build up the industries and develop the resources of this region," the *Oregonian* assessed the influence of nature and culture in Portland's development:

Nature has done a great deal for Portland. The railroads have done a great deal more. But Nature and the railroads can't do it all. It is well enough to have influential friends, if we don't depend on them too exclusively; but a man must do something for himself. It is about that way with a community.

What the larger region needed, the editors insisted, were energetic and industrious people to till its valleys, to shear its sheep, to fatten its cattle, to dig its mineral resources, and to make "lumber out of its forests, shoes out of its hides, clothing out of its wool."[33]

The industrial modeling of the Oregon country at the onset of the twentieth century reflects the influence of cultural imperatives summarized by historian Donald Worster—a view of the natural world as capital, the obligation to use that capital for self-advancement, and a conviction that the social order should promote the accumulation of personal wealth.[34] The more imaginative among those articulating that new configuration envisioned a symbiosis of metropolis and countryside cooperating to mutual advantage. Nature's boundless wealth would flow from hinterland to processing center and then via railroad and the great blue corridor of the Columbia to oceanic markets. Under that set of arrangements, wheat, beef, minerals, logs, and other raw materials followed the natural gradients of the Willamette and Columbia rivers to Portland, while goods and merchandise flowed outward from the city to lesser towns in the interior districts. In his study of Chicago and its hinterland, William Cronon argues that a descending hierarchy of places—from metropolis to smallest town—was effected to carry out the "movement of goods and produce shuttling between city and country."[35] For Portland and the Pacific Northwest those expanding concentric rings of power also meant that distant and larger constellations of capital (and markets) heavily influenced the course of events in tributary territories, the material source of nature's industries.

The effects of the more advanced industrial transport technology — steam-powered locomotives, oceangoing vessels, and river steamers — strengthened Portland's already favored position in the exchanges between upriver resource communities and downstream metropolis. In addition to the attention it gave to the development of Portland's tributary area, the *Oregonian* also encouraged the city's business sector to expand its local manufacturing capacity, especially in "products, the raw material for which can be produced upon our own soil." The requisite natural resources existed in abundance; it required only entrepreneurial effort "to build an industrial empire upon the western slope." Factories, according to one writer, indicated progress, stamped a community as a city, and provided employment in the making of "goods and wares for home consumption and for shipment to tributary country."[36]

The Southern Pacific Railroad enthusiastically endorsed the effort to market Oregon's natural abundance. "Oregon probably has no equal in our Union for the number, size, and economical disposition of its water resources," the company claimed in a home-seekers' guide published in 1894. The pamphlet singled out the Columbia River for special attention, a stream with the potential to serve as an "artery of almost unbounded commercial relations with a vast domain north and east of Portland." The promotional tract contended that there was little land in the region that was "not good for something, being adapted to wheat, barley, oats, hay, pasture, fruits, vegetables, timber, mining." In many sections of Oregon the grass was green year-round, and its soil was "as black and rich as the mud of Egypt." The potential for the state's "latent or undeveloped agricultural wealth," the guide concluded, was "simply incalculable—almost beyond comprehension."[37]

The *Oregonian* again boasted in 1896 that Portland and its hinterland possessed "the essentials that go to make up a great industrial community." There was wheat to be ground, fruit to be canned, iron and coal seams to be worked, wool for clothing, and "untold quantities of timber to be converted into useful articles of commerce." Portland possessed the wealth, the enterprise, and the "unrivaled facilities to take advantage of the raw materials close at hand and the markets within easy reach." The newspaper offered up a utopian vision of a future industrial complex lining the banks of the Willamette River from its mouth to Oregon City, a stretch of twenty-six miles of river front where electric-powered factories would turn the productions of nature into finished goods.[38] But while some concerned themselves with Portland's prospects as a developing manufacturing center, there were others whose imaginations embraced larger, more ambitious programs.

Railroads and other symbols of the industrial world became increasingly apparent across the Oregon country as the nineteenth century drew to a close. Because certain forms of the new technology—the telegraph and the steam-powered locomotive—encouraged and quickened the union of rural, resource-abundant districts with urban centers, commercial organizations and an assortment of other enthusiasts took notice of those conditions to promote a more closely integrated regional economy. The potential for extending the influence of strategically located urban centers under the newly developing transportation and communication infrastructure gave flight to a soaring prose artistry and an expanding geography of commercial and industrial ambitions.

"WHERE ROLLS THE OREGON," an *Oregonian* headline blared in December 1896. "The mighty river [that] drains an empire" gave special advantages to the metropolis of the Northwest, benefits that would increase as developers refashioned the contours of the Columbia River and the landscape of the Oregon country to suit the new industrial imperatives:

Every railroad built, every steamer launched, every foot added to the channels of the river, every manufacturing industry started, every building erected, every store opened, every dollar brought into the country . . . has added to the growth and prosperity of Portland.

As for the great waterway itself, the recently completed Cascade Locks and Canal "improved" the river and "would be of inestimable benefit to the entire country." Employing the metaphor "an open river"—a slogan that became the great rallying cry of the early twentieth century—the *Oregonian* called for more improvements on the "water highway" to provide cost-effective competition to the rail carriers and to increase the overall capacity for goods shipped along the river corridor.[39]

River City's rail and water transportation promoters repeatedly argued that natural geographic features had preordained Portland's position as the preeminent commercial center in the Columbia River country. "All Roads Lead to Portland," the *Oregonian* proclaimed in 1899. Because "the great artery . . . which drains a vast region of rich and varied resources" followed the laws of gravity, logic and common sense suggested the importance of Portland. Even a casual glance at a map of the region, the newspaper contended, indicated how geography favored Portland: "As naturally as water run[s] down hill does the produce of the interior seek a market through Portland." In that sense, the city served as a transfer point because of "natural conditions that were recognized when the town was established."[40]

Fill the country beyond Portland with producers, the *Oregonian* argued, and the city itself would benefit enormously. The promotion of a sense of mutual and material interdependence between country and city should be the primary objective of Portland's investment community. The hinterland, with its "immense latent resources, which may be turned into wealth," was the true source of urban prosperity. Factories in the cities provided markets for the productions of the countryside, and transportation lines into the outback, in turn, contributed to the productiveness of rural areas and advanced the volume of exchanges between the two sectors. In a gesture toward sloganeering, the newspaper concluded: "The country will build the city—if you build the country."[41]

There was much work to be done on the big river, especially removing the principal "obstacle" to open commerce, the "wild stretch of river between The Dalles and Celilo." Removing that obstruction, according to the *Oregonian*, would make Portland "the great distributing point by water, as it is now the great distributing point by rail. All water highways, like all rail [roads] . . . have to come to the metropolis." For the local business community, the chief objective in opening the river to free navigation was the "area of productive country known as the Inland Empire, which is rich with all the resources that give wealth to the state."[42] Overcoming the impediments of nature, according to that logic, required a twofold effort: (1) building a rail line on the Oregon side of the river through the difficult section between The Dalles and the Cascades; and (2) creating an efficient water passageway in the same section to expand the volume of commerce and to protect against railroad monopoly. The open-river campaign, therefore, involved culturally prescribed alterations rooted in what its supporters deemed democratic and economic objectives.

Portland's commercial community worked tirelessly to correct nature's imperfections on the great waterway and to improve the channels that linked the Willamette metropolis "with the productive country of the interior basin." Building a canal system from The Dalles to Celilo would free the river "from the oppression of arbitrary and unnatural agreements between transportation agencies." Of the two great barriers to upriver traffic, that of the Cascade rapids had already been neutralized. Removing the last obstruction would enable the transport of goods along the natural corridor of the Columbia and provide shippers with an alternative to the "unnatural and costly route over the summit of the Cascade Mountains."[43]

Organized business groups in the Willamette metropolis were especially active in pressing the open-river campaign. The Portland Chamber of Commerce established an Open River Committee to address the question: "How can relief best be given the people of the Inland Empire?" The committee's seemingly selfless response was the need to build a government canal between The Dalles and Celilo. To expand its lobbying campaign with Congress, the chamber's Open River Committee met with representatives from eastern Oregon, eastern Washington, and Idaho to form the Open River Association. To facilitate travel along the river and to provide temporary relief from excessive "through" railroad rates, the two committees decided to build a portage railroad to bypass the falls and rapids, and secondly, to work for the completion of the canal and locks. To the Portland committee, the alternative means for shipping goods would create an open river and help regulate railroad rates more effectively.[44]

Couched in rhetoric that suggested environmental change, the meanings attached to the open-river campaign carried a commercial message: free traffic from economic monopoly and lower the financial costs of water travel. Both commercial and political discourse hinted that "natural" forces rather than federal regulation would provide a more effective means to curb monopoly influence. Reporting on a recent meeting of the National Rivers and Harbors Congress in 1907, Oregon's Gov. George Chamberlain told the Portland Chamber of Commerce that the great waterways of the United States were "natural regulators of freight." In a direct reference to the Open River Committee's effort, Chamberlain observed that an open waterway would serve as "a law provided by nature to regulate the freights of a country tributary to it." If the Columbia were open and unobstructed from its mouth to its headwaters, there would be no need "to regulate freight rates, because the river itself will regulate it."[45]

As the great artery of commerce for the Northwest, the Columbia River provided a "natural" passageway for tapping the wealth of the rich interior country and to advance Portland's economic interests. If the city was to be a great commercial seaport and if the interior country was "to reach its proper development," the Portland Chamber of Commerce argued, then reasonable transportation rates had to be established between upriver shipping points and the downstream metropolis. An open river upstream and "a deep and safe channel to the Sea" were necessary to the unrestricted navigation of Northwest waterways. In its *Report on an Open River,* the Chamber of Commerce raised the issue of the city's future trading prospects, especially with the opening of the Panama Canal and the potential for an expanded trade with Pacific Basin countries. Only with a considerably enhanced water transportation infrastructure would Portland be in a position to take advantage of that potential continental and oceanic flow of goods and materials.[46]

The discussions that centered on improving navigation on the Columbia River offered up complex and contradictory rhetorical messages, a confusing juxtaposition of the meaning of the natural and the unnatural that fused geography and economics into a larger industrial vision. The Portland business community talked about "tapping" into the resources of the unoccupied sections of the inland empire, thereby further enlarging the region tributary to the river and by extension to the city of Portland. Shortly after the turn of the century, the newly organized Portland Board of Trade

actively pursued several agendas: (1) railroad projects throughout the interior country; (2) advertising the region's agricultural production; and
(3) lobbying the federal government to continue canal-building work on
the mid-Columbia River.

Because modern communication and transportation technology had
revolutionized the region's commerce, the Portland Board of Trade announced in a 1902 promotional pamphlet that it intended to advertise the
city as a manufacturing and commercial center, the mark of "every civilized
community in the world." Portland held an advantageous position because
it had mountains nearby filled with precious metals, streams to be har-
nessed for power, rich soil and ideal climatic conditions, and inexhaustible
forests to supply the construction needs of the nation. All of this combined
"to make the Pacific Northwest a country of the greatest opportunities of
any in the world." To promote the development of the territory, the board
urged Congress to retain funding in the current "Rivers and Harbor Bill"
to improve navigation on the Columbia River. With improved access to the
interior, its resources could be brought to market "by the cheap transportation . . . afforded by . . . an open river."[47]

At the turn of the century new urban rivals for commercial supremacy in
the Pacific Northwest prompted Portland bankers and the Board of Trade to
intensify their promotional activity. When the Klondike gold rush boomed
the Seattle economy and helped it recover quickly from the depression of
the early 1890s, the Portland business community moved aggressively to re-
assert its preeminence as the leading city in the region. The most elaborate
example of Portland's resurgence was the city's sponsorship of a commemo-
rative commercial fair in 1905, the celebrated Lewis and Clark Centennial
Exposition. Civic leaders, especially the local business community, saw the
exposition as an international advertisement, heralding the promise that
Portland and its hinterland held for prospective settlers and investors.[48]

The most ambitious circular promoting the development of the Oregon
country was the *Portland Board of Trade Journal,* subsequently appearing
under a number of titles, including the *Chamber of Commerce Bulletin.* As
the opening of the Lewis and Clark Centennial Exposition approached in
1905, the board celebrated Oregon's virtues in its monthly publication:

No where in the world is there such a land of promise and opportunities as in the State of Oregon. She has countless store of mineral wealth hidden in her broad bosom awaiting the touch of capital to convert it into material tangible wealth. . . . she has the soil, climate and all other conditions unsurpassable that guarantees the successful pursuance of every industry.

Although references to turning the natural world to account in the market-place were stratagems that date from the earliest observations about the region, there was a new buoyancy, an aggressive, even strident tone to the commercial literature published in the early twentieth century.[49]

Jefferson Myers, president of the organizing committee in charge of the Lewis and Clark Exposition, hinted to local audiences that the celebration would bring many thousands of visitors, "the best class of immigration," and that those who made the trip might find themselves a new home. Oregon alone, he said, had "more native underdeveloped resources than any other commonwealth within the United States." Its virtually untouched and immense forests, its mines barely past the stage of discovery, and its fisheries were "only producing a small part of the revenue" they were capable of. What the state required, Myers reported, was the "industry, ambition, and wealth" to turn those resources to its advantage. To the *Oregonian*, the exposition represented an opportunity to "appeal to the country" and a means to concentrate attention on the Pacific states "and upon their vast and yet undeveloped resources." The Portland fair, due to run from June 1 to October 15, 1905, would be a true exhibition of nature's wares; it would allow the region to show its "products of field, forest, mine and sea." [50]

From a civic and commercial standpoint, the Lewis and Clark Exposition was a striking success. When the final tally was in, there were 1,588,000 paid admissions with another 966,000 attending through courtesy passes. The *Oregonian* called the exposition "a great financial success," one that "surpassed every expectation." The event drew the attention of the entire nation to the region, the newspaper reported, and in the succeeding months and years would be certain to contribute "to the advantage, development and progress of the Northwest." The urban historian Carl Abbott calculates that the exposition's stockholders got a 21 percent return on their investments. "Portland put itself in the mainstream of American boosterism with its decision to support the exposition," he concludes. In an editorial opinion one year after the event, the *Oregonian* provided a summary commentary: "the Lewis and Clark Exposition officially marked the end of the old and the beginning of the new Oregon."[51]

A few months after the close of the exposition, the *Oregonian* published a lengthy series of letters to the local chamber of commerce, applauding the effort to put on the fair and praising Portland's scenic splendors and the potential of the Oregon country. The most commonly reflected sentiment in that correspondence focused on Portland's industrial and commercial prowess, the abundant resources of its tributary areas, and the benefits that railroad building would bring to the city. All writers predicted future greatness for the city and the region: Portland held promise to be the New York of the Pacific Coast; with its wealth of resources, it offered greater opportunities than any other section of the United States; and, as Nathan Weill of the Pennsylvania Railroad put it, visitors were particularly "impressed with the cooperation in that section between man and nature."[52]

A businessman from San Francisco applauded the "many attractions" the region offered to farmers, miners, lumbermen, stockmen, and especially to capitalists who would find "unlimited opportunities for profitable investment in every direction." The general agent for the Northern Pacific Railroad reiterated a theme common to many of the letters, predicting that Portland's future was assured because it was "surrounded on all sides by that which makes and supports large cities." Its agricultural and horticultural resources, its lumber manufacturing, and its deep-water outlet to the Pacific were "advantages given to few cities in the world." But it was W. F. Holton, an otherwise obscure passenger agent from Indiana, who offered the finest of rhetorical embellishments. As the "natural market and shipping center for an empire," Portland was the "jeweled crown" of a magnificent region:

Ah, that we were all Oregonians, loving, hospitable, with an open-heartedness that envelopes the stranger like a great coat. I am positive, from all that I have heard, that Saint Peter, who greets us with a smile and a handshake as we knock at the golden gate, is surely an Oregonian.[53]

In the midst of the rhetoric associated with the Lewis and Clark Exposition, the Portland business community continued to push for the extension of railroads to sections of the state that might ultimately benefit River City.

When San Francisco capitalists proposed extending the Southern Pacific line from Weed to the Klamath Basin, the *Oregonian* worried that such a connection would "drain away to California the rich and rapidly growing traffic of the Klamath country." Portland's commercial community was chagrined, the newspaper reported, that the Harriman railroad interests would persist in such an out-of-date "method of extracting wealth from a country." But even if Portland lost the Klamath and Lakeview districts to the big California markets, the *Oregonian* reflected that "a portion of Central Oregon . . . can be saved for Portland if action is not too long deferred." Several years later when the Southern Pacific announced that it would construct a railroad from Eugene to Coos Bay on the Oregon coast, the newspaper hinted that the route had the potential to open a vast timber belt and provide a way for Portland to seize a large portion of that trade as well, an exchange that otherwise might have been destined for San Francisco.[54]

To take full advantage of the region's natural abundance, therefore, mandated the continued expansion of the region's new industrial infrastructure; it also required labor and capital. The Portland commercial community continued a long-standing tradition when it issued repeated calls for investment capital to take profitable advantage of the region's "undeveloped" resources. Through the "magic of capital" the Oregon country would realize its full potential, expand its industrial capacity, and manufacture its own products from the natural bounty of forest and farm. As one business executive put it: "Capital . . . is our one great need—to us the need of needs." Chamber of Commerce publications coupled those pleas for capital with more conventional requests: deepening the Columbia River bar and building the much-discussed canal between The Dalles and Celilo Falls.[55] As the marketing and distributing point for a vast tributary area, business interests in Portland emphasized that those improvements to the region's transportation infrastructure would facilitate the movement, processing, and marketing of nature's productions.

Although the construction programs of railroad barons James J. Hill and Edward H. Harriman attracted a great deal of attention, those projects shared space with the equally ambitious efforts to turn the Columbia River into an industrial corridor. An open river to the sea, Portland lawyer Joseph

Nathan Teal told a Lewiston audience in October 1905, would better enable "the mighty river rolling past your doors . . . to bear the burdens of the commerce of an empire."[56] For Teal, the Portland business community, and upriver shippers, turning the Columbia River into an industrial corridor—through a series of canals and locks, and eventually slack-water lakes—remained a primary objective from the funding and building of The Dalles–Celilo Canal in 1915 to the construction of dams following the Second World War.

According to its promoters, removing obstructions and channelizing the river would allow freight traffic to pass along the "course of least resistance . . . by the water-level route, instead of over lofty mountain ranges." When the Seattle *Post-Intelligencer* claimed that the "natural logic of events" dictated that farmers in the interior should ship by "the direct route from the wheat belt, not by the roundabout way of the Columbia River," the *Oregonian* objected. Invoking the "natural logic" theme, the newspaper argued that wheat could be shipped or "rolled down the grade to Portland . . . cheaper than it can be lifted over the Cascade Mountains." The forces of nature, or gravity in this case, mandated that freight be moved "over the line of least resistance." Furthermore, the Great River, the "made for man . . . water-level route to the sea," would act "as a safety valve to prevent railroad rates rising above normal heights."[57]

Those early twentieth-century ambitions to physically alter the Columbia River were only one component of an array of industrial designs planned for the Oregon country. During the first decade of the twentieth century, railroad building still was considered the essential ingredient to industrial and commercial growth. Railway development in the next decade, Portland physician Stephen Wise argued, would provide the "foundations of industrial quickening." Another Portlander remarked that railroads had the potential to link together "a city surrounded by a tremendous territory, rich in everything that nature provides." The Northwest could realize its vast natural promise, according to Portland Chamber of Commerce manager Tom Richardson, only when it was "gridironed railroads."[58]

During the first years of the new century, rail projects abounded everywhere. Boosters claimed that the proposed lines would "penetrate . . . into undeveloped field and forest" and open opportunities for people from crowded eastern cities, older farming districts, and depleted forest regions. Hitherto untapped by the railroad, that "new country" had existed in "almost perfect isolation" and would be effectively "bottled-up" until it was linked "to civilization and the markets of the world." But progress was being made, according to the Portland Chamber: the Great Southern Railroad had completed thirty miles of road from The Dalles to Dufur, "at the portals of empire"; the Oregon Railway and Navigation Company had built a line into the Wallowa Valley from Elgin; work was underway to open a route from Portland to Tillamook on the Oregon coast; and in a more imposing achievement, the Chicago, Milwaukee, and St. Paul Railway was working its way through the Bitterroot Mountains on its proposed link to Puget Sound.[59]

For its part, the *Oregonian* pointed out that railroads were the key to industrial growth and progress. It called for the construction of roads to hinterland areas to access "the marvelously rich resources of the country, which for untold ages have been awaiting transportation." Upon the railroad, it contended, "depends . . . the progress of every other industry." Creating a modern transportation infrastructure was "the one great energy necessary to all the rest. . . . Great possibilities of wealth are there; but the railroad must go and make it."

In addition to the new railroad lines' potential for creating wealth and their ability to bring the products of nature to Portland, they also were capable of redeeming the countryside. The *Oregonian* cited the case of the recently completed Columbia and Southern Railroad into Sherman County, which had "transformed an isolated and nonproductive region into a wonderfully rich country." The newspaper urged those who controlled Oregon's railroad destinies to "relieve other equally rich portions of the state from the bondage in which they are now held." More trunk lines through the arid regions, *Pacific Monthly* added, would bring settlement, the development of water power, and "work marvelous transformations in the far west."[60]

Newspapers and chambers of commerce in the Portland area and beyond continued to praise railroad development, especially as the James J. Hill and Edward H. Harriman interests girded for control of transportation along the Columbia River and the winding corridor up the Deschutes gorge. The prospect of central Oregon's industrial development unleashed rhetorical excesses that linked the "natural" industry of sawmilling with the rich ponderosa pine belt that stretched from the greater Bend area southward to the Klamath Basin. Private timber speculators blocked up thousands of forested acres in the early 1900s, ownerships that became infinitely more valuable when it became known that the area would soon have a railroad.[61]

From the vantage point of the Portland business community, a railroad from the Columbia River through the upper Deschutes country to Klamath Falls would bring an increased volume of trade to Oregon's preeminent city. Portland boosters expressed a sense of injury when the Southern Pacific completed a road from Weed in northern California to Klamath Falls in 1909, and many believed the Deschutes line would rectify that loss and keep some of central Oregon's wealth at home. To the magazine *Pacific Monthly,* the proposed route would "open up that railroadless central area of the State," the largest region in the nation without a railroad. When it appeared at first that only the Harriman consortium would build a road from the Columbia River to Klamath Falls, the *Oregonian* remarked that the move would " 'nail down' a large portion of the unoccupied Oregon territory for the Harriman interests."[62]

Allusions to "unoccupied" districts, "untapped" wealth, and "opening up" the country were common rhetorical ploys of the nineteenth century that lasted at least through the first two decades of the twentieth century. Those expressions were pervasive in the literature describing the central Oregon region after 1905. In the midst of the Hill-Harriman struggle to control traffic through the Deschutes corridor, *Pacific Monthly* boasted about the benefits to be derived from "this wonderful power and irrigation stream" once the railroad breached the canyons into the upper country. The journal foresaw "big irrigation projects," the appearance of new towns, an expansion in the acreage planted to wheat, and the region's "vast timber and mineral wealth . . . tapped for the first time."[63]

Instrumentalist rhetoric also filled the pages of Portland's commercial press. "Portland may well be pleased," Charles H. Carey wrote for *The Chamber of Commerce Bulletin,* "to see the interior of the state opened to settlement." Hay, grain, fruits, and products from the garden, he predicted, "will naturally go to the metropolis." The development of central Oregon, in Carey's view, would fix "another great agricultural district as extensive as the Willamette Valley in Portland's *hinterland*." Writing in the same issue of the *Bulletin*, Thomas Neuhausen noted that the trains soon to be in operation between the Willamette metropolis and Bend would be hauling lumber products down the grade of the Deschutes to the Columbia River and then on to Portland.[64]

As the Hill railroad crept toward the middle Deschutes country (after forging a jurisdictional truce with the Harriman interests), rumors abounded about federal reclamation projects and the development of irrigation districts, extending dry farming into the semiarid country southeast of Bend, and large timber purchases by syndicates like the Weyerhaeuser group. The "opening" of central Oregon was important to the Portland banking community, because it would "add greatly to the state's wealth." And the Portland Chamber of Commerce joined the chorus extolling the area's natural wealth when it published a series of essays on central Oregon. Here were "wealth-making possibilities" in timber, wheat growing, irrigated acreages, water power, and range lands, resources sufficient to make the interior country prosperous. Moreover, the prospects were bright that its productions would find their way to Portland.[65]

But the Portland *Oregonian* surpassed all others in superlatives about the events unfolding in the Deschutes region. In an extended series of articles in its inaugural issue for 1910, the newspaper declared that the James J. Hill and Edward H. Harriman interests "had begun a race for an awakened empire." Rail lines into the middle and upper Deschutes region would release a "land long dormant," an area possessing untouched mineral riches, incomparable stands of ponderosa pine, and a stream with a waterpower potential four times that of Niagara Falls. Because it lacked a railroad, the interior region was largely a vast undeveloped sagebrush range given over to grazing, swarms of jackrabbits, and where over the front of "nearly every barn in the settled districts is spread the drying skin of the coyote." When the railroad performed its magic on the country, the *Oregonian* predicted, the Deschutes "will become Portland territory," and its riches would follow the "downhill pull" to Oregon's metropolitan center "and contribute to the further growth and prosperity of this city."[66]

Boosters and promoters were especially active after the turn of the century, praising the Oregon country as a vast storehouse abundant with fruits, bulbs, fish, birds, and game animals. If Oregon deserved the title "storehouse" during the Indian period, *Pacific Monthly* remarked, the state was "no less deserving of the term today," because few areas had such variety in natural resources. The magazine advised, however, that Oregon wanted no loafers. But if people were willing to use intelligence and industry and cooperate with nature, they would be abundantly rewarded for their labor.[67] And if nature's abundance were proof, the timbered regions of Oregon offered greater potential rewards for hard work than any other section of the country.

Industrializing the Woodlands

The Southern Pacific railroad extends from one end of the State to the other in Western Oregon, and logging roads with up-to-date equipment are being built from it into the valuable forests of the western portion of the State. It is the beginning of development and fortunes will be made by those wise enough to see their opportunities. — *The Pacific Monthly (January 1904)*[1]

T he immense trees growing to the water's edge, some of them 500 years of age and 300 or more feet in height, impressed the earliest Europeans who traveled along America's northwest coast. John Ledyard of the British Royal Marines, a member of Captain James Cook's voyage into North Pacific waters in 1778, reported that the crew outfitted the ship with a new mizzenmast and other spars from the excellent timber growing along the shores of Nootka Sound on Vancouver Island. British sea captain George Vancouver, who sailed north from the mouth of the Columbia River in 1792, described the coastal forests in terms of a "luxuriant landscape":

The country now before us . . . had the appearance of a continued forest extending as far north as the eye could reach, which made me very solicitous to find a port in the vicinity of a country presenting so delightful a prospect of fertility.

When one of the topsail yards on his vessel, the *Discovery*, proved defective, Vancouver wrote in his log that it was their good fortune to notice the defect in a land where wood materials were abundant, "having only to make our choice from amongst thousands of the finest spars in the world." [2]

While the land-based newcomers who followed shared similar perceptions about the abundance and *potential* of the coastal rain forest, their earliest descriptions were more ambivalent and grudging. The journals of the overland explorers and fur traders suggests both frustration with the tangled density of the region's vegetation and humility toward the immensity of the elemental forces of nature. Meriwether Lewis, who reached the lower Columbia River estuary more than a decade after Vancouver's voyage, was ecstatic about a fir tree forty-two feet in circumference with 200 feet of clear timber to the lowest branch. The journals of Lewis and his second-in-command, William Clark, include several references to pine trees (actually Douglas fir) and spruce in the area around present-day Astoria. And despite the obstacles the dense underbrush posed for the travelers, the captains were impressed with immensity of the surrounding forest. On one occasion, after struggling through "intolerable thickets" and fallen timber to ascend a small mountain to gain a better visual vantage, Clark reported: "The Timber on those hills are of the pine Species large and tall maney of them more than 200 feet high & from 8 to 10 feet through at the Stump." [3]

A few years later the trader Alexander Ross, of John Jacob Astor's American Fur Company, confided to his journal that the party had difficulty falling trees near the mouth of the Columbia. After many days work with the ax, a tree would finally give way:

but it seldom came to the ground. So thick was the forest, and so close the trees together, that in its fall it would often rest its ponderous top on some other friendly tree; sometimes a number of them would hang together, keeping us in awful suspense, and giving us double labour to extricate the one from the other, and when we had so far suceeded, the removal of the monster stump was the work of days.

In two months of labor, according to Ross, the group had cleared less than one acre: "In the mean time three of our men were killed by natives, two were wounded by falling trees, and one had his hand blown off by gunpowder." [4]

David Douglas, the Scot who identified the species that bears his name, measured the dimensions of a tree in the vicinity of Fort Astoria in the

"Oregon's Easter Hat," cartoon by Harry Murphy in the *Oregonian*, 1909

Ponderosa forest, Central Oregon. *Deschutes County Historical Society*

Facing page: (Top) One season's "take," twenty miles east of Cottage
Grove. (Bottom) Hydraulic mining. *Gerald Williams Collection*

Celilo Falls, Columbia River. *Gerald Williams Collection*

Facing page: (Top) "A money-making proposition": sheep, Eastern Oregon. (Bottom) "Fish stories I have told": Columbia River sturgeon. *Gerald Williams Collection*

Steam donkey. *Gerald Williams Collection*

Facing page: (Top) Fish wheel, Columbia River. (Bottom) Cascade Locks,
Columbia River, completed in 1895. *Gerald Williams Collection*

Shevlin-Hixon Mill, Bend, Oregon. *Deschutes County Historical Society*

Facing page: (Top) Logging train, old "Two Spot," near Detroit, Oregon.
(Bottom) Forest fire burning through cutover slash.
Gerald Williams Collection

Owyhee Dam (early 1930s). *Gerald Williams Collection*

Facing page: (Top) Deschutes River filled with logs. (Bottom) Stauffer
homestead, Central Oregon. *Deschutes County Historical Society*

Diversion canal, Owyhee Dam, near Nyssa, Oregon (circa early 1930s).
Gerald Williams Collection

Facing page: (Top) Aerial view of Bonneville dam area and Columbia
River Highway (late 1930s). (Bottom) Klamath Irrigation Project, near
Tule Lake, California. *Gerald Williams Collection*

15-438   Aerial View of Bonnev___ ___ Area - Columbia River Highway

Near Tulelake, California.   EASTMAN'S STUDIO B-1605

Willamette Valley Project, Detroit Dam (late 1940s).
Gerald Williams Collection

"Deer season opens." *Gerald Williams Collection*

Photo courtesy of Sandy Brooke

mid-1820s with a circumference of forty-eight feet, one yardstick measure above the ground. Douglas reported that the tree had been "burned down to give way to a more useful vegetable, namely potatoes." The United States Exploring Expedition under the command of Lt. Charles Wilkes sailed into the Strait of Juan de Fuca in 1841 through stupendous evergreen forests. Finally anchored in the southern end of Puget Sound, one crew member recorded that "forrist trees of the largest size grow to the Very Waters Edge where you may cut a mast . . . for a Line of Battle Ship." The missionary John Frost crafted a vivid sketch of dense forest undergrowth when he traveled from the Clatsop Plains through the coastal mountains to the Willamette Valley. Laboring for a full day to gain a mere four or five miles through the dense brush, fallen trees, and numerous ravines, Frost reported that on one occasion, the small party ascended a stream and had to cut their way "through the thicket which skirted the creek on either side."[5] In a letter to the secretary of the interior, Indian superintendent J. Ross Browne complained about the thick forest undergrowth that proved as "impregnable" as "the great Chinese Wall."[6]

In addition to his detailed observations about early agricultural efforts in the Umpqua Valley, Jesse Applegate provided an equally impressive description of the area's densely wooded forests of fir, pine, and cedar, a setting that would "perhaps forever defy the art of many to bring them into a state of cultivation." Calvin West, who arrived in nearby Scottsburg a few years later, thought the area "an uninviting place" of "thick forest and close canyon with a few rods only of valey."[7] A newcomer to the Willamette Valley complained of "to much timbered country," and an early visitor to Coos Bay on Oregon's southern coast remarked that the hillsides away from water's edge abounded with the timber of the finest quality in Oregon. Another witness took notice of the "abundance of white cedar timber, well calculated for lumber," the extensive forests in the region promising to make "Koose Bay . . . a place of great importance."[8]

This is not to argue that the Douglas fir country was a blanket of dense forest from northern California to southern British Columbia. As numerous studies indicate, a series of great fires periodically burned over broad areas of the coastal region in Oregon and Washington during the historic period. William Morris's pioneering study of 1934 provides specific references about the year and approximate location of the more notable burns that have occurred since the 1840s. The first of those widespread conflagrations to appear in the historical records was an 1849 fire that burned the area from the southern reaches of the Siletz drainage to the Siuslaw River. There were no additional extensive burns until newspapers reported several fires raging in southwestern Oregon in 1867. The following year, one of the driest summer seasons on record, witnessed smoke and fire everywhere from Oregon northward to British Columbia. Several locations in western Oregon still show the effects of the fires of 1868. Finally, the fire season of 1902 proved to be the most destructive in terms of lives and property lost in western Oregon and western Washington.[9]

The several federal land surveys carried out during the 1850s provide at best a mixed estimate of the extent of forested land in western Oregon; indeed, some of the surveys appear to have been based on supposition rather than detailed field reconnaissance. The celebrated railroad survey of western Oregon carried out in the mid-1850s inaccurately described the area from Port Orford to the Columbia River as "everywhere covered with a dense forest."[10] Although the report's general characterizations of the Willamette, Umpqua, and Rogue valleys are consistent with other contemporary accounts, the railroad reconnaissance party very likely made assumptions about the mountainous regions (except for the specific areas actually traversed), rather than careful observations. The more detailed General Land Office survey notes for the same period reveal brush and oak openings scattered throughout the Coast Range, but with extended, densely forested areas as well.[11] A more realistic and accurate portrayal of the mountainous areas may have to wait the completion of numerous computer-generated Geographical Information Systems (GIS) mapping projects.

The first commercial inroads into Oregon's extensive coastal and riverine forest areas did not appear until sometime after the 1850s. And for most people of that time and place, the abundant timber stands seemed endless, blanketing much of the North Pacific slope. Moreover, it was widely believed that the trees grew so rapidly that the resource would quickly be renewed. That perception was especially apparent to midcentury loggers working at the fringes of the forests near estuaries and rivers and in the extensive waterways around Puget Sound. Distant forces were at work, however, that would soon see the forest begin to recede from water's edge. The West Coast lumber market, especially the big wholesale yards around San Francisco Bay, consumed a huge amount of timber. San Francisco capitalists were also active in establishing mills in the rich timber region adjacent to Puget Sound, Willapa Bay, the lower Columbia River, and Coos Bay.[12]

But those early commercial years of the industry, powered by human and animal energy, did not appreciably diminish the individual's relative sense of powerlessness in the forest environment. The technology was elemental, slow, and laborious. Logging with ax and crosscut saw, with human muscle and bull teams, required nearly superhuman effort, and few in that time and place questioned the essential rightness of it. Those who struggled daily through the tangled and dense undergrowth remained in awe of the majestic trees. With abundance all around them, they took only the best timber, leaving numerous culls that served as cover for animal life and inadvertently providing seed stock for regeneration. Although the accumulated debris left on the ground increased the potential for fires, Richard White argues that bull-team logging did not necessarily lead to serious deterioration of the forest environment. With only a limited disruption of local forest ecosystems, therefore, the degree of regeneration remained very high.[13]

Although Puget Sound, Grays Harbor, and lower Columbia River mills dwarfed the volume of lumber shipped over the Coos Bay bar, the southern Oregon coastal region provides a glimpse into the technical ability to move logs to waterways and to mill the huge timbers into lumber. The incipient industry originated with Daniel Giles and a partner who began operating a two-man whip-saw mill on Coos Bay in 1853. At about the same time, George Wasson built a water-powered Muley sash saw on the Coquille River a short distance to the south. Using oxen to haul logs to water's edge, the productive capacity of those water- and human-powered operations was sufficient to satisfy only the local market. But those crude enterprises became obsolete when Henry Heaton Luse and Asa Mead Simpson opened steam-powered mills in the late 1850s, establishing a pattern of trade geared to California markets that lasted for more than a century. Simpson's sawmills and shipbuilding yards, extending from Santa Cruz to Puget Sound, turned the abundant forests of the coastal region into extractive tributaries of the California construction industry.[14]

The number of loggers passing through the communities on Coos Bay testified to the activity taking place in the immense forests that lined its extensive waterways. The Coos Bay *News* reported in 1874 that there were about twenty-five logging camps in the region, with crews of eight to twelve workers each. In that same year, a California-based firm, E. B. Dean and Company, purchased a small mill in the town of Marshfield and promptly built a new steam-powered facility with a daily capacity of 50,000 board feet. Nine logging camps served the Dean operation, by far the largest producer on the bay. The combined daily capacity of Coos Bay mills at the onset of the 1880s was 100,000 feet, mostly rough-cut timbers that were shipped in the cargo trade to San Francisco finishing mills. A writer for the Portland *Oregonian* grumbled in 1884 that Coos Bay should properly be considered "a part of California" because its industries were "made and directed in San Francisco."[15]

With its extensive forests of Douglas fir, spruce, cedar, and pine, the Pacific Northwest was part of a larger continental landscape that was increasingly subject to industrial forces with the passage of time. As the once magnificent white pine forests of the Great Lakes states diminished in size and volume in the late nineteenth century, lumber capitalists who had accumulated considerable savings serving the Chicago and Midwestern economy began to look to the Gulf Plain forests of the south and then west to the fir and cedar country along the North Pacific slope. The *Oregonian* reported in 1882 "that the lumber supply of the Lakes States . . . can hold out only a few years longer," and because southern trees were inferior, lumbermen would turn to the Pacific Northwest, the "last great supply of first-rate timber." Two years later the Portland *Telegram* observed that timber supplies in the states of Michigan, Wisconsin, and Minnesota were nearly exhausted. Moreover, where lumbermen had cut only the best pine in the past and left the remainder to fire, now they were taking everything. In a commentary on the rate of cutting "and the unwarrantable waste" in the Northwest, the *Telegram* wondered "how long will it be before we shall be making a similar report?"[16]

In their concern about diminishing timber supplies elsewhere, the regional press reflected the arguments of a growing number of studies indicating that forest cover and timber stands in the United States were rapidly disappearing. In his 1864 classic, *Man and Nature*, George Perkins Marsh influenced a generation of scientific thinking about the relationship between forest depletion and flooding. At the same time, a Department of Agriculture employee, Frederick Starr, predicted that the nation would face a timber famine in thirty years. Still other natural scientists examined the association between soil erosion and the siltation of streams and declining salmon runs in New England rivers.[17] To many people in the scientific community, mounting evidence indicated that industrial influences were disrupting forest and stream environments alike.

The most significant of those early inquiries was the work of Franklin B. Hough, a New York physician with broad intellectual interests in scientific discourse. When he assisted the Bureau of the Census in gathering data for its 1870 report, Hough noticed a dramatic decline in the volume of lumber produced in the northeastern states. He expressed concern about what he believed to be the finite nature of the nation's woodlands in his famous 1873 address, "On the Duty of Governments in the Preservation of Forests," to the American Association for the Advancement of Science. The essay urged state regulation of forest practices, the establishment of forestry schools, and congressional action to oversee forest protection. The Secretary of Agriculture appointed Hough the federal government's first forestry agent in 1876 and subsequently chief of the Division of Forestry in 1881.[18]

The first national forest survey to include some reference to the Pacific Northwest was Charles Sprague Sargent's monumental *Report on the Forests of North America*, published in 1884. A member of several leading scientific societies and a participant in early forestry conferences, Sargent gave special attention to the diminishing stands of white pine in the Great Lakes states. In his discussions about forest conditions in western Oregon and western Washington, he singled out Douglas fir as the most important commercial species and made passing reference to the less extensive but equally valuable stands of spruce and red and Port Orford cedar. For the forested areas east of the Cascade Mountains, however, Sargent was less informed. According to the report, most timber in the great western pine belt was confined to the higher elevations and the stands were "open, scattered, and generally composed of comparatively small trees."[19] Even a casual review of the published surveys available in the early 1880s shows that Sargent was simply wrong in describing the pine forests east of the mountains.

In the ensuing years, the regional press continued to print summaries about federal studies of cutover lands in the eastern United States. Except for the more extreme booster publications, most journals were ambivalent about the lumber industry's apparent migratory character. Although newspapers and magazines occasionally warned about repeating old patterns of profligacy and waste, more often they praised the region's natural advantages as the repository of the last remaining "virtually untouched" timber on the continent. The *Oregonian* worried in 1880 that the Northwest might repeat the experiences of the state of Maine where timber "was thought to be inexhaustible" fifty years earlier. Now, the newspaper reported, "the old 'pine tree state'" was little more than "a figure of speech." Farther west there were also indications that large sections of Michigan and Wisconsin also were "being rapidly denuded of timber."[20]

For most citizens of western Oregon, the *Oregonian* argued, the problem was the abundance of timber and the tendency of people to want "to destroy it rather than save it." In a somber note on "future prospects," the newspaper concluded that forests were like other resources—potentially exhaustible—even though they grew back quickly:

Like all others, we shall not begin to husband our resources till our resources diminish to an extent that will cause inconveniences. We shall continue to deal with our timber as with our fish—drawing recklessly on both our forests and our streams, and not thinking of the reckless waste till it is too late to repair it.

But the enormous consumption of lumber in the eastern and midwestern United States and the huge harvests in Michigan, Wisconsin, and Minnesota suggested advantages for heavily timbered states like Oregon. Because Northwestern forests held "the most considerable source of supply remaining on the continent," the *Oregonian* predicted that the lumber industry would surpass both the fisheries and wheat trade. The use of the region's forest wealth was legitimate, the newspaper suggested on another occasion, "it is only its waste that is to be deplored." Hence, it would be wise for citizens to protect and preserve their timberlands for future markets.[21]

At the onset of the steam era *West Shore* boasted that the forests of the Douglas fir district were "practically unlimited and inexhaustible." With the end of the great pine forests of the Great Lake states in sight, the journal noted that "the Pacific coast [had] an inexhaustible fund upon which to draw." In subsequent issues *West Shore* writers argued that the region's difficult physical character was no hindrance to progress: "No country, considering its rugged aspect, is more easily subjugated." And in the midst of those advances in technology and production, the *Oregonian* continued to push publicity about the region's forested abundance, "more extensive and more valuable than those of any other state."[22] Widely read newspapers and magazines such as the *Oregonian* and *West Shore* unquestionably helped fuel the rampant speculation in Northwest timberland that took place between 1890 and the first years of the twentieth century.

Technological developments soon proved that speculative activity fortuitous when loggers introduced a revolutionary productive force, steam power, to woods operations. Once again, the influences of a distant industrializing world — an expanding market demand for lumber and the increased mechanization of production processes — spurred the adaptation of the machine to woods operations. Although steam-powered sawmills had been in use along the Northwest coast since the 1850s, operators did not begin adapting steam-driven machines to hauling in felled timber until the 1880s. As early as 1884, only four years after California redwoods logger John Dolbeer patented the first steam-powered yarding machine, *West Shore* observed that industrial technology was supplanting human and animal power in Pacific coastal forests. Under the heading, "Our Industries and Resources," the magazine reported that railroads and steam engines were replacing skid roads and bull teams in some logging operations. The new machines, one logger reported, were capable of hauling "logs from three to four . . . miles to river or bay, at no greater cost than ox teams have done it one or two miles."[23]

The increasing use of the steam "donkey" to yard and load logs vastly stepped up both the pace of activity in the woods — and disturbance to the ecology of coastal forests. The changeover from animal to steam power was incremental, with steam emerging by the early the twentieth century as the predominant technology for moving logs. Loggers in Washington, where the heaviest cutting was taking place, were using three steam donkeys for every one used in Oregon and California.[24] Speed and productivity were part of that new industrial environment, and adapting steam power to the logging end of the production system cut the technological gap between logging and milling operations. Stewart Holbrook reflected in his classic study, *Holy Old Mackinaw,* that the revolution in West Coast logging technology originated with the introduction "of small donkey engines and wire cable." The slow-moving oxen, he noted, "could not compete with the speedy yarding of logs by steam." George Emerson, a Grays Harbor lumberman and the first to use steam donkeys north of the Columbia River, was enthusiastic about their performance:

When one considers [that] . . . they require no stable and no feed, that all expense stops when the whistle blows, no oxen killed and no teams to winter, no ground too wet, no hill too steep, it is easy to see they are a revolution in logging.

With "no ground too wet, no hill too steep," the donkey engines began what Richard White has called "The Creation of a New Forest."[25]

When the powerful donkey engines replaced bull teams, loggers were able to work through the rainy winter months, thereby providing a steady supply of logs to the mills. Operating in terrain where oxen sank to their knees in mud, the "bull donkeys" pulled logs clear of the soggy ground, stumps, underbrush, and other obstructions. From the perspective of a century later, we can say that the steam donkey offered mixed blessings for the future: it greatly increased log production *and* it dramatically expanded cultural influences in the forests of the Pacific Northwest. But at the time, the technological prowess of the new steam-powered machines gave further conviction and assurance to capitalists who had been nurtured with propaganda about the region's abundance.

The proliferation of donkey engines enabled loggers to gain access to particular species and to increase the kind and volume of timber harvested. And if the laborious bull-team methods were relatively benign to the forest environment, donkey logging was quite the opposite. Set up along estuaries, rivers, or railroad tracks, the increasingly powerful engines hauled logs from up to a mile away. When operators added an aerial twist—the high lead—early in the twentieth century, they were able to haul logs to landings with one end suspended in the air, a technique that greatly increased both the volume of timber that could be moved and the incidence of injury and death to workers. "At the end of a steam logging operation," writes Richard White, "the ground would be gouged into a collection of hummocks and hollows covered with a tangled mass of rotten wood, branches, small timber, broken trees, stumps, and tops." In the process, donkey logging destroyed young trees and species of less market value and left in its wake a huge volume of waste that increased the chances of fire. And when the slash burned, as it often did, the fires were much hotter and more destructive than those that burned through standing timber where understory foliage and rotting debris on the forest floor provided most of the fuel.[26]

But the productive and highly efficient yarding machines represented only one segment in the industrial movement of logs to lumber manufacturing centers. As the most visible symbol of industrial activity in the western United States, the railroad had an even greater and more dramatic influence in altering the forested landscapes. Railroads provided access to timberlands a considerable distance removed from waterways, thereby linking abundant sources of raw materials with sawmilling settlements; they liberated the transportation of logs from the restrictions of natural geography, enabling operators to build roads into hitherto inaccessible terrain. As instruments of industrial production, therefore, rail lines freed loggers from topographical and seasonal constraints. In that sense, logging railroads partly replaced waterways as transportation arterials and vastly extended the industrial presence in the forest environment. "The railroad," historian William Cronon remarked in an understatement, "left almost nothing unchanged: that was its magic."[27]

When industrial logging first made its appearance in the Oregon country, the heaviest cutting was taking place in Washington, around Puget Sound and in the vicinity of Grays Harbor, places where timber grew to the water line. For logging operators who wanted to take advantage of the insatiable appetite of the increasingly more productive sawmills, it became apparent well before the turn of the century that logging railroads were the answer. "Nature and markets," historian Robert Ficken observes, "combined to create a demand for another new technological device, the logging railroad." Two company managers who built a rail line from Shelton on Puget Sound into the Grays Harbor district agreed that railroads had become indispensable to successful mill operations by the mid-1880s.[28]

Trullinger's, one of the many logging camps on the lower Columbia River during the late 1880s, employed a blend of old and new technologies as access to timber and terrain dictated. Located on the Walluska River, a tributary to Young's Bay about seven miles by land from Astoria, the J. C. Trullinger camp used both oxen and a standard-gauge, temporary railroad to haul logs from the immense stands of timber along the Walluska waterway to the company's mill at Astoria. A writer for the *Oregonian* visited the camp in the summer of 1887 and reported that loggers were working in a "maze of timber so dense and tangled" that it made negotiating travel by horseback difficult: "From the midst of this maze, made up of small firs, scattered cedars, hemlock, bushes of many kinds, and a tangle of vines, the giant firs were standing, from twenty to sixty per acre." Several of the standing trees in the vicinity, according to the superintendent in charge, measured from seven to nine feet in circumference.[29]

Once loggers felled and bucked the trees, oxen then "snaked" the logs a short distance downhill to a platform of skids where the crew rolled the huge timbers onto a railroad car. Despite the extensive waterways on the lower Columbia, the Portland journalist was convinced that railroads were critical to the future of logging: "By their use distance is practically annihilated, and timber fields back from water are made scarcely less valuable than those which lie along creek or river bottoms." As for the Trullinger railroad, when the forest in "the immediate district through which it runs is exhausted it will be an easy matter to take up the rails and put them down in another place." The writer also pointed out that although oxen could profitably haul logs up to a mile or more from water, loggers were finding it cheaper "to build . . . short roads than to employ cattle."[30] Because of the easy access to timber and its proximity to oceanic markets, logging practices in the greater Astoria area were probably typical of large producers

Northwest Oregon. *University of Wisconsin Cartographic Lab*

further upriver and in cargo export centers like Coos Bay. It is obvious that the new steam technology enhanced the commodity value attached to trees.

After a tour through the most productive logging districts in 1905, Richard Kennedy informed readers of the magazine *Pacific Monthly* that the largest and best-equipped operations were located on Puget Sound and the lower Columbia River. Donkey engines and short-line railroads, he pointed out, had completely changed the way logging was done. Although Columbia River logger Simon Benson was not the first to experiment with the new technology, Kennedy indicated that Benson was the first operator to make use of steam donkeys. After the donkey engines hauled logs to a "landing," Benson and others adopted a variety of techniques to move the huge timbers to milling sites. One method used on steep slopes involved the construction of extended chutes of parallel timbers down which logs hurtled to a waterborne landing. At one camp, Kennedy estimated that logs traveled seven-eighths of a mile in forty-five seconds: "The water displaced by the logs is thrown into the air in a column thirty to seventy-five feet high."[31] As relatively natural and inexpensive transportation arterials, waterways continued to be the most popular means to move logs. It was simply more profitable to "drive" logs on streams where they were convenient than to operate a railroad.

But in situations where difficult terrain dictated that logs had to be transported some distance over land, Kennedy remarked that the more productive operations used railroads. During his tour, he also noticed a new development in moving timber:

In recent years an aerial cable tramway has been successfully used in logging over deep canyons. A strong cable is stretched from the top of one hill to another. A block on this carries another cable, which it lowered into canyons to lift up the logs and carry them across.[32]

In the first decade of the new century, the technical development and elaboration of what eventually became known as the "high-lead system" were being worked out in several settings in the coastal forests of the Douglas-fir region. The *West Coast Lumberman* reported in 1903 that operators were using an aerial logging system near Montesano, adjacent to the busy Grays Harbor logging district. If it proved successful, the trade journal argued, the new technique of suspended cables would enable loggers to save labor and machinery and to work in otherwise inaccessible canyons. A writer for *Pacific Monthly* believed the system of aerial cables would "prove one of the most potent factors in introducing a new era in lumbering."[33]

Late-nineteenth-century commercial loggers on the Columbia River combined ingenuity with natural forces to maneuver timber to sawmills. In the mountainous country that became Columbia County south of Scappoose Bay, several small family logging operations began cutting timber along the tributaries to Milton Creek during the 1880s. Those modest undertakings used a system of skid roads and streams to move logs to mill sites. Herbert Howard, who owned a farm on a small tributary to Milton Creek, expanded his enterprise to include a sawmill that produced a small volume of rough-cut lumber; his crew used the small streams on the five square miles of Dart Creek to splash logs to the mill site. But Howard was only one of several families who used Milton Creek and its tributaries to run logs following heavy winter rains. As the main route for moving logs to market, Milton Creek served as a kind of natural commercial artery, joining the abundance of lower Columbia River forests with the industrial center around Scappoose Bay and oceanic markets beyond. One Milton Creek resident referred to the spectacular river drives as "harvest time for the logging crews." After the logs were "sluiced down" Milton Creek to the bay, crews sorted them by ownership brands, placed the timber in booms, and towed them to purchasing mills.[34]

When steam power entered Columbia County around the turn of the century, the more heavily capitalized operations began building logging railroads into the interior to gain access to the rich timber stands in the Nehalem Valley. Portland-based logging magnate Simon Benson was among the first to finance the construction of a railroad from Clatskanie toward the Nehalem Valley. One authority estimates that there were about thirty logging railroads in the Nehalem district in the early twentieth century, with each road averaging about four miles of track. Virtually all of the Nehalem logging camps were using steam donkeys to haul timber to railroad sidings. As the rail lines pressed further into the interior valleys, Benson and other large investors, including the Northern Pacific Railroad, were active in blocking up huge acreages of timberland for speculative purposes.[35]

The face of the Nehalem Valley landscape changed slowly at first as a trickle of white settlers began taking up bottomland claims during the 1860s. Clearing land for agricultural purposes, as one early valley farmer recalled, required long hours of hard work: "We have to burn down the trees here. Some of them are six and eight feet through; to burn them in two, bore with a auger, start the fire, and let them rip." According to a local historian, "Columbia County land had a lot of stumps." And despite what everyone recognized as a prodigious effort to clear land, the acreages of "improved" holdings listed in the Columbia County tax records actually diminished between 1890 and 1910. Although the number of farms more than doubled between 1890 and 1910, their average size dropped from more than 200 acres to less than 100 acres during the same period. Despite the establishment of several small orchards and a few dairy farms producing for the local market, the county's principal attraction remained its magnificent stands of timber.[36]

The building of logging railroads into Columbia County timberlands dramatically accelerated changes to the surrounding landscape. The construction of the railroad into Nehalem Valley opened up "twenty billion feet of standing timber," according to *Pacific Monthly;* continuing the line into Tillamook County would give loggers access to another 13 billion feet. As the figures in Table Nine indicate, the introduction of large-scale, industrial logging operations in Columbia County contributed to a sharp increase in population in the first decade of the twentieth century. Without question, as the twentieth century advanced, the county's chief business was increasingly vested in logging and lumbering. Egbert Oliver, who grew up in Columbia County, points to that new social and economic reckoning: "Up and down the county the plant whistle was the heartbeat of people."[37]

Although it was far removed from Oregon's most productive center of logging on the Columbia River, San Francisco capitalists continued to show interest in the timber-rich Coos Bay district when they funded the construction of a railroad from Coos Bay to Myrtle Point, a small town on the Coquille River. Completed in 1893, the twenty-seven-mile rail line funneled logs from some of the finest timber on the North Pacific slope to the sawmills on Coos Bay. But the big cargo mills on the bay—especially the Simpson Lumber Company, and after its opening in 1908, the C. A.

TABLE NINE

Population of Columbia County, 1860–1910

Year	Population
1860	532
1870	863
1880	2,042
1890	5,191
1900	6,237
1910	10,580

Smith Lumber Company—cut a prodigious amount of timber. The Coos Bay *Times* acknowledged that new reality with a 1913 headline: "Last of the Operations on Tidewater on Coos Bay Is in Sight." When the heavy cutting adjacent to the sloughs and estuaries around the bay began to take its toll, the C. A. Smith Company made plans to move deeper into its immense holdings in the Coquille River drainage. Here, too, the railroad was critical. The far-flung C. A. Smith operation constructed a railroad up the South Fork of the Coquille River to an old ranch that was subsequently turned into the company town of Powers.[38] For the next several decades the massive timber stands in the Coquille drainage provided much of the log supply for the C. A. Smith mills and their successors on Coos Bay. The railroad from Powers to Myrtle Point and then across the low divide into the Coos estuary was the principal link between the abundant forests on the Coquille and the manufacturing centers on the bay.

But the great Northwest rainforest was not the sole object of speculative interest to distant lumber capitalists. For several decades, sojourners along the Oregon Trail had recorded glowing descriptions of the pine forests in the Blue Mountains and in the upper Deschutes River drainage. "It is a sight for our eyes to behold the timber," S. B. Eakin confided to his diary shortly after crossing the Snake River in August 1866, "it is so long since we have seen any. These mountains are covered with a dense forest of timber,—

pine, and fir." Although Eakin was among the last to travel the Oregon Trail, his expression of relief at the sight of trees was typical of those who preceded him. After crossing the Snake River on the Oregon Trail in 1845, Joel Palmer wrote in his journal that he had observed "beautiful groves of yellow pine timber" along the mountain slopes. By the time he reached the crest of the Blue Mountains west of the Grand Ronde Valley, he concluded that the region might "strictly be termed a timber country." Eleven years earlier and from the vantage of the Grand Ronde Valley, the naturalist John Kirk Townsend penned a similar assessment: the mountains to the west and northwest were "densely covered with tall pine trees." George Wilkes, who passed through the Powder River Valley in the early 1840s, was awed by the scenery after an early season snowfall: "a beautiful valley surrounded on all sides by the overtopping ridges of the Blue Mountains, their huge bases clothed with immense forests of majestic pines, and their stupendous tops gleaming with everlasting snow." Departing from the Grand Ronde Valley four days later, Wilkes reported again that his party "passed . . . through large bodies of pine timber." [39]

Among those westbound travel observations, United States Army Capt. John Charles Fremont's descriptions of the Blue Mountains were the most detailed. According to Fremont, a great variety of "timber exhibits a luxuriance of growth unknown to the eastern part of the continent and to Europe" covered much of the mountainous region north and west of the Snake River. In the "well-timbered" mountains west of the Grand Ronde Valley Fremont identified "large and stately trees [most likely *Pinus ponderosa*] more than 200 feet in height and from three to seven feet in diameter." He also reported seeing a "white spruce" at twelve feet and a larch ten feet in circumference. [40]

The same great pine forests attracted the lumberman David Eccles to the Powder River Valley in the early 1890s and Brooks-Scanlon and Shevlin-Hixon to the upper Deschutes country twenty years later. When the expedition followed an old Indian trail from The Dalles to the Klamath Lake region in November and December 1834, Fremont wrote in his journal one of the earliest narrative descriptions of the eastern slope of the Cascade Mountains. At the point where references to trees once again appear in his journal, Fremont acknowledged that the country was "far more interesting . . . than the route along the Snake and Columbia rivers." As the expedition ascended the Deschutes drainage, the captain reported snowy mountain peaks looming to the party's right above "dark pine forests," serving as "grand beacons" to guide them southward.[41]

Just before the reconnaissance party reached the Metolius River, Fremont reported seeing pines in the bottomland, among them "an immense one, about twelve feet in diameter." Two days beyond the junction with the Metolius the trail "entered a beautiful pine forest through which we travelled for several hours." On the following day, December 5, Fremont recorded more of the same: "Today the country was all pine forest. . . . The timber was uniformly large; some of the pines measuring 22 feet in circumference, and 12 to 13 feet at six above." In the vicinity of the Little Deschutes River on December 7, the expedition encountered broad, open meadows, "rich soil and excellent water, surrounded by noble forests," a picture "sufficient to delight the eye of the farmer." And still more of the same the next day: "Our direction was a little east of south, the trail leading constantly through pine forests." Although the soil was barren, it was capable of "producing varieties of magnificent pines." And the day before the expedition reached Klamath Lake, Fremont wrote: "The trail leads *always* [author's emphasis] through splendid pine forests."[42]

The federal railroad surveys of the mid-1850s render even more detailed accounts of the extensive pine forests on the eastern slopes of the Cascade Mountains. Lt. Henry Abbott, who directed the section of the survey from Klamath Lake northward through the Deschutes drainage in the late summer of 1854, made frequent reference to hills "heavily timbered with pine" and areas of "open pine timber." On August 26 the Abbott party left the Deschutes and "followed the trail for about seven miles through a pine forest . . . . the country . . . [having] been recently burned over by the Indians." Elsewhere in the middle Deschutes region, Abbott referred to the surveyors emerging "from the forest" and the "thickly timbered foothills of the Cascade Range."[43]

The botanical section of the 1855 railroad surveys through the Washington Cascades (known as the "Stevens Report") portrays a forested landscape similar to that south of the Columbia River. The report's representation of the ponderosa-pine dominated area is especially pronounced, even poetic in temper:

There is [so] little underbrush in these forests that a wagon may be drawn through them without difficulty, forming a striking contrast to the dense thickets of the western slopes. . . . the level terraces, covered everywhere with good grass and shaded by fine symmetrical trees of great size, through whose open foliage the sun's rays penetrate with agreeable mildness, give to these forests the appearance of an immense ornamental park.

Near the base of Mount Adams the Stevens surveyors observed that "one pine almost exclusively prevails, (P. PONDEROSA, called 'Yellow Pine')." The tree normally grew to more than 100 feet high, "with a straight clear trunk three to five feet thick, branching at the height of about forty feet."[44]

What is most striking about those midcentury railroad survey narratives is their similarity to the turn-of-the-century forest reserve reports and the investigations of the United States Geological Survey (USGS). With the exception of newly introduced grazing ungulates to the forests—sheep and cattle—and the continued influence of natural and human-caused fire, the descriptions of the ponderosa-dominated forests are much the same. Except for the Oregon Lumber Company's operation in the Powder River country, market and industrial influences in the interior forests were still relatively limited. That was especially true of the most impressive and spectacular of those forests, the immense ponderosa pine belt that extended from the middle Deschutes region to the Klamath Basin.

As the twentieth century dawned, the extensive "yellow pine" region attracted the attention of United States government officials and private speculators alike. The federal interest in Cascade Mountain forests originated in a rider attached to an agricultural appropriations bill in 1891. That seemingly insignificant clause authorized the president to set aside designated sections of the public domain in reservations of various kinds, including lands valuable for timber. President Grover Cleveland's creation of the Cascade Forest Reserve in 1893 and his subsequent additions to Oregon's forest reserve system just before he left office in 1897 reflected the influence of that powerful new authorization.[45] The president's action also kindled a series of federal investigations and surveys to determine forest conditions, and it triggered parallel inquiries into the influence of graziers in the reserves. Those extended investigations of Oregon's Cascade Forest Reserve reveal a great deal of information about the composition and species characteristics of the forests.

H. D. Langille, who headed one of the turn-of-the-century USGS investigations of forest conditions in the central Cascades, compiled one of the better descriptions of the great ponderosa district. On the lower slopes of the mountains, the surveyors observed forests "of pure growth . . . [which] are generally open, without much litter or undergrowth, and for those reasons are almost immune from fire." In the yellow pine country, the report continued, "the forest floor is often as clean as if it had been cleared, and one may ride or even drive without hindrance. As the hills are approached the brush increases." The Langille team estimated that in the "yellow-pine region bordering the timberless area of eastern Oregon," 10 percent of the timbered area had burned recently, and 90 percent of the forest "at some remote period." [46]

Another turn-of-the-century survey, John B. Leiberg's inquiry into forest conditions in the southern Cascades, provides additional evidence of the importance of fire in shaping ponderosa-dominated landscapes. Leiberg described a forest composed of trees that varied greatly in age, a clear indication of "their origin as reforestations after fires." The Leiberg surveyors reasoned that during the period of "Indian occupancy [fires] were not of such frequent occurrence nor of such magnitude as they have been since the advent of the white man." During the early days of white settlement, the report continued, fires were "more numerous and devastated much larger areas." But in those extensive places where ponderosa pine were dominant, frequent fires suppressed undergrowth and seedling trees. Leiberg concluded with what has become the standard scientific judgment on the maintenance of healthy ponderosa forests:

The yellow pine is by all odds the best fire-resisting tree in the sylva of the North Pacific slope [author's emphasis]. Repeated conflagrations may run through stands of the yellow-pine type without serious damage to the older trees of this species, provided the litter and humus be not too great. On the eastern side of the Cascades, especially, fires have run through the yellow-pine timber many times. The absence or relative scarcity of young growth and underbrush is here very noticeable and striking.[47]

At the time the USGS conducted its surveys of the Cascade Range forest reserves, there were only a few sawmills scattered through the ponderosa region, all of them cutting lumber for local consumption. Leiberg estimated in 1900 that of the 1,450,420 acres of "yellow-pine type," only 33,700 acres had been logged. Small production mills selling mostly to local settlers and ranchers operated in the Klamath Basin, in the vicinity of the future town of Bend. Two or three mills were located further down the Deschutes drainage, including one on the Warm Springs Agency that sawed timber "when needed." But for the ponderosa district there were rumors of change in the air, circumstances that forest inspector H. D. Langille acknowledged in his 1904 report on the northern section of the Cascade Reserve. The area to the east of the reserve, he remarked, was "rapidly being settled up," irrigation projects were bringing "water to the thirsty plains," and railroad surveyors were traversing the countryside. "In short," Langille predicted, "an era of prosperity is beginning which will bring the Cascade Range Reserve into close and important relations with the state at large." [48]

Even before the advent of large-scale industrial logging along the Cascade Mountains ponderosa belt, Oregon had emerged as a leading lumber producing state, ranking third to Washington's first-place position by 1910. At the time of the USGS investigations of the newly created forest reserves, the Douglas-fir region was the scene of heaviest cutting and the center of production. However, a sizable volume of lumber that had been shipped by sea to California and the Pacific Basin was now being sold in Midwestern markets. The completion of James J. Hill's Great Northern Railway in 1893 and plummeting lumber production in the Great Lakes states enabled aggressive Washington and Oregon producers to supply Midwestern buyers. The regional press boasted about those new and expanding marketing opportunities. On Puget Sound, the *Washington Standard* observed that because nature had "been generous toward all, a future of unlimited prosperity" awaited: "The timber is here; the men are here to manufacture it; and the country . . . wants the lumber." The Portland *Oregonian* remarked in late 1902 that "the lumber industry has made greater progress than anything else in the state for the past year." In terms of the dollar value returned to the state, the newspaper indicated that the industry had already become Oregon's leading income producer.[49]

Despite the state's expanding lumber output, *Pacific Monthly* complained in 1903 that Oregon suffered in comparison with Washington and the California redwood districts because it lacked adequate railroad facilities. The existing lines were inadequate and made "it possible to reach but an absurdly small part of the tremendous timber sections of the state." But the future held greater promise, the magazine reported, because railroad companies were making plans to "extend their lines into the interior of the state" to promote their own interests and the citizens they serve. The new transportation routes were necessary, *Pacific Monthly* concluded, to meet healthy export markets and increasing calls from eastern buyers. With very little surplus stock on hand and few complaints about overproduction, there was "every reason to believe that the industry will continue to thrive."[50]

With the numerous investigations of western forest conditions before him, USGS director Henry Gannett estimated in 1903 that Oregon held some of the finest forests in the world. Moreover, the state had two and a half times more standing timber than Washington, where more cutting had taken place and the lumber industry was further advanced. A writer for the *Oregonian* acknowledged that there was a geographical pattern at work in which forests in the Far West were now supplying the lumber needs of midwestern and eastern states. New York, the leading producer until 1865, had fallen to seventeenth place by 1904, with Wisconsin ranked first and Michigan second, "notwithstanding the rapid depletion" of their forests. But the Pacific coastal region was different from the Midwest and the East because there was no pressure to clear forest land for food production. The newspaper reflected, however, "that these conditions will arrive, no one can doubt."[51]

The experiences of the Great Lakes states sometimes tempered even the most unabashed boosters of lumbering in the Northwest. Portland's *Chamber of Commerce Bulletin* agreed that the general tenor of the Gannett report was accurate: that forests were potentially exhaustible; and that knowledgeable people could anticipate with some accuracy when the United States would be importing lumber from Canada. Before that shift occurred, however, the *Bulletin* predicted that "the tremendous timber country in the Pacific Northwest" would fill the nation's lumber needs. The chamber publication observed that the government's creation of the forest reserves had "thrown out a protecting arm" to slow the rate of exhaustion. Moreover, the *Bulletin* pointed out, federal reserves were far removed from transportation arterials and very likely would not be marketable for several decades.[52]

Despite some ambivalence in the regional press, the huge extent and volume of Northwest forests and their potential value in distant markets impressed almost everyone. An editorial in the *Oregonian* in 1904 repeated what was becoming a familiar litany: "Oregon has more standing timber, of commercial value, than any other state." According to the census for 1900, the Portland newspaper contended, nearly half of the state was economically valuable for its timber. The region's Pacific marine climate enhanced that natural abundance, enabling timber to grow more rapidly in Oregon and Washington than elsewhere. The *Oregonian* pointed to the observations of the first settlers, who "now find great forests of fir in places that were quite open in the times of their early observation"; lands that were formerly bare of timber now grew trees more than two feet in diameter and over 100 feet tall. The newspaper concluded: "Nature here will effect the renewal if only given a chance."[53]

Coupling those abundant timber stands with distant markets was the prospect that most excited newspapers and the region's numerous booster organizations. Businessman Frank Ira White estimated a potential log supply sufficient to keep local mills running for 150 years. Citizens had every right to expect that Oregon's magnificent stands would provide a continuous supply of lumber to the "enormous demand of the states lying between the Mississippi River and the Rocky Mountains." But potentially more important than domestic markets "and greater than all else," White contended, was "future traffic with the Orient," the teeming populations of China, Japan, and markets elsewhere around the Pacific Rim. Although railroads were jousting with each other for "control of the Northwest," White urged potential investors to remember that there were lucrative prospects in trade with the Orient as well. Traffic, after all, was "the pot of gold at the end of the railroad rainbow."[54] Here was the imperial language of capital, defining both the natural world and agglomerations of people (markets) in instrumentalist terms, indeed, as agencies to be manipulated at will for purposes of profit-making.

On another occasion the *Oregonian* observed that the state's "still almost untouched" forests would "become the basis of an immense activity," while nearby Washington's fortunes would decline because of its diminishing supply of timber. "Oregon," the newspaper bragged, "has an industry in coming which in Washington within a few years will be practically exhausted." The Portland daily also speculated that in another twenty-five years Oregon's population might again exceed that of its northern neighbor, because "in this state so little has been done upon the resources which Nature has offered to industry and enterprise."[55]

Portland Chamber of Commerce publications enthusiastically joined in boasting about Oregon's natural abundance, with a special eye toward attracting eastern investors. Chamber writers used data printed in Henry Gannett's USGS report — and then embellished those statistics — to draw attention to the impressive timbered wealth of the lower Columbia River. In its monthly bulletin for October 1905, the chamber reported that the largest volume of high-quality forest land lay outside the forest reserves in the hands "of speculative men who are holding for the coming investors." The greater portion of Oregon's timber, the bulletin indicated, was situated west of the Cascade Mountains, "or, more properly, west of the summit of the Cascades, as they are heavily wooded practically to their peaks." Although there was also a considerable volume of timber on the eastern slope of the Cascades and in the foothills of the Blue Mountains, the chamber publication concluded that of the state's enormous quantity "of embryonic building material over 80 percent is in Western Oregon."[56]

The *Oregonian* emphasized the growing importance of forest productions, especially for foreign markets, when it reported early in 1905 that several grain vessels had been retrofitted to make them suitable for hauling lumber. Because orders for grain were down, "the opening afforded by the foreign lumber demand" mandated the change. The Portland Chamber of Commerce proudly added that lumber had surpassed wheat in both shipping tonnage and in money value returned to the state.[57] Indeed, the Portland Chamber of Commerce and its allied business interests held an expansive and ambitious territorial vision that embraced coastal forests, the agricultural productions of the Willamette Valley and the interior, and the great pine forests on the eastern slopes of the Cascades.

If the railroad represented the opening wedge of industrial influences in the Douglas-fir region, the coming of steel rails to the central and eastern Oregon pine districts had an even more dramatic effect in remaking the physical and social landscape. Distant markets had little influence on the extensive ponderosa districts until the Southern Pacific Railroad reached Klamath Falls from the south in 1909 and the Oregon Trunk Line was completed up the Deschutes River to Bend in 1911.[58] In extending steel rails to central and southern Oregon, railroads reconfigured the demographic map of the area, concentrating population in strategic processing and manufacturing centers such as Bend and Klamath Falls. The newly constructed and efficient transportation arterials linked the magnificent stands of ponderosa pine—referred to by *Pacific Monthly* as "the finest body of pine in the State and probably in the world"[59]—with outside markets. That sudden industrial presence in the region set in motion the large-scale production of lumber.

For some time the Portland *Oregonian* had urged railroad interests to build a line from the Columbia River south into the Klamath country, to prevent "the possibilities of this splendid region" being surrendered to California. As Hill's Great Northern and Edward R. Harriman's Union Pacific interests waged their infamous construction battle through the Deschutes gorge, *Pacific Monthly* devoted its regular column, "Development News," to the benefits the project would bring to Oregon. The new road would "tap the rich Central Oregon country" and provide access to the "visible natural wealth" of its ponderosa forests. A writer for Portland's *Chamber of Commerce Bulletin* added that natural forces made the ponderosa pine forests of central Oregon an excellent investment opportunity, largely because of the low risk of fire: "The one great drawback in considering an investment in timber is largely eliminated . . . on account of the absence of underbrush in the yellow pine country of Eastern Oregon."[60]

Anticipating that Bend would develop into an important lumber manufacturing center, the *Oregonian* pointed to its convenient location at the apex of a massive timber belt that extended along the foothills of the Cascades "spreading out into an elongated 'V' " toward the southern boundary of the state. And it seemed that nature, too, had conspired to make Bend the center of production, because the Deschutes River formed "a natural mill pond," a perfect location for large lumber manufacturing facilities. And beyond the town, including the federally reserved portions, the newspaper estimated that 50 percent of the pine belt "has reached the stage of maturity when cutting is demanded." [61]

For George Palmer Putnam, editor of the Salem *Capital Journal,* the year 1910 was filled with the promise of prosperity, especially for the great "traffic producing area" of central Oregon. With the greatest "railroad development ever witnessed in the West" nearing reality, the newly opened region would soon be sending its riches out to the world. Among the many great natural assets of the Deschutes Valley, Putnam asserted that timber was the most important among "Central Oregon's dormant resources and chiefly responsible for the railroad's coming." He predicted that the forest belt stretching beyond Bend would undergo heavy cutting as soon as railroads provided an opening to outside markets. Like so many of his contemporaries, Putnam pointed to the ideal natural conditions that existed in the region: "No timber in the world can be logged more easily, due to the level and unbroken character of the land, permitting the introduction of logging railroads at the minimum expense." With the nearby Deschutes River available for water power and "well adapted for mill pond making," the town of Bend was "destined to be a great milling point." As an added benefit, in his view, the productions of the "new land" would eventually find their way to Portland, and thereby "add to the commercial wealth of that city." [62]

Railroad construction activity in central Oregon accelerated an already busy investment and speculative environment, especially in the area's timberlands. The process of "privatizing" the public domain, of transferring land title from public to private ownership, began in the mid-1890s and culminated in the first decade of the new century when lumbermen moved aggressively to block up huge acreages into private holdings.[63] The writer Philip Cogswell has provided a synopsis of the wheeling and dealing that took place:

Details of how hundreds of thousands of acres of timberland were obtained by private interests are vague, and the information that has been passed down reflects a confusing variety of names, shifting ownerships and trades. It appears, however, that there were several methods by which timberland moved from public to private ownership, some completely legal and aboveboard, others ranging from questionable to deliberate fraud.[64]

Ultimately a few large ownerships emerged out of those multiple title transfers. Among timberland holders who eventually dominated production in the upper Deschutes/Klamath pine district were Shevlin-Hixon and Brooks-Scanlon in the Bend region and Weyerhaeuser in the Klamath region.

The newspaper accounts reporting the extension of railroads to central Oregon and the building of state-of-the-art sawmills celebrated the "commercial greatness" that would attend the opening of the area's "latent wealth . . . in magnificent forests." The *Oregonian*'s Frank Ira White praised the far-sighted lumbermen who were about to convert "the forests of the great Northwest into merchantable products." From Michigan, Wisconsin, and Minnesota, they came to a timber belt "of almost staggering proportions" opened by the Hill and Harriman railroads. The great heroic figures in this drama, White told his readers, were the railroad builders and the timberland and mill owners who were about to commence "the gigantic industrial task of converting this timber into lumber."[65]

Technology, competitive advantages over rival producing regions, and the virtual absence of constraints on private timber harvesting (except for the market) contributed to the halcyon production years in the Bend/Klamath Falls pine district. But more than any other factor, the nearly pure stands of ponderosa pine explain the booming productivity of the area's mills. The USGS survey listed 1,450,420 acres of harvestable sawtimber on the eastern slopes of the Cascades in 1900; of that huge quantity, only 33,700 acres had been cut. Similar to the pine forests in the greater Bend area, the richest commercial timber in Klamath County grew on terrain ideally suited to railroad and truck-road construction, much of it within a thirty-mile radius of processing plants in Klamath Falls.[66]

But it is Bend that provides the more fascinating story of the conjuncture between culture and nature, between economics and ecology, between a thriving lumber town and the forested wealth within reach of an extensive transportation system. Bend's large-volume pine manufacturers, according to historian Thomas Cox, "represented the last, spectacular flowering of the old order," a production system predicated on liquidating standing timber as quickly as markets and the technical ability to produce permitted. The story of the Brooks-Scanlon and Shevlin-Hixon operations parallels that of other Great Lakes lumber capitalists who began purchasing large tracts of timber in the Pacific Northwest in the early years of the twentieth century. Through mergers and buyouts, Shevlin-Hixon had amassed more than 200,000 acres of prime ponderosa timber when its immense mill began cutting lumber along the Deschutes River on March 3, 1916; Brooks-Scanlon, with a small but rapidly expanding acreage, opened sawmill facilities with a similar productive capacity on the opposite side of the river the following month. The Bend *Bulletin* was ecstatic about those developments:

The dream, Bend, the sawmill and lumbering center of Central Oregon is now an actuality. . . . After years of "watchful waiting" by men who were possessed with faith that one day saws would be humming and that the vast area of Deschutes timber would be manufactured at Bend, they have today to take a 10-minute walk from the center of town to see that realization of their dreams.[67]

Each of those large pine manufacturing facilities employed about 600 men, with a ratio of perhaps two workers engaged in the logging end of the business for every mill operative.[68] The expanding cutting capacity of the plants eventually reached 200 million board feet a year, a prodigious amount. For nearly three decades, the town and the surrounding countryside bustled with the kind of activity that prompted the Forest Service to proclaim: "The history of the economic development of Deschutes County is largely the history of its lumber industry."[69] A strong case can be made that Bend was the most timber-dependent community in Oregon, or at least until the timber began to run out after the Second World War and entrepreneurs launched an effort to capitalize on a resource of another kind, the area's scenic and recreational attractions, including snow.

The industrial world of logging and lumbering came to the upper

Deschutes and Klamath country long after livestock and farming had gained a foothold. And especially in the Bend area, it came to dominate all other forms of activity in terms of income. Production boomed and operators gave little thought to permanence of operation; only the condition of the market and the restraints imposed by federal ownership curtailed harvest levels. On the upper Deschutes, cutting first took place on prime timber south and west of Bend, much of it in private ownership. And then as the private supply dwindled, logging operations moved farther to the west and south and into accessible areas in the national forests. In the process, economies of production and access to a quality resource reconfigured the landscape of the greater Bend area: the larger trees on lower slopes and in private ownership, ultimately representing a huge volume of excellent timber, were the first to go.[70]

In a delightful essay published in *Pacific Monthly* in 1908, the journalist Fred Lockley reminisced about nearly twenty years of travel through the Oregon country. His wanderings took him through the Blue Mountains and along the eastern slope of the Cascade Mountains and through what he called the "Southern Oregon timber belt." But what most excited his poetic imagination was the magnificent and inspiring scenery of the coastal mountains, "nature untouched by man." Travel the picturesque and winding Trask, Siletz, and Coquille rivers from mountain crest to estuary, he urged his readers, and you will find "trees straight as a lance, six feet, yes often eight or ten feet in diameter, their smooth trunks unbroken by limbs for a hundred feet." Beneath the huge trees, standing on a carpet of soft and deep century-old moss, one stood "in a mysterious semi-twilight," notwithstanding the noonday sun. And wherever one looked, Lockley wrote, "dim cathedral-like aisles radiate in all directions."[71]

Mingled with Lockley's sylvan vision, however, were statistical references to Oregon's timbered wealth: forests covered 57 percent of the state; its 54,300 square miles of woodlands held 15 percent of the standing timber in the United States; and despite "our wasteful system of lumbering," Oregon still had 3 billion feet of standing timber. Lockley's mixed references to the natural and untrammeled character of the coastal forests and his paral-

TABLE TEN

Population of Oregon and Washington, 1880–1920

Year	Oregon	Washington
1880	174,768	75,116
1890	317,704	357,232
1900	413,536	518,103
1910	672,765	1,141,990
1920	783,389	1,356,621

lel allusions to the potential commodity value of the state's woodlands, attached contradictory and ambivalent meanings to those timbered settings.[72]

Removed from the realm of rhetorical fancy, a very different material reality prevailed in early twentieth-century Oregon. For the rapidly increasing population in the heavily forested counties, production figures and the commercial values of the day put the lie to much of Lockley's preindustrial description. By the close of the First World War, the ever-present sound of the steam whistle and the squeal of the yarding machine reverberated through coastal forest and inland pine district alike. Although not all of the region's increasing population was employed directly in the lumber industry, the new industrial technology with its vast productive capacity was most apparent in the fastest growing counties.

From the onset of the industrial era through the second decade of the twentieth century, the comparative population figures for Oregon and Washington reflect dramatic growth for both states, with the largest increases taking place in Washington, the leading lumber producing state in the nation. Washington's population grew by nearly 500 percent during the 1880s, another 150 percent during the 1890s, and then more than 200 percent between 1900 and 1910 (see Table Ten). The coming of transcontinental railroads, the granting of statehood, the Klondike gold rush, and the expanding wheat production in eastern Washington explain some of that population increase. But the key attraction for newcomers rested in the

Board Feet of Logs Delivered
to C. A. Smith Mills, 1907–1911

1907	25,000,000
1908	65,000,000
1909	85,000,000
1910	100,000,000
1911	150,000,000

burgeoning number of jobs in the logging camps and lumbering towns in the western sections of the state. Oregon's population growth, although less impressive than that of its neighbor, also mirrored an expanding industrial presence in the woods.

The Coos Bay region on Oregon's relatively isolated southern coast provides an excellent case study of the relationship between a magnificent and lush forest environment and the building of modern production facilities in the area. The volume of timber delivered to the big C. A. Smith sawmills indicates the scale of the increasing timber harvests away from the extensive waterways and the highly productive industrial facilities on Coos Bay. When the company's newly built, state-of-the-art sawmill began cutting lumber on February 29, 1908, it was the centerpiece of an industrial production system that included several miles of logging railroads, logging camps, extensive booming and rafting facilities, docks and equipment for loading ships, and modern vessels for shipping the finished product to Pacific buyers. The productive capacity of the highly integrated operation, as Table Eleven indicates, was impressive.[73] And while the statistics reveal little flesh-and-blood information about the company's logging infrastructure, the sharply augmented volume of logs delivered to the manufacturing facilities on the bay points to an increasingly intrusive human presence in the forests beyond.

Although the expanding acreages of cutover timberlands in Oregon's Douglas-fir and ponderosa country serve as powerful symbols of the increased pace of industrial activity in the woods, equally extensive culturally induced changes were taking place elsewhere across the state. None were more environmentally intrusive, ambitious, and expansive than the multitude of plans to manipulate rivers and streams for industrial purposes: to improve navigation, to generate hydroelectric power, and to provide water for irrigation. Those imaginative and ambitious designs to remake the regional landscape involved an expansive sense of hubris about the positive social benefits that would be gained from transforming the natural world.

Engineering Nature

Oregon is the undiscovered Paradise of practical business men and women who are alive to the undeveloped resources of our country, and have the far-seeing eye of an Astor that looks into the future and sees spread upon time's unfailing scroll the things that are to be. — *The Chamber of Commerce Bulletin (1908)*[1]

Men are born, not made," William Bittle Wells wrote in the *Pacific Monthly* in March 1905. "The qualities of manhood are inherent. A man masters his environment because there is stuff in him to do it, and it must come out." The achievement of manhood, of progress, he argued, required unending struggle against delay and discouragement, yet men were fully capable of mastering their surroundings. "Environment melts before the man who is in earnest. All things are possible to him who believes."[2] While those words combine elements of social Darwinism, masculine bravado, and strong praise for the importance of individual enterprise, they also suggest, albeit in exaggerated form, the significant role that language plays in clarifying the perceptions and fundamental assumptions of culture. Although the sentiments published in *Pacific Monthly* were symbolic, they also included references that were weighty with meaning about human intentions. In the material world, they become a kind of social reality.

"Language, by its very nature, even when it wants humbly to transcribe, must tell a story," contends William Truettner of the National Museum of American Art. "Stories are what we impose on the world." Because language is so heavily infused with cultural meaning and attribution, it is a powerful vehicle for assigning significance, purpose, and value to *things* and happenings in the material world. Human activity, William Cronon argues, takes place "within a network of relationships, processes, and systems that are as ecological as they are cultural."[3] Because our language, our rhetorical expressions, are culture bound, reflecting the perceptions and values that influence human behavior toward physical nature, it is imperative that we pay close attention to the narratives that represent and give meaning to those realities.

The stories associated with conquest and expansion into the American outback are deeply embedded in our national mythology. As such, they point to an almost transcendental belief that it is right and proper to engage in the unlimited manipulation of nature to promote the welfare of humankind. By the early years of the twentieth century the conceptual framework to that pragmatic, instrumentalist (and commercial) view of nature embraced the conservationism of the Progressive era, the assumption that orderly, systematic, scientific, and engineering approaches toward the natural world would bring greater material benefits to a greater number of people. Progressives valued nature for its production of commodities for human use. As such, conservation ideology preached virtues that were consistent with the modernizing world of industrial capitalism: efficiency, the elimination of waste, and the development and scientific management of resources. As the historian Samuel Hays has argued: "The apostles of the gospel of efficiency subordinated the aesthetic to the utilitarian."[4] In that calculus, economic imperatives were transcendent, a reality that was especially apparent in resource-abundant regions like the Pacific Northwest.

Early-twentieth-century conservation ideology in the Oregon country paralleled similar arguments at the national level, a discourse that was primarily utilitarian, instrumentalist, and development oriented. Gifford Pinchot, who established the ideological parameters for the national debate, stated the case for the federal forests—and by extension other resources as well: "The object of our policy is not to preserve the forests because they are beautiful or because they are refuges for wild creatures or the wilderness, but the making of prosperous homes. . . . Every other consideration becomes secondary." An apostle of scientific efficiency and orderly administration, Pinchot, according to Donald Worster, "saw the world as badly in need of managing." Oregon governors George Chamberlain and Oswald West, who supported the conservation policies of Pinchot and President Theodore Roosevelt, both advocated federal control and management of natural resources "in the public interest." Oswald West's inaugural message to the Oregon legislature in 1911 illustrates that utilitarian ideology:

It is most vital to the future prosperity of this state and of its people that its natural resources be conserved to the fullest extent in order so that they may be fully utilized and developed for the benefit not only of this but of future generations.[5]

The Oregon Conservation Commission, a quasi-public body appointed by Governor Chamberlain with a nonexistent budget, provides another example of that instrumentalist attachment to the natural world. In its published report for 1908, the commission defined the conservation of resources as "the highest utilization of them," the implementation of practices indicating "that man has attained a more commanding position over the forces of nature." As such, it urged the state of Oregon to proceed along the path of orderly development. In its second biennial report, the commission described its work as having a "most practical meaning"; indeed, "it would have been almost equally appropriate to call it a 'development' commission," whose responsibilities and duties were to formulate "a definite policy for the fullest and most permanent use by the people of Oregon's natural resources."[6]

A careful reading of those early twentieth-century narratives reveals yet another caveat, one especially important to the Pacific Northwest. To realize its potential, the region required a comprehensive and integrated infrastructure that included a wide array of "improvements": energy-producing facilities, water and land-based transportation arterials, educational institutions, and the technical ability to engineer the regional landscape to better serve human need. Here the world of developer and engineer, of promoter and scientist, the uninhibited language of the booster and the cool rhetoric of the bureaucrat became one. The federal government was to be a partner to those enterprises, providing the capital, much of the technical proficiency, and in some instances the land itself to those willing to "tame" the region for agricultural and industrial development.[7]

For the Pacific Northwest, few aspects of human cultural activity were more visibly obvious than the myriad efforts to divert and control the region's extensive waterways. Although the region's major streams—the Columbia, Snake, and Willamette—were the focal point of much of the attention, developers, commercial shippers, engineers, and a broad array of agricultural groups expressed interest in virtually every stream and waterway. Collectively that industrial modeling of Northwestern rivers included the dredging and channeling of streams, building jetties, and erecting dams to improve navigation, control flooding, provide water for irrigation, and generate electricity.

The efforts to manage waterways originated in the nineteenth century with a few privately built canals in the Willamette Valley, the construction of miners' "ditches" in eastern and southwestern Oregon, and finally publicly funded snag pulling and dredging in the Willamette River, especially in the Portland Harbor area. Beyond those fledgling private and state projects, the federal government, through the Army Corps of Engineers, financed dredging activity and the construction of jetties at the mouth of the Columbia River, Yaquina Bay, Coos Bay, and the entrances to the Coquille and Umpqua rivers. In newspaper reports, booster publications, and in volumes of published material, the Corps promoted those activities in terms of "improvements" and the monetary "benefits" they would bring to local people. The completion of the Cascades Locks Canal on the Columbia River in November 1896 was the most ambitious of those early public-works projects.[8] The small private projects and the more grandiose (and expensive) federal works, however, were only the beginning of far more extensive efforts to redesign the region's waterways.

Some of the proposals to manipulate river environments reflected intuition and unanchored imagination rather than careful scientific investigation. William Adolph Baillie-Grohman's grand scheme to build a canal from the upper Kootenay River in British Columbia to the headwaters of the Columbia River during the 1880s was artful and adroit. But as the writer

William Dietrich indicates, the proposal was also a harbinger of the future, a plan that clearly suggested a growing enthusiasm for orchestrating waterways to serve human ends. Baillie-Grohman wanted to divert the Kootenay River's spring freshets into the Columbia in order to reclaim potential agricultural land in the upper Kootenay Valley. Completed in 1889, the 6,700-foot canal proved to be a white elephant for its private investors. Dietrich points out, however, that Baillie-Grohman's naive but bold plan was born of purpose and conviction bred by the Industrial Revolution, a belief in the human ability "to improve the environment through engineering." In subsequent decades that kind of confidence would lead to the dramatic transformation of the Great River of the West.[9]

The upper Columbia River was not alone in its esoteric and quixotic engineering proposals. At the time Baillie-Grohman was formulating his plans, a civil engineer suggested an even more fanciful scheme for the lower Columbia: building a series of canals that would link Grays Harbor, Willapa Bay, and the lower Columbia River. Those who supported the idea wanted to avoid the treacherous bar at the mouth of the Columbia by bringing vessels "through the deep and unchanging channel" of Grays Harbor via Willapa Bay and then to Bakers Bay inside the bar. In 1909 a Seattle promoter circulated a similar plan to accommodate "light draft vessels." The new proposal dropped any reference to accommodating large ships entering the Columbia; instead, the plan argued that a such canal would connect "a section hitherto isolated from the outer world with the larger markets" and help develop southwest Washington as "a summer playground for the Northwest."[10]

For the Portland commercial community and upriver shippers on the Columbia, the building of The Dalles–Celilo canal, completed in 1915, was the greatest engineering venture prior to the construction of Bonneville Dam. The result of Army Corps of Engineers' studies dating to the mid-1870s and long in the planning stages, construction of the 8.5-mile canal did not begin until 1905. Then inefficient contractors, a lack of funds, design modifications, and "open-river improvements" delayed completion for another decade.[11] But the grand moment finally arrived when the assembled dignitaries stood amidst the swirling winds and dust at Big Eddy to commemorate the formal opening of The Dalles–Celilo Canal. The celebrants, public and private officials alike, heralded the event as the culmination of more than forty years of hopes and dreams and prodigious effort. The May afternoon affair is interesting today for its lofty speech-making and rhetorical chest-beating. The imagery and symbolism evoked on the occasion also represent what would become standard in the discourse about landscape in the Oregon country. That is, the region's material well-being would best be advanced through technical and instrumentalist strategies. In the case of the celebration at Big Eddy, that meant the creation of appropriate physical infrastructures.[12]

In his remarks at the ceremony, Marshall Dana, the editor of the Portland *Daily Journal,* told the crowd that the Celilo Canal was a triumph from both an engineering and a public perspective. Although the engineering expertise to develop the Columbia River required "big men capable of doing things in a big way," efforts such as the newly completed canal would prove to be projects of great community benefit. Building dams, canals, and locks, Dana concluded — subduing "the splendid river . . . to assist the ends of transportation and the progress of civilization" — meant the generation of electrical power and providing water to bring life to arid lands. "The verdant field, the orchard, and the vineyard," he said, "will soon replace the cactus thorns and sagebrush." Portland attorney, conservationist, and progressive political figure Joseph Nathan Teal told the gathering that the Army Corps of Engineers' work in building the water bypass "demonstrates that where the engineers have the opportunity they secure results." The opening of the canal had eliminated the time-consuming portage around the Long Narrows and Celilo Falls. "The shackles are broken," Teal observed. "The river is free at last."[13]

The river may have been freed from natural obstructions to commercial shipping, but its new physical reality did little to alter traditional patterns of river traffic. Charles Francis Adams, a member of the famous family and a railway magnate in his own right, predicted to a Portland audience in 1900 that while the completed canal "would do little business," on the other hand, it would keep railroad rates reasonable for shippers. Subsequent developments proved Adams to be correct. The Dalles–Celilo Canal never proved the boon to river traffic that its forecasters had predicted. The canal, whose configuration and upstream bulkheads can still be seen along Interstate 84 upriver from The Dalles, carried virtually no commercial traffic during the 1920s and only a limited volume after the completion of the lock at Bonneville in July 1938. But an Army Corp of Engineers history insists that the alternative provided by the two canals and locks on the mid-Columbia kept railroad rates for shipping wheat at a reasonable level prior to the era of the big dams.[14]

Those who promoted development in the Oregon country were epic poets of sorts, harbingers of change, visionaries whose imaginations knew few restraints other than those dictated by the most obvious limits of technology and natural obstacles. The publicists all agreed that the state of Oregon was blessed with water power; the big issue was how to make that latent energy available for use. The *Oregonian* called for a statewide engineering study in 1904 and the implementation of a resource strategy that would develop the natural forces of the state's waterways to serve the public good. "This great resource of Nature should be held for the use of all the people," the newspaper remarked in a burst of Progressive-era rhetoric.[15] To those who shared the *Oregonian*'s view, river systems in the Pacific Northwest had the potential to yield great public benefit if they were developed properly.

Effusive references to the potential for cheap hydropower flowed literally everywhere through the region's booster community. The big problem with Northwest rivers, an *Oregonian* editorial contended, was the huge volume of power that had been "running to waste at Celilo, The Dalles and the Cascades since the world began." Harnessing and putting to work the "vast power that has been lying dormant . . . for ages" was a task for progressive-minded citizens. Hitherto the swift waters of the Columbia had been "nothing but an obstruction to commerce." The Portland *Chamber of Commerce Bulletin* added its view that Oregon's abundant water power offered "ground-floor opportunities" for enterprising people who were willing to take advantage of "industrial man's most valued auxiliary."[16]

Producing electrical power, providing water for agricultural development in arid regions, and controlling and manipulating river systems also served the capitalist marketplace. Indeed, those who articulated a development ideology for the Oregon country argued that the region's "unlimited water power" was a great source of industrial wealth, providing opportunities to develop electrical power at comparatively little expense. "No power on earth," Portland's leading newspaper contended, "possesses the economic advantages of that provided by Nature." The *Oregonian* pointed out that nature was generous in other ways too, providing abundant quantities of rock and gravel "within convenient distance for use in making concrete dams." Those natural conditions provided ideal circumstances to make Oregon attractive to investors seeking lucrative opportunities in manufacturing or power development. The key to Oregon's future was to take advantage of its many streams "yet running to waste."[17]

Proposals to control and manage waterways, according to the regional press, ranked high in public interest. Although it was distant from the Pacific Northwest, the completion of the Panama Canal served as a symbol of possibilities, of the intrinsic promise to be gained through engineering landscapes. Shortly after the canal opened, Oregon's Gov. James Withycombe urged Northwesterners to join with California in celebrating the closing of the spatial distance between Atlantic and Pacific waters: "The barriers set up by Nature have been cast aside and, as it were, our coast line has been made continuous from Portland, Maine, to Portland, Oregon." The larger meaning of the great isthmus canal implied the availability of "water routes to all the world," but especially commercial benefits to the Pacific coastal states. The governor predicted that Oregon could expect more immigrants, the creation of new industries, and further development.[18]

But events closer to home — on the Columbia River and its tributaries, in Oregon's Deschutes watershed, the Klamath Basin country, and desert-like Malheur County — dominate the stories about human efforts to redesign the regional landscape. Water for transportation, water for irrigation, water for hydroelectric power — water ran everywhere through the region's promotional and development publications during the interwar years. Engineers and their allies in the business community were especially cognizant of the potential for waterpower development in the Northwest. Oregon's state engineer, John Lewis, echoed what was becoming a common refrain when he observed in 1915 that the Columbia River drainage embraced "one-third of all the water power of the United States." To unlock what he called "the door to large scale water power development" — canalization, dam construction, and the building of irrigation systems — required the commitment of sizable amounts of public funding. The engineer deplored "our present loss through wasting water power" and money in temporary, small-scale projects.[19]

Those who promoted more comprehensive and ambitious water development programs persistently drummed home the theme of wasting nature — wasted water flowing unused to the sea and thousands of acres of wasted land that could be made productive through the application of water. In the case of low-lying areas in the western portion of the state, the developers' arguments centered on reclaiming wetlands. To turn those idle lands into productive enterprises, however, required an investment of low-interest public funds and settlers to colonize the reclaimed lands. Making acreages available at reasonable rates, boosters believed, would have social and economic benefits: it would provide land to energetic colonists of modest means; it would add productive acreages to the tax rolls; and it would reduce the overall assessment burden. By expanding its irrigated land base and by reclaiming wetlands, the *Oregon Journal of Commerce* argued, the state had the potential to create more wealth. The chamber publication assured its readers that barriers to reclamation were financial and technical rather than agricultural.[20]

But even the most enthusiastic of promoters sometimes suffered pangs of ambivalence, a recognition that progress came at a price. In the midst of development fever in the 1920s, an editorial in *Oregon Business* — exhibiting both arrogance toward the past and assurance about the future — acknowledged the disappearance of the passenger pigeon and the near extinction of the buffalo, both victims of the relentless "pioneers [who] pushed westward in search of free land." Although the newcomers found "millions of fertile acres upon which the new empire of the Northwest has been built," the time of free land had passed; there was no "farther west" to enter and occupy:

This is called progress. The world moves unceasingly. New eras dawn; old forms pass. The buffalo, the passenger pigeons, free land — these are symbolic of the old order. We look back and smile tolerantly at the simple philosophy of the pioneers just as future generations will look back and smile tolerantly at us.

The editorial conceded that change, "this progress," had come about at a dizzying pace. The development of Oregon, the continued influx of new residents, the filling in of its empty spaces, meant that the present moment was the ideal time to enjoy Oregon, to fish favorite streams, to camp in special places, to enjoy the blessings of the Oregon coast. "If you do not," the writer warned in a rather curious assessment of future prospects, "it will soon be too late." [21]

None were more active in promoting the development of the region than organizations representing the business and investment community. The Portland and Oregon Chambers of Commerce and their respective publications were an advance guard of sorts, urging a myriad of promotional activities: deepening and widening the bars at the entrance to rivers, expanding rail lines through the arid eastern country, and building irrigation works across many of the same areas. In their efforts to capitalize the hinterland, to commodify the great outback of the Oregon country, the commercial community worked closely with like-minded professionals in state and federal agencies—with the state water bureau, with departments of agriculture and forestry, and with federal offices such as the Bureau of Reclamation, the Army Corps of Engineers, the Forest Service, and the United States Fish and Wildlife Service.

Those commercial and government-agency groups produced a strikingly analogous literature in terms of its rationalized, instrumentalist approach to the natural world. While the focal point of many of their ambitions centered on turning the Columbia River into a canalized and controlled techno-artifice, other strategies fastened on developing hydroelectric power, applying the techniques of scientific management to the region's agricultural and forest lands, and reclaiming arid sections. The latter involved a variety of irrigation schemes for areas hitherto unfit for commercial use. The fundamental objective of those efforts was civic "improvement," to fully develop the region's resources and to advance the material welfare of Northwesterners.

In that public discourse the business community focused most of its attention on efforts to reshape the natural world to advance the interests of commerce. In addition to their enthusiastic support for extending rail arterials to remote, less populated districts, Portland commercial interests and the region's most widely circulated newspaper aggressively promoted irrigation projects in central and far eastern Oregon. As the Newlands reclamation bill worked its way toward congressional passage, the *Oregonian* praised President Theodore Roosevelt and the National Irrigation Association for promoting "useful and honest legislation . . . for western development." It also singled out for special commendation Oregon congressman Malcolm Moody, who conducted a tour through the eastern districts of the state for Roosevelt's advisers, Gifford Pinchot and Frederick H. Newell.[22]

When Congress passed the Reclamation Act in 1902, it triggered a flurry of surveys and investigations, with most of the attention focused on the Malheur, Willow Creek, and Owyhee projects in far eastern Oregon, the Umatilla drainage in the northeastern section, and the Klamath Basin in the southcentral part of the state. The *Oregonian,* a consistent supporter of those drawing-board proposals, argued that completing the projects would effectively transform the driest sections of Oregon into areas "peopled with prosperous farmers and orchardists." In its view, reclamation had the potential to perform "magical effects on seemingly worthless land." And the irrigated districts promised even more: because agriculturalists required only a few acres to make a comfortable living, the new settlements would be clustered together, promoting neighborliness and helping to break down "the dreary isolation of farm life."[23]

For the next several decades, the *Oregonian*'s writers employed the rhetoric of military struggle, of mastering difficult obstacles, of overcoming adversity, to describe reclamation achievements. In a 1905 article that opened with the line, "New territory may be secured only by conquest," the newspaper compared the work of reclamation engineers to the conquering armies of ancient Rome:

Uncle Sam's war of conquest is being waged upon the arid lands of the great West. His weapons are water. Flooding the desolate sagebrush wastes with a liquid army, he will transfigure them into blooming Edens where happy, contented people thrive in the erstwhile haunts of venomous rattlers and wary, lonely jackrabbits.[24]

In editorials the following year, the *Oregonian* celebrated the bright prospects for the interior country, a region "to be redeemed by man's intel-

ligence," a place where human labor would reclaim the desert and "overcome the obstacles of nature." Following an argument reminiscent of the
nineteenth-century slogan, "Rain Follows the Plow," the *Oregonian* praised
the "wonderful transformation" that "new conquests" would bring:

The plow would open the way; the tree and the garden and the field of grain or grass
would cool the air and increase the moisture. Fertility in the highest degree would
appear where to superficial observation no fertility seemed possible.[25]

The Newlands Reclamation Act authorized the secretary of the interior
to designate irrigation sites and to set up a reclamation fund from the sale
of public lands to finance specific undertakings. Administered by the Reclamation Service, the federal projects required those settling reclaimed land
to repay the costs of constructing irrigation works within ten years.[26] For
the duration of its existence, the Oregon Conservation Commission enthusiastically supported the Reclamation Service and its projects. The state's
waterpower potential, according to the commission, was "of far greater
importance to the people than any other resource." It urged the rapid development of irrigation in the Willamette Valley and the enactment of a
water law to protect power resources from monopoly. The commission repeatedly pressed the argument that the growth of the state depended on
an increasing agricultural population. Hence, developing the state's water
resources for irrigation was a prerequisite to an expanding farm acreage.
"The highest type of agricultural development," the commission asserted,
"is found in irrigated sections."[27] Historian Donald Pisani contends that
boosters viewed irrigation as a way to reach a balance between agriculture
and industry, "to make the West more like the East."[28]

Despite the enactment of federal legislation to encourage the development of irrigation projects, most reclamation effort in Oregon was volun-
tary and cooperative, and involved private capital investment. Until well
into the twentieth century, privately financed irrigation acreage far surpassed lands reclaimed under the provisions of the Carey Act (1894) or
the Newlands Reclamation Act (1902). Although he called the Reclamation
Act "the boldest piece of legislation ever enacted" for the American West,
Pisani points out that it had little effect for more than three decades. For its
part, the Oregon Conservation Commission recommended more aggres-

sive federal and state activity in the development of water resources in its 1912 report. The commission feared that private capital would "not lead the way to lowering prices."[29]

The first federally sponsored reclamation project in Oregon took place in the Klamath Basin, an area with an average annual precipitation between ten and twelve inches. With an unusual and irregular topography, the upper Klamath River Basin is made up of several sub-basins joined by the waters of the Klamath River and its tributaries. Before private and public irrigation projects completely changed the face of the landscape, the Klamath Basin was an extensive series of valleys with shallow lakes and swamps, comprising roughly 185,000 acres of natural wetlands and providing one of the most prolific waterfowl breeding areas in North America.[30] The early-twentieth-century naturalist, photographer, and public lecturer William L. Finley described the unreclaimed tule marshes and club-rushes that covered much of the area "a great nursery for game birds."[31]

Stock raisers and homesteaders began occupying the upper Klamath region in the 1860s, and as in Oregon's southwestern quadrant, the intensive grazing of too many cattle and sheep on limited acreages dramatically changed the original grassland communities. Exotic invading annual grasses replaced the native perennials that once dominated the area. Although water diversions for agricultural purposes did not begin until the mid-1880s, the pace of converting lands to more intensive farming gained momentum after the turn of the century. At the same time, appropriating water became increasingly more complex, with specified amounts reserved for agriculture and hydropower production, and eventually an indeterminate amount to sustain the wildlife refuges.[32]

Formally designated as a federal undertaking in 1905, the Klamath Irrigation Project eventually remade the ecological landscape of the basin area to the south and east of Klamath Falls. That early Reclamation Service effort, the second oldest in the nation, built a system of canals and ditches that delivered water to 233,625 acres of potentially irrigable land. A series of dams, dikes, ditches, and drainage arterials subsequently eliminated the vast marshland areas, including Lower Klamath Lake and Tule Lake which lie mostly in northern California. Fewer than 75,000 acres of the original

185,000 acres of natural wetlands remain.[33] Far to the east in the Warner Valley, an ecological setting with striking similarities to the Klamath Basin, the writer William Kittredge crafted a striking word picture about his family's work at diking and ditching and converting the remnants of ancient tule beds into almost 8,000 acres of irrigated land:

The headgates were opened when the spring runoff waters came, and those fields were flooded and pumped dry again. We were reinventing the land and the water-flow patterns of the valley on a model copied from industry, and irrevocably altering the ecology of everything.[34]

The Klamath project originated with Reclamation Service surveys in 1903 and 1904, and then, following considerable local interest, the Oregon and California legislatures ceded their rights to Lower Klamath Lake and Tule Lake early in 1905. The Reclamation Service approved the proposed works the same year amidst suggestions that California support was crucial to getting the project started. Frederick Newell, a reclamation official who visited the Klamath country and then traveled on to Portland, thought the project was the most "feasible and probable" of Oregon's reclamation proposals. The engineering features of the Klamath works, Newell told a Portland audience, were proving less difficult than area landowners who were unwilling to subdivide their sizable acreages. The very large single ownerships in the Klamath Basin threatened to contravene provisions of the 1902 law that required 160-acre limitations for land irrigated under federal projects. "Nearly all of the good land to be watered by the various projects," Newell observed, "is owned in large tracts." The specific acreages in question were large swamp and marsh areas that were to be drained, subdivided into smaller holdings, and then watered by the Klamath project's system of canals and ditches.[35]

Portland interests enthusiastically supported the development of "that large, rich section known as 'the Klamath country.'" The *Chamber of Commerce Bulletin* described Upper Klamath Lake as "a vast natural reservoir" that would provide an abundance of water for the ambitious reclamation project. The arrival of Edward R. Harriman and the Southern Pacific Railroad in Klamath Falls in 1909 and the continued expansion of the irrigation works provided "the things that Klamath has lacked." As soon as engineers drained Lower Klamath and Tule lakes, the *Bulletin* informed its readers, they would commence building the canal system that would carry water from the upper lake to the newly reclaimed lands. The Portland business journal regarded the opening of the Klamath country as a simple matter: "Here the problem is merely one of conveying the water from the great natural reservoir to the places where it is needed for growing crops." The *Bulletin* writer praised the Klamath region for providing "the greatest duck and goose hunting country in the world,"[36] but apparently missed the obvious effect that draining marshlands would have on waterfowl populations.

Before human structures altered its course, water from Upper Klamath Lake exited through a natural basalt dike at the southern end of the lake into Link River, a short stream that empties into Lake Ewauna, the actual headwaters of the Klamath River (see maps pp. 256–57). During periods of high water, Lake Ewauna overflowed into Lower Klamath Lake, a large natural marsh that covered approximately 94,000 acres and extended into California. Agriculturists, who had long been interested in the area, had put up some of the earliest private irrigation works in the bed of Lower Klamath Lake. According to the Portland *Oregonian*, the government's Klamath project involved two major engineering schemes: (1) impounding the flow of Lost River and irrigating several small valleys; and (2) draining Tule and Lower Klamath lakes and then diverting water through a canal from Upper Klamath Lake to irrigate the reclaimed lands.[37]

A Reclamation Service decision to build a dike to control the overflow from the Klamath River into Lower Klamath Lake contributed to significant alterations to the basin landscape. Federal officials negotiated with the Southern Pacific Railroad and the latter agreed to allow use of portions of its rail bed to serve as a dike to prevent the river from spilling over into Lower Klamath Lake.[38] The gates regulating the water were subsequently closed in 1917 and a process that one local history calls "the unwatering of Tule Lake and Lower Klamath Lake" proceeded apace. Lower Klamath, directly affected by the Southern Pacific dike and gates, receded 1.9 feet the first year and the drying-up process was complete by 1922. The great marshlands that once comprised the lower lake disappeared with the diminishing waters.[39]

The new technical ordering imposed on Lower Klamath destroyed much of the breeding and nesting area for bird populations. In an article published in the *Oregon Sportsman* in 1925, William and Irene Finley lamented that the project left in its wake "a great desert waste of dry peat and alkali." The Klamath engineering works had destroyed "one of the most unique features of North America," the Finleys charged; the end result was "a crime against our children." There were still other problems: fire, which ravaged the area annually, had burned to a depth of three feet; and for the thousands of waterfowl and insect-eating birds that formerly nested in the marsh area, "the public got nothing in return." After the water evaporated, the Finleys pointed out, a great infestation of grasshoppers covered the country to the east of the lake in 1922, a phenomenon that illustrated the important role that birds played in insect control. "In the annihilation of the great marsh areas of the Klamath country," the Finleys concluded, "the balance of nature has undoubtedly been overthrown to a considerable extent."[40]

William Finley's long familiarity with the basin spurred his opposition to draining Lower Klamath Lake and convinced him that the benefits of reclamation were not worth the sacrifice of the great marshland. Although Finley was a well-known naturalist, photographer, and writer and held leadership positions in organizations like the Audubon Society and the Izaak Walton League, his opposition to the Klamath Project was ineffective. A local history published in 1941 acknowledged Finley's criticisms, and those of other "nature lovers," but argued that the reclaimed land was cost-effective because it supported valuable grain crops. "Be that as it may, and might-have-beens to the contrary," the volume concluded, "it remains true that it was the Government Reclamation Project that transformed the unforested parts of Klamath County from a grazing to an agricultural area."[41]

The gradual extension of reclamation work in the basin continued apace, first to the main valley near Klamath Falls and then to the Poe Valley and the north section of Tule Lake. Project engineers next extended irrigation works to the Yonna and Langell valleys and finally canals were completed to the remainder of the Tule Lake area and Lower Klamath Lake. Klamath County's growing population, especially during the first decade of the twentieth century, should rightly be attributed to the extension of the Southern Pacific Railroad into the basin and the increasing acreages of re-

TABLE TWELVE

Population of Klamath County,
1890–1930

1890	2,444
1900	3,970
1910	8,554
1920	11,413
1930	32,407

claimed land. As Table Twelve indicates, during the critical first decade of the project (1900–1910), the county's population grew by more than 200 percent, a growth rate that reflected the expanding agricultural base more than any other factor. The continued development of irrigation agriculture and the opening of Weyerhaeuser's huge state-of-the-art sawmill in Klamath Falls explain the nearly 200 percent additional increase during the 1920s.[42]

Until the decade of the Great Depression, agricultural activity brought the most significant alterations to the Klamath Basin, especially to the region's waterways and marshlands. Some of the old wetland areas subsequently served as storage reservoirs where water levels fluctuated sharply. And even in the small, remnant areas of the original marshlands, wetlands depended on the return flow of irrigation water, or whatever was available after users with prior rights satisfied their needs. As the twentieth century draws to a close, the water that once covered extensive waterfowl breeding areas is now reused on cropland from two to seven times before it is returned to the Klamath River.[43]

The federal census of 1890 issued a word of caution for agriculturalists attempting to establish successful dryland farms in the arid sections of Oregon.[44] As one might expect, those warnings went largely unheeded in the presence of boundless optimism about the potential for agricultural expansion. Barbara Allen's perceptive book, *Homesteading the High Desert,* illustrates the complexities of the link between James J. Hill's call to "get people into this country" and the complex and changing nature of Oregon's arid landscape. Urged on through an active marketing campaign in newspapers, magazines, and promotional brochures, railroads and land companies strived mightily to sell central Oregon as an ideal setting for dry farming, especially the growing of wheat. That effort resulted in a great inrush of settlers to pursue what the dry-farming promoters referred to as "scientific soil culture," and an equally sudden and dramatic exodus when crops failed and the wells ran dry.[45] Where the proponents of irrigation agriculture preached the unlimited extension of farming in arid regions, dry-farming enthusiasts urged adaptation to natural conditions. The problem was that adaptation to natural conditions failed because human imagination (and promotion) often moved beyond the constraints of climate and landscape.[46]

Lured by the blandishments of the Hill railroad interests and the Enlarged Homestead Act of 1909, immigrants rushed to settle the high desert country. In Barbara Allen's words, settlement "receded almost as abruptly, leaving the inevitable debris in its ebb." When Isaiah Bowman made the 135-mile highway trip through the sagebrush country from Bend to Burns in August 1930, he counted seventy "shanties," only nineteen of them occupied. Those mostly deserted, doorless, and windowless dwellings were the remnant "improvements" of homesteaders who were attempting "to turn sagebrush country into grainfields and ranches." Bowman traced the beginning of the settlement period to about 1905 when farmers first began to occupy the open land in the Bend-Prineville area. With the arrival of the railroad in 1911 a period of expansion followed when newcomers moved into the sage desert to the southeast of Bend.[47]

In a final note to his essay, "Western Zones of Experiment," Bowman concluded that the effort to settle the high desert did little more than to widely extend "the limits of unprofitable wheat production." In the end, he concluded, the rush to establish homesteads on the sage plains drew "much narrower limits to cultivation than the settlers of this twentieth century were long willing to believe." The margins to successful wheat growing, Bowman contended, lay somewhere to the north of the Deschutes-Jefferson county line. The Oregon State Planning Board published a report in the late 1930s confirming Bowman's assessment: the land north and south of

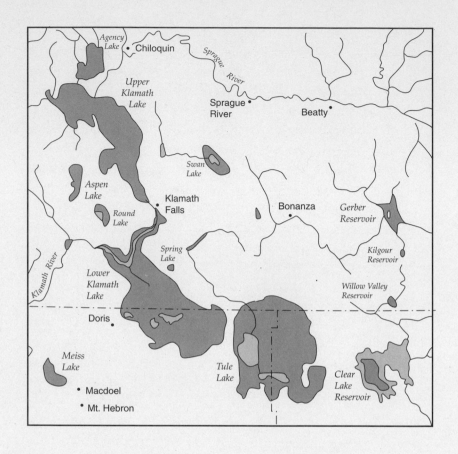

Klamath Basin, circa 1904

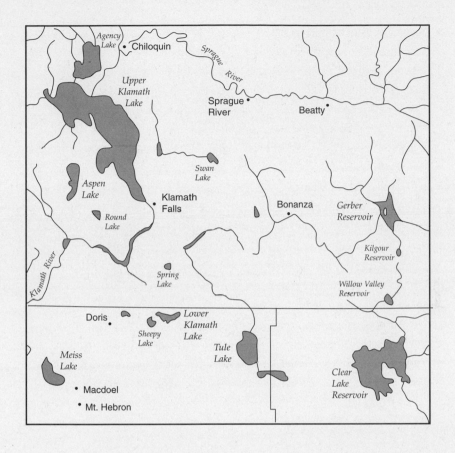

Klamath Basin, 1970

Madras for several miles was best adapted to wheat production under dry-farming conditions. The profitable cultivation of wheat, the Planning Board warned, required the use of "energetic" and scientific dry-farming practices, sufficient precipitation, and an adequate price for grain. Those conditions, the report cautioned, "occur probably two years out of five." [48]

According to Barbara Allen, only half of the homesteaders in the Fort Rock–Christmas Valley–Silver Lake area remained long enough to gain title to land; far fewer managed to eke out a permanent existence. The key element in the recent history of the high desert, Allen contends, was to link the success of homesteading in a fairly direct way to cyclical patterns of wet and dry years. In the end, it "was a failed effort." Isaiah Bowman pointed out that the problem originated when farmers listened to the propaganda of the railroad and land companies and began to venture "out of the safe zone to the edge of the juniper and into desert sage." [49] When the already marginal precipitation pattern failed, as it did between 1916 and 1920 when the weather turned dry, the failed homesteaders simply moved on to new settings, many of them to the booming town of Bend and its newly opened sawmilling operations. If nature failed to provide satisfactory conditions for a productive agriculture, at the least it would afford, for a time, the prospects of making a living from the abundant forests along the eastern slope of the Cascade Mountains.

As an identifiable watershed area, the upper Deschutes country covers approximately 8,700 square miles and includes Deschutes and Crook counties and most of Jefferson County. It embraces the Crooked River drainage, a major tributary to the Deschutes, and the communities of Bend, Prineville, Redmond, and Madras. Several mountain masses divide the region into scattered sections of relatively level but extensive bench lands ranging in elevation from 2,500 to 4,000 feet. Rich volcanic soils cover some of the area, but thousands of acres of basaltic bedrock—"scab land" the locals call it—are interspersed throughout the potential agricultural districts and precipitation is often less than ten inches per year. [50]

But if the desert proved too arid for dry farming, the promoters asserted, that did not imply that the region lacked potential for other forms of agriculture. The census for 1890 indicated that there was "no question as to the permanence of the water supply, the fertility of the land when irrigated, . . . [or] the favorable character of the climate" in the Deschutes country.[51] Indeed, farmers began diverting small amounts of water from area streams to irrigate hay crops well before 1900. By the early years of the twentieth century, the abundant water available in the upper Deschutes system began to attract agricultural promoters interested in building irrigation works. With the obvious failures of dry farming, Isaiah Bowman noted, farmers looked to the streams for salvation and promoted irrigation as "the solution to agricultural development."[52]

Although it never achieved the agricultural productivity that took place in the Klamath Basin (nor the one promised in booster literature), reclamation proposals for the upper Deschutes country attracted a great deal of attention for a prolonged period of time. The first filing for Deschutes River water took place in 1892, but the more significant claims were the turn-of-the-century reservations of developers Charles C. Hutchinson and A. M. Drake (a wealthy Minnesota capitalist). The two men and their associates vied for control of a variety of irrigation projects in the greater Bend area. Eventually both organizations sold out to a single successor firm, the Deschutes Irrigation and Power Company, but not before the volume of water appropriated was so great that the United States Geological Survey reported in 1914 that filings for stream withdrawals vastly exceeded the annual flow of the Deschutes.[53]

As it did for developments elsewhere, the Portland *Oregonian* served as an advance agent, touting the virtues of irrigated agriculture in the Deschutes Valley. In a lengthy article published in 1905 the newspaper praised the region for its equable climate, unsurpassed "fertility of soil," and "abundance of water such as exists in few arid portions of the world." The development of the Deschutes region, it argued, would lead "within a few years" to an immense population increase. Its healthful and invigorating climate produced "sound sleep, . . . improved appetite and digestion," and made the area ideally suited to growth. The Deschutes Valley Land and Investment Company, an early real estate group, published an equally fanciful brochure that envisioned "great tracts of land reclaimed from the desert wilds . . . groaning under the weight of fruit, vegetables, hay, and grain."[54]

Newspapers and other promotional agencies, and the prospect of a railroad, spurred speculative interest in upper Deschutes agricultural lands. Real estate and development firms—among them the Deschutes Irrigation and Power Company and the Deschutes Valley Land and Investment Company—took advantage of wagon road and railroad grant lands to block up contiguous acreages with irrigation potential. Although hints about inflated prices and suggestions of fraud abounded, a State Land Board inquiry turned up empty handed. The land companies boosted the fortunes of two new railroad communities, Culver and Metolius, located on the level plain to the east of the Deschutes and Crooked rivers. Because Culver served as the point where the Hill and Harriman railroads converged on their up-river route to Bend, Portland's *Chamber of Commerce Bulletin* promoted the town as the "Junction City" of the Deschutes Valley. With irrigation water applied to the sage plains in the vicinity of Culver, the *Bulletin* enthused, the surrounding area would prove to be "one of the most beautiful and fertile regions in the entire Central Oregon country." [55]

Despite the business community's efforts to engage the Reclamation Service in the upper Deschutes region, federal interest lagged far behind private endeavors. Moreover, the early private irrigation projects, most of them in the greater Bend and Prineville area, were carried out under the Carey Act. Under its provisions the state of Oregon contracted with development corporations to build irrigation works on public lands and then sold the developed acreages to settlers in 160-acre units. Except for Ochoco Creek, a tributary to the Crooked River, none of those efforts provided water storage. A Federal Power Commission study in 1922 attributed the relatively constant annual flow of the Deschutes to the "large proportion of underground inflow [from Spring River and Fall River] as well as to the well sustained low-water surface flow derived from the high crest of the Cascades." At the time of the investigation, the commission reported that several ditch and irrigation companies were delivering water to about 42,800 acres. Engineers built the dam and distribution works of the Ochoco project in 1917 and 1918 with a storage reservoir sufficient to irrigate approximately 22,000 acres.[56]

The physical work of reshaping the central Oregon landscape was difficult, elemental, dangerous, and labor intensive. The lava surface in the Bend and Prineville area proved resistant to dynamite, black powder, and hand drills. A recent history of the Deschutes country remarked that building the lengthy canals, ditches, and laterals required large crews, teams of horses, and rudimentary equipment such as scrapers and fresnos. To advance its construction work, the Deschutes Irrigation and Power Company purchased two portable steam boilers to provide the energy to drive the rock drills, a technological innovation that vastly speeded the process of boring through the tough strata of lava. There is also evidence that work crews demanding reasonable wages took advantage of their special expertise and moved on to other irrigation projects where the pay was better.[57]

Despite considerable construction activity, there were few successes. In some instances engineering efforts to control waterways in the upper Deschutes turned into outright debacles. One of the more widely advertised and highly acclaimed ventures, the Tumalo project, suggested that there were physical limits to what could be accomplished in natural settings of porous volcanic rock. The controversial works on Tumalo Creek, a tributary of the Deschutes, originated as a private, Carey Act undertaking shortly after the turn of the century. Because of numerous delays, dissatisfied investors, and angry settlers, the state of Oregon assumed control of the project in 1913, promptly drafted a new design, and then issued new contracts to its constituents. Engineers completed the system of dams, canals, and diversion works in late 1914 and the 22,000-acre-foot reservoir filled with water. And then disaster struck when pressure in the bottom of the reservoir opened a fissure and most of the water drained into the ground. After further geological investigations, state officials decided that only a small portion of the reservoir was capable of holding water. Ultimately, the state's grand scheme to irrigate more than 27,000 acres had to be reduced to about 8,000 acres.[58]

Although federal reports and surveys of river development projects lack the imagery and poetic fancy of the booster publications, they were no less sanguine in their ambitions about engineering landscapes in the interests of economic improvement. Federal surveyors carried out the first in the series of engineering studies of the upper Deschutes Basin in 1912 under a co-operative agreement between the state of Oregon and the Reclamation Service.[59] Although the survey proved abortive, a 1922 report by the Board of Engineers (comprised of representatives from the Reclamation Service, the

Army Corps of Engineers, and the United States Geological Survey) proved far more important. The study offered up a bit of technical balancing in the debate between reclamation development and hydropower production on the Deschutes River. The volume of water in the Deschutes, according to the report, was inadequate to support both irrigation and hydropower, because the latter required a fairly constant storage capacity to produce electricity. Moreover, there were geological problems in the middle and upper portions of the river basin where porous volcanic rock caused considerable water loss in the existing irrigation canals.[60]

Beyond those difficulties, the Board of Engineers determined that irrigation along the Deschutes and its tributaries would be possible only in the upriver areas, because the lower eighty miles of the stream ran through a deep canyon, with the arable land at a much higher elevation. "Storage on the upper Deschutes," the report estimated, "can probably at an early date be beneficially used for the irrigation of 110,000 to 140,000 acres" in addition to about 130,000 acres that potentially could be watered under existing rights. Because storing water would "diminish the possibilities of power development along its entire course," the board opted for the more immediate prospect of land reclamation. The value of Deschutes hydropower, therefore, would depend on its sales potential, in markets that did not exist under the present circumstances. Because the benefits of irrigation would attract "a most desirable class of citizens," create markets, and contribute to the growth of nearby towns, the engineers supported agricultural development over that of power production. Besides, the board concluded, further speculation would be redundant: "The popular sentiment in the West is strongly in favor of irrigation use of water where feasible as against power use."[61]

Several factors, immediate and distant, intervened to delay federal support for the Deschutes reclamation projects. Because landowners in the vicinity of Redmond and Madras refused to accept the government's limitation on the size of farm units, the Reclamation Service abandoned its effort. Local proposals to build what became known as the North Unit Irrigation Project surfaced again in the late 1920s, but the government blocked those initiatives when it threw financial support behind the huge engineering works in the Umatilla Basin and in far eastern Oregon on the

Malheur and Owyhee rivers. Jarold Ramsey, whose grandparents came to the Agency Plains area overlooking the Deschutes Canyon and the Warm Springs Reservation in 1900, recalls the family's struggles to raise wheat on a half section of land (with half of that summer-fallowed each year): "Farming then was not without its tensions, but it was hardly agribusiness or the physically and economically frantic enterprise it became when irrigation arrived in the late 1940s." Compared to Umatilla and Palouse farmers, he remembers, "ours were piker yields." That seasonal rhythm of dry farming—fall plowing, harrowing, and seeding, late spring weeding, and summer harvesting—did not come to an end until the formal opening of the North Unit Irrigation Project in the late 1940s.[62]

Although the federal government finally authorized the big Deschutes irrigation scheme in 1938, the outbreak of the Second World War delayed the project again. When district engineers completed the imposing system of dams, canals, aqueducts, and power-generating facilities in the late 1940s, a critic remarked that one question remained: would there be an adequate supply of irrigation water at a cost farmers could afford to pay? The irrigation schemes planned for the upper Deschutes, according to Sheldon Erickson, were overly optimistic. The engineering plan erred in its calculations of stream flow: "Expectations were based upon short records during the wet cycle, and in many cases streams have fallen considerably short when water was most needed."[63]

Reclamation issues dominated discussions about the dryland Northwest from the Columbia Basin to the Oregon/California border in the 1920s.[64] In addition to the Klamath Basin, a similar claim can be made for the arid stretches of eastern Oregon during the same decade. Federal engineers and reclamation boosters also expressed interest in projects on the lower Umatilla River and proposals for Harney and Malheur counties. Turning those "undeveloped" sections of the state into productive agricultural landscapes, its advocates believed, would "mark a new era in state development." That effort would require a commitment from financial institutions, federal reclamation engineers, Oregon Agricultural College, county extension agents, and the Oregon State Chamber of Commerce.[65]

The promotional literature of the 1920s defined reclamation work as the magic ingredient in creating prosperity and greater wealth and attracting enterprising new settlers. The Oregon Development Board and the Oregon Irrigation Congress proposed a series of "colonization projects" to secure settlers for the "undeveloped sections of the state." A carefully planned development program, the promotional groups believed, would lead to "the upbuilding of the state." The manager of the Oregon State Chamber of Commerce argued that the state's future agricultural growth would depend largely "on the reclamation of millions of acres of arid and semi-arid lands." Settling newly reclaimed land "would being 150,000 new families to the state," William Ide reported in the Portland *Oregonian* in 1927. Irrigation projects, he noted, had already added millions of dollars in agricultural assets and were "worth many times what they cost." [66]

The general objective of reclamation proposals, according to its advocates, was to put to useful purposes thousands of acres that otherwise were "producing nothing at present." The *Oregon Journal of Commerce* called such lands potential "sources of wealth of enormous proportions." And because irrigation offered the promise of prosperity, Oregon needed more "people to make its idle land productive" and to get those acreages on the tax rolls and thereby reduce the burden on others. The strategies necessary to fulfill those requirements involved technical and financial considerations, rather than matters of the natural order. According to some irrigation boosters, nearly all agricultural progress during the twentieth century had been "advanced through reclamation." Water worked miracles, the president of the Oregon Reclamation Congress argued, and was well worth its cost both in economic and social terms. Wilford Allen observed:

We reclaim acres only that some man and some woman may find their opportunity to found a home; opportunity to produce from the soil enough that a family may be properly clothed, fed and schooled, and something of the things we term luxuries provided.[67]

No single individual pursued the reclamation of arid land with greater zeal than Marshall Dana, editor of the Portland *Daily Journal*. Dana, elected president of the National Reclamation Association at its organizational meeting in 1932, combined the virtues of missionary and practical politico in his promotion of western irrigation projects. His articles about the redeeming virtues of reclaiming arid lands sparkled with optimism, emphasized the potential for social transformation, and embraced themes of ecological renewal and rebirth. When Congress approved the initial appropriations in 1924 for the Owyhee and Vale reclamation projects in far eastern Oregon, Dana saw the move as part of "the great westward shift of men and the machinery of development."[68]

Marshall Dana and other like-minded water developers had grandiose ambitions for both arid and humid sections of the Pacific Northwest. In their view, the region's future agricultural and industrial growth depended on several initiatives: reclaiming millions of acres of arid, semiarid, and wetland areas; developing the hydroelectric potential of its principal streams; providing oceangoing vessels with better access to the Columbia River and other coastal harbors; and improving transportation on inland waterways. Their passion for engineering landscapes grew increasingly bold as humans advanced their technical ability to manipulate the natural world.

In that headlong rush to refashion the water world of the West, developers and engineers focused their initial efforts on rivers that were easiest to control and where the task of diverting water through canals and ditches was relatively simple. The work carried out in the Klamath Basin, the Umatilla district in northeastern Oregon, and Reclamation Service projects on the Snake River are the most prominent of those early efforts. But, as Donald Worster has pointed out, when the easily accessible sources of water no longer satisfied their appetite, reclamation boosters and their engineering friends began looking further afield for new supplies. At that point, they turned to the federal government, "which alone could provide the capital, technical expertise, and political power to tap more inaccessible or formidable watersheds."[69]

The big water development projects—Grand Coulee is probably the best example—were far too complex and expensive for local developers. The great hydroelectric projects and big reclamation works and the new cost-benefit schemes that provided the political muscle for the giant multipurpose water development enterprises implied, as Donald Pisani has indicated, comprehensive planning "and the imposition of the state as a major component in support of the mega-projects."[70] Filled with optimism about the prospect of producing cheap electricity, reclaiming "wasted" lands, and

converting deserts into blooming Edens, the supporters of those engineering enterprises firmly believed in the efficacy of a human controlled and
managed natural world, calculated and strategically designed environments
that would be capable of turning out an ever-increasing volume of goods
and material.

Toward Systemic Change

The new and oncoming generations must set their faces toward the morning. The old existence was idyllic, indeed, and may be remembered as ideal; but no state or stage of life, especially in a new country, is fixed and permanent; nor ought it to be. — *Oregonian, June 16, 1909*

The Oregon country was becoming an increasingly complicated place as the twentieth century advanced. The emergence of a truly global economy had vastly accelerated the scope and pace of intercontinental and interregional associations and exchanges. Market articulations and the intrusions of the industrial world were rapidly integrating this once remote corner of the globe into an international web of relationships. Both country and city, arid and humid sections of the Northwest had become mutually interdependent in their economic attachments, in their relations with global cultures, and in their links to the natural world.[1] That web of economic, industrial, technical, and biological relationships reflected the influences of transcontinental enterprises, technological breakthroughs, and marketing and commodity initiatives that reverberated far beyond the confines of individual political units.

For the Western industrial world, and the United States in particular, that international flow of ideas involved the increasing application of scien-

267

tific and engineering principles to problems of manufacturing and production.[2] In the effort to articulate those processes and to convince skeptical public audiences, promoters and developers adopted a common language that promoted the notion that landscapes could be endlessly manipulated to benefit humankind. In that ongoing discussion, the larger issue was not limits *per se,* but the application of human technical and scientific genius to move beyond physical and material restrictions. Although that more aggressive spirit toward the natural world did not emerge full blown until after the Second World War, its meaning and essence were clearly apparent before the close of the nineteenth century.

For the Oregon country those ambitions began in a modest way. In the Willamette Valley, beginning in the 1840s farmers ditched and drained prairies and wetlands, introduced exotic grasses, plants, and trees, built canals and more intrusive industrial transportation facilities, and constructed clusters of dwellings and mercantile and manufacturing structures. The more invasive of those nineteenth-century technical efforts involved dredging rivers, building small dams to power waterwheels and then generators, and the construction of a few fledgling irrigation works. With the passing of time there developed a growing literary hubris toward the natural world that suggested improvement, renewal, and physical betterment — even in the face of activities that some considered destructive. A reporter for the *Oregonian* suggested in 1890 that human influences, even those that appeared to desecrate the natural world, were in effect signs of progress. Traveling up the Clackamas River in March, the writer observed great changes everywhere: a farmhouse where a few weeks earlier none existed; stately trees falling victim to "the settler's ruthless axe"; and lush grasses leveled by clearing operations. Whole acres of a once verdant forest, the reporter noted, were now blackened ruins covered with "charred stumps and prostrate trunks" of once living trees. But in a matter of weeks, all would be changed:

The debris will be removed, the stumps pulled up, and what is now rough and unsightly, will be a green waving stretch of wheat, and the scene, instead of being marred, will be even more beautiful by the marked contrast.[3]

With advances in industrial technology, those ideas quickly expanded to embrace more ambitious and environmentally intrusive activities. Scientists and engineers—in addition to the customary groups of railroad promoters, dreamers, pitchmen, and land company boosters—were convinced of the essential rightness of their effort to remake the physical landscape. As a group, they fixed on the notion that the sole purpose and function of the natural order was to serve human material needs. In the struggle for existence, according to an early 1920s study of energy resources, humans had advanced to their present position "through a facility for turning the forces of nature to account." To further perfect the human condition required changes in attitude that would bring "scientific control to the direction" of everyday activity.[4]

Oregon's development community focused many of its proposals on efforts to build dams on the Willamette and Columbia rivers. There were other suggestions in that arsenal of instrumentalist ideas: assisting farmers through extension outreach programs; expanding the agricultural base by reclaiming arid land; educating timberland owners in the principles of scientific forestry; and providing the most advanced engineering expertise to logging operators. Although Congress had shown little interest in big, multipurpose dam projects at the onset of the 1920s, a national and international economic crisis quickly moved those seemingly visionary propositions to the forefront.

In North America only the Mississippi, the Saint Lawrence, and the Mackenzie rivers surpass the Columbia in volume of water. The Columbia system drains 259,000 square miles, wends its way through sharply differing climatic zones and ecosystems, and embraces seven states and the Canadian province of British Columbia. Its source is inconspicuous Columbia Lake, nestled 2,650 feet above sea level between the mineral-rich Selkirks and the northern Rocky Mountains, eighty miles north of the United States border. Its major tributary, the 1,038-mile Snake River, begins at the roof of the continent in Wyoming's Jackson Lake and passes through a vast and varied landscape before joining the Columbia.[5] To know the River of the West and the human groups that have settled along its waterways is to recognize that the great Columbia system has been a significant force in human as well as geological history. The writer Don Holm remarked nearly two decades ago that the Columbia defied easy definition:

It is more than a waterway filled with fish, exploited by hydroelectric plants, dancing with pleasure and commercial boats and measured out for irrigation. It is, as some- one once commented, an expression of a nation's dynamic economic and social movements. . . . It is more than just a river.[6]

More than fifty years ago Peter Noyes, a respected elder in the Colville tribe, related a story about the formation of the Columbia River that he first heard as a small child. According to Noyes, long, long ago, when Coy- ote was the really big man on earth and when there was no Columbia River, a big lake covered much of the Colville country. To the west, a long ridge of mountains prevented the waters of the lake from flowing to the ocean. Coyote was wise enough to see that if he could make a passageway through the mountains, the salmon would come up from the ocean and provide food for his people. So Coyote put his great powers to work and, starting near where Portland is presently located, dug a hole through the mountains that allowed the Columbia River to flow to the ocean as it does today. The salmon were then able to swim up the river and Coyote's people had plenty to eat ever after.[7]

It is proper that stories about transforming landscapes and controlling the region's waterways include something about the infamous trickster and guru, the animal-being so central to Native American lore in the Pacific Northwest. But Coyote's imagination and ingenuity in moving mountains and redirecting rivers were only slightly more venturesome and ambitious than the engineering schemes that began to emerge as the twentieth cen- tury advanced. Although the majestic and powerful Columbia River was the focal point for many of those ambitions, developers and promoters were interested in virtually every waterway in the region. Beyond the rivers and streams were arid wastelands in need of reclamation, virgin timber stands to be opened up, mineral deposits to exploit, and a myriad other natural phenomena that might be turned to advantage at market.

Arnold Bennett Hall, the president of the University of Oregon, was among the public figures who advised a broad-based development strategy for the state. In a speech to a Portland-area commercial audience in 1927, Hall directly addressed the ties between scientific research and economic development. He told the urban business community that Oregon's material well-being was linked to university training, extension work, and research. Although little could be done to alter the state's natural resource base, the prospects for developing "the constructive genius, to make those resources yield their profit" were infinite. Hall's central message was that "the day of scientific investment" was at hand; no longer were the great business interests of the country willing to extend financial offerings on a "hunch." By applying scientific principles and research to industrial and business problems, Oregon would be in a better position to develop and calculate more efficiently the productive use of its vast resources.[8]

Gov. Walter M. Pierce, who subsequently became one of the foremost public power advocates as a U.S. congressman, set the tone for the development of Oregon's waterways. In his address to the legislative assembly in 1925, Pierce called for the public to invest in the "Creator's wonderful gift to the people." With the finest undeveloped rivers in the union, "Oregon's splendid power streams" opened the possibilities for cheap electrical energy that would attract hundreds of industries to the state. "The stage is set," the governor told the legislators, "for the hydro-electric drama in Oregon." Pierce asked the lawmakers to create a commission to study the prospects for hydropower development and the establishment of public utility districts. Projects such as the one proposed for the head of the McKenzie River and another at Umatilla Rapids on the Columbia, according to Pierce, had the potential to "revolutionize Oregon." When he left office two years later, Pierce again urged the legislature to promote the development of water power sufficient to turn factory wheels, to provide electricity to cities and towns, and to "bring a new era of prosperity to the state." The outgoing governor also recommended extending irrigation systems to increase the amount of arable land for agricultural uses.[9]

"Water is the greatest undeveloped resource in America today," Secretary of Commerce Herbert Hoover told a Seattle audience in 1926. The United States embraced hundreds of miles of inland waterways that could be to put to use, and the arid portions of the West included approximately 300,000 acres of land capable of being reclaimed. "The undeveloped resources now going to waste each year," the secretary pointed out, "amount to billions of dollars." With the nearby Columbia Basin in mind, Hoover urged his audience to think big, to think in terms of large-scale, comprehensive, coordinated, and long-term development projects.[10] Although that kind of rhetoric became commonplace among regional planners during the late 1930s and after, some government agencies and commercial organizations shared those sentiments at an even earlier date.

For a decade generally associated with laissez-faire policies, the 1920s proved to be a remarkably fruitful period for federally inspired regional planning, particularly for large-scale development projects. And the great Columbia River system, historian William Willingham points out, was the central focus of much of that attention. The more venturesome federal interest in Northwest waterways can be traced to the River and Harbor Act of 1925 and its provision for authorizing surveys of the nation's major streams. As one of ten river basins targeted for future study in the famous House of Representatives Document 308, the Columbia system provided one of the earliest laboratories for multiple-purpose development. The 308 Report for the Columbia recommended the construction of ten dams, with Grand Coulee the principal upriver undertaking and a dam at Bonneville the lowermost project. According to Willingham, "the document's concise presentation of dam sites formed the basic plan for the Columbia River's development over the succeeding 40 years."[11]

Despite Corps of Engineers' surveys and the technical expertise of the Bureau of Reclamation, the private sector was the driving force in most of the discussions about imposing giant engineering schemes on the region's waterways. The state's leading commercial publication, *Oregon Business,* argued that the problem of development was merely a technical issue. Oregon possessed the requisite raw materials and production capacity to feed, clothe, shelter, and otherwise care for its own people. The state also boasted a considerable potential for hydroelectric power; it had excellent ocean, river, rail, and highway transportation facilities; and its educational institutions were sufficient to support future development. "The primary collective problem before the people of Oregon," the journal declared in 1928, "is simply one of successful management of the commonwealth." Oregon's future was assured "providing we . . . do a good job of state management."[12] Like other commercial developers in the West, however, writers for *Oregon Business* were ambivalent about the role of the central government—complaining about excessive federal control of land in the region, while they also called for larger congressional appropriations for river development and reclamation projects.

One of the more eloquent voices calling for the comprehensive remodeling of Northwest rivers was R. H. Kipp, executive secretary of the Columbia Valley Association. Kipp supported the "development of any and all units of the Columbia River and its tributaries, including the elements of navigation, power, reclamation, and flood control." Mindful of upriver wheat farmers who were at a competitive disadvantage because of transportation costs, Kipp worried in a 1930 essay that the completion of a nine-foot channel on the Mississippi River to Minneapolis and St. Paul and a similar shipping channel into the Dakotas on the Missouri would worsen the situation for upper-Columbia River farmers. He urged the federal government to look at the Pacific Northwest river system as an integral "connecting link of the entire national inland waterway system."[13] Kipp's novel suggestion that the Columbia system was part of a larger organic whole was couched in language that appealed to the national interest. To develop the vast inland waterways—the St. Lawrence, Mississippi, Missouri, and the Columbia—in Kipp's view, was a patriotic and national commitment.

Because Kipp was a key executive player in several of the river development schemes initiated during the early 1930s, his correspondence and public pronouncements provide insights to the commercial community's growing enthusiasm for big, multipurpose dam projects. For the Columbia, the Snake, and the Willamette rivers, Kipp proposed "the development of every element and every unit of every element that is possible on the three rivers." He urged the federal government to commence its big projects on the Columbia at that point "which would be of the greatest good to the greatest number." Building a dam at "the first obstacle going up river" would provide hydroelectric power and "be of the greatest aid to navigation." Beyond the work proposed for the Cascades, Kipp recommended that the Columbia and Willamette be developed "as far up each river as is possible."[14]

The rolling landscape of the Umatilla region had been the centerpiece to some of the more active and enduring Columbia region development proposals since the turn of the century. One of the earliest Reclamation Service efforts, the Umatilla Irrigation Project, involved the construction of a ninety-eight-foot-high, earth-fill dam that promised to serve water to a triangle-shaped area east of the Columbia River. Although the canals began delivering water to the expanding acreages of reclaimed land between 1908 and 1910, the Umatilla Project generally languished for lack of interest and the poor quality of the volcanic soils.[15] But navigation and irrigation interests in the region launched more ambitious plans in the early 1920s with the formation of the Umatilla Rapids Association. The emergence of the new organization marked the onset of more aggressive lobbying efforts to build a big dam on the Columbia River above Celilo Falls. By the close of the decade the association's supporters were touting the project for its multiple benefits: irrigation, hydropower, and navigation. And then, when the Army Engineers published the 308 Report in the early 1930s, mid-Columbia promoters added the centrality of navigation and power production to their earlier arguments.[16]

Portland's irrepressible Marshall Dana supported the Umatilla Rapids dam proposal. With an eye cast toward the project's reclamation possibilities, he argued that such public works promised to be "the Boulder dam of the Pacific Northwest." The Umatilla proposal, in his view, embodied the multiple features necessary to attract federal funding: reclamation, power generation, and navigation improvements. The construction of such a dam would pool water in the Columbia channel to its union with the Snake, "thus correcting one of the most difficult links in boat operation between Lewiston, Idaho, and the Pacific." The Umatilla project also would provide the means to expand fertile agricultural land in an area that was potentially "one of the most productive and agreeable" on the continent.[17]

Even before he became the chief executive of the Portland General Electric Company, Franklin T. Griffith spoke passionately about the issue of Columbia River hydropower development. A business-minded visionary with an affection for eloquent phrase-making, Griffith asserted that nature had lavishly endowed Oregon with an astounding abundance that awaited "only the productive genius of man" to turn its natural wealth to the benefit of its citizens. As one who was committed to incremental growth, he believed that electrical utilities should pursue policies that would anticipate demand. Furthermore, they should "exert every legitimate effort to increase demands by encouraging the establishment of new industries and the increased use of energy." Using water power to generate electricity, according to Griffith, "is real conservation in that it makes use of a natural resource without destruction."[18]

Official proposals to dam the Cascades section of the Columbia River for hydroelectric power generation actually predate the Army Corps of Engineers' 308 Report. E. G. Hopson of Washington, D.C., an engineer formerly with the Reclamation Service, submitted a preliminary permit to the Federal Power Commission in 1926 to build a waterpower project immediately west of Cascade Locks. Hopson's plan called for a spillway dam with regulating gates that would build a twenty-foot head of water. The *Oregonian* reported that Hopson's idea could expect opposition from several quarters, because promoters had already advanced other proposals for big dams, one a reclamation project in the Columbia Basin and the second the construction of the Umatilla Rapids power project.[19] Although Hopson's quiet proposal disappeared from the record in the face of more ambitious hydropower and navigation projects, his scheme and others like it suggest the increasingly bold and ambitious blueprints being proposed for the Columbia River and its tributaries.

Engineering feats in distant places, especially the Boulder/Hoover Dam project on the Colorado River, boosted the confidence and fueled the convictions of river developers in the Pacific Northwest. Assuming that it would be included in the Corps of Engineers' 308 Report, the Columbia Valley Association's board of directors supported an especially daring proposal, a giant dam across the Columbia River at Celilo Falls that would pool water as far distant as fifteen miles up the Snake River. Under the bold headline, "Construction of Plant at Celilo Unit of Project . . . Will Dwarf Boulder Dam," the *Oregonian* contended that the undertaking would store huge amounts of water for power production and irrigation, and provide convenient navigation for large boats to the upper reaches of the river. As events unfolded, no such proposal was included in the 308 Report. However, that did not deter the association from announcing that it would support any plan that would gain legislative funding and carry out the engineers' recommendations.[20]

Former governor and Progressive-era conservationist Oswald West threw his support behind the increasingly ambitious engineering proposals for the Columbia River. To put the state's water resources fully to work, West called for the development of ten potential power sites between Warrendale and Umatilla Rapids: "The good old river," he observed, "is available for the use of all those who would increase our prosperity through hydroelectric development." West pointed to other possibilities that deserved attention as well, especially proposals to exploit the water power potential of the Deschutes and Metolius rivers. West brushed aside the political charges of the 1930 Democratic candidate for governor, Julius Meier, who claimed that the power trust already controlled the better sites on Oregon's rivers.[21]

Voted into office in the fall of 1930, Meier turned out to be a passionate crusader for public power who believed that developing the Columbia River was the best route to economic recovery and social revitalization. Speaking before a hearing of the House Rivers and Harbors Committee in Washington, D.C., in 1932, Meier urged the government to "select a feasible project from an engineering standpoint" to build a dam on the river to produce hydroelectric power. Meier argued that such an undertaking should be strictly a business proposition, because its navigation, reclamation, and flood control features would repay the construction costs in a few years. But most important, it should be a federal project:

> The Columbia is both a national and international stream. It is because of this feature, the nature of the proposed development and the magnitude of the financial undertaking that this river should be developed by the federal government for the benefit of the people of the great Pacific Northwest.[22]

Private capital alone could not accomplish the task, Meier concluded. Moreover, the government had an additional obligation to the region because it had withdrawn vast reserves of the public domain from private use, thereby retarding growth and "removing the lands themselves from the state tax rolls." Meier asked for "development and not delay" in taking advantage of the river's hydropower and in canalizing the river from its mouth to Idaho. "Canalization," he told the committee, "means cheap water transportation for agriculture." Meier directed the committee's attention to the huge potential markets of the Pacific Rim and the bright prospects that those held for Northwest agriculture. The Columbia River had sufficient cheap power to revolutionize the social and economic life of an entire region, but for the moment, he told the committee, "all this power is now rolling in waste to the sea." [23]

While regional promoters, engineers, and politicians refined and elaborated their ambitions for the Columbia River, other federal and local officials were busy extending earlier water development and land reclamation projects. In the Klamath Basin, water users themselves had a falling out when the California-Oregon Power Company floated a proposal to construct hydroelectric facilities on the Klamath River. The power company's proposition divided the Klamath population. Agricultural interests opposed appropriation for power generation unless the project fully protected the water rights of reclamation users. The *Oregonian* reported that most residents on irrigation projects opposed further appropriation of Klamath water, one of the farmers charging that the California-Oregon company had rushed in to file claims to sections of the Klamath River, "grabbing while the grabbing was good." On the other hand, many local business people argued in favor of granting a permit, because it would create a new payroll and bring more revenue into the community.[24] In all of the debate over legal rights to water, however, there were no discussions about potential dangers to fish migrations or to the remaining waterfowl nesting areas in the basin. The legal struggle over control of the river was argued and metered out in water units for a variety of industrial uses.

Of all those pre–Depression era "miracles worked by water," [25] the Vale-Owyhee project in the desert country of southeastern Oregon was the largest and most ambitious. The potential for physically transforming the landscape of the eastern Oregon desert country excited Marshall Dana, always a reclamation enthusiast: "You can take a sagebrush plain and convert it by the magic of water into green fields, neat homes, tree fringed roads and peaceful agrarian outlooks." But Dana was not only devoted to promoting the idea of Jeffersonian yeoman farmers in their "neat homes." He supported with equal passion big hydroelectric projects and water development schemes to improve navigation on the region's major rivers. The eastern Oregon projects required a dramatically reconfigured landscape, reconstructing the natural contours of the Owyhee and Malheur river valleys through a series of tunnels, canals, and giant siphons. The two rivers were to be controlled and managed, to be made over into instruments of human will and design for the social and economic welfare of all citizens.[26]

Like other water development works in the Northwest, Vale-Owyhee was a spin-off of even larger reclamation enterprises — in this case, the nearby Snake River projects. Although the Reclamation Service conducted surveys of the Malheur and Owyhee rivers in 1903, the government did not appropriate funds for the project until 1924. Two years later a local booster, Dalton Biggs, remarked that progress in building the dams, canals, and laterals was the work of thousands of people who had labored "to see the waste lands of the Malheur and Owyhee brought under irrigation." For such a large effort to succeed, Biggs observed, an enterprise required the proper climate, soil, water, and settlers. The Malheur County project had the first two, "the third is promised, and . . . we should readily get the settlers."[27]

Writing for the journal *Oregon Business,* Biggs predicted that the Owyhee and Vale projects would add three times the present taxable wealth to Malheur County's assessment rolls. The proposed acreages to be irrigated, he noted, were greater than the combined total of all other government projects in the state. Writing in the same issue, Marshall Dana added that the eastern Oregon reclamation works had the potential to grow corn and other crops that would surpass production in the Midwest in size, quality, and yield per acre. Dana, who thought the day of large irrigated farms was in the past, envisioned the establishment of one-family units, "where every member helps, where they feed the family first and sell only their surplus." The objective in attracting settlers to the projects, at least for its more idealistic promoters, was to create new farms and homes and to discourage speculation in land.[28]

Ranking behind only the Salt River and North Platte projects in the

1920s, the federally funded Vale-Owyhee works involved a vast engineering scheme for the lower Owyhee and Malheur valleys: a 360-foot-high dam on the Owyhee River, a diversion tunnel 3.5 miles long, 5 miles of additional tunnel, 2.5 miles of steel siphon, and nearly 200 miles of distribution canals. At its maximum extent, the venture was to reclaim 105,000 acres of desert and provide supplementary water to an additional 63,000 acres. The reclamation plan embraced two separate units: (1) the larger Owyhee development along the Owyhee and Malheur rivers and on the west side of the Snake River; and (2) the adjacent Vale project further up the Malheur Valley.[29]

The promoters of Vale-Owyhee mixed nature, myth, and engineering fancy in their praise of the big federal enterprise. The "State Reporter" columnist in *Oregon Business* likened the works to "the marvels of ancient times" with its tunnels, irrigation system, and contoured canals. Visiting "America's Valley of the Nile" in 1929, the writer predicted that water would begin flowing through the seventy-five-mile Vale unit canal by 1930. The project, "one of the most remarkable irrigated land propositions ever offered to people in America," promised to fill up with settlers "the moment water is ready for the land." Local officials predicted that the area's population would increase to 80,000 people within ten years. When construction workers completed the canals and laterals for the first unit of the Vale project in 1930, the resident engineer announced that "the ditches and water are ready" to irrigate 3,700 acres. At the March ceremonies, Oregon's outgoing governor, Walter Norblad, turned a valve releasing water into the canal and marking the official opening of the Vale-Owyhee reclamation project.[30]

Because Owyhee Dam and its accessory system of siphons and canals involved immense construction requirements, that segment of the reclamation plan was much slower in coming on line. When engineers completed the giant dam and its system of tunnels in the late 1930s, the works set in motion the subsequent transformation of Malheur-Vale sage lands into productive row-crop enterprises. The Owyhee, Vale, and Snake River projects eventually delivered low-cost water to some of the largest agribusiness corporations in the Pacific Northwest. As an artifact of the pre–Depression era, however, Owyhee is significant for its bold engineering scheme and because it was a harbinger of even more grandiose multipurpose dam proposals that emerged during the 1930s.

They were both special moments in time, gathering places for thousands of curious people who came to witness the genius of two magnificent engineering feats: gigantic Boulder Dam (later renamed Hoover Dam) on the Colorado River in the arid Southwest, and the even more gargantuan Grand Coulee Dam on the northern rim of the Columbia plain. A crowd in excess of 10,000 gathered in the desert heat along the rock wall on the Nevada side of the Colorado River gorge on the morning of September 30, 1935, to hear President Franklin D. Roosevelt extol the virtues of the work that had recently been completed (funding and construction, of course, predated Roosevelt's election). This "twentieth-century marvel," he told the assembled senators, business leaders, and thousands of ordinary citizens who had driven hundreds of miles to the remote location, was a striking example of "altering the geography of a region" to serve the common good.[31] The largest federally funded project to that moment, Hoover Dam would protect against flooding, provide waters for farmers and urban dwellers, and produce cheap electric power for the health and comfort of generations of future Americans.

Just one year earlier more than 20,000 people had gathered on October 4, 1934, to hear the president speak at the early stages of a second construction site, the even more ambitious and grandiose Grand Coulee Dam. Later dubbed "the biggest thing on earth," Grand Coulee, in the president's words, would give a living presence to Horace Greeley's axiom, "Go West, young man, go West." The completion of the project would help "develop" the Far West and at the same time provide "opportunity to many individuals and families back in the older, settled parts of the nation to come out here and distribute some of the burdens which fall on them more heavily than fall on the West."[32] In later addresses in the Pacific Northwest, Roosevelt praised the rehabilitative social and economic benefits of both Bonneville and Grand Coulee dams: the amenities that cheap electrical power would bring to common people; the end to the ravages of downstream flooding; and the reclamation of once unproductive lands through the great pumping systems that would distribute water to the parched acres of the Columbia Basin.

Franklin Roosevelt got his first glimpse of the Northwest in 1914 when he toured the region as Woodrow Wilson's Assistant Secretary of the Navy. When the more mature and seasoned Roosevelt next visited the region in 1920 as the Democratic Party's vice-presidential candidate, his special interest focused on the Columbia River. At a campaign stop in Spokane, he emphasized the importance of developing the river and urged that a "Columbia Valley Authority" be established to coordinate planning for dam-building and reclamation projects; the federal government, he suggested, should be a significant partner. As his railroad car rolled down the Columbia River in that first unsuccessful try for national office, Roosevelt reflected that he "could not help thinking, as everyone does, of all that water running down unchecked to the sea."[33]

When he returned to the Northwest as the Democratic Party's presidential candidate in 1932, Roosevelt enthusiastically embraced a variety of development proposals, including public power projects and the establishment of public utility commissions; the latter, he believed, would have the potential to serve as "tribunes of the people." Roosevelt also promised that the federal government's next big hydroelectric construction project would be on the Columbia River. Once in office, he released money in the summer of 1933 through the Federal Emergency Relief Administration to begin the work of building Bonneville and Grand Coulee dams.[34] Although the Pacific Northwest included only 3 percent of the nation's population, the region possessed an abundance of natural wealth and the best hydropower sites in the United States. As an administration interested in measures that promised to stimulate economic recovery, it made sense for New Dealers to focus on developing infrastructures that would expand job opportunities and attract new industries.

The Bonneville and Grand Coulee undertakings were the most notable of the New Deal engineering projects in the Pacific Northwest. As such, they represented a vastly expanded and more intrusive federal presence on the Columbia River and elsewhere in the region. For dreamers and visionaries, the Great River stood as a shining beacon, a symbol of opportunity for a region suffering from unemployment, social dislocation, hunger, and privation. For the more purposeful and material minded, the potential of the big waterway was vested in statistics: of costs and benefits, of dams and hydropower, of improved navigation and flood control. Through harnessing nature's power to human objectives, Richard White argues, the proponents of dam building believed that nature's most destructive tendencies could be curbed and the river would be developed to its fullest potential.[35]

As the economy continued its downward spiral and the specter of suffering and want settled across the Pacific Northwest, the idea of transforming the Big River, indeed *any* river, was deemed high-minded public enterprise, not merely profitable opportunity for developers. One powerful example underscores this point. By most measures, Lewis Mumford is one of the more significant American thinkers of the twentieth century. An intellectual, a social progressive and visionary, a man of immense humanistic learning, Mumford gained public attention during the Depression for promoting region-wide planning as a socially redeeming virtue. His premise was that human modifications of nature were "a part of the natural order." The moment was ripe, in his view, for the remodeling of both nature and society. The new power dams and other development projects being built across the country represented what he called "the thrust and sweep of the new creative imagination." Regional planning, he believed, had the capacity "to bring the earth as a whole up to the highest pitch of perfection and appropriate use."[36]

Mumford's ideas attracted the attention of the Pacific Northwest Regional Planning Commission, especially Benjamin Kizer, who wrote Mumford that his book, *The Culture of Cities,* was "causing young men to see visions and old men to dream dreams." At Kizer's suggestion, the commission invited Mumford to advise the group about the role of the Columbia River in future planning efforts. Mumford agreed and toured the region in 1938. In his journey from the McKenzie River to Puget Sound, he reported "breath-taking landscapes, the great simplicity of the towering Douglas firs, the genial farm-and-orchard landscape of the Willamette Valley, the subtle and manifold beauties of the Columbia Gorge." But he found something unsettling as well, "a sense of unoccupied space," as though one might still expect to see a covered wagon and "a weatherbeaten pioneer family" walking alongside. "The whole 'Oregon Country,'" Mumford concluded, "is a region that has been partly defaced but not yet, one feels, fully mastered."[37]

When Lewis Mumford made his summertime trip through the Willamette Valley in 1938, there was little physical evidence that the new federal largesse had dramatically altered the physical landscape despite five years of New Deal engineering works. But appearances were deceiving. The seemingly bucolic setting that Mumford described was in the process of being pre-scripted for change: an engineering scheme that eventually would remodel the valley's contours, attempt to eliminate flooding, remove the remaining floodplain forests, and transform the composition of local ecosystems. The inception of what became known as the Willamette Valley Project reflected the combined efforts and initiatives of local business and commercial inter-ests who collectively sought to create a new river system, to impose a design on the Willamette River that more closely approximated utilitarian and in-strumentalist purposes.

Although they were peripheral to the great works on the Columbia River, the engineering efforts directed at western Oregon's major waterway provide insights to the integration of politics and economics and to the complex of motives that inspired the infinitely more intrusive human pres-ence in the Willamette Valley landscape. The water development project that began to take form in the 1930s fits Samuel P. Hays's classic descrip-tion of conservation as "scientific enterprise." Firmly grounded in exten-sive engineering surveys and planning, the system of dams was designed to promote the efficient development of *all* the resources in the Willamette Basin.[38] The proposals that emerged in the 1930s represented the efforts of farmers, industrialists, and commercial interests in the valley as well as the Army Corps of Engineers. Their combined lobbying eventually gained fed-eral funding for a series of multipurpose dams on the Willamette system.

The Willamette Valley proper and the mountains that border its west-ern and eastern limits are notorious for their heavy seasonal precipitation. In the past, heavy rainfall in the valley has combined with melting snow from the mountain slopes to produce frequent wintertime floods, some of them of major significance. As the population of the Willamette region grew, the annual floods wrought increasing havoc upon business and industrial life from Eugene and Springfield at the head of the valley downstream to Portland. During the late nineteenth and the early years of the twentieth century, private citizens and occasionally urban governments constructed revetments, retaining walls, and levees to contain the worst excesses of flooding. However, as human numbers and the corresponding pressure on the valley's land base increased, the clamor for federal action intensified. By the early 1930s an organized letter-writing campaign was beginning to force the issue. Addressed to Oregon's senators and congressmen, the lobbying groups requested federal intervention to curb the ravages of flooding.[39]

In the midst of a rapidly collapsing economy, bank and business failures, and increasing unemployment, an interrelated group of private organizations and public agencies proposed a series of resolutions that promised to foster economic rehabilitation. Local chambers of commerce and development-oriented agencies in the valley eventually garnered the support of a receptive Congress and a sympathetic president who were willing to underwrite their proposals for economic revitalization. At the center of the comprehensive plan was a scheme for water resource development. The redoubtable R. H. Kipp, with ties to the promoters of the Willamette project, wrote Oregon's Sen. Charles McNary: "It is not a question of 'can' or 'will' we develop these Northwest rivers, we just 'must' do it in order to place ourselves on an equal with other similar river districts."[40]

When the Corps of Engineers released its famous 308 Report for the Columbia River in 1932, the document included a preliminary survey of the Willamette River. The study cited the potential for irrigation storage and power development on tributary streams and listed six potential reservoir sites capable of producing hydroelectric power. Corps Division Engineer Thomas M. Robins reported that "navigation is the most important use of the Willamette River . . . [but] there is no flood problem on the Willamette of sufficient magnitude to necessitate formulation of a general plan for flood control." Robins recommended that power development be left to private enterprise, "subject to existing laws which safeguard the interests of navigation," and that "local agricultural interests" should be responsible for developing irrigation projects. The preliminary inquiry concluded, however, that adopting a plan to control the Willamette River system would have to await a more comprehensive survey.[41]

The shifting political winds that brought expanded opportunities for the Corps elsewhere eventually prompted Robins to reverse his position on flood control. Through the influence of Oregon Congressman James Mott and Senator McNary, the Corps completed its final survey of the Willamette system in April 1937. Adopted as *House Document No. 544* (hereafter, the 544 Report), the plan recommended the development of water resources in the Willamette basin to control flooding, to improve navigation, to provide water for irrigation and power development, and to flush pollutants from the stream.[42] In the subsequent months and years, the promoters' media releases, their exchanges of correspondence, and official government reports emphasized the need to control the natural forces of the Willamette River. The various interest groups seeking that end were supremely confident about the feasibility of the coordinated water development plan and the benefits it would bring to the valley.

Commercial and industrial supporters of the project argued that it would brighten business prospects, speed industrial growth, and enhance agricultural development. Proponents advertised the plan as the way to adjust natural conditions in the valley to suit human purposes. The organizing activities and lobbying campaigns of local groups, especially their intimate connections with elected and appointed government officials, eventually succeeded in garnering federal support to fund the vast engineering plan.[43]

The most influential supporters of the project were a conglomerate of loosely aligned commercial and business organizations interested in promoting economic growth. Among those cohorts, the Columbia Valley Association, Willamette River Waterways Association, Willamette Valley Flood Control Association, county chapters of the Farmers Union, Grangers, local chambers of commerce, and a valley-wide business group, the Greater Willamette Valley Association, were the most prominent. Many of the leaders of those organizations later held prominent positions in public agencies associated with the Willamette Valley Project and its operating body, the Willamette River Basin Commission (created by the Oregon legislature in 1939).[44]

In the eyes of those who wanted to regulate the Willamette system, the waterway was dysfunctional and unreliable in its natural condition. Its seasonal fluctuations hampered progress: destructive torrents of water during the winter months and meager summer flows hindered navigation and allowed municipal and industrial pollutants to build up in the lower river. Indeed, the Pacific Northwest Regional Planning Commission reported in 1935 that, alone among all the region's rivers, the Willamette was polluted to the point that it was injurious to both the public and the fishery.[45]

In the initial effort to obtain federal funds, proponents centered their attention on improving navigation. Aware of the ongoing Army Corps of Engineers' survey, business groups informed Oregon's Sen. Charles McNary that improving the channel would augment shipping on the Willamette River. In a letter to McNary in early 1931, R. H. Kipp expressed fear that navigation interests might be slighted in the pending Army Engineers' preliminary report. Kipp urged McNary to use his influence in Congress to get the necessary appropriations for the final survey of the Willamette River system. He cautioned that "every inch of the way must be fought for."[46]

Kipp's letter went beyond navigation concerns and requested a survey that included flood control and irrigation, "two very important development features on the Willamette River." Holding water in tributary reservoirs, he emphasized, would "make irrigation possible which . . . is the one biggest undeveloped feature of the Willamette Valley."[47] Kipp's ties with Oregon's congressional delegation in Washington, D.C., and his contacts with political and business groups at home made him an important player in the Willamette Valley Project's formative years. In addition to his position with the Columbia Valley Association, Kipp was an official of the Willamette River Waterways Association, an organization of lumbermen and farmers who wanted to improve the channel for shipping. One of the Willamette Valley's more pressing transportation needs, the association argued, was to "improve" the river for barge traffic.[48]

The earliest proponents of regulating the Willamette were broadly distributed through the length of the valley. H. E. Maxey, publisher of the *Springfield News*, argued that the project was "born by public demand in Lane County" at the organizational meeting of the Willamette Valley Flood Control Association on October 30, 1933. Congressman James Mott, who was present, outlined the necessary legislative steps to secure congressional authorization for an engineering survey and the subsequent implementation of the engineers' findings.[49] Those preliminary meetings, coupled with the ongoing Army Engineers' surveys, enabled organizations backing river development work to broaden their support. In the late summer of 1934 the Willamette Valley Flood Control Association turned to the lower valley for allies, and together with commercial groups in Portland they formed a nine-county flood control association. From that point, events moved to the governor's office and the formation of the State Planning Board and its auxiliary, the Willamette Valley Project Committee.[50]

A few months after Gov. Charles Martin appointed the Oregon State Planning Board in February 1935, the board submitted a preliminary report recommending a "comprehensive program for the development of the Willamette Valley." The planning board urged the "greater utilization of the natural resources of this watershed" for the benefit of all its inhabitants. The board's report called for the "conservation and use of water resources through storage of rainfall and run-off during the rainy months." The most important feature of the valley's development, according to the board, was the need to regulate the flow in the main river. The Planning Board also emphasized the Willamette Valley's potential as a "resettlement area," a ploy that may have been designed to make the project more attractive to New Deal politicians.[51] Integrating environmental with social engineering, the Planning Board believed, would rehabilitate a badly damaged economy and extend the helpful hand of promise to newcomers.

The essence of R. H. Kipp's earlier suggestions to Senator McNary appear in the Planning Board's preliminary report and ultimately became key features of the Willamette Valley Project. For immediate action, the Planning Board recommended building storage dams on Willamette tributaries to store water for irrigation use, to prevent flooding, and to regulate flow in the main river. The board further urged Congress to commission the Army Corps of Engineers to carry out the task.[52] To help obtain federal financing for the multipurpose dam scheme, Governor Martin appointed a nonsalaried Willamette Valley Project Committee to "awaken interest in the Valley's development and to obtain public support for the project." Over the next months and years, the committee lobbied strenuously to generate support, urging people to attend public hearings, issuing news updates about congressional authorization and appropriation bills, and writing promotional articles for local newspapers about the economic benefits of the undertaking.[53]

The Corps began field surveys in August 1935 to determine suitable locations for dam and reservoir sites on the Willamette system. With an expanded authority, the Corps worked through the final details of the coordinated water regulatory plan during the next several months. The Willamette Valley Project Committee, the Corps, and pro-development organizations kept each other informed about surveying reports and legislative progress. The collective efforts of the chambers of commerce and other promotional groups bore fruit when Congress approved the 544 Report in March 1938.[54] The lobbying activities that took place in the months prior to congressional authorization provide insights to the political power and influence of those who had everything to gain from approval of the plan. The combined influence of the valley's most significant economic groups and the political influence they wielded in Washington, D.C., eventually gained federal endorsement for the project.

Before the Corps drafted its final report, the agency scheduled a February 1937 hearing in Salem to discuss the engineering details of the valley project. In the weeks before the hearing, the Greater Willamette Valley Association, an umbrella organization representing business and commercial groups, gave its full support to the flood-control and river-development program. In an effort to attract capital and homeseekers, the association advertised the valley's assets in western magazines and journals. And finally, its call for member affiliates to attend the Corps of Engineers' hearing was a rousing success, with more than 400 people present to show their support for the project. Representatives from nearly every chamber of commerce in the valley attended, as well as spokespersons for city and county governments, farmers' groups, the Columbia Valley Association, and the Greater Willamette Valley Association.[55]

Enthused about the Corps' expanded authority, Col. Thomas Robins called the Salem hearing one of the finest ever held in the Willamette Valley. Robins was obviously pleased that the project committee's development plan followed closely the pending recommendations of the Portland Division of the Army Engineers. To the Columbia Valley Association, the hearing represented "the start of a unified movement for comprehensive and sound development of the Willamette Valley." Newspapers added their unqualified support and praised the economic benefits the project would bring to the valley.[56] But the hearing's principal success rested in the large and enthusiastic turnout. For its part, the business community was increasingly confident that it would obtain federal funds for the plan.

From his Portland office, Marshall Dana heralded the project "A National Opportunity," because it included "so many features for prosperity and human happiness." The *Eugene Register-Guard,* a longtime advocate of controlling the flow of the Willamette River, referred to the prospective work as "environment refinement and development," the mark of an "energetic and vital people . . . remaking their physical surroundings to better fit their needs." Only a handful of sports and commercial fishers and the outdoor photographer William L. Finley spoke out against building high dams on the Willamette system. Those who endorsed the project dismissed opponents as backward looking, their complaints the nostalgic and irrational murmurings of cranks and nature lovers. One of Finley's critics, C. A. Rockhill, accused the naturalist of throwing a "monkey wrench" in the way of progress. He wrote Senator McNary that most people "place human life above that of fish."[57]

After the Corps completed its survey of the Willamette Basin, its report was literally dumped into the congressional pork-barrel. The Board of the U.S. Army Corps of Engineers then held a series of hearings, the most significant being a second Salem gathering in December 1937, where local groups protested the board's refusal to recommend the project for immediate consideration. Fearing that the move threatened to shelve the plan, R. H. Kipp requested yet another hearing and urged board members to make personal visits to the valley to assess the potential benefits of the project. The *Oregon Statesman,* a strong supporter of the water control scheme, repeated its call for immediate flood control and bank protection works. And the redoubtable Kipp mailed some 350 circulars to commercial, civic, and farmer groups, urging them to send representatives to the late December hearing. Kipp advised supporters to contact the Corps and to praise the flood control benefits and other values of the project. The circular closed with the admonition: "This is the greatest opportunity we have ever had to bring the Willamette Valley Project to the attention of the Board of Army Engineers and the entire nation! WE MUST NOT FAIL!"[58]

Kipp's effort to pack the Salem hearing with enthusiastic supporters was a rousing success. "This is the first time the Willamette Valley people were ever organized and ready to fight for something," Kipp told Congressman Walter Pierce. Proponents of the water control plan touched upon all the benefits the project would bring: flood control for agriculture and urban centers, an increased summer flow to aid industrial expansion, water for more intensive irrigation agriculture, and increases in farm acreage for the valley's growing population. Following the meeting, the peripatetic Kipp worked with Senator McNary and congressmen Pierce and Mott to urge the Board of Army Engineers to approve the project. His tactics succeeded; the board approved the plan and the House of Representatives made it a reality and endorsed the Willamette Valley Project (*House Document No. 544*) in June 1938 as part of the omnibus flood control bill.[59]

The 544 Report proposed the construction of seven storage reservoirs, a levee, and bank revetment work at an estimated cost of $62 million. The initial authorization bill called for the state of Oregon to provide a matching fund ("local contribution") of $18,645,000, but through Kipp's forceful lobbying and the influence of Senator McNary and Congressman Mott, the state's share was considerably reduced. In a letter to McNary, R. H. Kipp assured the senator that the project had the enthusiastic approval "of the larger interests of the state as well as the upvalley districts." Kipp mentioned his contacts with J. C. Ainsworth of the United States National Bank in Portland, Franklin T. Griffith of the Portland General Electric Company, two pulp and paper firms in Oregon City, and the publisher of the *Oregonian*. "Each have urged us to go the limit in securing this project for Oregon and have offered their full support." Kipp added that those who had been inactive were "now urging all forces to join in the necessary steps to bring about the general construction." J. C. Ainsworth, for one, wrote McNary that "no development has ever had such unanimous active support on the part of all interests as this Willamette Valley Project."[60]

The Oregon legislature created the Willamette River Basin Commission in 1939 to coordinate federal allocations and to provide liaison among other state and federal agencies. In the following weeks and months the quasi-official Willamette Valley Project Committee continued issuing an avalanche of circulars and press releases to assure that funding for the public works project would be forthcoming. One circular, signed by state Sen. Douglas McKay and R. H. Kipp, anticipated full cooperation from the state legislature but informed readers that no stone should be left unturned: "Upon our state action will depend what favorable action we can secure in Congress." [61] The creation of the Willamette River Basin Commission guaranteed that state money would be available to lobby for federal funds and to administer those appropriations.

Newspapers, public agencies, and promoters of the Willamette Valley Project were ecstatic about congressional approval. The short-lived Oregon State Planning Board believed the engineering works would bring "continuing long range benefits through greater development of land and water resources . . . and . . . opportunities for more intensive production and settlement." The project was "putting money to work." [62] The *Eugene Register-Guard* printed a special supplement applauding the prospects for increased economic opportunity that the project would bring to the valley. One contributor claimed that the water development scheme would "carry the valley to heights heretofore reached only in the dreams of the more progressive politicians." Another saw the possibility of a "brilliant future . . . as keen business minds take advantage of unfolding possibilities." [63]

Letters to Oregon's senators and congressmen and newspaper editorials emphasized that jobs for the unemployed would give an immediate boost to the Oregon economy. W. F. Buse, an Oregon City lumberman, wrote to Rep. Walter Pierce that "this project constitutes the finest type of work that our government can do to help bring about a better economy and put men to work." Another urged Senator McNary to speed up the process of getting the project started "in order to give the badly needed employment." Although the idea of providing additional jobs was not part of the argument presented to Congress in the 544 Report, Thomas Robins of the Corps advised McNary that a favorable recommendation from Congress would bring "increased prosperity not only for the farms throughout the Willamette Valley but in the cities and towns as well." [64] Finally, just as construction was beginning on Fern Ridge Reservoir to the west of Eugene in the summer of 1939, the *Eugene Daily News* praised the long and "valiant" effort of R. H. Kipp, "who stayed in the fight to the end."[65]

As an expression of a vastly expanded federal presence in Oregon and the Pacific Northwest, public works programs such as the Willamette Valley Project served immediate social and economic purposes: creating jobs and regenerating local economies. Less observable, but perhaps more important, the big construction works established in the public mind a perception of movement, of accomplishment, of using the federal largesse to serve the needs of citizens. As such — and this was especially true of the federally funded water projects — New Deal funding provided the necessary infrastructure for the region's emergence as an important industrial center during the Second World War and subsequently as an important player in the global economy in the years that followed.

But the great river projects initiated during the 1930s were much more. The vast new engineering designs imposed on the Columbia River and its major tributaries, the Snake and Willamette, ultimately reconfigured those waterways into instrumentalized, mechanized units of production. The multiple dams converted those rivers from seasonally fluctuating, free-flowing streams into functional segments designed to augment an expanding industrial economy. The Willamette Valley Project dams, although of a lesser scale than the massive Columbia and Snake river enterprises, reflected similar objectives. In the end the Army Engineers turned the Willamette River into a technically understood phenomenon, known through the transit, through its flow per cubic foot, and through its seasonal fluctuations. The largely regulated flow of today's river did not emerge from whole cloth; it was a cultural creation, reflecting the conscious planning and collective ambitions of a society that sought to alter the physical world to suit its material objectives.

Pressures from local interest groups and wartime dislocations caused modifications to the original Army Corps of Engineers' proposals. The eventual construction of thirteen main-stem and tributary dams has curbed the worst ravages of the once seasonal floods. And although the dams with hydropower facilities produce an insignificant amount of electricity, the reservoirs store sufficient amounts of water during normal seasons to provide an adequate minimum flow in the main stem of the Willamette River and enough water for an extensive irrigation agriculture. The social and ecological costs are evident as well. High dams now block hundreds of miles of spawning and rearing grounds for migrating salmon and steelhead trout, and long sections of the once-scenic tributary valleys and hundreds of acres of timber and agricultural land are now inundated. The reservoir pools themselves also cover hundreds of prehistoric and historic Indian sites.

In the midst of the Great Depression, the idea of fusing scientific/engineering expertise with strategies to right a badly faltering economy had great social appeal. Moreover, on the eve of the Second World War there was a growing national confidence that the natural world could be endlessly manipulated to the advantage of humankind. That emerging article of faith was vested in the increasing technical ability to move mountains, dam rivers, and build huge physical constructions. Oregon and the Pacific Northwest represented a laboratory of sorts, a region with a relatively low person-to-land ratio and a wealth of natural abundance where engineering and scientific expertise could be put to work to remake the environment to better serve human ends. Especially manifest among those proposals were the building of multipurpose dams.

Despite the economic disaster of the Great Depression and the concomitant crisis of overproduction—especially for agricultural products and wood construction materials—those who supported the public-works engineering schemes were optimists, firm believers that building dams, reclaiming arid lands, and other environment-altering enterprises held great social promise. Whether they were in the private or public sector, project developers were convinced that the combined forces of human enterprise and engineering genius could effectively advance the public welfare. That belief infused discussions about expanding the Klamath Reclamation Project, building the North Unit of the Deschutes irrigation works, pushing construction of the Owyhee-Malheur and Umatilla projects, and controlling and regulating the flow of the Willamette River system.

The numerous writings of Richard Neuberger best expressed that spirit as the 1930s drew to a close. Rising through his news-reporting and writing skills to a leadership position in the Oregon legislature and, subsequently, election to the United States Senate, the tall, angular, and bespectacled Neuberger was an optimist who saw great prospects for the region. To the University of Oregon–trained journalist, the Pacific Northwest, with its un-limited opportunity, represented "the last great frontier of this country." More than any other public figure of his time, Neuberger articulated the heroic vision of development for the old Oregon country. Strong explorers and courageous builders of empire course through the pages of his late-Depression-era book, *Our Promised Land.* A master at employing Turnerian metaphors, Neuberger traced the story of the Columbia region through a succession of Darwinian stages: from "raiding and pillaging savages"; to the explorers who "inexorably and relentlessly . . . forged westward"; to the small farms that replaced the trapper's bivouac; to the plow and hoe that superseded the trap and rifle. Although that "genesis of civilization" had replaced "the ephemeral framework of the trading-post system" by the late nineteenth century, Neuberger still viewed the region as little more than a wilderness.[66]

From the time he converted to New Deal liberal activism in the mid-1930s, Neuberger became one of the foremost advocates of turning the re-gion's "almost limitless . . . undeveloped natural resources" to productive public use. Most of his attention (and admiration) focused on the giant engineering projects on the Columbia River. Describing the great water-way's passage through the Columbia Basin as "a living force in a dead land," Neuberger praised the big federal works taking place on the river and ar-gued that water would transform an area that supports "only desert weeds and bushes, and coyotes and rattlesnakes and prairie dogs" into a land of poplar trees, corn fields, farmhouses, and small communities.[67]

But it is the rhetoric and metaphor in Neuberger's writing that is most intriguing and instructive. Those qualities are especially important because more than anyone else of his generation — and largely through his talents as a writer — Neuberger was the region's master at literary synthesis. Cast in the instrumentalist rhetoric so characteristic of his time, Neuberger's Columbia River was part of wild nature, and as such, it was an environment to be manipulated and turned to better service. The purpose of impos-ing the new technological vision on the river was to effect life from death, to bring civilization to "the dead desert." For Neuberger, that human-engineered landscape marked a shift from the elementary and simple to the more complex and sophisticated, a world better suited to the purposes of its designers.

Like the prevailing sentiments of the wider public audience he wrote for, Neuberger's language was neither one of caution nor reflection. His descriptions of the physical and cultural worlds of Oregon and the Northwest were consistent with the dominant political and economic interests of his time. Under proper engineering design, rivers would function to irrigate immense basins, to light cities, to run factories, and to mechanize farms. The only requirement to reach those collective objectives, in Neuberger's view, was a public will to tame waterways and put them to work. Insofar as he defined nature as servant and handmaiden to humankind, Neuberger was at one with the larger economic culture that saw nature as capital to be put to productive use.[68] As such, Richard Neuberger was the exemplary spokesperson for his age, giving emphasis to the values and attitudes of the late Depression years that would ultimately find expression in an even more confident mood in the period following the Second World War when both public agencies and private institutions committed huge expenditures toward the further transformation of the Oregon country.

Epilogue: One Moment in Time

The Northwest corner of the U.S. is a rich and rugged region which boasts of being America's "last frontier." This is the land of Oregon and Washington that Thomas Jefferson predicted would be a "great independent empire" and that Daniel Webster said wasn't worth a dollar.
— *Life, October 13, 1947*

As the United States posed on the brink of a climactic two-ocean war in 1940, the Depression-born Oregon Writers' Project completed its contribution, *Oregon: End of the Trail*, to the American Guide Series. A land with a greater variety of climate, scenery, and vegetation than all the other states, the Guide proclaimed, Oregon was "still the most unspoiled and most uncluttered spot in America." While the California and Alaska gold rush phenomena had bypassed Oregon, it seemed obvious that hydropower development, the arrival of dust-bowl immigrants, and "the boosting activities of chambers of commerce" would soon bring great change to the state. The contributors to the Oregon Guide feared that the peaceful beauty of the land would be transformed into something less:

. . . a network of highways, clogged with cars and defaced with hot dog stands, the groves littered with tin cans and papers, the hills pock-marked with stumps and the cities cursed with the slums that seem to accompany industrial progress.[1]

What, then, would happen to the behavior and values of its citizens? Would they appreciate nature and "rooted living" less? Would they become "more avid and neurotic in the pursuit of wealth?"[2]

From the vantage of the late twentieth century, we can say that the Oregon Guide's writers offered up an ambiguous vision of the future of the state and the broader region. But observers from beyond the Northwest who wrote for national circulation magazines following the close of the Second World War were much less ambivalent. That is especially true of major journals where romance and nostalgia, intermixed with soaring and imaginative rhetoric about the prospects of the region, saturated the periodic print media. Theirs was neither the language of reason nor restraint, but rather a prose imbued with a particular fix on the material world, one replete with suggestions that humans were fully capable of controlling the future through continued and systemic alterations to the world about them. Collectively, those postwar journalistic salvos suggested that further remodeling of the regional landscape through ever more powerful and intrusive technologies would lead to the good society.

"Out of the wilderness," exclaimed *Time* magazine in 1950. "World War II tripped off the biggest influx in the Northwest's history; it had gained a million and a half people." According to *Time,* the region had emerged from "raw wilderness in little more than a century," and "rather than a mere outpost of Eastern manufacturing and finance," it now appeared on the verge of industrial prominence. The magazine pointed to the symbols of enterprise and expansion that were especially apparent in "clean and airy cities" like Richland, the brand-new town of 24,000 people that had blossomed in the desert near the Hanford plutonium works. The *Time* article went on to extol the revolution in production in the timber industry where caterpillar tractors "crashed through fir jungles, yanking new-cut logs along," and where loggers still wore "tin" pants but now felled trees with power saws, lived in town, and drove to work each day.[3]

Although the weekly magazine praised "big companies" for practicing reforestation and developing new wood products, *Time* cautioned that—like the purse seiners and salmon trollers on the Columbia River—neither agricultural operations nor the lumber industry "could expand beyond certain rigid limits without inviting disaster." With wheat and cattle producers and fruit orchardists already facing saturated markets, federal expenditures for the likes of the Boeing complex, the expanding hydroelectric projects, and the Hanford operation were responsible for keeping the region prosperous.[4] But those words of caution were peripheral to the central discourse about the United States in the immediate postwar years. American successes in the Second World War and the booming economic conditions that followed ushered in an era of supreme self-confidence, a belief that landscapes could be perfected, that scientific and technical expertise could be employed to improve the material and social condition of humankind, and that the natural world could be endlessly manipulated to achieve that end.

In the years following the close of the war, there emerged in the United States an era of unquestioning, even imperious scientific approaches toward the natural world. For the Pacific Northwest, *Time* magazine reported again in 1951, the control and management of its forest lands and waterways had created a new frontier "made ready for man by spectacular engineering." *Time* cited the scientific work of the Forest Service and the engineering genius of the Bureau of Reclamation and the Army Corps of Engineers, whose combined achievements meant that the United States could "expand almost indefinitely within its present boundaries." The magazine offered its full endorsement to the federal agencies who were "making rivers behave," whose dams were accomplishing great works through "geographical judo." Although "the big blue river," the region's symbol of unity, "seemed to hold the key to real prosperity," there was a general sense of confidence elsewhere in the Northwest — in the Willamette Valley and east of Oregon's Cascade Mountains — that reclamation and hydropower projects, the implementation of modern scientific and management techniques in agriculture and forestry, and human technical genius would combine to forge the good society, to provide decent, stable living for future generations.[5]

Such thinking represented the technocratic optimism of a supremely confident and unreflective culture during the postwar era, the idea that it was the mission of scientists and bureaucrats to overcome limits, not to establish them. That enthusiasm for unlimited economic growth and the endless engineering of nature also reflected Cold War concerns about an adequate resource base in the fight against communism. Warren Smith of the Oregon Academy of Sciences joined in that general optimism in a 1949 Portland *Oregonian* column, challenging those he called "prophets of doom" such as Oswald Spengler and José Ortega y Gasset. "We have a responsibility," he said, "to use our brains and not be continually 'passing the buck' to the Almighty." With "greater knowledge of the physical universe," Smith concluded, "we can guide our evolution toward something better."[6]

In truth, postwar Oregon was both a piece of its own past and a regional representation of a superpower political economy that stood astride a large portion of the globe. Reed College historian Dorothy Johansen, who explored the region's history in search of an essentialist theme in a 1947 essay, found no radical departures or startling new traditions. Nineteenth-century Americans who came to the Oregon country, she contended, "were well trained for their tasks of hewing forests, of plowing the land, of building their homes." In the westward push from the Atlantic to the Pacific, they took for granted that the continent was "theirs for the taking." Those who made the trek to the Pacific Northwest along the Oregon Trail were no different; their ancestors "had been in the process of doing so since they landed on the shores of America." Both Washington and Oregon, Johansen argued, grew as territorial appendages to the transportation empires of Henry Villard, James J. Hill, and Edward R. Harriman. The Oregon country existed, she concluded, "solely because the nation had need of its resources." As for the state of Oregon, it was "an economic and social fiction"; it had no economy except as the nation's needs "dictated the exploitation of its natural resources."[7]

If the requirements of industrial capitalism demand radical indifference to place,[8] then Johansen's assessment provides historical context for the changes that took place across the Pacific Northwest after the Second World War. Development planners, investment capitalists, and politicians alike viewed the region's agricultural and forested landscapes and waterways as undifferentiated and instrumentalist segments of the natural world. What distinguished the immediate postwar decade from the Depression years, however, was the growing confidence in the human ability to effect environmental change without consequence, a firm belief in what the environmental historian Paul Hirt calls the "technological manipulation of natural systems."[9]

Postwar politicians and technocrats went about their work with an overweening exuberance and confidence, constructing their arguments on an aggressive faith in science and a long-standing and extensive literature promoting the development of the natural world. During the Depression years, state and regional planning bodies advanced the idea that technical, instrumentalist approaches could resolve economic, social, and environmental problems. The Pacific Northwest Regional Planning Commission boldly confided its faith in technical solutions in a mid-1930s report: "The planning attack on a problem is practically the 'scientific approach' — of systematically observing the facts, studying their relationships, and deducing laws or new facts." Planning strategies, the commission believed, required the formation of "advisory technical committees" on land, minerals, water, hydroelectric resources, and other categories appropriate to the natural world. The objective of planning was to coordinate the development of resources for social and economic benefit.[10]

As the United States moved closer to war and Grand Coulee Dam neared completion in 1940, planners gave increasing attention to the region's potential for "undeveloped power." With an emphasis that stressed unused energy and wasted power flowing to the sea, the Northwest Regional Council (a short-lived group comprised of elected state officials) called for building regional power grids to accord with "the behavior of rivers and the peculiarities of electricity." The Northwest needed to develop a system of dams and electrical grids that took advantage of both "glacial-melt streams and those that responded immediately to seasonal precipitation." Under the present system, according to the council, the "whims of Nature instead of the rules of engineers govern the availability of power." An interlocking regional grid system would "wipe out this seasonal obeisance to Nature."[11]

Shortly after the onset of the Second World War, the Pacific Northwest Planning Commission issued a broad set of objectives that embraced a multiple-point regional development program that included "the full use of human and physical resources to augment the welfare and security of the people, now and in generations to come." Under land development, the commission cited the need for agricultural production to keep pace with advances in other fields. To achieve that objective, the region had to "reclaim by irrigation, clearing, drainage, diking, and flood control, at least one million acres of fertile cropland." The commission's goal for managing the region's forest resources was "to continue to supply a substantial part of the Nation's needs." For water development, the planning group recommended a "construction program to provide fullest practicable control and use of stream flow in all major drainages."[12] Although both the lingering pangs of depression through the late 1930s and then the huge costs of prosecuting the two-front war delayed regional planning, the end of the European and Asian conflicts opened the way for the wholesale investment of capital, advanced technology, and human energy that would further reshape the face of Oregon.

Richard Neuberger was the most prominent among Oregon's public figures to promote the idea that the state and the larger region would continue to benefit and prosper from the "frontier of modern technology" introduced by industrial development during the Second World War. Writing for the *New York Times Magazine* in 1945, Neuberger noted that Northwesterners were "buoyant and cheerful" about the future. With its rich treasure-trove of hydroelectricity, with half the nation's forest reserves, and with a diverse and solid agricultural foundation, Neuberger was confident that the region was on the verge of achieving Thomas Jefferson's dream of becoming "a great, free and independent empire."[13]

Two years after the end of the war *Life* magazine referred to the Pacific Northwest as "a land of promises come true," promises centered in industries linked to the natural world:

. . . of reclaimed soil from deserts or sagebrush; of cheap hydroelectric power; of fabulously fertile valleys; . . . of snow-covered mountain peaks and timber-topped hills.

To the editors of *Life,* the region was "the peaceful last frontier which, in time of war, lived up to its potentials." Human genius had transformed its mountain streams into hydroelectric units; its hydropower in turn produced metals and explosives; its great stands of timber were sawed into plywood for airplanes; and its harbors rang with the building of ships. *Life* predicted that Oregon and Washington had the potential to serve as "a land of opportunity unlimited for generations to come."[14]

That sense of *permanence,* the notion that humans could effect a built environment that would last for generations, was linked to virtually every postwar proposal to manage and control the natural world. Those wildly optimistic schemes (such as building dams on every free-flowing river), only occasionally acknowledging negative social and environmental consequences, illustrate the overweening confidence of postwar culture and its woefully unreflective sense of its own history. An ideology based on illusions of abundance and the logic of the marketplace drove the economic life of Oregon and the Northwest during those years. What the historian Paul Hirt calls an "artifice of optimism" and a narrow instrumentalist mentality directed public and private policy toward forested landscapes, rivers and streams, and other natural phenomena.[15]

As a culture we tend to be nostalgic about the past, of a quieter time in a slower-paced era, indeed a mythical age where our forebears enjoyed a strong sense of self-identity and place, an independent spirit, a seemingly self-sufficient way of life. Most of us agree that such a view falls short of reality. We forget, for instance, that in the Oregon country influences far beyond the region have constructed and then reconstructed its demographic and ecological character since the early days of the fur trade and the first agricultural settlements. It is important to remember that the conditions and circumstances transforming the Oregon landscape today — as they did a century ago — reflect national and global developments, especially those associated with market and industrial forces. To grasp the transformation that has taken place across the Pacific Northwest during the last two centuries is to know something of relations between the countryside, its urban centers, and distant constellations of capital and markets. Capitalism has been, in brief, the most powerful determinant of environmental change during the last two centuries.[16] Great expanses of the American West, it should be remembered, including much of the Oregon country, originally developed as urban/industrial, dependent economies centered in mining, agriculture, fishing, and timber.

What has emerged in the late twentieth century is an integrated web of exchange relationships that is at once regional, national, and global. To fix one's focus on a particular place, therefore, is to understand something of the dynamic of change, its common features over a broad area, and its relationship to a vibrant and persistently innovative set of economic relations and technological forces over time. The repeated introduction of new and more productive technologies brought stunning advances in goods produced for the market, escalated intrusions in the natural world, and introduced what eventually became systemic alterations to landscapes and ecosystems. In the early years of the Euro-American conquest, change was slow and geographically limited. Except for the exogenous diseases that ravaged the native population across the Northwest, the effort to modify nature was circumscribed and local in character. But the pace of change accelerated with increases in population and the repeated introduction of an ever more powerful machinery of production.

The changes that took place in Oregon always reflected circumstances and conditions in distant places: the industrializing eastern United States in the last half of the nineteenth century and the continued demand for raw materials and foodstuffs in the twentieth century. Market relations— including the fluctuating demand for minerals, wheat, lamb, wool, beef, lumber, and salmon—determined the scale and intensity of human relationships with the physical world. Perpetually shifting outside forces and increasingly intrusive and sophisticated technologies prescribed the extent and degree of environmental change.

At the onset of the Second World War capital and technology had become the determining features in human approaches toward the natural world. Once daunting and imposing, physical nature seemed less fearsome in the face of a technology that further removed humans from the intimacy of the environment in which they labored. The ability to redirect waterways, move mountains, expand agricultural output, and produce an ever greater volume of material goods were heady accomplishments. The enhanced ability to effect those ends placed a premium on the efficient and orderly transformation of the productions of nature into market commodities. Collectively, those activities contributed to dramatically altered ecosystems, skewed the concentration of population increasingly into urban areas (especially in the Willamette Valley), stepped up the volume of goods moving from hinterland to metropolis, and vastly extended the built environment.

In that sense, the Second World War was a watershed in the introduction of technological innovations, particularly those in agriculture and lumbering. The increased use of tractors placed a premium on capital-intensive, mechanized procedures that drove people from the land. Similar advances in logging operations—the development of the chain saw and diesel-powered yarding machines—accelerated the technological displacement of workers. Those changes brought sharp increases in productivity, contributed to a decline in the rural population, and caused an equally impressive growth in the number of people living in cities and suburbs. The diminishing number of rural people, however, did not imply any lessening of human influences in the outback. Indeed, the increased market demand for the products of forest, soil, and water—combined with an enhanced technical capacity to take advantage of those resources—intensified the transformation of both natural and social environments. And then with the ending of the war, those advanced technical, mechanical, and engineering achievements were fused with a spiraling sense of human confidence and self-assurance.

For the place we call Oregon, the very physical conditions under which life is maintained have been dramatically altered over the course of the last two centuries. But the most dramatic, systemic, and pervasive changes have taken place since the onset of the big-dam era. First Bonneville (1938), then Grand Coulee (1941), and in the period following the Second World War, a series of dams on the main stem of the Columbia River and its major tributaries has unleashed an era of unprecedented manipulation of the natural world. Although this book only hints at the sources and magnitude of that transformation, the period from 1940 to the present stands by itself as a subject worthy of inquiry. The last sixty years of this century have served up mixed sentiments about the scope and direction of environmental change. Until the publication of Rachel Carson's *Silent Spring* in 1962, there were few who questioned the essential rightness of the belief that human technical effects would contribute to improvements in the quality of life. But persisting smog alerts in the Los Angeles Basin, burning rivers such as Cleveland's

Cuyahoga, and a host of other environmental stresses apparent by the late 1960s ushered in a period of escalating social protests about deteriorating air and water quality and other livability issues.

"Salmon," Richard White argues in *The Organic Machine,* "symbolize nature in the Pacific Northwest. . . . they are tokens of a way of life."[17] If White is correct in that assessment—and I think he is—then the story of the region's anadromous fish may provide the best insight to the tremendous physical changes that had taken place the region prior to the Second World War. Because the fish travel such great distances to reach their spawning grounds, human activities in virtually every corner of the region affected migrating salmon and steelhead trout. Large-scale industrial mining activity, some of it dating from the nineteenth century, turned out huge piles of tailings that in subsequent decades released toxic metals (especially lead) into waterways. As early as 1894 the United States Fish Commission reported that placer mining on the Boise River, a tributary to the Snake, had seriously depleted salmon runs. On other rivers—the Snake, Malheur, and Owyhee—early reclamation projects began diverting water to irrigate semiarid lands, and tributary streams sometimes dried up because of the volume of water used to irrigate fields. In addition to altering and drastically simplifying the species composition of reclaimed agricultural land, the expanding irrigation systems increased the sediment load in streams.[18] All of those changes preceded the big dam projects on the Columbia River.

And then there were the numerous small dams—seemingly everywhere across Oregon—that altered the flow of water and obstructed fish from upstream breeding grounds. The dams, especially those that blocked access to lakes, were particularly detrimental to sockeye salmon, a species that requires lake systems for their young to mature. Some of those early dams stored water for irrigation; others, especially those built as the twentieth century advanced, were designed to produce hydroelectricity. Even before the behemoths of the 1930s came on line, one fishery authority observed that dams had made nearly 50 percent of the Columbia basin inaccessible to salmon.[19] While that estimate may be exaggerated, it does testify to extensive alterations to natural stream flows in the region at the onset of the Great Depression. It also proved ominous for the future when large dams increasingly began to dot the landscape of Oregon's Willamette, Owyhee, Deschutes, and Klamath systems.

Untreated industrial wastes, urban sewage, and logs dumped directly into rivers and streams further added to the degradation of water quality, thereby further damaging salmon breeding habitat. Such practices prompted the Oregon Board of Health early in this century to declare the lower portions of the Willamette River "an open sewer." The board's report for 1911 disclosed that in some instances pollutants in the river made fish unsuitable for food. Indeed, in the Portland Harbor area the dissolved oxygen content of water was so low during the late summer months that trout died within minutes when they were lowered into the river in wire cages. The *Oregon Sportsman,* the official publication of the Oregon Fish and Game Commission, observed in 1914 that pollution in the Willamette River was destroying fish life. Dumping urban sewage, mill and factory wastes, and filth into public waters, the agency concluded, "is a factor that will completely deplete our streams of fish, if it is allowed to continue. These things are wrong, both morally and legally."[20]

While stream pollution has not been a major feature of this study, what happened to Oregon's waterways indicates the wide-ranging, *systemic,* and *multifaceted* environmental changes that were taking place everywhere in the region. And that is precisely why salmon are important to this discussion. Individually, none of those industrial practices — mining, agriculture, logging, or dumping mill and municipal wastes into streams — threatened salmon in the vast Columbia system or in the streams that flowed westward through Oregon's coastal range.[21] Collectively, they would eventually imperil *all* anadromous fishes. The roots to those changes resided in the commodity-oriented perspective of a modernizing, industrial-like vision that viewed altering stream flows and "developing" landscapes in terms of progress and human improvement.

The new environmental conditions of the late twentieth century centering on the salmon controversy represent strikingly different historical circumstances from the glowing visions of progress promised in an earlier day, a time when the salmon ran red in the streams and the abundant stands of timber seemingly mocked those who urged restraint. Today it is difficult to grasp the optimism that accompanied the move to capitalize on nature's bounty. That sense of confidence may have peaked in the years immediately following the end of the Second World War when virtually every technical, engineering, and development scheme carried with it implications of permanence. Managing and controlling the region's waterways, expanding hydropower and reclamation projects, implementing sustained-yield timber practices, and encouraging farmers to follow the scientific expertise of the Agricultural Extension Service were seemingly the wave of the future.

For a time the buoyant postwar economy provided large numbers of Oregonians with modest incomes, the ability to accumulate savings, and to enjoy the good life. The principal factor driving working-class well-being was a booming California economy, especially its demand for lumber products. The years from 1945 to the 1970s witnessed a robust and energetic culture of hard work, a general optimism about the future, and in the region's mill towns, an uninhibited boasting about production records.[22] Less obvious at the time was any widely shared concern about limits, about the sustainability of "nature's industries."

With the emergence of the civil rights movement in the 1960s and the growing opposition to the war in Vietnam, that heady sense of well-being and optimism about the future began to erode. For a variety of reasons, some of them related to a heightened sense of social activism, environmental issues moved to the forefront of public concern during the 1970s. Wilderness preservation, wild and scenic rivers, air quality, water pollution, and other issues related to land use were at the center of those discussions. And for a time, the state of Oregon proved to be a leader in enacting environmental legislation (albeit some would charge that it was largely of the cosmetic kind). The state's political leadership, especially in the person of Gov. Tom McCall (1967–75) gained national renown through the enactment of several pieces of environmental legislation. The most prominent of those included elevating the former State Sanitary Authority to a Department of Environmental Quality in 1969; the creation of the nation's first "land-use" legislation with the establishment of the Land Conservation and Development Commission in 1973; and perhaps the most celebrated of all, the Oregon bottle bill, a measure that required purchasers to pay a cash deposit on beer and soft-drink containers.[23]

McCall, the son of an eastern Oregon ranching family and a journalist news broadcaster by training, was an outspoken and flamboyant public figure with a gift for turning a phrase. He was committed and seriously engaged in issues of livability. In one of his more enduring rhetorical expressions, he told a gathering of visiting business people that his state was not for sale: "Oregon has not been an over-eager lap-dog to the economic master. Oregon has been wary of smokestacks and suspicious of rattle and bang. Oregon has not camped, cup in hand, at anyone's affluent doorstep. Oregon has wanted industry only when that industry was willing to want what Oregon is." On other occasions McCall characterized the right to the unrestricted use of land as the "Buffalo Hunter mentality," and he referred to the garish stretch of Oregon Highway 101 through the coastal community of Lincoln City as "a model of strip city grotesque."[24]

During and after his tour in the governor's office, McCall's relations with local and national media were exceptional. When he left office, the media proclaimed the ex-governor one of the nation's leading environmentalists, bringing special attention to his role in the clean-up of the Willamette River. A *National Geographic* article in 1972 praised the McCall administration for bringing the river "from shame to showcase." During his tour as governor, the article claimed, Oregon accomplished "the most successful river-juvenation program in the country." The governor was quoted as saying that fall runs of chinook salmon were unable to make their way upstream "until we cleaned up the Willamette River." Most pollution was eliminated from the river, according to *National Geographic,* after McCall's election in 1966. "Shortly thereafter, leadership and legislature kept their promise to the people by eliminating loopholes in existing laws and writing more forceful ones."[25]

As one might expect, the story of pollution abatement in the Willamette River — eliminating municipal and industrial wastes from the waterway — was a difficult, prolonged, and problematic endeavor. Indeed, the major actions and decisions that improved water quality in the Willamette took place many years before McCall became governor; it was merely the cumulative effect of the "clean-up" effort that became apparent during the McCall administration. The effort to improve the water quality in the river dates to the 1920s and 1930s, the establishment of the State Sanitary Authority in 1938, and the lengthy struggle to limit the dumping of municipal and industrial pollutants. Most cities along the Willamette River had primary treatment facilities by 1957 and secondary facilities a decade later.[26] Another major factor in the improved quality of the Willamette River was the construction of numerous storage reservoirs on tributary streams, which provided flushing action during the low-water months of autumn.

Exploding urban growth during the postwar era eventually worsened what many viewed as Oregon's famous livability. Metropolitan areas such as Portland extended their reach into the countryside—slowly at first and then more aggressively as population and the number of high-tech industries multiplied. A new built environment of sprawling residential developments, shopping malls, and industrial plants intruded into lands formerly devoted to agricultural production. Built chiefly of wood, the new suburbs continued the old dialectical relationships between metropolis and countryside, with the products of nature moving to urban centers and in the process transforming both environments.[27] But for the thinly populated outback, for those settlements dependent on traditional resource industries, the sands began to run out. Depleted resources, shifts in capital investments to more lucrative portfolios, the consolidation of production, educational, even health care facilities into fewer units, and labor-saving technological advances, especially in agriculture and timber, explain the unraveling of the older, extractive-based economies. In brief, the more rural and less traveled of our communities were facing the sunset of an era—and mixed messages about the future.

The experience of the central Oregon community of Bend provides a stark example of the newly emerging reality for some of the old extraction and processing centers. The population of the small but thriving town in the early 1960s was about 12,000; the community had one large operating sawmill, the huge Brooks-Scanlon operation, still turning out a prodigious volume of lumber from the ponderosa forests along the eastern slope of the Cascade Mountains. Then in 1994, with its timber supplies sharply diminished following more than seventy years of unprecedented lumber production, the Brooks-Scanlon operation closed its facilities along the Deschutes River.[28]

But Bend lives on, and in its present reincarnation the business community dominating the town has turned from milling lumber to mining tourists and otherwise selling nature's amenities in clean air, breathtaking scenery, and affordable real estate prices. Brooks-Scanlon, too, has returned in a second life as Brooks Resources, Inc., one of the leading development groups in central Oregon. The town that once prospered through sending the products of nature to the city is now surviving in a weird kind of exchange. Retirees, affluent refugees from metropolitan areas, and business people made mobile through the telecommunications revolution are driving the current boom. Set free and footloose by money, easy air travel, and information-age technology, the new émigrés are independent of the traditional requirements of a centralized work place. But in a sense they are no more free of the forces of nature than their counterparts of the previous century. When a fire erupted in the woody forest debris on the outskirts of Bend in 1993, the resulting conflagration destroyed more than twenty houses, most of them the new homes of the recently arrived.

On the western side of the Cascade Mountains rapidly rising temperatures and torrential rains in early February 1996 caused the Willamette River and its tributaries to wreak havoc across farmland and urban centers alike. The rising floodwaters were reminders of the power and unpredictability of nature and pointed to the shortcomings of overconfidence in the human capacity to find technological and engineering solutions to *all* natural phenomena. The consequences of that techno-vision are also reflected in the recent findings of deformed fish in the Willamette River and the high incidences in bottom sediment of residue from the herbicide atrazine and the insecticide diazinon. Indeed, the waterway may be a miner's canary of sorts. If culture is now a factor in climate change, if instrumentalism is the ultimate mark of value, and if human ingenuity oftentimes leads so easily to tragedy, then I agree with Simon Schama: we may be caught up in an out-of-control mind-set.[29] When the Willamette system overflowed its banks in February 1996, the meandering waters not only exposed connections to an early-nineteenth-century landscape, but it also revealed the flaws of a culture that assumed it had bested the river.

Notes

Prologue: The Essence of Place

1. Yi-Fu Tuan, *Space and Place: The Perspective of Experience* (1977), 136.

2. Raymond Williams, *The Year 2000* (1983), ix.

3. These ideas are adapted from Richard White, "Frederick Jackson Turner and Buffalo Bill," in *The Frontier in American Culture*, James R. Grossman, ed. (1994), 7–66.

4. *Columbian*, February 12, 1853; Gustavus Hines, *Life on the Plains of the Pacific: Its History, Condition, and Prospects* (1851), 319; and *Oregon Spectator*, December 19, 1850. Campbell is quoted in Ellis A. Stebbins and Gary Huxford, *Since 1856: Historical Views of the College at Monmouth* (1996), 47.

5. White, "Frederick Jackson Turner and Buffalo Bill," 26.

6. Dayton Duncan, *Out West: American Journey along the Lewis and Clark Trail* (1987), 392–93.

7. Elliott West, *The Way to the West: Essays in the Central Plains* (1995), 83 and 86. Although his study did not focus on the physical environment, Earl Pomeroy's *The Pacific Slope: A History of California, Oregon, Washington, Idaho, Utah, and Nevada* (1965) also found great complexity in western development.

8. Peter James, "Ecotopia in Oregon?" *New Scientist* 81, no. 113 (January 4, 1987), 28–30. Also see Ernest Callenbach, *Ecotopia: The Notebooks and Reports of William Weston* (1975).

9. Tuan, *Space and Place*, 85.

10. James, "Ecotopia in Oregon?" 29.

11. Portland *Oregonian*, April 25, 1993.

12. See especially William Cronon, *Changes in the Land: Indians, Colonists, and the Ecology of New England* (1983); Richard White, *Land Use, Environment, and Social Change: The Shaping of Island County, Washington* (1980); and Donald Worster, *Dust Bowl: The Southern Plains in the 1930s* (1979).

13. Timothy W. Silver, *A New Face on the Countryside: Indians, Colonists, and Slaves in South Atlantic Forests, 1500–1800* (1990), ix–x, 2.

14. My thanks to Don Wolf for these insights. Richard White insists that environmental historians should ground their work "in the larger life of the planet." See White, "Environmental History, Ecology, and Meaning," *Journal of American History* 76 (March 1990), 1116.

15. Dan Flores, "Place: An Argument for Bioregional History," *Environmental History Review* 18 (Winter 1994), 6.

16. Hines, *Life on the Plains of the Pacific,* 318.

17. *Columbian,* November 20, 1852.

18. For an excellent survey of the *historical* context of this discussion, see Carlos A. Schwantes, *The Pacific Northwest: An Interpretive History* (1989), 59, 97–99.

19. Ibid.

20. For a parallel argument that underscores the complexities of environmental change that resulted from the expansion of the world capitalist system, see Cronon, *Changes in the Land,* 14–15.

21. See Colin A. M. Duncan, "On Identifying a Sound Environmental Ethic in History: Prolegomena to Any Future Environmental History," *Environmental History Review* 15 (Summer 1991), 13.

22. Fernand Braudel, *The Perspective of the World,* trans. by Sian Reynolds (1984), 20, 27, 622.

23. The following sources have shaped my thinking on these issues: Peter Berger, *The Capitalist Revolution: Fifty Propositions about Property, Equality, and Liberty* (1986); Worster, *Dust Bowl;* and Eric Wolf, *Europe and a People without History* (1982).

24. See Donald Worster, "Transformations of the Earth: Toward an Agroecological Perspective in History," *Journal of American History* 76 (March 1990), 1101.

25. I am indebted to Robert Bunting for these observations.

26. I am indebted to Donald Wolf for these observations.

27. Richard White, "Discovering Nature in North America," *Journal of American History* 79 (December 1992), 888.

28. Flores, "Place: An Argument for Bioregional History," 10–11.

29. For the further elaboration of this argument, see Leften S. Stavrianos, *The Promise of the Coming Dark Age* (1976), 168–69.

30. On this point, I agree with Richard White. See White, "The Made and Unmade Worlds: Labor and Western Places," Annual Meeting of the Western History Association, Albuquerque, New Mexico, October 20–23, 1994. This reference is based on the author's notes.

31. Cronon, *Changes in the Land,* 13; and Flores, "Place: An Argument for Bioregional History," 12.

32. Edward O. Wilson, *Biophilia* (1984), 11; and Simon Schama, *Landscape and Memory* (1995), 14. Also see Donald Worster, "Nature and the Disorder of History," *Environmental History Review* 18 (Summer 1994), 1–15.

33. For an interesting commentary on this question, see Betsy Blackmar, "Contemplating the Force of Nature," *Radical Historians Newsletter,* no. 70 (May 1994), 1, 4, 16.

34. E. R. Jackman, *Oregon: A State of the Mind* (Corvallis: Friends of the Library, 1961), 5–16.

35. Ibid., 16.

36. This argument is adapted from William Cronon, "Frontier and Region in Western History," address to the Conference on Power and Place in the Northern West, University of Washington, November 4, 1994.

37. Robin Cody, "The Northwest Voice," *Oregon Quarterly* (Spring 1995), 18.

38. Samuel N. Dicken and Emily F. Dicken, *The Making of Oregon: A Study in Historical Geography* (1979), xiii.

39. William Kittredge, *Hole in the Sky: A Memoir* (1992), 40.

40. William Kittredge, *Owning It All* (1987), 62–63.

41. Barry Lopez, "A Sense of Place," *Old Oregon* (Autumn 1991), 16.

42. James P. Ronda, "Calculating Ouragon," *Oregon Historical Quarterly* 94 (Summer–Fall 1993), 121.

43. For a discussion of the erosion of optimism in the American West, see William Howarth, "America's Dream of the Wide Open Spaces," *Book World,* January 4, 1987, 4.

The Native Ecological Context

1. John Kirk Townsend, *Narrative of a Journey across the Rocky Mountains to the Columbia River* (1839; rpt., 1978), 161, 163.

2. John Davies, ed., *Douglas of the Forests: The North American Journals of David Douglas* (1980), 94–96. For information about those accompanying Douglas, see Robert Boyd, "Strategies of Indian Burning in the Willamette Valley," *Canadian Journal of Anthropology* 5 (Fall 1986), 70.

3. Davies, ed., *Douglas of the Forests,* 94; and David Douglas, *Journals of Travels in North America, 1823–1827* (1953), 237.

4. Carl O. Sauer, "A Geographical Sketch of Early Man in America," *Geographi-*

cal Review 34 (1944), 529–73; Sauer, "The Agency of Man on Earth," in *Man's Role in Changing the Face of the Earth*, William L. Thomas, ed. (1956), 1:54–56; Sauer, *Seventeenth Century North America* (1980), 211; and Stephen J. Pyne, *Fire in America: A Cultural History of Wildland and Rural Fire* (1982; rpt., 1997), 75.

5. Henry Dobyns makes this point in *From Fire to Flood: Historic Human Destruction of Sonoran Desert Riverine Oases* (1981), 27.

6. Ibid., 28.

7. Stephen W. Barrett, "Indians and Fire," *Western Wildlands* 6, no. 3 (Spring 1980), 17–21.

8. For a select number of scholars who argue this point, see Carl O. Sauer, "Man in the Ecology of Tropical America," *Proceedings of the Ninth Pacific Science Congress* 20 (1957), 104–10; Sauer, "Man's Dominance by Use of Fire," *Geoscience and Man* 10 (1975), 1–13; William Cronon, *Changes in the Land: Indians, Colonists, and the Ecology of New England* (1983); and Richard White, *Land Use, Environment, and Social Change: The Shaping of Island County, Washington* (1980).

9. William Cronon, "Comments on 'Landscape History and Ecological Change,'" *Journal of Forest History* 33 (July 1989), 125; and Norman L. Christensen, "Landscape History and Ecological Change," ibid., 119.

10. For an excellent review, see Karl W. Butzer, "The Americas before and after 1492: An Introduction to Current Geographical Research," *Annals of the Association of American Geographers* 82, no. 3 (1992), 345–66.

11. For an example of the Indian manipulation of a specific environment, see White, *Land Use, Environment, and Social Change*, 19–25. Also see William K. Stevens, "An Eden in Ancient America? Not Really," *New York Times*, March 30, 1993.

12. William M. Denevan, "The Pristine Myth: The Landscape of the Americas in 1492," *Annals of the Association of American Geographers* 82, no. 3 (1992), 370. The second Denevan quote is in the *New York Times*, March 30, 1993.

13. Neil Roberts, *The Holocene: An Environmental History* (1989), 57–113. For the plausibility of overkill as explanation for Pleistocene extinctions, see Paul S. Martin, "Pleistocene Overkill," *Science* 179 (1973), 969; J. E. Mosimann and P. S. Martin, "Simulating Overkill by Paleoindians," *American Scientist* 63 (1975), 304–13; and Donald K. Grayson, "Pleistocene Avifaunas and the Overkill Hypothesis," *Science* 195 (1977), 691–93.

14. Roberts, *The Holocene*, 71; and Donald Worster, *The Wealth of Nature: Environmental History and the Ecological Imagination* (1993), 54–55.

15. The physiographic region that embraces the present states of Washington, Oregon, and Idaho, northern California and Nevada, western Montana, and British

Columbia. The greater Columbia River system also provides a definitive outline for the region.

16. Eugene S. Hunn, *Nch'i-Wana, "The Big River": Mid-Columbia Indians and Their Land* (1990), 19–21; C. Melvin Aikens, *Archaeology of Oregon* (1986), 41–42; Ewart M. Baldwin, *Geology of Oregon* (1981), 52–53; and Leroy E. Detling, *Historical Background of the Flora of the Pacific Northwest* (1968), 35–36.

17. Aikens, *Archaeology of Oregon,* 9–10; and Peter J. Mehringer, "Late-Quaternary Pollen Records from the Interior Pacific Northwest and Northern Great Basin of the United States," in *Pollen Records of the Late-Quaternary North American Sediments,* Vaughan M. Bryant, Jr., and Richard G. Holloway, eds. (1985), 169.

18. Peter G. Boag, *Environment and Experience: Settlement Culture in Nineteenth-Century Oregon* (1992), 7–8; and Aikens, *Archaeology of Oregon,* 109–10.

19. For a brief account of the Fort Rock and other Northwest archaeological excavations, see Luther S. Cressman, *The Sandal and the Cave: The Indians of Oregon* (1962; rpt., 1981).

20. Roberts, *The Holocene,* 67; and Aikens, *Archaeology of Oregon,* 9.

21. Aikins, *Archaeology of Oregon,* 9–10.

22. Butzer, "The Americas before and after 1492," 346.

23. For a discussion of these issues, see Roberts, *The Holocene,* 5.

24. Ibid., 122; Carlos Schwantes, *The Pacific Northwest: An Interpretive History* (1989), 19. For the reference to Neo-European settlements, see Alfred W. Crosby, *Ecological Imperialism: The Biological Expansion of Europe, 900–1900* (1986).

25. Dean A. Shinn, "Historical Perspectives on Range Burning in the Inland Pacific Northwest," *Journal of Range Management* 33 (November 1980), 418–19. For the absence of Neolithic agriculture in the Pacific Northwest, see Butzer, "The Americas before and after 1492," 348; White, *Land Use, Environment, and Social Change,* 14–34 (quote on p. 32); Philip Drucker, *Indians of the Northwest Coast* (1955), 35–55; and Cressman, *Sandal and the Cave,* 40–54.

26. Hunn, *Nch'i-Wana,* 19, 21; Hunn, "The Plateau," in *The First Oregonians,* Carolyn M. Buan and Richard Lewis, eds. (1991), 14; and Richard White, "The Altered Landscape: Social Change and the Land in the Pacific Northwest," in *Regionalism and the Pacific Northwest,* William G. Robbins, Robert J. Frank, and Richard E. Ross, eds. (1983), 114–15.

27. The term "Oregon Country," a vaguely conceived geographic region, became current in the United States during the early years of the nineteenth century. See Oscar O. Winther, *The Great Northwest: A History* (2d ed., 1950), 3.

28. White, *Land Use, Environment, and Social Change,* 21; and White, "The Altered Landscape," 111.

29. James K. Agee, *Fire Ecology of Pacific Northwest Forests* (1993), xi, 3, 11, 25; and Shinn, "Historical Perspectives on Range Burning," 415–17. A fire regime embraces the role of fire in an ecosystem.

30. Agee, *Fire Ecology of Pacific Northwest Forests,* 54–55; and Henry T. Lewis, "Reconstructing Patterns of Indian Burning in Southwestern Oregon," *Living with the Land: The Indians of Southwest Oregon,* Nan Hannon and Richard K. Olmo, eds. (1990), 80–83.

31. Pyne, *Fire in America,* 84–85. For Oregon's Willamette Valley, see Boag, *Environment and Experience,* 12–15.

32. Leslie M. Scott, ed., "John Work's Journey from Fort Vancouver to Umpqua River, and Return, in 1834," *Oregon Historical Quarterly* 24 (1923), 242, 249.

33. Boyd, "Strategies of Indian Burning in the Willamette Valley," 66.

34. Ibid., 66–67.

35. Ibid., 71.

36. Peel is quoted in James R. Gibson, *Farming the Frontier: The Agricultural Opening of the Oregon Country, 1786–1846* (1985), 129. Wilkes is quoted in Boyd, "Strategies of Indian Burning in the Willamette Valley," 71. Also see James R. Habek, "The Original Vegetation of the Mid-Willamette Valley, Oregon," *Northwest Science* 35, no. 2 (May 1961), 74–75.

37. Robert R. Bunting, "Landscaping the Pacific Northwest: A Cultural and Ecological Mapping of the Douglas Fir Region, 1778–1900" (Ph.D. diss., University of California, Davis, 1993), 261–62.

38. Boyd, "Strategies of Indian Burning in the Willamette Valley," 67–69. Also see Kathryn Anne Toepel, "The Western Interior," in *The First Oregonians,* Buan and Lewis, eds. (1991), 15–20.

39. Habek, "The Original Vegetation of the Mid-Willamette Valley," 75; and James R. Sedell and Judith L. Froggatt, "Importance of Streamside Forests to Large Rivers: The Isolation of the Willamette River, Oregon, U.S.A., from Its Floodplain by Snagging and Streamside Forest Removal," *Vera. Interna. Verein. Limnol.* 22 (December 1984), 1830. The land survey notes were transcribed from microfiche in the Marion County surveyor's office by Susan Kolar, Corvallis, Oregon.

40. See S. M. Galatowitsch, "Using the Original Land Survey Notes to Reconstruct Presettlement Landscapes in the American West," *Great Basin Naturalist* 50, no. 2 (1990), 181–91.

41. Toepel, "The Western Interior," 16; and Boyd, "Strategies of Indian Burning in the Willamette Valley," 69.

42. Boyd, "Strategies of Indian Burning in the Willamette Valley," 72.

43. Ibid.

44. Ibid.; and Toepel, "The Western Interior," 16.

45. George Riddle, *History of Early Days in Oregon,* 45. Reprinted from *The Riddle Enterprise,* 1920.

46. Henry Zenk, "Contributions to Tualatin Ethnography: Subsistence and Ethnobiology" (M.A. thesis, Portland State University, 1976), 58; and Boyd, "Strategies of Indian Burning in the Willamette Valley," 76.

47. Bunting, "Landscaping the Pacific Northwest," 46–48.

48. Overton Johnson and William H. Winter, *Route across the Rocky Mountains* (1846; rpt., 1982), 46–48.

49. Jeff LaLande, *An Environmental History of the Little Applegate Watershed* (1995), 17–18. The *Ashland Tidings,* March 4, 1892, quoted in ibid., 18.

50. Stephen Dow Beckham, *Land of the Umpqua: A History of Douglas County, Oregon* (1986), 34–36.

51. This is the title to Donald W. Meinig's *The Great Columbia Plain: A Historical Geography, 1805–1910* (1968), still the best book of its kind for the Pacific Northwest.

52. Lee Eddlemann, "Oregon's High Desert: Legacy for Today," in *Oregon's High Desert: The Last 100 Years* (1989), 2; and J. B. Kauffman and D. B. Sapsis, "The Natural Role of Fire in Oregon's High Desert," in ibid., 15.

53. James A. Young and B. Abbott Sparks, *Cattle in the Cold Desert* (1985), 19–22.

54. Ibid., 27–32; Kauffman and Sapsis, "The Natural Role of Fire in Oregon's High Desert," 15; and Shinn, "Historical Perspectives on Range Burning," 416–17.

55. Young and Sparks, *Cattle in the Cold Desert,* 22; T. C. Elliott, ed., "The Peter Skene Ogden Journals," *Oregon Historical Quarterly* 11 (June 1910), 207; and Eddleman, "Oregon's High Desert," 2.

56. Reuben Gold Thwaites, ed., *Original Journals of the Lewis and Clark Expedition, 1804–1806* (1959), 4:290, 345–46.

57. K. G. Davies, ed., *Peter Skene Ogden's Snake Country Journals, 1826–27* (1961), 7, 19, and 126–27.

58. Explorer and discovery accounts of the Americas dating from the time of Columbus, according to Richard White, appraised objects in the physical environment in terms of their value as commodities. See White, "Discovering Nature in North America," *Journal of American History* 79 (December 1992), 879–80.

59. Kauffman and Sapsis, "The Natural Role of Fire in Oregon's High Desert," 15; and Shinn, "Historical Perspectives on Range Burning," 416 and 419.

60. C. S. Fowler, "Subsistence," in *Great Basin,* Warren L. D'Azevedo, ed. (1986), 79, 93–94; and Margaret M. Wheat, *Survival Arts of the Primitive Paiutes* (1967), 91.

61. Townsend, *Narrative of a Journey across the Rocky Mountains,* 246.

62. Samuel Parker, *Journal of an Exploring Tour beyond the Rocky Mountains*

(1838; rpt., 1967), 272, 274; Donald Jackson and Mary Lee Spence, eds., *The Expeditions of John Charles Fremont* (1970), 1:550–51; and Eddlemann, "Oregon's High Desert," 2.

63. Hunn, *Nch'i-Wana*, 130–31.

64. For a recent study that confirms the role of Indian-caused fire in shaping the complex forested landscape of the Blue Mountains, see Nancy Langston, *Forest Dreams, Forest Nightmares: The Paradox of Old Growth in the Inland West* (1995), 45–49.

65. Townsend, *Narrative Journey across the Rocky Mountains,* 163.

66. Washington Irving, *The Adventures of Captain Bonneville, U.S.A., in the Rocky Mountains and the Far West* (1837; rpt., 1961), 339–41.

67. Archer Butler Hulbert and Dorothy Printup Hulbert, eds., *The Oregon Crusade: Across Land and Sea to Oregon* (1935), 178; and Thomas J. Farnham, *An 1839 Wagon Train Journal: Travels in the Great Western Prairies, the Anahuac and Rocky Mountains and in the Oregon Territory* (1843; rpt., 1977), 73.

68. James Clyman, *Journal of a Mountain Man* (1928; rpt., Missoula: Mountain Press Publishing Company, 1984), 120.

69. Langston, *Forest Dreams, Forest Nightmares,* 47.

70. Young and Sparks, *Cattle in the Cold Desert,* 27; James K. Agee, "The Historical Role of Fire in Pacific Northwest Forests," in *Natural and Proscribed Fire in Pacific Northwest Forests,* John D. Walsted, Steven R. Radosevich, and David V. Sandberg, eds. (1990), 26–27; and White, "Discovering Nature in North America," 882.

71. Archibald Campbell to William H. Seward, Secretary of State, Feb. 3, 1869, RG 76, Records Relating to the First Northwest Boundary Survey Commission, 1853–1869, National Archives, T-606, roll 1.

72. *Reports of Explorations and Surveys . . . for a Railroad from the Mississippi River to the Pacific Ocean,* 1853–55, (1857), 6 (Abbott): 75; and diary of B. J. Pengra, entries for July 1865, in Stephen Dow Beckham, *The Oregon Central Military Wagon Road: A History and Reconnaissance,* U.S. Department of Agriculture, Forest Service, Heritage Research Associates Report no. 6, 1 (1981): 28–34.

73. J. G. Cooper and G. Suckley, *The Natural History of Washington Territory* (1859), 9–11. This privately published volume includes segments of the larger report. Also see Thomas M. Quigley, *Forest Health in the Blue Mountains: Social and Economic Perspectives,* U.S. Department of Agriculture, Forest Service Technical Report (1992), 1.

74. Francis Haines, "The Northward Spread of Horses among the Plains Indians," *American Anthropologist* 40 (1938), 431, 435–36; and Hunn, *Nch'i-Wana,* 22–26.

75. "Wilson Price Hunt's Diary of His Overland Trip Westward to Astoria in

1811–12," in *The Discovery of the Oregon Trail: Robert Stuart's Narratives,* Philip Ashton Rollins, ed. (1935), 301–2.

76. Nesmith Ankeny, *The West as I Knew It* (1953), 27.

77. Farnham, *An 1839 Wagon Train Journal,* 74–75; and Parker, *Journal of an Exploring Tour beyond the Rocky Mountains,* 281.

78. Jackson and Spence, eds., *The Expeditions of John Charles Fremont,* 1:551 and 584; Raymond W. Settle, ed., *The March of the Mounted Riflemen as Recorded in the Journals of Major Osborne Cross and George Gibbs and the Official Report of Colonel Loring* (1940), 229; and George Belshaw, *Diary of the Oregon Trail, 1853* (1960). John W. Evans, who has compiled an excellent volume of the early travel accounts of the Blue Mountains section of the Oregon Trail, contends that Indians fired the prairie in the late summer to ensure "an abundance of new grass for their horse herds." See Evans, *Powerful Rocky: The Blue Mountains and the Oregon Trail* (1991), 29n.

79. See Richard White, *The Roots of Dependency: Subsistence, Environment, and Social Change among the Choctaws, Pawnees, and Navajos* (1983), 100, and 247–48; Dan Flores, "Bison Ecology and Bison Diplomacy: The Southern Plains from 1800 to 1850," *Journal of American History* 78 (1991), 481; Barrett, "Indians and Fire," 21; Elliott West, *The Way to the West: Essays on the Central Plains* (1995); and Langston, *Forest Dreams, Forest Nightmares,* 47–49.

80. Hunn, *Nch'i-Wana,* 19; Philip Shabecoff, *A Fierce Green Fire: The American Environmental Movement* (New York: Hill and Wang, 1993), 24; and *Congressional Globe,* 29th Cong., 1st sess., 1846, p. 342.

81. Helmut K. Buechner, "Some Biotic Changes in the State of Washington, Particularly during the Century 1853–1953," *Research Studies of the State College of Washington* 21 (1953), 154; and White, "The Altered Landscape," 111.

The Great Divide

1. Overton Johnson and William H. Winter, *Route across the Rocky Mountains* (1846; rpt., 1982), 49.

2. Gary E. Moulton, ed., *The Journals of the Lewis and Clark Expedition,* 5 (1988), 287–88, 327, and 335. The estimate of the number of fishing stations that Lewis and Clark encountered is in Anthony Netboy, *The Columbia River Salmon and Steelhead Trout: Their Fight for Survival* (1980), 4–5.

3. For Jefferson's long-standing and imperial interests in western North America, see James P. Ronda, *Lewis and Clark among the Indians* (1984); William Appleman Williams, *The Contours of American History* (1961); Henry Nash Smith,

Virgin Land: The American West as Symbol and Myth (1950); and Bernard DeVoto, *The Course of Empire* (1952).

4. Jefferson is quoted in James P. Ronda, *Astoria and Empire* (1990), 43.

5. Donald Jackson, ed., *Letters of the Lewis and Clark Expedition with Related Documents, 1783–1854* (rev. ed., 1978), 319, 321–22; and John Logan Allen, *Passage through the Garden: Lewis and Clark and the Image of the Northwest* (1975), 394.

6. Dorothy O. Johansen and Charles M. Gates, *Empire of the Columbia: A History of the Pacific Northwest* (2d ed., 1967), 49; and John Ledyard, *A Journal of Captain Cook's Last Voyage to the Pacific Ocean* (1783; photocopy rpt., Corvallis, OR, 1963), 69–70.

7. The first Vancouver quote is in Robert E. Ficken, *The Forested Land: A History of Lumbering in Western Washington* (1987), 8; the second quote is in Johansen and Gates, *Empire of the Columbia*, 45.

8. Ross Cox, *The Columbia River*, Edgar I. and Jane R. Stewart, eds. (1957), 71, 80, 157, 256.

9. Alexander Ross, *Adventures of the First Settlers on the Oregon or Columbia River, 1810–1813* (1904; rpt., 1986), 89, 108, 114; and Philip Ashton Rollins, ed., *The Discovery of the Oregon Trail: Robert Stuart's Narratives* (1935), 32, 52.

10. Robin Fisher, *Contact and Conflict: Indian-European Relations in British Columbia, 1774–1890* (1977), 35.

11. Robert R. Bunting, "Landscaping the Pacific Northwest: A Cultural and Ecological Mapping of the Douglas Fir Region, 1778–1900" (Ph.D. diss., University of California, Davis, 1993), 85.

12. For a survey of this relatively well-known history, see Carlos A. Schwantes, *The Pacific Northwest: An Interpretive History* (1989), 53–60.

13. Work came to the Columbia River country with Peter Skene Ogden in 1823 and was chiefly responsible for fur-trading activities in the Upper Columbia region. Between 1823 and 1825 he was busy establishing a farm and building Fort Colville, and in 1830 he succeeded Ogden as the head of the Snake River trapping brigade. See Leslie M. Scott, ed., "John Work's Journey from Fort Vancouver to Umpqua River, and Return, in 1834," *Oregon Historical Quarterly* 24 (September 1923), 238–39.

14. Ibid., 242, 247, 249.

15. Johansen and Gates, *Empire of the Columbia*, 127–30.

16. Bunting, "Landscaping the Pacific Northwest," 97–100; and Burt Brown Barker, ed., *Letters of Dr. John McLoughlin, Written at Fort Vancouver, 1829–1832* (1948), 185.

17. "Dispatch from George Simpson, Esq., Governor of Rupert Land," *The Pub-*

lications of the Hudson's Bay Record Society (n.d.), 66–67; and E. E. Rich, ed., *The Letters of John McLoughlin from Fort Vancouver to the Governor and Committee* (1941), 37.

18. Eugene S. Hunn, *Nch'i-Wana, "The Big River": Mid-Columbia Indians and Their Land* (1990), 31–32.

19. Much of this discussion is based on my notes from Robert Boyd, "Disease as a Factor in Native Population Decline," a talk presented at Oregon State University, February 1988. Also see Alfred W. Crosby, *The Columbian Exchange: Biological and Cultural Consequences of 1492* (1972), 30–31; and Robert Boyd, "Demographic History, 1774–1874," in Wayne Suttles, ed., *Northwest Coast* (1990), 137.

20. Boyd, "Disease as a Factor in Native Population Decline"; and Boyd, "Demographic History, 1774–1874," 137–38. Also see Schwantes, *The Pacific Northwest*, 36–37.

21. Boyd, "Disease as a Factor in Native Population Decline"; Boyd, "Demographic History, 1774–1874," 137; and Moulton, ed., *The Journals of the Lewis and Clark Expedition*, 6 (1990), 81, 286–87.

22. Boyd, "Disease as a Factor in Native Population Decline"; Boyd, "Demographic History, 1774–1874," 139; and Robert T. Boyd, "Another Look at the 'Fever and Ague' of Western Oregon," *Ethnohistory* 22 (Spring 1975), 135–54.

23. James L. Ratcliff, "What Happened to the Kalapuya? A Study of the Depletion of Their Economic Base," *Indian Historian* 6 (Summer 1973), 31.

24. John Kirk Townsend, *Narrative of a Journey across the Rocky Mountains to the Columbia River* (1839; rpt., 1978), 224–25.

25. Rich, ed., *The Letters of John McLoughlin*, 88; Frederick G. Young, ed., "The Correspondence and Journals of Captain Nathaniel J. Wyeth," *Sources of Oregon History*, 1, pts. 3–6 (1899), 148, 175. David Douglas is quoted in H. H. Stage and C. M. Gjullin, "Anophelines and Malaria in the Pacific Northwest," *Northwest Science* 9, no. 3 (1935).

26. Samuel Parker, *Journal of an Exploring Tour beyond the Rocky Mountains* (1838; rpt., 1967), 191–92; and Schwantes, *The Pacific Northwest*, 37.

27. Boyd cites a mortality rate between 1830 and 1841 on the lower Columbia River of 92 percent (see "Demographic History, 1774–1874," 139; and "Disease as a Factor in Native Population Decline").

28. Rich, *The Letters of John McLoughlin*, 125–26.

29. "The Diary of Reverend Jason Lee," *Oregon Historical Quarterly* 17 (1916), 262–63.

30. James R. Gibson, *Farming the Frontier: The Agricultural Opening of the Ore-*

gon Country, 1786–1846 (1985), 130; and Lois Halliday McDonald, ed., *Fur Trade Letters of Francis Ermatinger* (1839; rpt., 1980), 163.

31. Don Johnson, ed., *The Journals of Captain Nathaniel J. Wyeth to the Oregon Country, 1831–1836* (1899; rpt., 1984), 33.

32. "Occupation of the Columbia River: A Report of the Committee to Inquire into the Situation of the Settlements upon the Pacific Ocean," *Oregon Historical Quarterly* 8 (1907), 60–62, 66–67, 70–71.

33. Schwantes, *The Pacific Northwest*, 78–79.

34. Thomas Hart Benton, *Thirty Years' View* (1897), 1:13.

35. For this argument, see Schwantes, *The Pacific Northwest*, 79.

36. Alfred Crosby, *Ecological Imperialism: The Biological Expansion of Europe, 900–1900* (1986), 193–94.

37. See William E. Doolittle, "Agriculture in North America on the Eve of Contact: A Reassessment," *Annals of the Association of American Geographers* 82 (September 1992), 386.

38. Richard White, *"It's Your Misfortune and None of My Own": A New History of the American West* (1991), 212–13.

39. Crosby, *Ecological Imperialism*, 7.

40. This argument is based on an adaptation of Richard White's general ideas to the Willamette Valley. See White, *"It's Your Misfortune and None of My Own,"* 214–15.

41. Crosby, *Ecological Imperialism*, 6–7.

42. Phoebe Goodell Judson, *A Pioneer's Search for an Ideal Home*, John M. McClelland, Jr., ed. (1966), 42.

43. Thomas J. Farnham, *An 1839 Wagon Train Journal: Travels in the Great Western Prairies* (1843; rpt., 1977), 79.

44. Letter of Talmadge B. Wood, April 1844, in "Documents," *Oregon Historical Quarterly* 3 (December 1902), 395–96; Nesmith Ankeny, *The West as I Knew It* (1953), 30–31 (the author is quoting from the diaries of James Nesmith); and Joel Palmer, *Journal of Travels on the Oregon Trail in 1845* (1847; rpt., 1992), 116–18.

45. Elliott West, *The Way to the West: Essays on the Central Plains* (1995), 32–33.

46. M. M. McCarver to C. A. Dodge, in "Documents," *Oregon Historical Quarterly* 4 (March 1903), 78–79.

47. Palmer, *Journal of Travels on the Oregon Trail*, 152–53.

48. Ibid., 154–57.

49. White, *"It's Your Misfortune and None of My Own,"* 90; and Richard White, "Trashing the Trails," in *Trails: Toward a New Western History*, Patricia Nelson Limerick et al., eds. (1991), 26–27.

50. Boyd, "Demographic History, 1774–1874," 141.

51. Ibid., 141.

52. James Douglas to Board of Governors, October 18, 1838, in Rich, ed., *The Letters of John McLoughlin*, 241–42.

53. Charles Wilkes, "Report on the Territory of Oregon," *Oregon Historical Quarterly* 12 (September 1911), 290–93, 299.

54. Peter G. Boag, *Environment and Experience: Settlement Culture in Nineteenth-Century Oregon* (1992), 105; Gibson, *Farming the Frontier*, 131–33; and Oscar O. Winther, *The Great Northwest: A History* (2d ed., 1950), 77.

55. Peter H. Burnett, *Recollections and Opinions of an Old Pioneer* (1880; rpt., 1969), 141; and Rich, ed., *The Letters of John McLoughlin*, 141.

56. Gibson, *Farming the Frontier*, 136–37, 152–53.

57. Johnson and Winter, *Route across the Rocky Mountains*, 42, 46.

58. Palmer, *Journal of Travels*, 158–59. The population estimate is in Gibson, *Farming the Frontier*, 137.

59. Gibson, *Farming the Frontier*, 135; and Boag, *Environment and Experience*, 47–48.

60. Jerry C. Towle, "Changing Geography of Willamette Valley Woodlands," *Oregon Historical Quarterly* 83 (Spring 1982), 74–75.

61. William A. Bowen, *The Willamette Valley: Migration and Settlement on the Oregon Frontier* (1978), 74–75; and Richard White, *Land Use, Environment, and Social Change: The Shaping of Island County, Washington* (1980), 41–43.

62. Bowen, *The Willamette Valley*, 79–80; C. L. Camp, ed., *James Clyman, American Frontiersman* (1928), 134; and "Report of Lieutenant Neil M. Howison on Oregon, 1846," *Oregon Historical Quarterly* 14 (March 1913), 52.

63. Bowen, *The Willamette Valley*, 80.

64. Raymond F. Dasmann, *The Destruction of California* (1965), 60, 62, 65.

65. Salem *Oregon Statesman*, February 24, 1862; and J. C. Nelson, "The Grasses of Salem, Oregon and Vicinity, *Torreya* 19, no. 11 (1919), 216–27. Also see Bunting, "Landscaping the Pacific Northwest," 261–62.

66. The quotation on the Indian population is in Russell Thornton, *American Indian Holocaust and Survival: A Population History since 1492* (1987), 212–13.

67. U.S. Department of Commerce, Bureau of the Census, *The Seventh Census of the United States: 1850* (1853), lxxxii.

68. Waldo is quoted in Bowen, *The Willamette Valley*, 75.

69. White, *Land Use, Environment, and Social Change*, 48–49; and Boag, *Environment and Experience*, 62–63. Also see William G. Robbins, "Some Perspectives

on Law and Order in Frontier Newspapers," *Journal of the West* 17 (January 1978), 53–62.

70. "Report of Lieutenant Neil M. Howison," 51.

Prescripting the Landscape

1. Theodore Winthrop, *The Canoe and the Saddle* (1862; rpt., 1913), 104.

2. Donald Worster, "Transformations of the Earth: Toward an Agroecological Perspective in History," *Journal of American History* 76 (March 1990), 1096. For a further elaboration of this notion, see Richard White, *Land Use, Environment, and Social Change: The Shaping of Island County, Washington* (1980), 35–53.

3. White, *Land Use, Environment and Social Change*, 32–33; and Samuel Parker, *Journal of an Exploring Tour beyond the Rocky Mountains* (1842; rpt., 1990), 288.

4. For a discussion of these issues on a larger regional scale, see William G. Robbins, *Colony and Empire: The Capitalist Transformation of the American West* (1994).

5. William A. Bowen, *The Willamette Valley: Settlement on the Oregon Frontier* (1978), 69–70.

6. The Organic Code is printed in ibid., 70.

7. Oregon City *Spectator,* February 22, 1849; and Malcolm Clark, Jr., *Eden Seekers: The Settlement of Oregon* (1981), 236–37.

8. Clark, *Eden Seekers,* 237; and Jerry A. O'Callaghan, *The Dispossession of the Public Domain in Oregon* (1960), 19, 34. Also see "Petition of Citizens of Oregon Praying That the Laws of the United States May Be Extended over That Territory," in Priscilla Knuth and Charles M. Gates, eds., "Oregon Territory in 1849–1850," *Pacific Northwest Quarterly* 40 (1949), 5–7.

9. For the background to this discussion, see William G. Robbins, "The Indian Question in Western Oregon: The Making of a Colonial People," in *Experiences in a Promised Land: Essays in Pacific Northwest History,* G. Thomas Edwards and Carlos A. Schwantes, eds. (1986), 51–67.

10. The provisions of the boundary treaty and the territorial act are reprinted in "The Coos, Lower Umpqua and Siuslaw Indian Tribes: An Historical Perspective," unpublished pamphlet distributed by the Coos, Lower Umpqua, Siuslaw Indian Tribes, Inc., Coos Bay, Oregon. Copy in the author's possession.

11. Alvin Josephy, Jr., *The Nez Perce Indians and the Opening of the Northwest* (1965), 286; *Congressional Globe,* 31st Cong., 1st sess. (1850), 41D; and Stephen Dow Beckham, "History of Western Oregon since 1846," in *Northwest Coast,* Wayne Suttles, ed. (1990), 180.

12. Beckham, "History of Western Oregon since 1846," 182–83; and Beckham, *Requiem for a People: The Roque Indians and the Frontiersmen* (1971), 147–67.

13. C. F. Coan, "Federal Indian Relations in the Pacific Northwest: The Second Stage, 1853–1856," *Oregon Historical Quarterly* 23 (1922), 14–16; U.S. Department of Interior, *Annual Report of the Commissioner of Indian Affairs* (1855), 110, and (1856), 12.

14. Coan, "Federal Indian Relations in the Pacific Northwest," 4–5. The army officer is cited in Preston E. Onstad, "The Fort on the Luckiamute: A Resurvey of Fort Hoskins," *Oregon Historical Quarterly* 65 (1964), 175.

15. Robert R. Bunting, "Landscaping the Pacific Northwest: A Cultural and Ecological Mapping of the Douglas Fir Region, 1778–1900" (Ph.D. diss., University of California, Davis, 1993), 236, 240.

16. For a discussion of this issue, see Robbins, "The Indian Question in Western Oregon," 51–67.

17. Carlos A. Schwantes, *The Pacific Northwest: An Interpretive History* (1989), 92, 166; and Donald W. Meinig, *The Great Columbia Plain: A Historical Geography, 1805–1910* (1968), 201–4.

18. Jesse Applegate, "Umpqua Agriculture, 1851," *Oregon Historical Quarterly* 32 (June 1931), 142; Wilson Blain to David Kerr, December 30, 1853, typescript in Wilson Blain folder, Letters, 1853–1855, Oregon Historical Society Manuscript 1208 (hereafter OHS 1208), Portland; and Wallace D. Farnham, "Religion as an Influence in Life and Thought: Jackson County, Oregon, 1860–1890" (Ph.D. diss., University of Oregon, Eugene, 1955), 25.

19. See, for example, Applegate, "Umpqua Agriculture, 1851," 135.

20. Ibid.

21. Sheba Hargreaves, ed., "The Letters of Roselle Putnam," *Oregon Historical Quarterly* 29 (September 1928), 243, 246–47, 252.

22. Ibid., 250–51; and Applegate, "Umpqua Agriculture, 1851," 137.

23. Hargreaves, ed., "Letters of Roselle Putnam," 256.

24. Donald Worster, *Nature's Economy: A History of Ecological Ideas* (1977; 2d ed., 1994), 258–65.

25. George Riddle, *History of Early Days in Oregon,* 30–31, 36. Reprinted from *The Riddle Enterprise,* 1920.

26. Ibid., 37–41.

27. Verne Bright, "The Lost County, Umpqua, Oregon, and Its Early Settlements," *Oregon Historical Quarterly* 51 (1950), 120–22; Douglas County, Oregon, *Proceedings of the Board of County Commissioners of Umpqua County,* Book A (December 1851); Oregon *Statesman,* July 4, 1851.

28. Farnham, "Religion as an Influence in Life and Thought," 25; and Joseph Gaston, *The Centennial History of Oregon, 1811–1912* (1912), 1:452.

29. James R. Robertson, "The Social Evolution of Oregon," *Oregon Historical Quarterly* 3 (1902), 11.

30. Applegate, "Umpqua Agriculture, 1851," 135.

31. Bunting, "Landscaping the Pacific Northwest," 266–67.

32. Portland *Oregonian,* December 24, 1950.

33. Jack H. Blok, "The Evolution of Agricultural Resource Use Strategies in the Willamette Valley" (Ph.D. diss., Oregon State University, Corvallis, 1974), 51; Peter Boag, *Environment and Experience: Settlement Culture in Nineteenth-Century Oregon* (1992), 106–8; *Oregonian,* November 4, 1900; and Michael L. Olson, "The Beginnings of Agriculture in Western Oregon and Western Washington" (Ph.D. diss., University of Washington, Seattle, 1970), 112.

34. *Oregonian,* July 10, 1852.

35. Ibid., September 18, 1852, and March 26, 1853.

36. George O. Goodell, "The Upper Calapooia," *Oregon Historical Quarterly* 4 (March 1903), 70.

37. Jerry C. Towle, "Changing Geography of Willamette Valley Woodlands," *Oregon Historical Quarterly* 83 (1982), 77; Joseph Brown is quoted in Bunting, "Landscaping the Pacific Northwest," 285; and John Minto, "From Youth to Age as an American," *Oregon Historical Quarterly* 9 (June 1908), 140.

38. William G. Robbins, *Hard Times in Paradise: Coos Bay, Oregon, 1850–1986* (1988), 4, 12.

39. Oregon *Statesman,* October 18, 1853; and Oregon *Spectator,* September 16, 1853.

40. Coos Bay *News,* January 2 and September 24, 1884, July 31, 1889, and May 7, 1890.

41. J. R. Caldwell, "The First Fruits of the Land: A Brief History of Early Horticulture in Oregon," *Oregon Historical Quarterly* 7 (March 1906), 28. For the argument that settlers sought to implement conventional agricultural practices, see Richard White, "The Altered Landscape: Social Change and the Land in the Pacific Northwest," in *Regionalism and the Pacific Northwest,* William G. Robbins et al., eds. (1983), 111.

42. Caldwell, "First Fruits of the Land," 29–30.

43. Ibid., 32–33.

44. Ibid., 34–35; Blok, "The Evolution of Agricultural Resource Use," 53; and *Oregonian,* January 1, 1995.

45. Hargreaves, ed., "The Letters of Roselle Putnam," 252. In his essay on early agriculture in the Umpqua Valley, Jesse Applegate emphasized that the settler's concern during the first year or two was "his own subsistence." During that period of "simple and primitive" culture, he advised farmers to focus on "breaking land," planting winter wheat, and then a vegetable garden for the summer. Although he failed to mention fruit in that 1851 essay, Applegate praised the wheat and vegetable production of the area. See Applegate, "Umpqua Agriculture, 1851," 137–40.

46. *Oregonian,* September 6, 1851, and November 4, 1900.

47. Bunting, "Landscaping the Pacific Northwest," 277–78. The quotation is in Boag, *Environment and Experience,* 122–23.

48. *Willamette Farmer,* March 16 and 23, 1872.

49. Minto, "From Youth to Age as an American," 131–32.

50. T. J. Dryer, publisher and editor of the Portland *Oregonian,* persistently argued for home manufactures that would aid "in the prosperity of the country." Home-produced goods would "keep the money in the country, in place of paying it out to those who come here temporarily to make all they can out of their speculations." *Oregonian,* September 6, 1851.

51. For an elaboration of this argument, see Bunting, "Landscaping the Pacific Northwest," 331–35.

52. *Oregonian,* February 15, 1861.

53. Ibid., October 5, 1869.

54. Ibid., February 4, May 20, and October 22, 1867.

55. These figures are cited in Boag, *Environment and Experience,* 115. Other sources differ only slightly from this assessment.

56. *Oregonian,* November 8, 1873.

57. Because of his interest in sheep husbandry and a variety of issues of interest to farmers, John Minto was named editor of the *Willamette Farmer.* See Minto, "From Youth to Age as an American," 147.

58. Minto, "From Youth to Age as an American," 138–39; and Dorothy O. Johansen and Charles M. Gates, *Empire of the Columbia: A History of the Pacific Northwest* (2d ed., 1967), 284.

59. *Oregonian,* October 8, 1853.

60. Oscar O. Winther, *The Great Northwest: A History* (2d ed., 1950), 169n; Samuel N. Dicken and Emily F. Dicken, *The Making of Oregon: A Study in Historical Geography* (1979), 81, 92; *West Shore* 1, no. 1 (August 1875), 4; and *Oregonian,* July 1, 1867.

61. Johansen and Gates, *Empire of the Columbia,* 279.

62. Boag, *Environment and Experience,* 115.

63. *Oregonian,* January 1, 1868; Dicken and Dicken, *The Making of Oregon,* 95; and *Willamette Farmer,* June 28, 1869.

64. Dean May argues that families settling in the vicinity of Sublimity (to the east of Salem) were "people of the soil" who took "pride in their independence gained through owning and operating their own land or shops" in their former places of residence. See Dean L. May, *Three Frontiers: Family, Land, and Society in the American West, 1850–1900* (1994), 43–44.

65. *Oregonian,* August 20, 1869.

66. *Willamette Farmer,* March 2, 1872.

67. Ibid., May 14, 1869; and *Oregonian,* October 5, 1869, and July 17, 1862.

68. *Oregonian,* May 20, 1865.

69. Ibid., October 25, 1871; and *Willamette Farmer,* February 1, 1866.

70. Boag, *Environment and Experience,* 112; *Willamette Farmer,* July 6, 1872; and Johansen and Gates, *Empire of the Columbia,* 309.

71. U.S. Department of Commerce, Bureau of Census, *Compendium of the Ninth Census* (1872), 772–73.

72. Dicken and Dicken, *The Making of Oregon,* 85; *Willamette Farmer,* September 8, 1865; and *Oregonian,* March 26, 1868.

Technology and Abundance

1. For a general discussion of the influence of railroads in the American West, see E. J. Hobsbawm, *The Age of Capital, 1848–1875* (1975), 39–41, 45; Alan Trachtenberg, *The Incorporation of America: Culture and Society in the Gilded Age* (1982), 6, 12, 19–20; and Carlos A. Schwantes, *Railroad Signatures across the Pacific Northwest* (1993), 17.

2. Dorothy O. Johansen and Charles M. Gates, *Empire of the Columbia: A History of the Pacific Northwest* (2d ed., 1967), 279; *Oregonian,* October 13, 1962; Jesse Applegate to J. W. Nesmith, November 15, 1863, printed in the *Oregonian,* November 21, 1863; and Schwantes, *Railroad Signatures across the Pacific Northwest,* 39–42.

3. *Oregonian,* June 28 and October 7, 1865; and *Willamette Farmer,* February 2, 1872.

4. Dean L. May, *Three Frontiers: Family, Land, and Society in the American West, 1850–1900* (1994), 252–53.

5. Newsom is quoted in the *Willamette Farmer,* July 27, 1872.

6. *Oregonian,* December 10, 1884.

7. For an elaboration of this theme, see William G. Robbins, *Colony and Empire: The Capitalist Transformation of the American West* (1994), 68–69.

8. Hobsbawm, *The Age of Capital*, 60–61.

9. Richard White, *"It's Your Misfortune and None of My Own": A New History of the American West* (1991), 128.

10. Carlos A. Schwantes, *The Pacific Northwest: An Interpretive History* (1989), 194.

11. *Oregonian*, April 24 and May 8, 1869.

12. Frances Fuller Victor, *All Over Oregon and Washington: Observations on the Country* (1872), 67.

13. Schwantes, *Railroad Signatures across the Pacific Northwest*, 38, 53–54; Michael L. Olsen, "The Beginnings of Agriculture in Western Oregon and Washington" (Ph.D. diss., University of Washington, Seattle, 1970), 175–77, 277; Samuel N. Dicken and Emily F. Dicken, *The Making of Oregon: A Study in Historical Geography* (1979), 85; and Peter G. Boag, *Environment and Experience: Settlement Culture in Nineteenth-Century Oregon* (1992), 115.

14. *Willamette Farmer*, June 28, 1869, and February 24, 1872.

15. These figures, based on the ninth (1870) and tenth (1880) census reports, are slightly exaggerated because portions of two counties (Benton and Lane) extended beyond the Willamette Valley. With the formation of Lincoln County just before 1900, among the counties in the Willamette Valley proper only Lane County still extended to the coast. For these various statistics, see U.S. Department of Commerce, Bureau of the Census, *Eighth Census of the United States: 1860*, 400; *Ninth Census of the United States: 1870, Compendium of the Ninth Census*, 772; and *Tenth Census of the United States: 1880, Compendium of the Tenth Census*, 723.

16. *Willamette Farmer*, June 20, 1874.

17. *West Shore* 1, no. 4 (November 1875), 2.

18. David Newsom, "Remarks about Oregon," *West Shore* 1 (January 1876), 1.

19. *Willamette Farmer*, October 26, 1877.

20. Denison's obituary is reprinted in E. Earl Newsom, comp., *David Newsom: The Western Observer, 1805–1882* (1972), 271–72.

21. Ibid., 167–69.

22. *Willamette Farmer*, March 2 and May 4, 1872.

23. Ibid., April 26, 1873.

24. Ibid., June 13, 1874.

25. Ibid., May 4, 1877.

26. Ibid., September 27, 1878, and June 13, 1879.

27. Ibid., June 15, 1877, September 16, 1881, and June 30, 1882.

28. Ibid., October 14 and 21, 1881.

29. Schwantes, *Railroad Signatures across the Pacific Northwest,* 60.

30. Randall Mills, "A History of Transportation in the Pacific Northwest," *Oregon Historical Quarterly* 45 (1946), 291–92; Johansen and Gates, *Empire of the Columbia,* 310–11; and Oscar O. Winther, *The Great Northwest: A History* (2d ed., 1950), 263–64.

31. *Oregonian,* January 13, 1880.

32. Mills, "History of Transportation in the Pacific Northwest," 292; Enoch A. Bryan, *Orient Meets Occident: The Advent of Railways to the Pacific Northwest* (1936), 162; and Winther, *The Great Northwest,* 264, 266.

33. Johansen and Gates, *Empire of the Columbia,* 311.

34. *Oregonian,* August 14, 1883.

35. Ibid., January 2, 1888.

36. Ibid.

37. Ibid.

38. Ibid., January 1, 1895.

39. Roseburg *Pantagraph,* August 10, 1872, June 7, 1873; and Roseburg *Plaindealer,* March 7, April 25, 1873.

40. *Plaindealer,* April 25, 1873.

41. A. G. Walling, *History of Southern Oregon* (1884), 412.

42. Stephen Dow Beckham, *Land of the Umpqua: A History of Douglas County, Oregon* (1986), 82, 210.

43. These statistics are listed in William G. Robbins, "The Far Western Frontier: Economic Opportunity and Social Democracy in Early Roseburg, Oregon" (Ph.D. diss., University of Oregon, Eugene, 1969), 68–71.

44. U.S. Department of Commerce, Bureau of the Census, *Sixteenth Census of the United States: 1940, Population.*

45. David Newsom to the *Pacific Christian Advocate,* December 8, 1881, reprinted in Newsom, comp., *David Newsom: The Western Observer,* 261.

46. U.S. Department of Commerce, Bureau of the Census, *Compendium of the Ninth Census,* 772–73; and *Compendium of the Tenth Census,* pt. 2, 723, 806, 899.

47. Katherine C. Atwood, *As Long as the World Goes On: Environmental History of the Evans Creek Watershed,* U.S. Department of the Interior, Bureau of Land Management, Medford District Office (1995), 26, 28; Jeff LaLande, *An Environmental History of the Little Applegate River Watershed,* U.S. Department of Agriculture, Forest Service, Rogue River National Forest, 1995, 19–20; and White, *"It's Your Misfortune,"* 232–33.

48. LaLande, *An Environmental History of the Little Applegate River Watershed*, 20; and Atwood, *As Long as the World Goes On*, 28, 51.

49. LaLande, *An Environmental History of the Little Applegate River Watershed*, 20, 44; and Atwood, *As Long as the World Goes On*, 28–30.

50. Cole M. Rivers, "History and Development of the Rogue River Basin as Related to Its Fishery Prior to 1941," typescript, Rogue River Fisheries, vol. 1, Salem, Oregon State Game Commission, quoted in LaLande, *An Environmental History of the Little Applegate River Watershed*, 44–45, 48.

51. Atwood, *As Long as the World Goes On*, 28–29; and LaLande, *An Environmental History of the Little Applegate River Watershed*, 22.

52. *Willamette Farmer*, April 6, 1872.

53. The *Intelligencer* is quoted in William G. Morris, "Forest Fires in Western Oregon and Washington," *Oregon Historical Quarterly* 35 (1934), 323.

54. David Newsom to the *Pacific Christian Advocate*, December 8, 1881, reprinted in Newsom, comp., *David Newsom: The Western Observer*, 262; and *Oregonian*, January 1, 1881.

55. Atwood, *As Long as the World Goes On*, 39.

56. George Catlin, *Episodes from "Life among the Indians" and "Last Rambles"* (1959), 144.

57. *Oregonian*, October 28, 1869, and September 8, 1881.

58. Don Holm, "Where Rolls the Columbia," *Oregonian*, July 20, 1975, 14; Anthony Netboy, *Columbia River Salmon and Steelhead Trout* (1980), 20–21; Schwantes, *The Pacific Northwest*, 164; and *Oregonian*, September 8, 1881. Robert D. Hume is the subject of Gordon B. Dodds's biography, *A Pygmy Monopolist: The Life and Doings of R. D. Hume* (1961).

59. Lisa Mighetto, *Saving the Salmon: A History of the U.S. Army Corps of Engineers' Role in the Protection of Anadromous Fish on the Columbia and Snake Rivers* (1994), 20–21; and Courtland Smith, *Salmon Fishers of the Columbia* (1979), 30–33.

60. David Johnson, "Salmon: A Legacy of Abundance," *What's Happening* (Eugene), January 31, 1991, p. 7; and Netboy, *Columbia River Salmon and Steelhead Trout*, 20–21.

61. Netboy, *Columbia River Salmon and Steelhead Trout*, 21.

62. Baird's letter was reprinted in the *Oregonian*, March 3, 1875.

63. Ibid.

64. Ibid.

65. *Willamette Farmer*, April 20, 1877; Livingston Stone to Spencer Baird, June 18, 1872, cited in Jay Taylor, "Making Salmon: Conjuring Nature across Time and

Cultures," paper delivered to the biennial meeting of the American Society for Environmental History, Las Vegas, Nevada, March 8–11, 1995, copy in the author's possession; and J. W. Collins, "Report on the Fisheries of the Pacific Coast of the United States," *Report of the Commissioner of Fisheries* (1893), 10–11. I am especially indebted to Jay Taylor's insights for the discussion of artificial propagation as the solution to the salmon crisis.

66. *Willamette Farmer,* April 13 and 20, 1877.

67. *Oregonian,* August 1 and September 8, 1881, and April 26, 1884.

68. Ibid., September 8, 1881.

69. The Board of Fish Commissioners' report is quoted in Netboy, *Columbia River Salmon and Steelhead Trout,* 35.

70. *Oregonian,* August 11, 1887.

71. Ibid.

72. Report of the Oregon Fish and Game Protector (1894), quoted in Netboy, *Columbia River Salmon and Steelhead Trout,* 36.

73. The Clarke quotation is in Mighetto, *Saving the Salmon,* 21. Also see Schwantes, *The Pacific Northwest,* 164; and Netboy, *Columbia River Salmon and Steelhead Trout,* 34–36, 105–55.

Into the Hinterland

1. For general information on mining in the interior Northwest, see Carlos A. Schwantes, *The Pacific Northwest: An Interpretive History* (1989), 106, 172–74; Donald W. Meinig, *The Great Columbia Plain: A Historical Geography, 1805–1910* (1968), 208–14; Oscar O. Winther, *The Great Northwest: A History* (2d ed., 1950), 220–26; and Dorothy O. Johansen and Charles M. Gates, *Empire of the Columbia: A History of the Pacific Northwest* (2d ed., 1967), 265–68.

2. Jerry Mosgrove, *The Malheur National Forest: An Ethnographic History,* U.S. Department of Agriculture, Forest Service, Pacific Northwest Region (1980), 35–41.

3. Theodor Kirchhoff, *Oregon East, Oregon West, 1863–1872,* Frederic Trautmann, ed. and trans. (1987), 85–86; Mosgrove, *The Malheur National Forest,* 173; and *An Illustrated History of Baker, Grant, Malheur, and Harney Counties* (1902), 137–66.

4. *An Illustrated History of Baker, Grant, Malheur and Harney Counties,* 380–86.

5. Johansen and Gates, *Empire of the Columbia,* 267, 269; and W. D. Lyman, *An Illustrated History of Walla Walla County, Washington* (1901), 101.

6. Lyman, *An Illustrated History of Walla Walla County,* 57; Schwantes, *The Pacific Northwest,* 106; and Meinig, *The Great Columbia Plain,* 215–17.

7. Meinig, *The Great Columbia Plain*, 220–22.

8. F. A. Shaver, comp., *An Illustrated History of Central Oregon* (1905), 2:636, 700.

9. The Dalles *Weekly Times* is quoted in ibid., 428–29.

10. Meinig, *The Great Columbia Plain*, 288–89. The Ohio reporter is quoted in *Willamette Farmer*, August 12, 1881.

11. Meinig, *The Great Columbia Plain*, 261.

12. *Willamette Farmer*, February 8, 1878.

13. *Oregonian*, September 27, 1879; and Enoch A. Bryan, *Orient Meets Occident: The Advent of the Railways to the Pacific Northwest* (1936), 162, 164.

14. Quoted in *Willamette Farmer*, August 8, 1879.

15. Eugene V. Smalley, *History of the Northern Pacific Railroad* (1883; rpt., 1975), 352–54; and Carlos A. Schwantes, *Railroad Signatures across the Pacific Northwest* (1993), 86–87.

16. Quoted in *Willamette Farmer*, August 12, 1881.

17. Ibid., June 13, 1879.

18. Ibid.; and *Oregonian*, May 26, 1886.

19. U.S. House of Representatives, *Reports on the Statistics of Agriculture in the United States: Agriculture by Irrigation in the Western Part of the United States and Statistics of Fisheries in the United States at the Eleventh Census: 1890* (1896), 202–3, 215.

20. John F. Due and Giles French, *Rails to the Mid-Columbia Wheatlands: The Columbia and Southern and Great Southern Railroads and the Development of Sherman and Wasco Counties, Oregon* (1979), 29–31.

21. Doyle is quoted in Shaver, comp., *An Illustrated History of Central Oregon*, 431.

22. Due and French, *Rails to the Mid-Columbia Wheatlands*, 46–51.

23. Ibid., 74, 85, 87.

24. Ibid., 103–6, 111.

25. Helmut K. Buechner, "Some Biotic Changes in the State of Washington, Particularly during the Century 1853–1953," *Research Studies of the State College of Washington* 21 (1953), 168–69.

26. *Oregonian*, July 3, 1899.

27. Robert Carlton Clark, "Harney Basin Exploration, 1826–60," *Oregon Historical Quarterly* 33 (June 1932), 110–11.

28. Ibid., 112–14; and Peter K. Simpson, *The Community of Cattlemen: A Social History of the Cattle Industry in Southeastern Oregon, 1869–1912* (1987), 5.

29. Simpson, *The Community of Cattlemen,* 5; and James A. Young and B. Abbott Sparks, *Cattle in the Cold Desert* (1985), 54–55.

30. Simpson, *The Community of Cattlemen,* 12, 19–21.

31. Ibid., 21.

32. Ibid., 18, 29–30.

33. Ibid., 39–40.

34. *An Illustrated History of Baker, Grant, Malheur and Harney Counties,* 635–37; and Simpson, *The Community of Cattlemen,* 33–34. The herd figures for southeastern Oregon are from the author's class lecture notes for History of the American West.

35. The quote is in the author's class lecture notes for History of the American West.

36. Simpson, *A Community of Cattlemen,* 24.

37. U.S. House of Representatives, *Reports on the Statistics of Agriculture . . . Eleventh Census: 1890,* 208–9.

38. U.S. Department of Commerce, Bureau of the Census, *Agriculture,* Vol. 5, *Farms, Livestock, and Animal Products,* pt. 1 (1902), 470–71; and Young and Sparks, *Cattle in the Cold Desert,* 220–21, 225.

39. Richard White, *"It's Your Misfortune and None of My Own": A New History of the American West* (1991), 226–27.

40. Young and Sparks, *Cattle in the Cold Desert,* 19–22.

41. Henry F. Dobyns, *From Fire to Flood: Historic Human Destruction of Sonoran Desert Riverine Oases* (1981), 114; and Karen Welcher, "Holocene Changes of Camp Creek, an Arroyo in Eastern Oregon" (M.S. thesis, University of Oregon, 1992), 26–29.

42. David Griffiths, *Forage Conditions on the Northern Border of the Great Basin,* U.S. Department of Agriculture, Bureau of Plant Industry, Bulletin no. 15 (1902), 26–29.

43. Ibid., 30–31.

44. Ibid., 55–56; and Israel C. Russell, *Bulletin of the United States Geological Survey,* no. 199 (1902), 145–46.

45. Israel C. Russell, *Notes on the Geology of Southwestern Idaho and Southeastern Oregon,* U.S. Department of the Interior, United States Geological Survey, Bulletin no. 217 (1903), 19–20.

46. Israel C. Russell, *Preliminary Report on the Geology and Water Resources of Central Oregon,* U.S. Department of the Interior, United States Geological Survey, Bulletin no. 252 (1905), 7, 62.

47. Geoffrey L. Buckley, "Desertification of the Camp Creek Drainage in Central Oregon," *Yearbook of the Association of Pacific Coast Geographers* 55 (1993), 98;

and E. E. Rich, ed., *Peter Skene Ogden's Snake Country Journals, 1824–25 and 1825–26* (1950), 106–13.

48. All of the quotations and the discussion of the Price Valley landscape are in Buckley, "Desertification of the Camp Creek Drainage in Central Oregon," 105–13. The reference to Oregon's surveyor general is in Harold H. Winegar, "Camp Creek Channel Fencing: Plant, Wildlife, Soil, and Water Response," *Rangeman's Journal* 4, no. 1 (February 1977), 10.

49. Russell, *Preliminary Report on the Geology and Water Resources of Central Oregon,* 63; and Buckley, "Desertification of the Camp Creek Drainage in Central Oregon," 115–19.

50. Buckley, "Desertification of the Camp Creek Drainage in Central Oregon," 116–17.

51. Statement Regarding W. T. Cox's Experiences and Observations in Forestry, 974, File "Cox, W. T.," Gifford Pinchot Papers, Collections of the Manuscript Division, Library of Congress. For a brief account of William T. Cox's career as state forester in Minnesota, see William G. Robbins, *American Forestry: A History of National, State, and Private Cooperation* (1985), 67–72.

52. Philip Ashton Rollins, ed., *The Discovery of the Oregon Trail: Robert Stuart's Narratives* (1935), 75; John Davies, ed., *Douglas of the Forests: The North American Journals of David Douglas* (1980), 70; and Frederick G. Young, ed., *The Correspondence and Journals of Captain Nathaniel J. Wyeth, 1831–6* (1899), 173.

53. John Kirk Townsend, *Narrative of a Journey across the Rocky Mountains to the Columbia River* (1839; rpt., 1978), 172; Thomas J. Farnham, *An 1839 Wagon Train Journal: Travels in the Great Western Prairies* (1843; rpt., 1977), 79; and Donald Jackson and Mary Lee Spence, eds., *The Expeditions of John Charles Fremont* (1970), 1:553.

54. Statement Regarding W. T. Cox's Experiences and Observations in Forestry, 5; and Jackson and Spence, eds., *The Expeditions of John Charles Fremont,* 1:553.

55. Young and Sparks, *Cattle in the Cold Desert,* xxi, 27–28; and Stephen Whitney, *A Sierra Club Naturalist's Guide: The Pacific Northwest* (1989), 254–55.

56. Donald K. Grayson, *The Desert's Past: A Natural History of the Great Basin* (1993), 301.

57. Ibid., 302; and J. A. Young and R. A. Evans, "Population Dynamics after Wildfires in Sagebrush Grasslands," *Journal of Range Management* 31 (1978), 288.

58. Randall V. Mills, "A History of Transportation in the Pacific Northwest," *Oregon Historical Quarterly* 45 (1946), 291–92; Bryan, *Orient Meets Occident,* 161–63; and James B. Hedges, *Henry Villard and the Railways of the Northwest* (1930; rpt., 1967), 123–26.

59. *Oregonian,* January 28, 1890.

60. Mallory Hope Ferrell, *Rails, Sagebrush, and Pine: A Garland of Railroad and Logging Days in Oregon's Sumpter Valley* (1967), 9–13; Mosgrove, *The Malheur National Forest,* 71; Baker City *Record Courier,* November 7, 1946; and Shirley T. Moore, ed., *Sumpter Valley Railroad,* U.S. Department of Agriculture, Forest Service, Wallowa-Whitman National Forest, Pacific Northwest Region, n.d., n.p.

61. Ferrell, *Rails, Sagebrush, and Pine,* 13–33.

62. Langille is quoted in Mosgrove, *The Malheur National Forest,* 71.

63. The *Timberman* is quoted in Ferrell, *Rails, Sagebrush, and Pine,* 49. Langille reported that stamp mills and mining were consuming a considerable amount of timber. See Mosgrove, *The Malheur National Forest,* 72.

64. See, especially, Nancy Langston, *Forest Dreams, Forest Nightmares: The Paradox of Old Growth in the Inland West* (1995).

65. Richard White, *Land Use, Environment, and Social Change: The Shaping of Island County, Washington* (1980), 88–91; and Stephen J. Pyne, *Fire in America: A Cultural History of Wildland and Rural Fire* (1982; rpt., 1997), 254–55, 336–42.

66. Donald Worster, *Dust Bowl: The Southern Plains in the 1930s* (1979), 83.

Nature's Industries and the Rhetoric of Industrialism

1. *Oregonian,* January 1, 1890.

2. For a further elaboration of this idea, see Donald Worster, "Nature and the Disorder of History," *Environmental History Review* 18 (Summer 1994), 2.

3. *Pacific Monthly,* 11, no. 1 (January 1904), 65.

4. Donald Worster argues that this complex material dialectic is a constantly shifting reference point, reflecting changes both in the world of nature and in the human expectations of nature. See Worster, "Nature and the Disorder of History," 2.

5. Alan Trachtenberg, *The Incorporation of America: Culture and Society in the Gilded Age* (1982), 19, 57.

6. "Documents," *Oregon Historical Quarterly* 3 (December 1902), 422; *Oregon Spectator,* October 4, 1849; and *Oregon Statesman,* July 3, 1852.

7. Overton Johnson and William H. Winter, *Route across the Rocky Mountains* (1846; rpt., 1982), 42, 69.

8. Olympia *Pioneer and Democrat,* July 18, 1856.

9. Theodore Winthrop, *The Canoe and the Saddle* (1862; rpt., 1913), 210. Samuel Bowles is quoted in the *Oregon Statesman,* November 6, 1865.

10. *Willamette Farmer,* June 28, 1869, and February 24, 1872.

11. *West Shore* 1, no. 6 (June 1876), 1.

12. *Oregonian,* January 1, 1890.

13. *Hood River Glacier,* February 23, 1895.

14. Frances Fuller Victor, *All Over Oregon and Washington: Observations on the Country* (1872), 67.

15. This point is made in Oliver Zunz, *Making America Corporate, 1870–1900* (1990), 39–40. The standard reference work to railroads in the region is Carlos A. Schwantes, *Railroad Signatures across the Pacific Northwest* (1993).

16. *West Shore* 6, no. 2 (February 1880), 39.

17. Carlos A. Schwantes, "The Concept of the Wageworkers' Frontier: A Framework for Future Research," *Western Historical Quarterly* 18 (1987), 43.

18. Yi-Fu Tuan, *Space and Place: The Perspective of Experience* (1977), 5, 85.

19. J. D. Cleaver, "L. Samuel and the *West Shore:* Images of a Changing Pacific Northwest," *Oregon Historical Quarterly* 94 (Summer–Fall 1993), 170, 189.

20. "Oregon: Past and Present," *West Shore* 1, no. 4 (November 1875), 1–2; and ibid., 3, no. 3 (November 1877), 41.

21. Ibid., 1, no. 10 (June 1876), 5; and 14, no. 8 (August 1888), 415.

22. Ibid., 1, no. 6 (January 1876), 1; 2, no. 5 (January 1877), 85, and no. 12 (August 1877), 223.

23. P. B. Simmons, "Oregon as Seen by a Philadelphian," *West Shore* 5, no. 1 (January 1879), 25; ibid., 15, no. 3 (March 1889), 152; and 16, no. 229 (October 25, 1890), 173.

24. *West Shore* 1, no. 6 (January 1876), 9, 11, and no. 10 (June 1876), 5; 2, no. 8 (April 1877), 150; 5, no. 1 (January 1879), 25; and 9, no. 6 (June 1883), 128.

25. Ibid., 6, no. 8 (December 1880), 315; and 10, no. 5 (May 1984), 136.

26. Ibid., 14, no. 8 (August 1888), 410.

27. *Oregonian,* January 2, 1888.

28. Ibid., March 23, 1888.

29. For a study of Portland's business elite, see E. Kimbark MacColl and Harry H. Stein, *Merchants, Money, and Power: The Portland Establishment, 1843–1913* (1988).

30. *Oregonian,* October 2, 1884, and January 2, 1888.

31. Ibid., January 1, 1889; and Carlos A. Schwantes, *The Pacific Northwest: An Interpretive History* (1989), 191–92.

32. *Oregonian,* August 16, 1894.

33. Ibid., August 11, 1900.

34. Donald Worster, *Dust Bowl: The Southern Plains in the 1930s* (1979), 6.

35. William Cronon, *Nature's Metropolis: Chicago and the Great West* (1991), 310–11.

36. *Oregonian,* January 2, 1888, and January 1, 1889.

37. *The Wealth and Resources of Oregon for the Home Seeker, Capitalist and Tourist* (St. Louis: Woodward and Tiernan Co., 1894), 8–9, 19–20.

38. *Oregonian,* December 19, 1896.

39. Ibid.

40. Ibid., July 3, 1899.

41. Ibid., July 4, 1904.

42. Ibid.

43. Ibid., January 1, 1903.

44. *Chamber of Commerce Bulletin* 3, no. 3 (September 1904), 1, and no. 8 (February 1905), 9.

45. "Address by Governor Chamberlain," *Portland Chamber of Commerce Bulletin* 7, no. 2 (February 1907), 35–37.

46. Portland Chamber of Commerce, *Report on an Open River* (1906), 3–5.

47. *Columbia River Basin Journal* (Portland: Board of Trade, 1902), 12–13.

48. Carl Abbott, *Portland: Planning, Politics, and Growth in a Twentieth-Century City* (1983), 33–34; and Schwantes, *The Pacific Northwest,* 216–17.

49. *Portland Board of Trade Journal* 1, no. 2 (March 1905), 5–6.

50. *Oregonian,* May 31, 1903, and January 1, 1904.

51. Abbott, *Portland,* 44; and *Oregonian,* October 14 and 15, 1905, and October 14, 1906.

52. *Oregonian,* January 22, 1906.

53. Ibid.

54. Ibid., July 7, 1905, and August 2, 1911.

55. Edward Ehrman, "The Coming of Capital," *Portland Chamber of Commerce Bulletin* 4, no. 2 (August 1905), 7; M. Mosessohn, "Portland as a Seaport," ibid., 4, no. 12 (June 1906), 7; and *Oregonian,* August 10, 1905.

56. *Oregonian,* August 10 and December 27, 1905; and Joseph Nathan Teal, "An Open River from Lewiston to the Sea," *Portland Chamber of Commerce Bulletin* 4, no. 5 (November 1905), 8.

57. *Oregonian,* December 27, 1905.

58. Stephen S. Wise, "Greater Oregon," *Portland Chamber of Commerce Bulletin* 5 (October 1906), 16–17; W. A. Mears, "Portland, Oregon, as a Jobbing and Exporting Center," ibid. (November 1906), 9; and Tom Richardson, "Prosperity, a Present Condition of Oregon," ibid. (September 1906), 15–16.

59. Ibid., 2 (July 13, 1903), and 4 (November 27, 1905); and Schwantes, *The Pacific Northwest*, 155.

60. *Oregonian*, December 17, 1904, and October 23, 1905; and *Pacific Monthly* 11 (January 1904), 65. Also see the *Oregonian* quoted in *Portland Chamber of Commerce Bulletin* 5 (September 1906), 20–21.

61. Sheldon D. Erickson, *Occupance in the Upper Deschutes Basin, Oregon* (1953).

62. "Development News," *Pacific Monthly* 22 (November 1909), 540h; and *Oregonian*, February 21 and June 14, 1909.

63. *Pacific Monthly* 22 (October 1909), 430.

64. Charles H. Carey, "The New Oregon Country," *Chamber of Commerce Bulletin* 11, no. 3 (September 1909), 113–14; and Thomas B. Neuhausen, "Putting Money into Oregon Timber," ibid., 117.

65. *Oregonian*, January 1, 1910; and George Palmer Putnam, "The Awakening of Central Oregon," *Chamber of Commerce Bulletin* 12, no. 5 (May 1910), 324–25, 327.

66. *Oregonian*, January 1, 1910.

67. Fred Lockley, "Oregon, My Oregon," *Pacific Monthly* 19 (June 1908), 676, 693. The irony of Lockley's words is a photograph (p. 693) showing a child sitting on one of about thirty huge sturgeon.

Industrializing the Woodlands

1. Richard H. Kennedy, "Money in Trees," *Pacific Monthly* 11, no. 1 (January 1904), 26.

2. George Vancouver, *A Voyage of Discovery to the North Pacific Ocean, and Around the World* (1798; rpt., 1984), 1:210, 258–59.

3. Gary E. Moulton, ed., *The Journals of the Lewis and Clark Expedition*, 6 (1990), 42, 44–45.

4. Alexander Ross, *Adventures of the First Settlers on the Oregon or Columbia River, 1810–1813* (1849; rpt., 1986), 91–92.

5. David Douglas is quoted in Athelston George Harvey, *Douglas of the Fir* (1947), 57–58. The member of the Wilkes expedition is quoted in George M. Colvocoresses, *Four Years in a Government Exploring Expedition* (1852), 257. Also see Nellie B. Pipes, "Journal of John H. Frost, 1840–43," *Oregon Historical Quarterly* 35 (1934), 357–59.

6. J. Ross Browne to the Secretary of the Interior, November 17, 1857, U.S. House, Indian Affairs in the Territories of Oregon and Washington, 35th Cong., 1st sess., 1858, H. Ex. Doc. 39, Serial 955, p. 13.

7. Jesse Applegate, "Umpqua Agriculture, 1851," *Oregon Historical Quarterly* 32 (1931), 135; and Grace D. Stuart and Reginald R. Stuart, eds., *Calvin B. West of the Umpqua* (1961), 41.

8. Horace Holden, "Oregon Pioneering," 1878, Bancroft Library, University of California, Berkeley, P-A 40, p. 2; *Oregon Statesman,* October 18, 1853; and *Oregon Spectator,* September 16, 1853.

9. William G. Morris, "Forest Fires in Western Oregon and Western Washington," *Oregon Historical Quarterly* 35 (December 1934), 322–33.

10. *Reports of Explorations and Surveys . . . for a Railroad from the Mississippi River to the Pacific Ocean,* 1853–55, vol. 6, pt. 2, p. 59.

11. County Surveyor's Records, Benton County, Oregon, vols. 1–3.

12. For the influence of San Francisco capital in the West Coast lumber industry, see William G. Robbins, *Hard Times in Paradise: Coos Bay, Oregon, 1850–1986* (1988), 12–25.

13. For an assessment of the ecological impact of bull-team logging, see Richard White, *Land Use, Environment, and Social Change: The Shaping of Island County, Washington* (1980), 88–92.

14. Stephen Dow Beckham, *Coos Bay: The Pioneer Period, 1850–1900* (1973), 31; Emil R. Peterson and Alfred Powers, *A Century of Coos and Curry* (1952), 425–26, 580; Stephen Dow Beckham, *The Simpsons of Shore Acres* (1971), 1–15; and Thomas R. Cox, *Mills and Markets: A History of the Pacific Coast Lumber Industry to 1900* (1974), 166–67, 171–72.

15. Coos Bay *News,* May 13 and June 21, 1874; A. G. Walling, *History of Southern Oregon* (1884), 494; and Portland *Oregonian,* January 1, 1884.

16. *Oregonian,* September 27, 1882. The Portland *Telegram* is reprinted in the Coos Bay *News,* June 25, 1884.

17. For the significance of these studies, see Harold K. Steen, *The U.S. Forest Service: A History* (1976), 8; William N. Sparhawk, "The History of Forestry in America," U.S. Department of Agriculture, *Trees: Yearbook of Agriculture* (1949), 703–4; and Henry Clepper, *Professional Forestry in the United States* (1971), 15.

18. Frank J. Harmon, "Remembering Franklin B. Hough," *American Forests* 86 (January 1977), 34–53; and Franklin B. Hough, "On the Duty of Governments in the Preservation of Forests," in *Conservation in the United States: A Documentary History,* ed. Frank E. Smith (1971), 1:688.

19. Charles Sprague Sargent, *Report on the Forests of North America,* U.S. Department of Agriculture (1884), 576–77.

20. *Oregonian,* October 17, 1880.

21. Ibid., June 9, 1881, November 10, 1887, and August 25, 1906.

22. *West Shore* 6 (March 1880), 70, and 7 (August 1881), 220; and *Oregonian*, January 1, 1905.

23. *West Shore* 10, no. 3 (March 1884), 75.

24. I have extensively discussed the influence of steam power in woods operations in *Hard Times in Paradise*, 28–29, 42, 56. Also see Richard A. Rajala, "The Forest as Factory: Technological Change and Worker Control in the West Coast Logging Industry, 1880–1930," *Labour/Le Travail* 32 (Fall 1993), 73–85.

25. Stewart Holbrook, *Holy Old Mackinaw: A Natural History of the American Lumberjack* (1938), 139; George H. Emerson, "Logging on Grays Harbor," *The Timberman* 8 (September 1907), 20; and White, *Land Use, Environment, and Social Change*, 94–112.

26. White, *Land Use, Environment, and Social Change*, 106. For an account of accidents in logging operations, see Andrew M. Prouty, *More Deadly Than War! Pacific Coast Logging, 1827–1981* (1985).

27. William Cronon, *Nature's Metropolis: Chicago and the Great West* (1991), 73.

28. *Oregonian*, April 11, 1893; and Robert E. Ficken, *The Forested Land: A History of Lumbering in Western Washington* (1987), 71–73.

29. *Oregonian*, August 25, 1887.

30. Ibid.

31. Richard H. Kennedy, "Logging Our Great Forests," *Pacific Monthly* 13, no. 1 (January 1905), 29–30.

32. Ibid., 31–32.

33. The *West Coast Lumberman* is cited in the *Pacific Monthly* 9, no. 6 (June 1903), 407.

34. Egbert S. Oliver, *Homes in the Oregon Forest: Settling Columbia County, 1870–1920* (1983), 12–15.

35. Ibid., 153–60.

36. Ibid., 188–91.

37. Kennedy, "Money in Trees," 26; and Oliver, *Homes in the Oregon Forest*, 191, 229–30.

38. Steve Greif, "A Century of Coos County Railroads," manuscript in Southwest Oregon Community College Library, Coos Bay; Victor Stevens, *The Powers Story* (1979), 16–17; and Coos Bay *Times*, February 20, 1914.

39. S. B. Eakin, Jr., *A Short Sketch of a Trip across the Plains by S. B. Eakin and Family, 1866* (1970), 25; Joel Palmer, *Journal of Travels on the Oregon Trail in 1845* (1847; rpt., 1992), 110; John Kirk Townsend, *Narrative of a Journey across the Rocky*

Mountains to the Columbia River (1839; rpt., 1978), 161, 163; and George Wilkes, *The History of Oregon, Geographical and Political* (1845), 86–87. The best description of the forest ecology of the Blue Mountains is Nancy Langston, *Forest Dreams, Forest Nightmares: The Paradox of Old Growth in the Inland West* (1995).

40. Donald Jackson and Mary Lee Spence, eds., *The Expeditions of John Charles Fremont* (1970), 1:541, 545, 547.

41. Ibid., 578–79.

42. Ibid., 583–85.

43. *Reports of Explorations and Surveys . . . for a Railroad from the Mississippi River to the Pacific Ocean,* vol. 6, Report of Lieut. Henry L. Abbott, *Explorations for a Railroad Route, from the Sacramento Valley to the Columbia River* (1855), reprinted in Bert and Margie Webber, *Railroading in Southern Oregon and the Founding of Medford* (1985), 194–200.

44. J. G. Cooper and G. Suckley, *The Natural History of Washington Territory* (1859), 9–11. This privately published volume includes segments of the longer report.

45. Samuel Trask Dana and Sally K. Fairfax, *Forest and Range Policy: Its Development in the United States* (2d ed., 1980), 56–59; and John Ise, *The United States Forest Policy* (1920), 110–15.

46. H. D. Langille et al., *Forest Conditions in the Cascade Range Forest Reserve, Oregon,* Department of the Interior, U.S. Geological Survey, Professional Paper 9 (1903), 78 and 87.

47. John B. Leiberg, "Cascade Range and Ashland Forest Reserves and Adjacent Regions," *Twenty-first Annual Report of the United States Geological Survey to the Secretary of the Interior, 1899–1900,* pt. 5, Forest Reserves, 277–78, 288. Also see Langston, *Forest Dreams, Forest Nightmares,* 28–37.

48. Leiberg, "Cascade Range and Ashland Forest Reserves," 273; Langille et al., *Forest Conditions in the Cascade Range Forest Reserve, Oregon,* 90; and H. D. Langille, "A Report on the Cascade Range Forest Reserve," June 4, 1904, filed in Box 1, National Forests, 1904–1906, Record Group 95, National Archives and Federal Records Center, Seattle, 1.

49. Thomas R. Cox et al., *This Well-Wooded Land: Americans and Their Forests from Colonial Times to the Present* (Lincoln: University of Nebraska Press, 1985), 167; Olympia *Washington Standard,* January 6, 1893; and *Oregonian,* October 18, 1902. The *Oregonian* listed several conventional agricultural categories—livestock, grain, hops, wool, fruit, and dairy production—under separate headings. Collectively, the value of those entities was nearly three times greater than the income from lumber.

50. *Pacific Monthly* 11 (April 1904), 281.

51. *Oregonian,* June 9, 1904.

52. "Portland's Lumber Interests," *Chamber of Commerce Bulletin* 4, no. 4 (October 1905), 9.

53. Gannett's estimates are mentioned in Kennedy, "Money in Trees," 19; *Oregonian,* June 9, 1904.

54. *Oregonian,* January 14, 1906.

55. Ibid., May 31, 1908.

56. "Portland's Lumber Interests," 9.

57. *Oregonian,* February 9, 1905; and "Portland's Lumber Interests," 9.

58. Thomas R. Cox, "Closing the Lumberman's Frontier: The Far Western Pine Country," *Journal of the West* 33 (1994), 59; and Philip Cogswell, Jr., "Deschutes Country Pine Logging," in *High and the Mighty: Sketches about the Deschutes Country,* Thomas Vaughan, ed. (1981), 239–41.

59. *Pacific Monthly* 11, no. 1 (January 1904), 19.

60. *Oregonian,* August 10, 1905; *Pacific Monthly* 22, no. 11 (November 1909), 540h; and *Chamber of Commerce Bulletin* 11, no. 3 (September 1909), 116.

61. *Oregonian,* January 1, 1910.

62. George Palmer Putnam, "The Awakening of Central Oregon," *Chamber of Commerce Bulletin* 12, no. 5 (May 1910), 324–25. The regional embrace and aspirations of the Portland business community knew few limitations. The *Bulletin* printed an article on railroad development in Oregon's far southwestern Illinois Valley under the title "Enlarging Portland's Tributary Territory." See *Chamber of Commerce Bulletin* 13, no. 3 (September 1910), 130.

63. The classic contemporary account of timber fraud is Stephen A. D. Puter, *Looters of the Public Domain* (1908; rpt., 1972).

64. Cogswell, "Deschutes Country Pine Logging," 236.

65. *Oregonian,* December 6, 1909, and January 1, 1910.

66. John B. Leiberg, "Cascade Range and Ashland Forest Reserves," 273; and U. S. Department of Agriculture, Forest Service, *Forest Statistics for Klamath County, Oregon* (1936), 3–6.

67. Cox, "Closing the Lumberman's Frontier," 61; Cogswell, "Deschutes County Pine Logging," 238–46; and Bend *Bulletin,* March 3, 1916. Cogswell also cites the *Bulletin.*

68. I made a similar calculation for the ratio of workers employed in sawmill and logging operations on Coos Bay during the days of steam-powered logging. That ratio changed when the chain saw and gasoline-driven engine were introduced to the woods. See Robbins, *Hard Times in Paradise,* 41.

69. Cogswell, "Deschutes Country Pine Logging," 246–47; and U.S. Department of Agriculture, Forest Service, *Forest Statistics for Deschutes County, Oregon* (1936), 6.

70. The direction and kind of harvesting that took place adjacent to Bend is outlined in Sheldon D. Erickson, *Occupance in the Upper Deschutes Basin, Oregon* (1953), 96–102.

71. Fred Lockley, "Oregon, My Oregon," *Pacific Monthly* 19, no. 6 (June 1908), 676, 679.

72. Ibid., 680, 693.

73. Coos Bay *Times*, February 26 and 29, 1908; Coos Bay *News*, October 6 and December 1, 1908; and Peterson and Powers, *A Century of Coos and Curry*, 430. Also see the chapter "The Big Mill and Its World," in Robbins, *Hard Times in Paradise*, 40–53.

Engineering Nature

1. *Chamber of Commerce Bulletin* 8, no. 2 (February 1908), 18.

2. William Bittle Wells, "Masters of Environment," *Pacific Monthly* 13, no. 5 (March 1905), 193.

3. William H. Truettner and Alexander Nemerov, "What You See is Not Necessarily What You Get: New Meaning in Images of the Old West," *Montana, the Magazine of Western History* 42 (Summer 1992), 75; and William Cronon, "A Place for Stories: Nature, History, and Narrative," *Journal of American History* 78 (March 1992), 1349.

4. Samuel P. Hays, *Conservation and the Gospel of Efficiency: The Progressive Conservation Movement, 1890–1920* (1959), 1–2, 127; and Gabriel Kolko, *The Triumph of Conservatism: A Reinterpretation of American History, 1900–1916* (1963), 110–11.

5. Gifford Pinchot is quoted in Grant McConnell, "Prologue: Environment and the Quality of Political Life," in *Congress and the Environment*, Richard A. Cooley and Geoffrey Wandesforde-Smith, eds. (1970), 6. Donald Worster, *Nature's Economy: A History of Ecological Ideas* (1977; 2d ed., 1994), 267; Oswald West, "The Battle of Life," *Oregonian*, November 14, 1937; and State of Oregon, *Messages of the Governor* (1911), 19.

6. State of Oregon, *Report of the Oregon Conservation Commission to the Governor* (1908), 7; and ibid. (1910), 5.

7. For a further elaboration of some of these ideas, see William Kittredge, *Owning It All* (1987), 62–63.

8. William F. Willingham, *Army Engineers and the Development of Oregon: A History of the Portland District, U.S. Army Corps of Engineers* (1983), 10–42.

9. William Dietrich, *Northwest Passage: The Great Columbia River* (1995), 186–87; and Stewart Holbrook, *The Columbia* (1956), 164–66, 176–77.

10. *Oregonian*, January 22, 1883, January 14, 18, and 19, 1909.

11. Willingham, *Army Engineers and the Development of Oregon*, 75–77.

12. I have argued this theme at greater length in "Narrative Form and Great River Myths: The Power of Columbia River Stories," *Environmental History Review* 17 (Summer 1993), 1–22.

13. Joseph Nathan Teal, "Address of Joseph N. Teal," *Oregon Historical Quarterly* 16 (1915), 125–29.

14. Willingham, *Army Engineers and the Development of Oregon*, 75–77; and Dietrich, *Northwest Passage*, 204. Charles Francis Adams is quoted in the *Oregonian*, April 25, 1900.

15. *Oregonian*, December 24, 1904.

16. Ibid., December 12, 1904; and *Chamber of Commerce Bulletin* 7, no. 3 (September 1907), 7.

17. *Oregonian*, February 28 and March 29, 1907.

18. James Withycombe, "Welcome to Oregon," *Oregon Country* 22, no. 5 (February 1915), 65. The Portland Chamber of Commerce regular monthly publications appeared under several different titles, including the *Portland Board of Trade Journal* and the *Oregon Country*.

19. *Oregon Country* 22, no. 2 (February 1915), 73. Two years earlier the state's attorney general estimated Oregon's water-power potential, presently "undeveloped and annually going to waste," at one-half the developed power of the United States. See ibid., 18, no. 1 (June 1913), 11.

20. *Oregon Journal of Commerce* 1, no. 10 (June 1923), 3–5.

21. *Oregon Business* 2, no. 9 (May 1924), 10.

22. Ibid., June 14, 1902.

23. Ibid., January 1, 1904, and February 11, 1905.

24. *Oregonian*, August 20, 1905.

25. Ibid., August 6 and 31, 1906.

26. Donald C. Swain, *Federal Conservation Policy, 1921–1933* (1963), 75.

27. State of Oregon, *Report of the Oregon Conservation Commission* (1908), 37, 46, 65; and ibid. (1909), 14, 25.

28. Donald Pisani, *To Reclaim a Divided West: Water, Law, and Public Policy, 1848–1902* (1992), 76.

29. Ibid., 322; and State of Oregon, *Report of the Oregon Conservation Commission* (1912), 17, 44.

30. "Upper Klamath River Basin Amendment to the Long Range Plan for the Klamath River Basin Conservation Area Fishery Restoration Program," Draft Statement Prepared for the Klamath River Basin Fisheries Task Force, October 1992, copy in the Oregon State University Marine Science Center Library, Newport, 2-A-20.

31. William L. and Irene Finley, "The Destruction of Lower Klamath," *Oregon Sportsman* 2, no. 1 (September 1925), 3.

32. U.S. Department of the Interior, *Upper Klamath River Basin, Oregon-California* (1954), 4–5.

33. U.S. Bureau of Reclamation, *Reclamation Accomplishments, 1905–1953: Klamath Project, Oregon-California,* prepared by Maurise K. Strantz (1953), 5–6; Arthur S. King, *A History of the Water Resources Congress* (1972), n.p.; and "Upper Klamath River Basin Amendment," 2-A-20 and 2-A-36.

34. Kittredge, *Owning It All,* 60–61; and Kittredge, *Hole in the Sky: A Memoir* (1992), 91.

35. U.S. Bureau of Reclamation, *Reclamation Accomplishments, 1905–1953,* 6; and *Oregonian,* August 13, 1905, and April 19, 1906. Also see the issues for May 12 and 17, 1905.

36. *Chamber of Commerce Bulletin* 10, no. 9 (January 1909), 24, 31.

37. U.S. Bureau of Reclamation, *Reclamation Accomplishments, 1905–1953,* 6–7; and *Oregonian,* January 1, 1910.

38. *Reclamation Accomplishments, 1905–1953,* 6–7; Finley and Finley, "The Destruction of Lower Klamath," 4; and Larry Rymon, "A Critical Analysis of Wildlife Conservation in Oregon" (Ph.D. diss., Oregon State University, Corvallis, 1969), 149–51.

39. Rachael Applegate Good, comp., *History of Klamath County, Oregon: Its Resources and Its People* (1941), 1:106–9.

40. Finley and Finley, "The Destruction of Lower Klamath," 3, 6.

41. Good, comp., *History of Klamath County,* 11–12.

42. U.S. Bureau of Reclamation, *Reclamation Accomplishments, 1905–1953,* 9; and Thomas R. Cox, "Closing the Lumberman's Frontier: The Far Western Pine Country," *Journal of the West* 33 (July 1994), 64.

43. "Upper Klamath River Basin Amendment," 2-A-20, 2-A-37.

44. U.S. House of Representatives, *Reports on the Statistics of Agriculture in the United States: Agriculture by Irrigation in the Western Part of the United States and Statistics of Fisheries in the United States at the Eleventh Census: 1890* (1896), 202–3.

45. Barbara Allen, *Homesteading the High Desert* (1987), 116–19, 129.

46. Pisani, *To Reclaim a Divided West*, 72.

47. Ibid., xii; and Isaiah Bowman, *The Pioneer Fringe* (1931), 93, 97.

48. Bowman, *The Pioneer Fringe*, 98, 101, 103; and Oregon State Planning Board, *Present and Potential Land Development in Oregon through Flood Control, Drainage and Irrigation* (1938), 141.

49. Allen, *Homesteading the High Desert*, xviii, 86–87; and Bowman, *The Pioneer Fringe*, 110.

50. Oregon State Planning Board, *Present and Potential Land Development in Oregon*, 140–41.

51. U.S. House of Representatives, *Reports on the Statistics of Agriculture in the United States . . . at the Eleventh Census: 1890*, 207.

52. Bowman, *The Pioneer Fringe*, 100.

53. *Bend Bulletin*, May 19, 1909; F. F. Henshaw, John H. Lewis, and E. J. McCaustland, "Water Rights and Appropriation," U.S. Geological Survey Paper no. 344, *Deschutes River, Oregon, and Its Utilization* (1914), 149; and F. A. Shaver, comp., *An Illustrated History of Central Oregon* (1905), 718.

54. *Oregonian*, August 20, 1905; and Deschutes Valley Land and Investment Company pamphlet, 3–4, in Special Collections, Knight Library, University of Oregon, Eugene.

55. *Oregonian*, August 4, 1907; and *Chamber of Commerce Bulletin* 13, no. 1 (July 1910), 20–21, and no. 2 (August 1910), 68.

56. Federal Power Commission, *Report to the Federal Power Commission on Uses of Deschutes River, Oregon* (1922), 10–11; and Rodman W. Paul, *The Far West and the Great Plains in Transition, 1859–1900* (1988), 247.

57. Keith and Donna Clark, "Pioneers of Deschutes Country," in *High and the Mighty: Select Sketches about the Deschutes Country,* Thomas Vaughan, ed. (1981), 47–48.

58. Ibid., 51–53.

59. L. K. Lamb, "The North Unit of the Deschutes," *Oregon Business* 6, no. 4 (December 1927), 3.

60. Federal Power Commission, *Report on Uses of Deschutes River, Oregon,* 10, 48.

61. Ibid., 48–53.

62. Jarold Ramsey, " 'New Era': Growing Up East of the Cascades, 1937–1950," in *Regionalism and the Pacific Northwest,* William G. Robbins et al., eds. (1983), 175–201.

63. Sheldon D. Erickson, *Occupance in the Upper Deschutes Basin, Oregon* (1953), 69–78.

64. Richard White, *The Organic Machine* (1995), 54–55.

65. *Oregon Journal of Commerce* 1, no. 2 (November 1922), 3–4, 11.

66. "Development Program Favorably Received," *Oregon Journal of Commerce* 1, no. 3 (November 10, 1922), 3, 11.

67. "Land Settlement Is Reclamation Problem," ibid., 1, no. 10 (June 10, 1923), 3–5.

68. Paul Pitzer, *Grand Coulee: Harnessing a Dream* (1994), 58; and Marshall N. Dana, "The Magic of Reclamation," *Oregon Business* 3, no. 11 (July 1925), 5–6.

69. Donald Worster, "A Dream of Water," *Montana, the Magazine of Western History* 36 (Autumn 1986), 73.

70. Pisani, *To Reclaim a Divided West*, 138.

Toward Systemic Change

1. For the interdependent relationships between country and city, see William Cronon, *Nature's Metropolis: Chicago and the Great West* (1991), 5–19.

2. For a further explication of this idea, see the classic argument in C. P. Snow, *Two Cultures and the Scientific Revolution* (1963), 30–32.

3. *Oregonian*, March 1, 1890.

4. Chester G. Gilbert and Joseph E. Pogue, *America's Power Resources: The Economic Significance of Coal, Oil, and Water-Power* (1921), 3, 317.

5. Anthony Netboy, *The Columbia River Salmon and Steelhead Trout: Their Fight for Survival* (1980), 4–5.

6. *Journal Kept by David Douglas during His Travels in North America, 1823–1827* (1959), 127; and Don Holm, "Where Rolls the Columbia," *Oregonian*, July 20, 1975, pp. 6–7.

7. "How Coyote Made the Columbia River," in Ella E. Clark, *Indian Legends of the Pacific Northwest* (1953), 88.

8. Arnold Bennett Hall, "Scientific Research a Need," *Oregon Business* 5, no. 6 (February 1927), 6, 14.

9. State of Oregon, *Message of Walter M. Pierce, Governor, to the Thirty-third Legislative Assembly, 1925*, 23–24, and *Message of Walter M. Pierce, Governor, to the Thirty-fourth Legislative Assembly, 1927*, 1–2, 11 (copies in the University of Oregon Archives, Eugene).

10. Hoover is quoted in "The Winning of the West," *Oregon Business* 5, no. 3 (November 1926), 3.

11. William F. Willingham, *Army Engineers and the Development of Oregon: A History of the Portland District, U.S. Army Corps of Engineers* (1983), 93–95.

12. *Oregon Business* 6, no. 11 (July 1928), 8.

13. R. H. Kipp, "Rivers *Are Great* Resources," *Oregon Business* 11, no. 2 (October 1930), 3.

14. Ibid., 6–7.

15. *Oregonian*, November 18, December 5, and December 11, 1905; April 8, 1906; June 10, 1907; and December 13, 1909. Also see George H. Upthegrove, "Umatilla Government Project, Hermiston, Oregon," *Chamber of Commerce Bulletin* 15, no. 1 (July 1911), 15–16.

16. William L. Lang, "The Engineered Columbia and the Problem of Locality" (unpublished manuscript in the author's possession), 9–11.

17. Marshall N. Dana, "America's *Greatest Power Stream*," *Oregon Business* 11, no. 1 (September 1930), 3.

18. Franklin T. Griffith, "Hydro-Electric Development," *Oregon Business* 3, no. 5 (January 1925), 7, 15–16.

19. *Oregonian*, November 11, 1926. It should be noted that Hopson's name does not appear in any of the indexes to studies of dam building on the Columbia River.

20. *Oregonian*, November 19, 1931.

21. Ibid., October 9, 1930.

22. Meier's testimony was reprinted in ibid., February 2, 1932.

23. Ibid.

24. *Oregonian*, August 1 and September 14, 1930. Hydropower companies, including the California-Oregon Power Company, subsequently built a series of small generating facilities on the upper river where natural falls existed. The only dams used exclusively to produce electricity are located downstream below the great reclamation projects. See State of California, *Interim Report on Klamath River Basin Investigation: Water Utilization and Requirements* (1954), 20–37.

25. Wilfred Allen, "Reclaiming Reclamation," *Oregon Business* 4, no. 6 (February 1926), 8.

26. Ibid., 3, no. 11 (July 1925), 6.

27. Dalton Biggs, "The Owyhee and Vale Projects," *Oregon Business* 5, no. 6 (February 1927), 7, 15–16.

28. *Oregon Business* 5, no. 6 (February 1927), 15; 3, no. 11, 6; and 4, no. 6 (February 1926), 8.

29. Harold M. Sims, "The Vale-Owyhee Project," *Oregon Business* 5, no. 11 (July 1927), 3–5.

30. State Reporter, "America's 'Valley of the Nile,'" *Oregon Business* 7, no. 6 (February 1929), 4; E. G. Harlan, "Water Ready at Vale," ibid., 10, no. 6 (February 1930), 4–5; and "New Land Productive," ibid., 11, no. 6 (February 1931), 4.

31. Peter Wiley and Robert Gottlieb, *Empires in the Sun: The Rise of the New American West* (1982), 3–6.

32. Roosevelt's address is quoted in Richard L. Neuberger, *Our Promised Land* (1938; rpt., 1989), 64.

33. Quote is in Neuberger, *Our Promised Land,* 3.

34. Michael P. Malone and Richard W. Etulain, *The American West: A Twentieth-Century History* (1989), 161; and Paul C. Pitzer, *Grand Coulee: Harnessing a Dream* (1994), 66–75.

35. Richard White, *The Organic Machine* (1995), 49. I have drawn on chapters two and three of White's book for some of the argument presented here.

36. Mumford is quoted in ibid., 64–67.

37. Lewis Mumford, *Regional Planning in the Pacific Northwest* (1939), 1–2.

38. Samuel P. Hays, *Conservation and the Gospel of Efficiency* (1959), 2.

39. On the issue of Willamette River flood control, see the correspondence to Oregon's Senator Charles McNary in the McNary Papers, box 6, Oregon Collection, Knight Library, University of Oregon, Eugene.

40. R. H. Kipp to Senator Charles McNary, March 17, 1931, in box 6, McNary Papers.

41. Henry R. Richmond, *The History of the Portland District Corps of Engineers, 1871–1969* (1970), 96–97; and U.S. Army Corps of Engineers, "Report from the Chief of Engineers on Willamette River, Oregon, Covering Navigation, Flood Control, Power Development, and Irrigation," 72d Cong., 1st sess., 1932, House Doc. 263, 16–17.

42. McNary to C. E. Williamson, April 28, 1938, box 6, McNary Papers; James W. Mott, "Legal Procedure of Valley Project Is Complicated," *Eugene Register-Guard,* July 31, 1938; Oregon, Willamette River Basin Commission, *Final Report* (1959), 5; U.S. Army Corps of Engineers, *General Information: Willamette Valley Project, Oregon* (1940), 5–9; and U.S. Army Corps of Engineers, "A Report on Willamette River and Tributaries, Oregon," 75th Cong., 3d sess., 1938, House Doc. 544.

43. See the promotional articles in the *Eugene Register-Guard,* July 31, 1938, and July 30, 1939; Portland *Oregon Journal,* February 25, 1937; and Eugene *Daily News,* July 5, 1939. Also see the Greater Willamette Valley Association, Inc., *Great Willamette Valley of Oregon* (n.p., n.d.), copy in the Oregon State Library, Salem.

44. Salem *Capital Journal,* April 2, 1940; and Willamette River Basin Commission, *Final Report,* 5.

45. Pacific Northwest Regional Planning Commission, *Progress Report: January 1934–January 1935* (1935), 81.

46. Kipp to McNary, March 17, 1931, box 6, McNary Papers.

47. Ibid. Kipp's correspondence with Oregon's senators and representatives is voluminous and most of it relates to a variety of river-development schemes.

48. Portland *Oregonian,* April 13, 1931.

49. *Eugene Register-Guard,* July 31, 1938. Maxey later served on the Willamette River Basin Commission.

50. Ibid.

51. Oregon State Planning Board, *Willamette Valley Project: A Regional Plan* (1936), 1; and Oregon State Planning Board, *The Willamette Valley Project* (1935), 1, 4.

52. Oregon State Planning Board, *The Willamette Valley Project,* 13.

53. *Eugene Register-Guard,* July 31, 1938, and July 30, 1939.

54. Oregon State Planning Board, *Willamette Valley Project: A Regional Plan,* 2, 19; Oregon, Willamette River Basin Commission, *Final Report,* 5; and *Oregonian,* February 24, 1936.

55. Salem *Oregon Statesman,* February 18, 25, and 26, 1937; and *Oregonian,* February 26, 1937.

56. *Oregonian,* February 26, 1937; and *Oregon Journal,* February 25, 1937.

57. *Oregon Journal,* February 25, 1937; *Eugene Register-Guard,* July 31, 1938; *Salem Capitol Press,* May 5, 1939; and C. A. Rockhill to McNary, circa 1938, in box 6, McNary Papers.

58. "Notice of Public Hearing, December 7, 1937: The Board of Engineers for Rivers and Harbors," in Walter Pierce Papers, Issues File, Oregon Projects, Knight Library, University of Oregon; R. H. Kipp to Board of U.S. Army Engineers, December 1, 1937, Pierce Papers; *Oregon Statesman,* December 9, 1937; Kipp to Pierce, December 8, 1937, and circular, December 7, 1937, Pierce Papers.

59. *Oregon Statesman,* December 21, 1937; Kipp to Pierce, December 28, 1937, Pierce Papers; McNary to J. C. Swan, March 9, 1938, box 6, McNary Papers; and *Cong. Rec.,* 75th Cong., 3d sess. (1938), 9504.

60. Oregon, Willamette River Basin Commission, *Final Report,* 5; Kipp to McNary, March 18, 1938, McNary to C. E. Williamson, April 28, 1938, and Ainsworth to McNary, June 11, 1938, box 6, McNary Papers.

61. Copy in Pierce Papers, Issues File, Oregon Projects.

62. Oregon State Planning Board, *Oregon Looks Ahead* (1938), 20, 56.

63. *Eugene Register-Guard,* July 31, 1938.

64. Buse to Pierce, January 5, 1940, Pierce Papers; Ray Steele to McNary, June 15, 1938, and Robins to McNary, November 1, 1937, box 6, McNary Papers.

65. *Eugene Daily News,* July 5, 1939.

66. Neuberger, *Our Promised Land,* 6, 8, 14–15, 17, and 24.

67. Ibid., 353–57.

68. Steve Neal, *They Never Go Back to Pocatello* (1988), 31–32. The relationship between capitalism and the natural world is suggested in Donald Worster, *Dust Bowl: The Southern Plains in the 1930s* (1979), 6. For a different view, see Peter Berger, *The Capitalist Revolution: Fifty Propositions about Prosperity, Equality, and Liberty* (1986).

Epilogue: One Moment in Time

1. Works Projects Administration, *Oregon: End of the Trail* (1940), vii–ix.

2. Ibid., ix.

3. *Time,* May 15, 1950, p. 23.

4. Ibid.

5. Ibid., July 30, 1951, pp. 48–51.

6. *Oregonian,* September 1, 1949.

7. Dorothy Johansen, "Oregon's Role in American History: An Old Theme Recast," *Pacific Northwest Quarterly* 38 (April 1949), 87, 89–90.

8. For an elaboration of this argument, see Colin A. M. Duncan, "On Identifying a Sound Environmental Ethic in History: Prolegomena to Any Future Environmental History," *Environmental History Review* 15 (Summer 1991), 13–14.

9. Paul Hirt, *A Conspiracy of Optimism: Management of the National Forests since World War Two* (1994), xxi–xxii.

10. Pacific Northwest Regional Planning Commission, *Progress Report: January 1934–January 1935* (1935), 20, 34, and 39.

11. Pacific Northwest Regional Planning Commission, *Pacific Northwest Problems and Materials: An Introduction* (1940), 29, 33, and 34.

12. Pacific Northwest Regional Planning Commission, *Development of Resources and of Economic Opportunity in the Pacific Northwest* (1942), 171–73.

13. Richard L. Neuberger, "The Land of New Horizons," *New York Times Magazine,* December 9, 1945, pp. 18 and 23.

14. *Life,* October 13, 1947, pp. 121–22.

15. Hirt, *A Conspiracy of Optimism,* xliv–xlvii.

16. Richard White, "Environmental History, Ecology, and Meaning," *Journal of American History* 76 (March 1990), 1112.

17. Richard White, *The Organic Machine* (1995), 90–91.

18. Charles H. Gilbert and Barton W. Evermann, "A Report upon Investigations in the Columbia River Basin, with Descriptions of Four New Species of Fish," *U.S. Fish Commission Bulletin* 14 (1894), 179; Oregon State Game Commission, *The Problems of Pollution of Oregon Public Waters and the Solution Offered under the National Recovery Act,* Bulletin 1 (1933); and Anthony Netboy, *Columbia River Salmon and Steelhead Trout: Their Fight for Survival* (1980), 57.

19. Marshall McDonald, *Salmon Fisheries of the Columbia River,* report prepared for U.S. Commission of Fish and Fisheries, 53rd Cong., 2d sess., 1894 (Senate Misc. Doc. 200), p. 155.

20. George Gleeson, *The Return of a River: The Willamette River, Oregon* (1972), 101–3; David B. Charlton to the author, November 13, 1975; and *Oregon Sportsman* (January 1914), 1.

21. See the *Oregonian,* October 10, 1994, and August 7, 1995.

22. For a discussion of postwar prosperity in resource-dependent communities, see William G. Robbins, *Hard Times in Paradise: Coos Bay, Oregon, 1850–1986* (1988), 107–21.

23. Carlos A. Schwantes, *The Pacific Northwest: An Interpretive History* (1989), 318–23.

24. Ibid., 322.

25. Ethel A. Starbird, "A River Restored: Oregon's Willamette," *National Geographic* 144 (June 1972), 816–19.

26. The best source on water-quality conditions in the Willamette River is Gleeson, *Return of a River.*

27. My argument here is derived from William Cronon, *Nature's Metropolis: Chicago and the Great West* (1992).

28. The story of Bend as a lumbering center is told in Philip Cogswell, Jr., "The Deschutes Country Pine Logging," in *High and the Mighty: Sketches about the Deschutes Country,* Thomas Vaughan, ed. (1981), 236–41; and Thomas R. Cox, "Closing the Lumberman's Frontier: The Far Western Pine Country," *Journal of the West* 33 (July 1994), 52–61.

29. Simon Schama, *Landscape and Memory* (1995), 14.

Bibliography

Government Documents, Reports, and Publications

Atwood, Katherine. *As Long as the World Goes On: Environmental History of the Evans Creek Watershed.* U.S. Department of the Interior, Bureau of Land Management, Medford District Office, 1995.

Beckham, Stephen Dow. *The Oregon Central Military Wagon Road: A History and Reconnaissance.* U.S. Department of Agriculture, Forest Service, Pacific Northwest Region, Willamette National Forest. Heritage Research Associates, Report no. 6. Vol. 1 (1981).

Benton County, Oregon. County Surveyor's Records. Vols. 1–3 (1855–57).

Browne, J. Ross, to the Secretary of the Interior, November 17, 1857. U.S. House, Indian Affairs in the Territories of Oregon and Washington. 35th Cong., 1st sess., 1858, H. Ex. Doc. 39, Serial 955.

Collins, J. W. "Report on the Fisheries of the Pacific Coast of the United States." *Report of the Commissioner of Fisheries.* Washington, D.C.: Government Printing Office, 1893.

Douglas County, Oregon. *Proceedings of the Board of County Commissioners of Umpqua County.* 1850–70.

Federal Power Commission. *Report to the Federal Power Commission on Uses of Deschutes River, Oregon.* Washington, D.C.: Government Printing Office, 1922.

Gilbert, Charles, and Barton W. Evermann. "A Report upon Investigations in the Columbia River Basin, with Descriptions of Four New Species of Fish." *U.S. Fish Commission Bulletin* 14 (1894): 170–97.

Griffiths, David. *Forage Conditions on the Northern Border of the Great Basin.* U.S. Department of Agriculture, Bureau of Plant Industry, Bulletin no. 15. Washington, D.C.: Government Printing Office, 1902.

Henshaw, F. F., John H. Lewis, and E. J. McCaustland. "Water Rights and Appropriation." U.S. Geological Survey, Paper no. 344, *Deschutes River, Oregon, and Its Utilization.* Washington, D.C.: Government Printing Office, 1914.

LaLande, Jeff. *An Environmental History of the Little Applegate Watershed.* U.S. Department of Agriculture, Forest Service, Rogue River National Forest, 1995.

Langille, H. D. "A Report on the Cascade Range Forest Reserve," June 4, 1904. Box 1, National Forests, 1904–1906. Record Group 95. National Archives and Federal Records Center, Seattle.

———, H. D., Fred G. Plummer, Arthur Dodwell, Theodore F. Rixon, and John B. Leiberg. *Forest Conditions in the Cascade Range Forest Reserve, Oregon.* U.S. Department of the Interior, U.S. Geological Survey, Professional Paper 9, Series H, Forestry. Washington, D.C.: Government Printing Office, 1903.

Leiberg, John B. "Cascade Range and Ashland Forest Reserves and Adjacent Regions." *Twenty-first Annual Report of the United States Geological Survey to the Secretary of the Interior, 1899–1900.* Part 5.

McDonald, Marshall. *Salmon Fisheries of the Columbia River.* Report prepared for the U.S. Commission of Fish and Fisheries. 53rd Cong., 2d sess., 1984, Senate Misc. Doc. 200.

Moore, Shirley T., ed. *Sumpter Valley Railroad.* U.S. Department of Agriculture, Forest Service, Wallowa-Whitman National Forest, Pacific Northwest Region, n.d.

Mosgrove, Jerry. *The Malheur National Forest: An Ethnographic History.* U.S. Department of Agriculture, Forest Service, Pacific Northwest Region, 1980.

Oregon. Willamette River Basin Commission. *Final Report.* Salem: n.p., 1959.

Oregon State Game Commission. *The Problems of Pollution of Oregon Public Waters and the Solution Offered under the National Recovery Act.* Bulletin 1. Portland: n.p., 1933.

Oregon State Planning Board. *Oregon Looks Ahead.* Salem: n.p., 1938.

———. *Present and Potential Land Development in Oregon through Flood Control, Drainage and Irrigation.* Published under the Auspices of the Works Progress Administration, 1938.

———. *Willamette Valley Project.* Salem: n.p., 1935.

———. *Willamette Valley Project: A Regional Plan.* Salem: n.p., 1936.

Pacific Northwest Regional Planning Commission. *Development of Resources and of Economic Opportunity in the Pacific Northwest.* Washington, D.C.: Natural Resources Planning Board, 1942.

———. *Pacific Northwest Problems and Materials: An Introduction.* Portland: Northwest Regional Council, 1940.

———. *Progress Report: January 1934–January 1935.* Portland: Natural Resources Board, District no. 11, 1935.

Quigley, Thomas M. *Forest Health in the Blue Mountains: Social and Economic Perspectives.* U.S. Department of Agriculture, Forest Service, Pacific Northwest Research Station, General Technical Report, PNW-GTR-296 (1992).

Reports of Explorations and Surveys, to Ascertain the Most Practicable and Economical Route for a Railroad from the Mississippi River to the Pacific Ocean. 1853–55. 12 vols. 33d Cong., 2d sess., 1857, Senate Ex. Doc. 78, Vol. 6 (Abbott). (Serial 763).

Russell, Israel C. *Bulletin of the United States Geological Survey,* no. 199. Washington, D.C.: Government Printing Office, 1902.

———. *Notes on the Geology of Southwestern Idaho and Southeastern Oregon.* U.S. Department of the Interior, United States Geological Survey, Bulletin no. 217. Washington, D.C.: Government Printing Office, 1903.

———. *Preliminary Report on the Geology and Water Resources of Central Oregon.* U.S. Department of the Interior, United States Geological Survey, Bulletin no. 252. Washington, D.C.: Government Printing Office, 1905.

Sargent, Charles Sprague. *Report on the Forests of North America.* U.S. Department of Agriculture. Washington, D.C.: Government Printing Office, 1884.

Sparhawk, William N. "The History of Forestry in America." In U.S. Department of Agriculture, *Trees: Yearbook of Agriculture.* Washington, D.C.: Government Printing Office, 1949.

State of California. *Interim Report on Klamath River Basin Investigation: Water Utilization and Requirements.* Sacramento: State Water Resources Board, 1954.

State of Oregon. *Messages of the Governor.* 1911.

———. *Message of Walter M. Pierce, Governor, to the Thirty-third Legislative Assembly, 1925.*

———. *Message of Walter M. Pierce, Governor, to the Thirty-fourth Legislative Assembly, 1927.*

———. *Report of the Oregon Conservation Commission to the Governor.* 1908–15.

U.S. Army Corps of Engineers. *General Information: Willamette Valley Project, Oregon.* Portland: Corps of Engineers, 1940.

———. "Report from the Chief of Engineers on Willamette River, Oregon,

Covering Navigation, Flood Control, Power Development, and Irrigation." 72d Cong., 1st sess., 1932, House Doc. 263.

———. "A Report on Willamette River and Tributaries, Oregon." 75th Cong., 3d sess., 1938, House Doc. 544.

U.S. Bureau of Reclamation. *Reclamation Accomplishments, 1905–1953: Klamath Project, Oregon-California.* Prepared by Maurise K. Strantz. July 1953.

U.S. Department of Agriculture, Forest Service. *Forest Statistics for Deschutes County, Oregon.* Forest Survey, Pacific Northwest Forest Experiment Station, 1936.

———. *Forest Statistics for Klamath County, Oregon.* Forest Survey, Pacific Northwest Forest Experiment Station, 1936.

U.S. Department of Commerce, Bureau of the Census. *Agriculture.* Vol. 5, *Farms, Livestock, and Animal Products.* Part 1. Washington, D.C.: Government Printing Office, 1902.

———. *Eighth Census of the United States: 1860.* Washington, D.C.: Government Printing Office, 1864.

———. *Ninth Census of the United States: 1870, Compendium of the Ninth Census.* Washington, D.C.: Government Printing Office, 1872.

———. *Seventh Census of the United States: 1850.* Washington, D.C.: Robert Armstrong, Public Printer, 1853.

———. *Sixteenth Census of the United States: 1940, Population.* Washington, D.C.: Government Printing Office, 1943.

———. *Tenth Census of the United States: 1880, Compendium of the Tenth Census.* Washington, D.C.: Government Printing Office, 1883.

U.S. Department of the Interior. *Annual Report of the Commissioner of Indian Affairs.* 1855.

———. *Annual Report of the Commissioner of Indian Affairs.* 1856.

———. *Twenty-first Annual Report of the United States Geological Survey to the Secretary of the Interior, 1899–1900.*

———. *Upper Klamath River Basin, Oregon–California.* Washington, D.C.: Government Printing Office, 1954.

U.S. House of Representatives. *Reports on the Statistics of Agriculture in the United States: Agriculture by Irrigation in the Western Part of the United States and Statistics of Fisheries in the United States at the Eleventh Census: 1890.* 52d Cong., 1st sess., Misc. Doc. 340. Washington, D.C.: Government Printing Office, 1896.

Works Projects Administration. *Oregon: End of the Trail.* Portland: Binfords and Mort, 1940.

Books

Abbott, Carl. *Portland: Planning, Politics, and Growth in a Twentieth-Century City.* Lincoln: University of Nebraska Press, 1983.

Abbott, Henry L. *Explorations for a Railroad Route, from the Sacramento Valley to the Columbia River* (1855). Reprinted in Bert and Margie Weber, eds., *Railroading in Southern Oregon and the Founding of Medford.* Fairfield, WA: Ye Galleon Press, 1985.

Agee, James K. *Fire Ecology of Pacific Northwest Forests.* Washington, D.C.: Island Press, 1993.

Aikins, C. Melvin. *Archaeology of Oregon.* Portland: Oregon State Office, U.S. Department of Interior, Bureau of Land Management, 1986.

Allen, Barbara. *Homesteading the High Desert.* Logan: Utah State University Press, 1987.

Allen, John Logan. *Passage through the Garden: Lewis and Clark and the Image of the Northwest.* Urbana: University of Illinois Press, 1975.

Ankeny, Nesmith. *The West as I Knew It.* Lewiston, ID: R. G. Bailey, 1953.

Baldwin, Ewart M. *Geology of Oregon.* Dubuque, Iowa: Kendall-Hunt, 1981.

Barker, Burt Brown, ed. *Letters of Dr. John McLoughlin, Written at Fort Vancouver, 1829–1832.* Portland: Binfords and Mort, 1948.

Beckham, Stephen Dow. *Coos Bay: The Pioneer Period, 1850–1900.* Coos Bay, OR: Arago Books, 1973.

———. *Land of the Umpqua: A History of Douglas County, Oregon.* Roseburg: Commissioners of Douglas County, 1986.

———. *Requiem for a People: The Rogue Indians and the Frontiersmen.* Norman: University of Oklahoma Press, 1971.

———. *The Simpsons of Shore Acres.* Coos Bay: Arago Books, 1973.

Belshaw, George W. *Diary of the Oregon Trail, 1853.* Eugene: Lane County Historical Society, 1960.

Benton, Thomas Hart. *Thirty Years' View.* 2 vols. New York: D. Appleton and Company, 1897.

Berger, Peter. *The Capitalist Revolution: Fifty Propositions about Prosperity, Equality, and Liberty.* New York: Basic Books, 1986.

Boag, Peter G. *Environment and Experience: Settlement Culture in Nineteenth-Century Oregon.* Berkeley: University of California Press, 1992.

Bowen, William A. *The Willamette Valley: Migration and Settlement on the Oregon Frontier.* Seattle: University of Washington Press, 1978.

Bowman, Isaiah. *The Pioneer Fringe.* Special Publication no. 13. New York: American Geographical Society, 1931.

Braudel, Fernand. *The Perspective of the World* (1979). Translated by Sian Reynolds. New York: Harper and Row, 1984.

Bryan, Enoch A. *Orient Meets Occident: The Advent of Railways to the Pacific Northwest.* Pullman, WA: Students Book Corporation, 1936.

Burnett, Peter H. *Recollections and Opinions of an Old Pioneer* (1880). New York: Da Capo Press, 1969.

Callenbach, Ernest. *Ectopia: The Notebooks and Reports of William Weston.* Berkeley: Banyan Tree Books, 1975.

Camp, C. L., ed. *James Clyman, American Frontiersman.* San Francisco: California Historical Society, 1928.

Catlin, George. *Episodes from "Life among the Indians" and "Last Rambles."* Norman: University of Oklahoma Press, 1959.

Clark, Ella. *Indian Legends of the Pacific Northwest.* Berkeley: University of California Press, 1953.

Clark, Malcolm, Jr. *Eden Seekers: The Settlement of Oregon.* Boston: Houghton Mifflin, 1981.

Clepper, Henry. *Professional Forestry in the United States.* Baltimore: Johns Hopkins University Press, 1971.

Clyman, James. *Journal of a Mountain Man* (1928). Missoula, MT: Mountain Press Publishing Company, 1984.

Colvocoresses, George M. *Four Years in a Government Exploring Expedition.* New York: Cornish, Lamport, and Company, 1852.

Cooper, J. G., and G. Suckley. *The Natural History of Washington Territory.* New York: Bailliere Brothers, 1859.

Cox, Ross. *The Columbia River,* edited by Edgar I. and Jane R. Stewart. Norman: University of Oklahoma Press, 1957.

Cox, Thomas R. *Mills and Markets: A History of the Pacific Coast Lumber Industry to 1900.* Seattle: University of Washington Press, 1974.

Cressman, Luther S. *The Sandal and the Cave: The Indians of Oregon* (1962). Corvallis: Oregon State University Press, 1981.

Cronon, William. *Changes in the Land: Indians, Colonists, and the Ecology of New England.* New York: Hill and Wang, 1983.

————. *Nature's Metropolis: Chicago and the Great West.* New York: W. W. Norton, 1991.

Crosby, Alfred W. *The Columbian Exchange: Biological and Cultural Consequences of 1492.* Westport, CT: Greenwood Press, 1972.

———. *Ecological Imperialism: The Biological Expansion of Europe, 900–1900.* New York: Cambridge University Press, 1986.

Dana, Samuel Trask, and Sally K. Fairfax. *Forest and Range Policy: Its Development in the United States.* 2d ed. New York: McGraw-Hill, 1980.

Dasmann, Raymond F. *The Destruction of California.* New York: Macmillan Company, 1965.

Davies, John, ed. *Douglas of the Forests: The North American Journals of David Douglas.* Seattle: University of Washington Press, 1980.

Davies, K. G., ed. *Peter Skene Ogden's Snake Country Journals, 1826–1827.* London: Hudson's Bay Record Society, 1961.

Detling, Leroy E. *Historical Background of the Flora of the Pacific Northwest.* Eugene: University of Oregon Museum of Natural History, Bulletin no. 13, 1968.

DeVoto, Bernard. *The Course of Empire.* Boston: Houghton-Mifflin Company, 1952.

Dicken, Samuel N., and Emily F. Dicken. *The Making of Oregon: A Study in Historical Geography.* Portland: Oregon Historical Society Press, 1979.

Dietrich, William. *Northwest Passage: The Great Columbia River.* New York: Simon and Schuster, 1995; paperback ed., Seattle: University of Washington Press, 1996.

Dobyns, Henry. *From Fire to Flood: Historic Human Destruction of Sonoran Desert Riverine Oases.* Socorro, NM: Ballena Press, 1981.

Dodds, Gordon B. *A Pygmy Monopolist: The Life and Doings of R. D. Hume.* Madison: Wisconsin State Historical Society, 1961.

Douglas, David. *Journals of Travels in North America.* New York: Antiquarian Press, 1953.

Drucker, Philip. *Indians of the Northwest Coast.* Garden City, NY: Natural History Press, 1955.

Due, John F., and Giles French. *Rails to the Mid-Columbia Wheatlands: The Columbia and Southern and Great Southern Railroads and the Development of Sherman and Wasco Counties, Oregon.* Washington, D.C.: University Press of America, 1979.

Duncan, Dayton. *Out West: American Journey along the Lewis and Clark Trail.* New York: Viking Penguin, 1987.

Eakin, S. B., Jr. *A Short Sketch of a Trip across the Plains by S. B. Eakin and Family, 1866.* Eugene: Lane County Historical Society, 1970.

Erickson, Sheldon D. *Occupance in the Upper Deschutes Basin, Oregon.* Research Paper no. 32, Department of Geography, University of Chicago, 1953.

Evans, John. *Powerful Rocky: The Blue Mountains and the Oregon Trail.* La Grande: Eastern Oregon State College, 1991.

Farnham, Thomas J. *An 1839 Wagon Train Journal: Travels in the Great Western Prairies, the Anahuac and Rocky Mountains and in the Oregon Territory* (1843). Monroe, OR: Monroe Publishing Company, 1977.

Ferrell, Mallory Hope. *Rails, Sagebrush, and Pine: A Garland of Railroad and Logging Days in Oregon's Sumpter Valley.* San Marino, CA: Golden West Books, 1967.

Ficken, Robert E. *The Forested Land: A History of Lumbering in Western Washington.* Seattle: University of Washington Press, 1987.

Fisher, Robin. *Contact and Conflict: Indian-European Relations in British Columbia, 1774–1890.* Vancouver: University of British Columbia Press, 1977.

Gaston, Joseph. *The Centennial History of Oregon.* 3 vols. Chicago: n.p., 1912.

Gibson, James R. *Farming the Frontier: The Agricultural Opening of the Oregon Country, 1786–1846.* Seattle: University of Washington Press, 1985.

Gilbert, Chester G., and Joseph E. Pogue. *America's Power Resources: The Economic Significance of Coal, Oil, and Water-Power.* New York: The Century Company, 1921.

Gleeson, George. *The Return of a River: The Willamette River, Oregon.* Corvallis: Water Resources Research Institute, Oregon State University, 1972.

Good, Rachael Applegate, comp. *History of Klamath County, Oregon: Its Resources and Its People.* 2 vols. Klamath Falls: n.p., 1941.

Grayson, Donald K. *The Desert's Past: A Natural History of the Great Basin.* Washington, D.C.: Smithsonian Institution Press, 1993.

Harvey, Athelston George. *Douglas of the Fir.* Cambridge: Harvard University Press, 1947.

Hays, Samuel P. *Conservation and the Gospel of Efficiency: The Progressive Conservation Movement, 1890–1920.* New York: Cambridge University Press, 1959.

Hedges, James B. *Henry Villard and the Railways of the Northwest* (1930). New York: Russell and Russell, 1967.

Hines, Gustavus. *Life on the Plains of the Pacific: Its History, Condition, and Prospects.* Buffalo: G. H. Derby and Company, 1851.

Hirt, Paul W. *A Conspiracy of Optimism: Management of the National Forests since World War Two.* Lincoln: University of Nebraska Press, 1994.

Hobsbawm, E. J. *The Age of Capital, 1848–1875.* New York: Charles Scribner's Sons, 1975.

Holbrook, Stewart. *The Columbia.* New York: Holt, Rinehart and Winston, 1956.

————. *Holy Old Mackinaw: A Natural History of the American Lumberjack.* New York: Macmillan Company, 1938.

Hulbert, Archer Butler, and Dorothy Printup Hulbert, eds. *The Oregon Crusade: Across Land and Sea to Oregon.* Denver: Colorado College, 1935.

Hunn, Eugene S. *Nch'i-Wana, "The Big River": Mid-Columbia Indians and Their Land.* Seattle: University of Washington Press, 1990.

An Illustrated History of Baker, Grant, Malheur, and Harney Counties. Spokane: Western Historical Publishing Company, 1902.

Irving, Washington. *The Adventures of Captain Bonneville, U.S.A., in the Rocky Mountains and the Far West* (1837). Rpt., edited by Edgeley W. Todd, Norman: University of Oklahoma Press, 1961.

Ise, John. *The United States Forest Policy.* New Haven: Yale University Press, 1920.

Jackson, Donald, ed. *Letters of the Lewis and Clark Expedition with Related Documents, 1783–1854.* Rev. ed., Urbana: University of Illinois Press, 1978.

————, and Mary Lee Spence, eds. *The Expeditions of John Charles Fremont.* 2 vols. Urbana: University of Illinois Press, 1970.

Johansen, Dorothy O., and Charles M. Gates. *Empire of the Columbia: A History of the Pacific Northwest.* 2d ed. New York: Harper and Row, 1967.

Johnson, Don, ed. *The Journals of Captain Nathaniel J. Wyeth to the Oregon Country, 1831–1836* (1899). Fairfield, WA: Ye Galleon Press, 1984.

Johnson, Overton, and William H. Winter. *Route across the Rocky Mountains* (1846). Fairfield, WA: Ye Galleon Press, 1982.

Josephy, Alvin, Jr. *The Nez Perce Indians and the Opening of the Northwest.* New Haven: Yale University Press, 1965.

Journal Kept by David Douglas during his Travels in North America, 1823–1827. New York: Antiquarian Press Ltd., 1959.

Judson, Phoebe Goodell. *A Pioneer's Search for an Ideal Home,* edited by John M. McClelland, Jr. Tacoma: Washington State Historical Society, 1966.

King, Arthur S. *A History of the Water Resources Congress.* Salem: Oregon Water Resources Congress, 1972.

Kirchhoff, Theodor. *Oregon East, Oregon West, 1863–1872,* edited and translated by Frederic Trautmann. Portland: Oregon Historical Society Press, 1987.

Kittredge, William. *A Hole in the Sky: A Memoir.* New York: Alfred A. Knopf, 1992.

————. *Owning It All.* Saint Paul: Graywolf Press, 1987.

Kolko, Gabriel. *The Triumph of American Conservatism: A Reinterpretation of American History, 1900–1916.* New York: The Free Press, 1963.

Langston, Nancy. *Forest Dreams, Forest Nightmares: The Paradox of Old Growth in the Inland West.* Seattle: University of Washington Press, 1995.

Lyman, W. D. *An Illustrated History of Walla Walla County, Washington.* Walla Walla: W. H. Lever, 1901.

MacColl, E. Kimbark, and Harry H. Stein. *Merchants, Money, and Power: The Portland Establishment, 1843–1913.* Portland: The Georgian Press, 1988.

McDonald, Lois Halliday, ed. *Fur Trade Letters of Francis Ermatinger.* Glendale, CA: Arthur H. Clark Company, 1980.

Malone, Michael P., and Richard W. Etulain. *The American West: A Twentieth-Century History.* Lincoln: University of Nebraska Press, 1989.

May, Dean L. *Three Frontiers: Family, Land, and Society in the American West, 1850–1900.* New York: Cambridge University Press, 1994.

Meinig, Donald W. *The Great Columbia Plain: A Historical Geography, 1805–1910.* Seattle: University of Washington Press, 1968.

Mighetto, Lisa. *Saving the Salmon: A History of the U.S. Army Corps of Engineers' Role in the Protection of Anadromous Fish on the Columbia and Snake Rivers.* Seattle: Historical Research Associates, 1994.

Moulton, Gary E., ed. *The Journals of the Lewis and Clark Expedition.* 8 vols. Lincoln: University of Nebraska Press, 1983–89.

Mumford, Lewis. *Regional Planning in the Pacific Northwest.* Portland: Northwest Regional Council, 1939.

Neal, Steve. *They Never Go Back to Pocatello.* Portland: Oregon Historical Society Press, 1988.

Netboy, Anthony. *The Columbia River Salmon and Steelhead Trout: Their Fight for Survival.* Seattle: University of Washington Press, 1980.

Neuberger, Richard. *Our Promised Land* (1938). Rpt., with an Introduction by David Nicandri, Moscow: University of Idaho Press, 1989.

Newsom, E. Earl, comp. *David Newsom: The Western Observer.* Portland: Oregon Historical Society Press, 1972.

O'Callaghan, Jerry A. *The Dispossession of the Public Domain in Oregon.* Washington, D.C.: Government Printing Office, 1960.

Oliver, Egbert S. *Homes in the Oregon Forest: Settling Columbia County.* Brownsville, OR: Calapooia Publications, 1983.

Palmer, Joel. *Journal of Travels on the Oregon Trail in 1845* (1847). Portland: Oregon Trail Coordinating Council, 1992.

Parker, Samuel. *Journal of an Exploring Tour beyond the Rocky Mountains* (1838). Minneapolis: Ross and Haines, 1967.

Paul, Rodman W. *The Far West and the Great Plains in Transition, 1859–1900.* New York: Harper and Row, 1988.

Peterson, Emil R., and Alfred Powers. *A Century of Coos and Curry.* Portland: Binfords and Mort, 1952.

Pisani, Donald. *To Reclaim a Divided West: Water, Law, and Public Policy, 1848–1902.* Albuquerque: University of New Mexico Press, 1992.

Pitzer, Paul C. *Grand Coulee: Harnessing a Dream.* Pullman: Washington State University Press, 1994.

Pomeroy, Earl. *The Pacific Slope: A History of California, Oregon, Washington, Idaho, Utah, and Nevada.* New York: Alfred A. Knopf, 1965; paperback ed., Lincoln: University of Nebraska Press, 1991.

Prouty, Andrew M. *More Deadly Than War! Pacific Coast Logging, 1827–1981.* New York: Garland Publishing, 1985.

Puter, Stephen A. D. *Looters of the Public Domain* (1908). New York: Arno Press, 1972.

Pyne, Stephen J. *Fire in America: A Cultural History of Wildland and Rural Fire.* Princeton: Princeton University Press, 1982; paperback ed., Seattle: University of Washington Press, 1997.

Rich, E. E., ed. *The Letters of John McLoughlin from Fort Vancouver to the Governor and Committee.* Toronto: Champlain Society, 1941.

———. *Peter Skene Ogden's Snake Country Journals, 1824–25 and 1825–26.* London: Hudson's Bay Record Society, 1950.

Richmond, Henry R. *The History of the Portland District Corps of Engineers, 1871–1969.* Portland: U.S. Army Corps of Engineers, 1970.

Riddle, George. *History of Early Days in Oregon.* Reprinted from *The Riddle Enterprise,* 1920.

Robbins, William G. *American Forestry: A History of National, State, and Private Cooperation.* Lincoln: University of Nebraska Press, 1985.

———. *Colony and Empire: The Capitalist Transformation of the American West.* Lawrence: University Press of Kansas, 1994.

———. *Hard Times in Paradise: Coos Bay, Oregon, 1850–1986.* Seattle: University of Washington Press, 1988.

———, Robert J. Frank and Richard E. Ross, eds. *Regionalism and the Pacific Northwest.* Corvallis: Oregon State University Press, 1983.

Roberts, Neil. *The Holocene: An Environmental History.* New York: Basil Blackwell, 1989.

Rollins, Philip Ashton, ed. *The Discovery of the Oregon Trail: Robert Stuart's Narratives.* New York: Charles Scribner's Sons, 1935.

Ronda, James P. *Astoria and Empire.* Lincoln: University of Nebraska Press, 1990.

————. *Lewis and Clark among the Indians.* Lincoln: University of Nebraska Press, 1984.

Ross, Alexander. *Adventures of the First Settlers on the Oregon or Columbia River, 1810–1813* (1849). Lincoln: University of Nebraska Press, 1986.

Sauer, Carl O. *Seventeenth Century North America.* Berkeley: Turtle Island Press, 1980.

Schabecoff, Philip. *A Fierce Green Fire: The American Environmental Movement.* New York: Hill and Wang, 1993.

Schama, Simon. *Landscape and Memory.* New York: Alfred A. Knopf, 1995.

Schwantes, Carlos A. *The Pacific Northwest: An Interpretive History.* Lincoln: University of Nebraska Press, 1989.

————. *Railroad Signatures across the Pacific Northwest.* Seattle: University of Washington Press, 1993.

Settle, Raymond. *The March of the Mounted Riflemen as Recorded in the Journals of Major Osborne Cross and George Gibbs and the Official Report of Colonel Loring.* Glendale, CA: Arthur H. Clarke Company, 1940.

Shaver, F. A., comp. *An Illustrated History of Central Oregon.* Spokane: Western Historical Publishing Company, 1905.

Silver, Timothy W. *A New Face on the Countryside: Indians, Colonists, and Slaves in South Atlantic Forests, 1500–1800.* New York: Cambridge University Press, 1990.

Simpson, Peter K. *The Community of Cattlemen: A Social History of the Cattle Industry in Southeastern Oregon, 1869–1912.* Moscow: University of Idaho Press, 1987.

Smalley, Eugene V. *History of the Northern Pacific Railroad* (1883). New York: Arno Press, 1975.

Smith, Courtland. *Salmon Fishers of the Columbia.* Corvallis: Oregon State University Press, 1979.

Smith, Frank E., ed. *Conservation in the United States: A Documentary History.* 2 vols. New York: Chelsea House, 1971.

Smith, Henry Nash. *Virgin Land: The American West as Symbol and Myth.* Cambridge: Harvard University Press, 1950.

Snow, C. P. *Two Cultures and the Scientific Revolution.* New York: Cambridge University Press, 1963.

Stavrianos, Leften S. *The Promise of the Coming Dark Age.* San Francisco: W. H. Freeman and Co., 1976.

Stebbins, Ellis A., and Gary Huxford. *Since 1856: Historical Views of the College at Monmouth.* Monmouth: Western Oregon State College, 1996.

Steen, Harold K. *The U.S. Forest Service: A History.* Seattle: University of Washington Press, 1976.

Stevens, Victor. *The Powers Story.* North Bend, OR: Wegford Publications, 1979.

Stuart, Grace D., and Reginald R. Stuart, eds. *Calvin B. West of the Umpqua.* Stockton: California History Foundation, 1961.

Swain, Donald. *Federal Conservation Policy, 1921–1933.* Berkeley: University of California Press, 1963.

Thornton, Russell. *American Indian Holocaust and Survival: A Population History since 1492.* Norman: University of Oklahoma Press, 1987.

Thwaites, Reuben Gold, ed. *Original Journals of the Lewis and Clark Expedition, 1804–1806.* 8 vols., 1904–5. New York: Antiquarian Press, 1959.

Townsend, John Kirk. *Narrative of a Journey across the Rocky Mountains to the Columbia River* (1839). Lincoln: University of Nebraska Press, 1978.

Trachtenberg, Alan. *The Incorporation of America: Culture and Society in the Gilded Age.* New York: Hill and Wang, 1982.

Tuan, Yi-Fu. *Space and Place: The Perspective of Experience.* Minneapolis: University of Minnesota Press, 1977.

Vancouver, George. *A Voyage of Discovery to the North Pacific Ocean, and around the World.* 3 vols, 1798. London: Hakluyt Society, 1984.

Vaughan, Thomas, ed. *High and the Mighty: Sketches about the Deschutes Country.* Portland: Oregon Historical Society, 1981.

Victor, Frances Fuller. *All Over Oregon and Washington: Observations on the Country.* San Francisco: John H. Carmany and Company, 1872.

Walling, A. G. *History of Southern Oregon: Comprising Jackson, Josephine, Douglas, Curry and Coos Counties.* Portland: A. G. Walling and Sons, 1884.

Webber, Bert, and Margie Webber. *Railroading in Southern Oregon and the Founding of Medford.* Fairfield, WA: Ye Galleon Press, 1985.

West, Elliott. *The Way to the West: Essays on the Central Plains.* Albuquerque: University of New Mexico Press, 1995.

Wheat, Margaret M. *Survival Arts of the Primitive Paiutes.* Reno: University of Nevada Press, 1967.

White, Richard. *"It's Your Misfortune and None of My Own": A New History of the American West.* Norman: University of Oklahoma Press, 1991.

————. *Land Use, Environment, and Social Change: The Shaping of Island County, Washington.* Seattle: University of Washington Press, 1980.

————. *The Organic Machine.* New York: Hill and Wang, 1995.

————. *The Roots of Dependency: Subsistence, Environment, and Social Change among the Choctaws, Pawnees, and Navajos.* Lincoln: University of Nebraska Press, 1983.

Whitney, Stephen. *A Sierra Club Naturalist's Guide: The Pacific Northwest.* San Francisco: Sierra Club Books, 1989.

Wiley, Peter, and Robert Gottlieb. *Empires in the Sun: The Rise of the New American West.* New York: G. P. Putnam's Sons, 1982.

Wilkes, George. *The History of Oregon, Geographical and Political.* New York: William H. Collyer, 1845.

Williams, Raymond. *The Year 2000.* New York: Pantheon Books, 1983.

Williams, William Appleman. *The Contours of American History.* Cleveland: World Publishing Company, 1961.

Willingham, William F. *Army Engineers and the Development of Oregon: A History of the Portland District, U.S. Army Corps of Engineers.* Washington, D.C.: Government Printing Office, 1983.

Wilson, Edward O. *Biophilia.* Cambridge: Harvard University Press, 1984.

Winther, Oscar O. *The Great Northwest: A History.* 2d ed. New York: Alfred A. Knopf, 1950.

Winthrop, Theodore. *The Canoe and the Saddle* (1862). Rpt., edited by John H. Williams. Tacoma: Franklin-Ward Company, 1913.

Wolf, Eric. *Europe and a People without History.* Berkeley: University of California Press, 1982.

Worster, Donald. *Dust Bowl: The Southern Plains in the 1930s.* New York: Oxford University Press, 1979.

————. *Nature's Economy: A History of Ecological Ideas* (1977). 2d ed., New York: Cambridge University Press, 1994.

————. *The Wealth of Nature: Environmental History and the Ecological Imagination.* New York: Oxford University Press, 1993.

Young, Frederick G., ed. *The Correspondence and Journals of Captain Nathaniel J. Wyeth, 1831–6.* Eugene: University Press, 1899.

Young, James B., and B. Abbott Sparks. *Cattle in the Cold Desert.* Logan: Utah State University Press, 1985.

Zunz, Oliver. *Making America Corporate, 1870–1900.* Chicago: University of Chicago Press, 1990.

Articles and Chapters

Agee, James K. "The Historical Role of Fire in Pacific Northwest Forests." In *Natural and Proscribed Fire in Pacific Northwest Forests,* edited by John D. Walsted, Steven R. Radosevich, and David V. Sandberg. Corvallis: Oregon State University Press, 1990.

Applegate, Jesse. "Umpqua Agriculture, 1851." *Oregon Historical Quarterly* 32 (June 1931), 135–44.

Barrett, Stephen W. "Indians and Fire." *Western Wildlands* 6, no. 3 (Spring 1980), 17–21.

Beckham, Stephen Dow. "History of Western Oregon since 1846." In Wayne Suttles, ed., *Northwest Coast,* vol. 7 of *Handbook of North American Indians,* edited by William C. Sturtevant. Washington, D.C.: Smithsonian Institution Press, 1990.

Blackmar, Betsy. "Contemplating the Force of Nature." *Radical Historians Newsletter,* no. 70 (May 1994), 1, 4, 16.

Boyd, Robert. "Another Look at the 'Fever and Ague' of Western Oregon." *Ethnohistory* 22 (Spring 1975), 135–54.

———. "Demographic History, 1774–1874." In Wayne Suttles, ed., *Northwest Coast,* vol. 7 of *Handbook of North American Indians,* edited by William C. Sturtevant. Washington, D.C.: Smithsonian Institution Press, 1990.

———. "Strategies of Indian Burning in the Willamette Valley." *Canadian Journal of Anthropology* 5 (1986), 65–86.

Bright, Verne. "The Lost County, Umpqua, Oregon, and Its Early Settlements." *Oregon Historical Quarterly* 51 (1950), 111–26.

Buckley, Geoffrey L. "Desertification of the Camp Creek Drainage in Central Oregon." *Yearbook of the Association of Pacific Coast Geographers* 55 (1993), 97–126.

Buechner, Helmut K. "Some Biotic Changes in the State of Washington, Particularly during the Century 1853–1953." *Research Studies of the State College of Washington* 21 (1953), 154–92.

Butzer, Karl W. "The Americas before and after 1492: An Introduction to Current Geographical Research." *Annals of the Association of American Geographers* 82 (1992), 345–66.

Caldwell, J. R. "The First Fruits of the Land: A Brief History of Early Horticulture in Oregon." *Oregon Historical Quarterly* 7 (March 1906), 28–51, 151–62.

Christensen, Norman L. "Landscape History and Ecological Change." *Journal of Forest History* 33 (1989), 116–25.

Clark, Robert Carlton. "Harney Basin Exploration, 1826–60." *Oregon Historical Quarterly* 33 (June 1932), 104–14.

Cleaver, J. D. "L. Samuel and the *West Shore:* Images of a Changing Pacific Northwest." *Oregon Historical Quarterly* 94 (Summer-Fall 1993), 170–91.

Coan, C. F. "The Adoption of the Reservation Policy in the Pacific Northwest, 1853–1856." *Oregon Historical Quarterly* 23 (1922), 1–38.

Cody, Robin. "The Northwest Voice." *Oregon Quarterly* 74 (Spring 1995), 18–23.

Cox, Thomas R. "Closing the Lumberman's Frontier: The Far Western Pine Country." *Journal of the West* 33, no. 3 (July 1994), 59–66.

Cronon, William. "Comments on 'Landscape History and Ecological Change.'" *Journal of Forest History* 33 (1989), 125–27.

————. "A Place for Stories: Nature, History, and Narrative." *Journal of American History* 78 (March 1992), 1347–76.

Denevan, William M. "The Pristine Myth: The Landscape of the Americas in 1492." *Annals of the Association of American Geographers* 82, no. 3 (1992), 367–79.

"The Diary of Reverend Jason Lee." *Oregon Historical Quarterly* 17 (1916), 240–66.

"Dispatch from George Simpson, Esq., Governor of Rupert Land." *The Publications of the Hudson's Bay Company Record Society.* London: The Hudson's Bay Record Society, n.d.

Doolittle, William E. "Agriculture in North America on the Eve of Contact: A Reassessment." *Annals of the Association of American Geographers* 82 (September 1992), 386–401.

Duncan, Colin A. M. "On Identifying a Sound Environmental Ethic in History: Prolegomena to Any Future Environmental History." *Environmental History Review* 15 (Summer 1991), 5–30.

Eddleman, Lee. "Oregon's High Desert: Legacy for Today." In *Oregon's High Desert: The Last 100 Years,* Special Report 841 (June 1989), Agricultural Experiment Station, Oregon State University, Corvallis.

Elliott, T. C. "The Peter Skene Ogden Journals." *Oregon Historical Quarterly* 11 (June 1910), 201–22.

Finley, William L., and Irene Finley. "The Destruction of Lower Klamath." *Oregon Sportsman* 2, no. 1 (September 1925), 3–6.

Flores, Dan. "Bison Ecology and Bison Diplomacy: The Southern Plains from 1800 to 1850." *Journal of American History* 78 (1991), 465–85.

————. "Place: An Argument for Bioregional History." *Environmental History Review* 18 (Winter 1994), 1–18.

Fowler, C. S. "Subsistence." In Warren L. D'Azevedo, ed., *Great Basin,* vol. 11 of *Handbook of North American Indians,* edited by William G. Sturtevant. Washington, D.C.: Smithsonian Institution Press, 1986.

Galatowitsch, S. M. "Using the Original Land Survey Notes to Reconstruct Pre-settlement Landscapes in the American West." *Great Basin Naturalist* 50, no. 2 (1990), 181–91.

Goodell, George O. "The Upper Calapooia." *Oregon Historical Quarterly* 4 (March 1903), 70–77.

Grayson, Donald K. "Pleistocene Avifaunas and the Overkill Hypothesis." *Science* 195 (1977), 691–93.

Habek, James R. "The Original Vegetation of the Mid-Willamette Valley, Oregon." *Northwest Science* 35, no. 2 (May 1961), 65–77.

Haines, Francis. "The Northward Spread of Horses among the Plains Indians." *American Anthropologist* 40 (1938), 428–41.

Hargreaves, Sheba, ed. "The Letters of Roselle Putnam." *Oregon Historical Quarterly* 29 (September 1928), 242–62.

Harmon, Frank J. "Remembering Franklin B. Hough." *American Forests* 86 (January 1977), 34–53.

Holden, Horace. "Oregon Pioneering." 1878. Bancroft Library, University of California, Berkeley, P-A 40.

Howarth, William. "America's Dream of the Wide Open Spaces." *Book World,* January 4, 1987.

Hunn, Eugene S. "The Plateau." In *The First Oregonians,* edited by Carolyn M. Buan and Richard Lewis. Portland: Oregon Council for the Humanities, 1991.

James, Peter. "Ecotopia in Oregon?" *New Scientist* 81 (January 1987), 28–30.

Johansen, Dorothy O. "Oregon's Role in American History: An Old Theme Recast." *Pacific Northwest Quarterly* 38 (April 1949), 85–92.

Johnson, David. "Salmon: A Legacy of Abundance." *What's Happening* (Eugene). January 31, 1991.

Kauffman, J. B., and D. B. Sapsis. "The Natural Role of Fire in Oregon's High Desert." In *Oregon's High Desert: The Last 100 Years.* Special Report 841 (1989), Agricultural Experiment Station, Oregon State University, Corvallis.

Knuth, Priscilla, and Charles M. Gates, eds. "Oregon Territory in 1849–1850." *Pacific Northwest Quarterly* 40 (1949), 3–23.

Lewis, Henry T. "Reconstructing Patterns of Indian Burning in Southwestern Oregon." In *Living with the Land: Indians of Southwest Oregon,* Proceedings of the 1989 Symposium on the Prehistory of Southwest Oregon, edited by Nan Hannon and Richard K. Olmo. Medford: Southern Oregon Historical Society, 1990.

McCarver, M. M. Letter to C. A. Dodge. In "Documents." *Oregon Historical Quarterly* 4 (March 1903), 78–79.

McConnell, Grant. "Prologue: Environment and the Quality of Political Life." In *Congress and the Environment,* edited by Richard A. Cooley and Geoffrey Wandesforde-Smith. Seattle: University of Washington Press, 1970.

Martin, Paul S. "Pleistocene Overkill." *Science* 179 (1973), 965–69.

Mehringer, Peter J. "Late-Quaternary Pollen Records from the Interior Pacific Northwest and Northern Great Basin of the United States." In *Pollen Records of the Late-Quaternary North American Sediments,* edited by Vaughan M. Bryant, Jr., and Richard G. Holloway. Dallas: American Association of Stratigraphic Palynologists, 1985.

Mills, Randall. "A History of Transportation in the Pacific Northwest." *Oregon Historical Quarterly* 45 (1946), 281–312.

Minto, John. "From Youth to Age as an American." *Oregon Historical Quarterly* 9 (June 1908), 127–73.

Morris, William G. "Forest Fires in Western Oregon and Washington." *Oregon Historical Quarterly* 35 (1934), 313–39.

Mosimann, J. E., and P. S. Martin. "Simulating Overkill by Paleoindians." *American Scientist* 63 (1975), 304–13.

Nelson, J. C. "The Grasses of Salem, Oregon, and Vicinity." *Torreya* 19, no. 11 (1919), 216–17.

"Occupation of the Columbia River: A Report of the Committee to Inquire into the Situation of the Settlements upon the Pacific Ocean." *Oregon Historical Quarterly* 8 (1907), 51–75.

Onstad, Preston E. "The Fort on the Luckiamute: A Resurvey of Fort Hoskins." *Oregon Historical Quarterly* 65 (1964), 173–96.

Pipes, Nellie B. "Journal of John H. Frost, 1840–43." *Oregon Historical Quarterly* 35 (1934), 348–75.

Rajala, Richard A. "The Forest as Factory: Technological Change and Worker Control in the West Coast Logging Industry, 1880–1930." *Labour/Le Travail* 32 (Fall 1993), 73–85.

Ratcliff, James L. "What Happened to the Kalapuya? A Study of the Depletion of Their Economic Base." *The Indian Historian* 6 (Summer 1973), 27–33.

"Report of Lieutenant Neil M. Howison on Oregon, 1846." *Oregon Historical Quarterly* 14 (March 1913), 1–60.

Robbins, William G. "The Indian Question in Western Oregon: The Making of a Colonial People." In *Experiences in a Promised Land: Essays in Pacific Northwest History,* edited by G. Thomas Edwards and Carlos A. Schwantes. Seattle: University of Washington Press, 1986.

———. "Narrative Form and Great River Myths: The Power of Columbia River Stories." *Environmental History Review* 17 (Summer 1993), 1–22.

———. "Some Perspectives on Law and Order in Frontier Newspapers." *Journal of the West* 17 (January 1978), 53–62.

Robertson, James R. "The Social Evolution of Oregon." *Oregon Historical Quarterly* 3 (1902), 1–37.

Ronda, James. "Calculating Ouragon." *Oregon Historical Quarterly* 94 (1993), 121–40.

Sauer, Carl O. "The Agency of Man on Earth." In *Man's Role in Changing the Face of the Earth,* edited by William L. Thomas. Chicago: University of Chicago Press, 1956.

———. "A Geographical Sketch of Early Man in America." *Geographical Review* 34 (1944), 529–73.

———. "Man in the Ecology of Tropical America." *Proceedings of the Ninth Pacific Science Congress* 20 (1957), 104–10.

Schwantes, Carlos A. "The Concept of the Wageworkers' Frontier: A Framework for Future Research." *Western Historical Quarterly* 18 (1987), 39–56.

Scott, Leslie M., ed. "John Work's Journey from Fort Vancouver to Umpqua River, and Return, in 1834." *Oregon Historical Quarterly* 24 (1923), 238–68.

Sedell, James R., and Judith L. Froggatt. "Importance of Streamside Forests to Large Rivers: The Isolation of the Willamette River, Oregon, U.S.A." *Vera. Interna. Verein. Limnol.* 22 (1984), 1828–34.

Shinn, Dean A. "Historical Perspectives on Range Burning in the Inland Pacific Northwest." *Journal of Range Management* 33 (November 1980), 416–20.

Stage, H. H., and C. M. Cjullin. "Anophelines and Malaria in the Pacific Northwest." *Northwest Science* 9, no. 3 (1935).

Teal, Joseph Nathan. "Address of Joseph N. Teal." *Oregon Historical Quarterly* 16 (1915), 125–29.

Toepel, Kathryn Anne. "The Western Interior." In *The First Oregonians,* edited by Carolyn M. Buan and Richard Lewis. Portland: Oregon Council for the Humanities, 1991.

Towle, Jerry C. "Changing Geography of Willamette Valley Woodlands." *Oregon Historical Quarterly* 83 (Spring 1982), 66–87.

Truettner, William H., and Alexander Nemerov. "What You See Is Not Necessarily What You Get: New Meaning in Images of the Old West." *Montana, the Magazine of Western History* 42 (Summer 1992), 70–76.

White, Richard. "The Altered Landscape: Social Change and Land in the Pacific Northwest." In *Regionalism and the Pacific Northwest,* edited by William G. Robbins, Robert J. Frank, and Richard E. Ross. Corvallis: Oregon State University Press, 1983.

———. "Discovering Nature in North America." *Journal of American History* 79 (December 1992), 874–91.

———. "Environmental History, Ecology, and Meaning." *Journal of American History* 76 (March 1990), 1111–17.

———. "Frederick Jackson Turner and Buffalo Bill." In *The Frontier in American Culture,* edited by James R. Grossman. Berkeley: University of California Press, 1994.

———. "Trashing the Trails." In *Trails: Toward a New Western History,* edited by Patricia Nelson Limerick, Clyde A. Milner, and Charles E. Rankin. Lawrence: University Press of Kansas, 1991.

Wilkes, Charles. "Report on the Territory of Oregon." *Oregon Historical Quarterly* 12 (1911), 269–99.

Winegar, Harold H. "Camp Creek Channel Fencing: Plant, Wildlife, Soil, and Water Response." *Rangeman's Journal* 4, no. 1 (February 1977), 10–12.

Wood, Talmadge B. Letter, April 1844. In "Documents." *Oregon Historical Quarterly* 3 (December 1902), 395–96.

Work, John. *See* Scott, Leslie M., ed.

Worster, Donald. "A Dream of Water." *Montana, the Magazine of Western History* 36 (Autumn 1986), 72–74.

———. "Nature and the Disorder of History." *Environmental History Review* 18 (Summer 1994), 1–15.

———. "Transformations of the Earth: Toward an Agroecological Perspective in History." *Journal of American History* 76 (March 1990), 1087–1106.

Young, Frederick G., ed. "The Correspondence and Journals of Captain Nathaniel Wyeth." *Sources of Oregon History* 1, pts. 3–6. Eugene: University Press, 1899.

Young, J. A., and R. A. Evans. "Population Dynamics after Wildfires in Sagebrush Grasslands." *Journal of Range Management* 31 (1978), 280–92.

Pamphlets

Jackman, E. R. *Oregon: A State of Mind.* Corvallis: Friends of the Library, 1961.
Portland Chamber of Commerce. *Report on an Open River.* 1906.
The Wealth of Resources of Oregon for the Home Seeker, Capitalist and Tourist. St. Louis: Woodward and Tiernan Company, 1894.

Periodicals and Newspapers

Bend Bulletin. 1909–18.
Columbian. 1850.
Columbia River Basin Journal. 1900–1904.
Coos Bay News. 1880–95.
Coos Bay Times. 1912–20.
Eugene Register-Guard. 1937–40.
Hood River Glacier. February 23, 1895.
New York Times. 1980–96.
Olympia Pioneer and Democrat. July 18, 1856.
Oregon Business. 1923–35.
Oregon Country. 1915–20.
Oregonian. 1850–1996.
Oregon Journal. 1935–40.
Oregon Journal of Commerce. 1920–23.
Oregon Spectator. 1848–50.
Oregon Sportsman. 1914–20.
Oregon Statesman. 1850–1940.
Pacific Monthly. 1892–1910.
Portland Board of Trade Journal. 1900–1905.
Portland Chamber of Commerce Bulletin. 1905–22.
Roseburg Pantagraph. 1872–74.
Roseburg Plaindealer. 1870–85.
Timberman. 1898–1910.
Time. 1945–52.
West Shore. 1875–91.
Willamette Farmer. 1869–82.

Theses, Dissertations, and Manuscripts

Blaine, Wilson. Letters. Oregon Historical Society Manuscript 1208. Oregon Historical Society. Portland.

Blok, Jack H. "The Evolution of Agricultural Resource Use Strategies in the Willamette Valley." Ph.D. dissertation, Oregon State University, Corvallis, 1974.

Bunting, Robert R. "Landscaping the Pacific Northwest: A Cultural and Ecological Mapping of the Douglas Fir Region, 1778–1900." Ph.D. dissertation, University of California, Davis, 1993.

Farnham, Wallace D. "Religion as an Influence in Life and Thought: Jackson County, Oregon, 1860–1890." Ph.D. dissertation, University of Oregon, Eugene, 1955.

McNary, Charles. Papers. Knight Library, University of Oregon, Eugene.

Olsen, Michael L. "The Beginnings of Agriculture in Western Oregon and Washington." Ph.D. dissertation, University of Washington, Seattle, 1970.

Pierce, Walter. Papers. Knight Library, University of Oregon, Eugene.

Pinchot, Gifford. Papers. Collections of the Manuscript Division. Library of Congress, Washington, D.C.

Robbins, William G. "The Far Western Frontier: Economic Opportunity and Social Democracy in Early Roseburg, Oregon." Ph.D. dissertation, University of Oregon, Eugene, 1969.

Rymon, Larry. "A Critical Analysis of Wildlife Conservation in Oregon." Ph.D. dissertation, Oregon State University, Corvallis, 1969.

Welcher, Karen. "Holocene Changes of Camp Creek, an Arroyo in Eastern Oregon." M.S. thesis, University of Oregon, Eugene, 1992.

Zenk, Henry. "Contributions to Tualatin Ethnography: Subsistence and Ethnobiology." M.A. thesis, Portland State University, 1976.

Index

Abbott, Carl, 197
Abbott, Henry L., 45, 223
abundance: nineteenth-century narratives of, 4; of Indian horses, 47; of salmon, 50, 140; promise of, 179, 184; link to manufactures, 182–83; marketing of, 191; and need for industrial infrastructure, 199; of timber supply, 213
Adams, Charles Francis, 243
Adams, John Quincy, 49
agriculture, 112; societies of, 6, 101, 116; and Neolithic revolution, 26; absence of, during Indian period, 29; Hudson's Bay Co. observes potential for, 55; subsistence activities, 61, 73; and biological and physical changes, 64, 71; disturbances created by, 65; western valleys favored, 65; in Willamette Valley, 70–74, 92; missionaries' practice of, 71; expansion of, 72, 91; as vanguard of ecological change, 81; practices in the last millennium, 81; and distant influences, 82; shift to commercial operations, 82, 174; technology, 89, 91, 101, 127, 184; requirements for success, 99; markets for, 100; destruction of pests, 106; and population, 107; speeds movement of goods, 115; railroads and golden age of, 115; in Douglas County, 127; boosters of, 149; beginnings on

Columbia Plateau, 155; federal census for, 162; clearing land for, 220; water diversions in Klamath Basin, 250; dryland, 254–58; in Deschutes Basin, 259; progress through irrigation, 264; interests oppose dam on Klamath River, 277
Ainsworth, J. C., 290
Alaska, 140
Allen, Barbara, *Homesteading the High Desert,* 254–58
Allen, John Logan, 52
Alvord Basin, 159
American Falls, 8
American Guide Series. *See* Oregon Writers' Project
Applegate, Jesse, 111; as immigrant to Umpqua Valley, 86; on Umpqua agriculture, 87–88; and killing deer, 88; on dense forest growth, 207
Applegate family, 87
archaeology, 28, 30
arid ecosystems, 38–45
Ashland *Tidings,* 38
Astor, John Jacob, 53, 54, 206
Athapascans, 38
Audubon Society, 253

Baillie-Grohman, William Randolph, 241–42
Baird, Spencer Fullerton, 135–36